Hong Kong
The World City and International Business Centre

This book has been written with the objective of providing an indispensable analysis and reference work regarding Hong Kong in order to enhance the performance of directors, managers and executives from companies of all sizes and types seeking to establish or further develop a presence in Hong Kong and Asia.

Hong Kong
The World City and International Business Centre

Andrew Mapp M.A, B.A. (HONS)

Andrew Mapp has spent many years living and working in Hong Kong, and has an in-depth knowledge and experience of the Hong Kong and Asian economy, as well as the social and political aspects of this area of the world. He has dual citizenship of Hong Kong and the United Kingdom.

© 2006 Andrew Mapp

First edition published by Cambridge Academic Ltd, The Studio, High Green, Gt. Shelford, Cambridge CB2 5EG.

The rights of Andrew Mapp to be identified as the author of this work have been asserted by him in accordance with the Copyright, Designs and Patents Act 1988.

All rights reserved. No part of this publication may be reproduced, stored in a retrieval system, or transmitted in any form or by any means, electronic, mechanical, photocopying, recording, or otherwise without prior permission of Cambridge Academic Ltd at:
The Studio, High Green, Gt. Shelford, Cambridge. CB2 5EG

ISBN 1-903-499-291

The contents of this publication are provided in good faith and neither The Author nor The Publisher can be held responsible for any errors or omissions contained herein. Any person relying upon the information must independently satisfy himself or herself as to the safety or any other implications of acting upon such information and no liability shall be accepted either by The Author or The Publisher in the event of reliance upon such information nor for any damage or injury arising from any interpretation of its contents. This publication may not be used in any process of risk assessment.

All images in this book (with the exception of the map) have been provided by the Hong Kong Trade Development Council, and are used with their express permission. No image in this publication may be reproduced, stored in a retrieval system, or transmitted in any form or by any means, electronic, mechanical, photocopying, recording, or otherwise without prior permission of the Hong Kong Trade Development Council.

Cover image courtesy of Graham Uden via Hong Kong Trade Development Council. Image subject to copyright as stated above.

Contents

1.	Introduction - Hong Kong - The World City (the city that means business)	1
2.	Strategic Advantages of Hong Kong	31
3.	Hong Kong's Service Industries & Business Sectors	49
4.	Why Hong Kong is a Business Paradise Why Choose Hong Kong as a Base?	102
5.	Unique Combinations	106
6.	Non Government Organisations	112
7.	The Hong Kong Monetary Authority	125
8.	The Mandatory Provident Fund	137
9.	The Legal System	143
10.	Exhibitions, Trade Fairs and Conventions	150
11.	Hong Kong Science and Technology Park	163
12.	Telecommunications	168
13.	Miscellaneous Points - Social Aspects	174
14.	Education	193
15.	Transport and Logistics	198
16.	The China Factor	215
17.	Investment Flows	243
18.	Integration of Hong Kong and China	247
19.	Invest Hong Kong	256
20.	Hong Kong Trade Development Council	268
21.	The Promotion of Hong Kong	278

22.	Regional Headquarters and Setting up a Company	289
23.	Recent Stories of Companies Setting Up in Hong Kong	312
24.	Useful Addresses and Contacts:	332
	Invest Hong Kong and Hong Kong Economic and Trade Offices	332
	Overseas Consultants	334
	Consulates	336
	Chambers of Commerce, Business Associations and Business Councils	346
	Associations, Federations, Institutes, Commissions, Councils, Committees and Agencies	350
	Hong Kong Trade Development Council (HKTDC) Offices	357
	Important Offices and Organisations	363
	Other Useful Websites	374
	Bibliography	377
	Index	389

Hong Kong skyline as seen from Kowloon

Daytime view of Hong Kong from the Peak

Night-time view of Hong Kong from the Peak

Hong Kong has a total area of 1092 square kilometres – 1042 km² of land and 50 km² of water. Its coastline is 733 km; its terrain is hilly to mountainous and its coordinates are 22° 15" North, 114° 10" East.

Map reproduced courtesy of and with express permission of Asia Web Direct Company Ltd.

*For Adena,
Richard and Zoe*

1. Introduction: Hong Kong – The World City (the city that means business)

When deciding whether or not to locate a regional headquarters or regional office in a particular city or country, companies need to determine the cost of fully establishing such a working office in the locality and assess the benefits that can be expected to be achieved. These costs and benefits then need to be compared to determine whether or not such an office is a financially viable option.

Companies also need to assess fully the cost impact, both short term and long term, of not establishing a regional office or regional headquarters in the particular city or country and the likely affect that will have on the level of competition experienced and rate of market penetration achieved. Companies need to consider whether or not competitors will enter and locate in the city or country and the effect this will have upon the company's market position and influence. In other words it may well be a situation where the first to enter gains the lions share of the market.

Multinationals will use Porters 5-forces model when assessing the suitability of a location for a regional headquarters or regional office. Porter's Five Forces Model together with a SWOT analysis may well be the starting point of any assessment. Prior to entering a market, firms will often conduct a number of analyses in order to determine whether or not to invest time and money pursuing a particular market entry strategy. A popular analysis is the SWOT analysis where the company will assess its strengths, weaknesses, opportunities and threats with regard to the proposed market. This essentially is a form of audit whereby the company can determine how to position itself and whether it would be expedient to enter the proposed market. It also serves to develop business direction for the company.

When conducting the SWOT analysis it is vital that the analysis be conducted rationally in a somewhat cold and calculated manner so as not to overestimate or underestimate aspects of the analysis. The company should first list its strengths, which for example may include product portfolio coordination, engineering capacity and capability, corporate identity, customer relations management, brandname reputation, etc. After having listed its strengths the company should then list its weaknesses, which for example may include poor product pricing, slow and reluctant innovation, lack of adherence to marketing strategy, poor presentation within the region, etc. The strengths and weaknesses are basically an internal assessment of the company and its capabilities, and as such are the foundation of the analysis.

After the internal analysis of strengths and weaknesses, the company must conduct an external analysis and consider the opportunities and threats presented by the proposed market. Opportunities may for example include potential market demand for product sector, brandname and corporate development prospects, market growth history, increasing affluence of population in target market, etc. Threats may for example include the level of competition and number of competitors as well as the nature of the competition, loss of market share and position if the company does not establish an office in the target market, deterioration of corporate image and position, strong retaliation from existing competitors already in the market if the company does try to enter the market, etc.

The SWOT analysis has often been regarded as a relatively simple and straightforward form of analysis and as such is often the preliminary analysis that companies will conduct when considering investing in the development of a new market or even developing an existing market where the company already has a position. This form of analysis often leads onto other forms of analysis such as the portfolio matrix, Porter's Generic Strategies, the Ansoff Growth Vector Matrix, Grand Strategy Matrix, Porter's Five Forces analysis, the Boston Consulting Group Matrix, the McKinsey market analysis, PEST analysis, etc. It is not the objective of this book to investigate these theories of market analysis. There are many good marketing textbooks that will cover these theories in detail and the reader should refer to these for explanation.

Nevertheless Porter's Five Forces analysis would be of particular assistance when considering whether or not to invest in the establishment of a regional headquarters or regional office in a new market or even the further development of such an already established office. Porter's Five Forces model is a competitive analysis covering internal rivalry, supplier power, buyer power, new entrants and substitutes. This analysis covers the threats to potential profits posed by these five forces and is something that all companies should consider very carefully.

Internal rivalry is an assessment of the level of competition within the market and the nature of the competition. Depending on the particular type of product or service that the company is supplying, competition may or may not be intense. The internal rivalry assessment will also cover the size of market competitors and their resources, market position and competitive capability, etc. Price is very often an important competitive element when competition is intense. For example, since the opening up of the telephone market in Hong Kong, more companies have entered this particular market sector and competition has become more intense with the result that prices have declined.

The supplier power analysis is an assessment of the size and power of companies supplying competitors within the market. The greater the bargaining power of suppliers, the higher will be overall costs. When supply is dominated by a few companies and the product or component that is being supplied is unique, suppliers have a very strong bargaining position and therefore the company's costs will be higher and profit margin lower. However, when the product or component being supplied to market competitors is freely and widely available, the bargaining power of suppliers will be reduced due to price competition and the margins of those companies competing in the market will be improved.

The buyer power analysis is an assessment of the size and strength of the bargaining power of buyers in the industry. When the product or service produced by the company is standard or undifferentiated with many competitors supplying the same or very similar products or services, the bargaining power of buyers is automatically increased because of their easy ability to switch to other companies. When buyers are concentrated and their order volumes are large, or when buyer margins are low and price is very important, the bargaining power of buyers will be stronger. However, the greater the level of uniqueness of the product or service supplied by the company, the lower will be the bargaining power of buyers due to their restricted ability to change to other companies in the market. Nevertheless, it should be remembered that it is a common tactic of buyers to try to play one company off against another in order to force them to compete on the basis of price by reducing or discounting their selling prices so as to obtain customer orders, thereby enabling the buyer to obtain a lower price for the product or service.

The substitutes analysis is an assessment of the level of substitutability of the product or service being supplied by the company. When profit margins are high, there will automatically be an increase in the number of substitutes within the market. The threat of substitutes will be determined by the willingness of buyers to accept a substitute, the closeness or similarity of the substitute when compared with the company's product or service, the price level and performance of substitutes, and the cost of switching to a substitute. When a buyer switches to a substitute product or service, the buyer has to be certain that the companies he is supplying further down the supply chain will accept the substitute product or service. In order to combat the threat of substitutes, the company should develop strong and distinctive brand personalities for its product or service. It becomes more difficult to substitute a product or service that has a strong brandname due to market acceptance.

The new entrants analysis is an assessment of the barriers to entry in a particular market and the level of investment in time and money that would be required in order to establish a feasible position within the market. The higher the barriers to entry, the less attractive the market will be, even though it might be quite lucrative for those already in the market. Companies already established within a particular market will always seek to raise or maintain barriers to entry so as to discourage competition from new entrants. If the company is considering entering a new market, it must carefully assess the required investment cost in its fullest sense covering the expense required and time envisaged in order to achieve company objectives.

After conducting a Porter's Five Forces analysis of the proposed market that the company is seeking to enter together with a SWOT analysis, the company will be in a much clearer position regarding the formulation of its business objectives and strategies. Many companies will have conducted such analysis prior to their establishing of a regional headquarters or regional office in Hong Kong. The vast majority of these companies will have concluded that being based in Hong Kong provides them with definite strategic advantage and as such clearly helps in the achievement of their corporate objectives. Being based in Hong Kong enables these companies to take full advantage of the market developments that are currently taking place in the region, particularly in China and South East Asia.

Before entering any market a company has to assess its core competencies as well as associated competencies to determine whether or not those competencies meet market entry requirements in order to be successful in the chosen market.

One of the key issues in globalised trade is the development and efficient use of networks at all levels from sourcing, purchasing, manufacturing, distribution and retailing. The use of these networks can add substantial strategic advantages both from the point of cost and hence eventual retail price, as well as rapid product distribution. Multinationals will place increasing emphasis upon precise development of strategic networks in order to increase corporate profitability.

Positioning of strategic networks can be used to minimise transportation costs depending upon the technology of the product and where materials and sub-assemblies are located and produced.

From the 1950s to the 1970s Hong Kong was China's eye on the rest of the world and the rest of the world's eye on China. Now Hong Kong is the rest of the world's gateway to China and China's gateway to the rest of the world. Hong Kong has often been referred to as the pearl of the Orient. A business man's paradise. Just how good or beneficial Hong Kong is to an international company will of course depend upon the objectives and strategy of that company. Nevertheless as an international city with global aspirations Hong Kong does offer many strategic advantages that do require investigation and consideration. The Hong Kong environment is extremely favourable with regard to business negotiations and contracts because of its stable government, low taxation and transparent administration. It is much more favourable than many other cities not only in Asia, but also throughout the world. Hong Kong has for a long time been regarded as the place where East meets West, but is now also seen as the place where East meets East. This is because of the information networks centred around Hong Kong, the excellent access to product and service sourcing in China, Asia and worldwide, as well as the access to markets in North America, Europe and elsewhere.

Companies are increasingly seeking to go global and search for new markets in order to develop profitability as well as develop market positions and brandname. Marketing objectives may include creation of brand awareness, brand development, regional control, corporate identity building, global structure alignment, sales support, etc. Profitability is a company concern and may be determined in terms of cash, image, name, short term and long term goals, etc. It can be defined in a broad number of ways depending upon corporate objectives. Simple profitability may mean increased cash flow and circulation making marketing decisions and expenditure so much easier due to a reduction in financial constraints. Or profitability may be defined on the basis of long term corporate objectives and company growth where immediate cash flow requirements are not the main concern, but nevertheless do aid such aspirations. In other words, whilst all companies seek to be profitable in order to remain in business the point of emphasis in such profitability will change overtime depending upon corporate objectives.

As an investment location Hong Kong offers a number of clear and positive advantages when compared with other locations. It has a very liberal and free investment regime, a well established legal system where the rule of law is supreme, capital is free to move into and out of the economy without restriction, regulations are clear and transparent, taxation is low and predictable, trade barriers do not exist and there is a clear policy of non-discrimination with regard to overseas investors.

Hong Kong is geographically located at the heart of East Asia and due to its well developed sea and air transport links it has developed an unrivalled position as the hub of Asia with regard to trade and investment. The city is also the main gateway to trade and investment opportunities in mainland China. As the eleventh largest trading economy in the world Hong Kong has a clear geographical advantage as a launch pad not just for the Chinese market, but also for markets throughout Asia.

Geographically Hong Kong is a relatively small area in South East Asia at the Southern tip of China bordering the South China Sea. It has a total area of 1,092 square kilometres, which is approximately six times the overall size of Washington DC in the United States of America, with land comprising 1,042 square kilometres and water 50 square kilometres. Hong Kong's geographical territory has more than 200 islands many of which are small and uninhabited. It has one border with

China that is 30 km long with the rest of the region being surrounded by water. The terrain is normally described as hilly to mountainous with steep slopes and lowlands in the north. Its coastline is approximately 733 km. Its geographical coordinates are 22° 15" N, 114° 10" E and its highest point is Tai Mo Shan at 958 metres.

The climate is that of tropical monsoon with winters being cool and humid, spring and summer being hot and rainy, and autumn being warm and sunny. In the summer temperatures can rise to 33, 34 or 35 degrees centigrade with humidity often being between 80 and 95 percent making life hot and sticky, and the need for air conditioning paramount. Whereas in winter the temperature can drop to 10° C or below, which due to the humidity makes it a lot colder than one would expect. The autumn period from September to November is often considered to be the best time of year in Hong Kong because temperatures are still warm, the summer rains and possible typhoons have finished and the humidity has declined to a level where it is no longer excessively sticky. It is an enjoyable time of the year, but nevertheless a busy time of the year when exhibitions and shows are in full swing. This is the best time of the year to visit Hong Kong.

Before the 1950s there was much more arable use of land in Hong Kong, but according to 2002 statistics only 5.05% of the land is arable with only 1.01% being for permanent crops. Now Hong Kong imports the vast majority of its food requirements with cuisine from around the world being freely and easily available at very reasonable prices. Nevertheless visitors and those planning to live in the territory should acquaint themselves with the local cuisine and become accustomed to eating in the manner that locals do as well as become accustomed to eating what the locals eat.

Hong Kong like many economies is now experiencing an aging population. In 1990 the median age of the population was 31.0 whereas in 2001 the median age had risen to 36.8. The proportion of children under 15 years of age in 1990 was 21.5% whereas in 2001 this figure had dropped to 16.4%. Also in 1990 the proportion of elderly aged 65 and over was 8.5% whereas in 2001 this figure had risen to 11.2%. Between 1990 and 1995 there were approximately 70,000 births per year, in 1999 this figure had dropped to 51,000 and in 2000 it was 54,000. In 1990 there were 12 live births per 1000 population whereas in 2000 there were only 8 live births per 1000 population. Between 1990 and 2001 the child dependency ratio decreased from 306 to 227 whereas the elderly dependency ratio increased from 122 to 155. It would appear that Hong Kong is not just experiencing an aging population, but also a decline in fertility.

In July 2002 it was estimated that Hong Kong had a population of 7,303,334 with a population growth rate of 1.26%. The age structure of the population was as follows:

Age Range	Population figure	% of Population
0 - 14	1,279,122	17.5
15 - 64	5,228,927	71.6
65 and over	795,285	10.9

The birth rate was 10.92 per 1000 population whereas the death rate was 6.11 per 1000 population and the net migration rate was 7.76 per 1000 population. Therefore Hong Kong in July 2002 still had an expanding population. As in most societies females tend to live longer than males and represent a slightly larger section of the community.

In July 2003 it was estimated that Hong Kong had a population of 7,394,170 with a population growth rate of 1.22%. The age structure of the population was as follows:

Age Range	Male	Female	% of Population
0 - 14	680,973	599,309	17.3
15 - 64	2,619,929	2,679,430	71.7
65 and over	375,058	439,471	11.0

The birth rate was 10.71 per 1000 population whereas the death rate was 6.19 per 1000 population and the net migration rate was 7.64 per 1000 population. Therefore Hong Kong still has an expanding population. The fertility rate in 2002 was estimated to be 1.3 children born per woman.

People in Hong Kong are now living longer than they did previously due to better medical provision and greater health consciousness. This has resulted in a noticeable decline in the death rate for all age groups. The infant mortality rate has decreased considerably from 6.2 per thousand live births in 1990 to only 3.0 in 2000 which is a very good indication of the health of the population and medical provision. Life expectancy has increased for both sexes with the year 2000 life expectancy for men being 77.0 years and for women 82.2 years. Compared with other parts of the world these life expectancy rates are rather high.

At least 95% of the population is ethnically Chinese with other nationalities representing 5% or less. Cantonese, the local dialect, Putonghua, the national language of China, and English are all recognised as official languages. Whereas Cantonese has been the main language of the native Hong Kong Chinese population and English was the only official language during much of the British occupation of Hong Kong, both these languages are now regarded as official languages to be used in courts and legislative activities. However, just prior to and since the handover of sovereignty in 1997, Putonghua has become a very important language due to the obvious relationship between Hong Kong and China.

With regard to literacy, in 2002 92.2% of the population were regarded as being literate of which 96% of the male population and 88.2% of the female population were literate. Primary education has been a compulsory requirement ever since the 1970s and most children do naturally progress through a full secondary education. There is also a growing emphasis upon attaining a tertiary education either in Hong Kong or overseas. Many graduates these days are highly qualified at tertiary level and are also fluent in both Cantonese and English, and in many cases Putonghua as well. The Chinese have always placed a high regard and emphasis upon education. The educated person has generally always been held in high esteem and therefore Chinese families have to a greater extent than western families placed a greater emphasis upon achieving and attaining a higher academic level than in many other societies. As such the working population of Hong Kong is well educated and well adapted to its working environment as well as being noted for the speed at which it accomplishes its tasks. For example, high rise buildings are built to recognised international standards at extremely quick speeds that have never been matched in the western world.

Since 1st July 1997, Hong Kong has been a Special Administrative Region of China with a high degree of autonomy. The Basic Law which was approved in March 1990 by the Chinese National People's Congress is Hong Kong's mini constitution. According to the Joint Declaration of 1984 signed by both China and Britain, Hong Kong will have a high degree of autonomy in all matters except foreign and defence affairs for the next 50 years. Foreign and defence affairs being of national interest remain within the authority of the national government. The socialist governmental system practised in China will not be introduced into Hong Kong. Instead Hong Kong will maintain its capitalist system with all that this entails, whilst China will further develop its socialist governmental system and all which that entails. The two systems will remain separate entities for all to observe. Hence, 'one country, two systems'.

The legal system in Hong Kong is based on English common law and all persons of 18 years of age and over who are permanent residents living in the territory have the right to vote in elections. To be classified as a permanent resident the individual has to either have been born in Hong Kong, have parents who are Hong Kong citizens or to have lived in Hong Kong for at least seven years and applied to become a permanent resident. If one's claim to being a permanent resident is due to having lived in Hong Kong for seven years, it must be remembered that such claim can be lost or forfeited if one is absent from the territory for more than three years. This was the ruling in force in May 2004.

Direct elections are conducted for a limited number of government posts where the total electorate can vote. The Democratic Party has often been the main choice of the electorate under direct elections. Indirect elections are also conducted for a number of government posts and such elections are limited to the votes of functional constituencies and an election committee drawn from broad regional groupings, municipal organisations and central government bodies. It is envisaged that in the coming years a greater number of government posts will be subject to direct election with the total electorate being the voting public. However, such development will to a large extent be determined by the economic environment and its future development, together with the need to ensure that the territory maintains political stability as well as economic stability thereby guaranteeing safety with regard to investment channels and commitments. The economic environment of Hong Kong is of critical importance to its future well being.

The Hong Kong Special Administrative Region (HKSAR) is led by a Chief Executive who is supported by an Executive Council and Legislative Council with a professional and impartial civil service. The concept of 'One Country, Two Systems' put forward by the late Deng Xiao Ping together with Hong Kong's mini constitution, the Basic Law, and the Joint Declaration signed by both China and Britain guarantee that the territory will enjoy a high degree of autonomy from China, except with regard to foreign affairs and defence. Under the Basic Law and Joint Declaration it is guaranteed that Hong Kong's economic and social systems, and way of life will not be changed for at least 50 years from the date of transfer of sovereignty (1st July 1997) and that Hong Kong's fundamental rights and freedoms will be respected and maintained.

The Joint Declaration was signed by Britain and China in 1984 and registered with the United Nations. It is a binding international agreement guaranteeing the preservation of the way of life in Hong Kong for at least 50 years. The Basic Law for Hong Kong was promulgated in China and came into effect on 1st July 1997 and is in effect a mini constitution. It gives legal effect to the provisions of the Joint Declaration in Hong Kong and China as well as expansion in certain areas.

The Joint Declaration on the Question of Hong Kong agreement between China and the UK was signed on 19/12/84 making Hong Kong into the Hong Kong Special Administrative Region of China. The 'one country, two systems' formula means China's socialist economic system will not be imposed on Hong Kong. Hong Kong will enjoy a high degree of autonomy in all matters except foreign and defence affairs for the next 50 years. The Basic Law was approved in March 1990 by China's National People's Congress (NPC) and became Hong Kong's mini constitution. It was adopted on 4th April 1990 by the NPC.

The Chief Executive is a Chinese citizen having lived in Hong Kong for not less than 20 years and is a permanent resident. The Chief Executive has executive and legislative powers, and is responsible for appointing his own principal officials subject to the confirmation of the Chinese government. The Chief Executive is chosen by an election committee composed of 800 citizens who are intended to be representative of Hong Kong. Under current legal arrangements, the Chief Executive can only serve a maximum of two consecutive five year terms.

According to the Basic Law it is an ultimate objective that the Chief Executive be elected by universal suffrage and also that the Legislative Council (LegCo) be elected by universal suffrage as well. Only local people can be members of the Legislative Council and recent elections held in 1998, 2000 and 2004 have demonstrated that the people of Hong Kong are determined to play a complete and proper role in the democratic process.

The judicial system in Hong Kong is based on the common law system of England with the only significant change since the handover of sovereignty being the establishment of the Court of Final Appeal. Under the current legal system the ruling of the Court of Final Appeal is the last and final interpretation of the law in Hong Kong. The Joint Declaration states that the courts of Hong Kong exercise their judicial powers independently and without any interference. Judges are appointed solely on their judicial qualities and capabilities, and may be appointed from any other common law jurisdiction.

On 1st July 2002, the Chief Executive implemented a new scheme for appointing top officials. The scheme allows for a more cabinet style of Executive Council where the Chief Executive chooses his 14 principal officials instead of them being permanent civil servants. The principal officials are appointed on fixed term contracts being directly responsible to the Chief Executive. The appointed principal officials are supported by a permanent, meritocratic and politically neutral Civil Service.

The rights and freedom of people in Hong Kong is enshrined in the rule of law that has been developed over many decades. The Basic Law and Joint Declaration both express safeguards and protection of the established civil rights regarding freedom of expression, assembly, religion, occupation as well as the right to strike and to own property. Application of the International Covenant on Economic, Social and Cultural Rights (ICESCR) and the International Covenant for Civil and Political Rights (ICCPR) in Hong Kong are also guaranteed under the Joint Declaration, and the Bill of Rights Ordinance also protects the implementation of the ICCPR. Regular reports regarding these covenants have been prepared by the

Hong Kong government and submitted to the Chinese Ministry of Foreign Affairs, which has then fulfilled its obligations and submitted the reports to the United Nations. Although China has previously been criticised for its human rights, the safety of human rights in Hong Kong are guaranteed in internationally recognised law and as such there will be no opportunity for contention.

In 2002 the Executive Council consisted of three ex-officio members and 10 appointed members. The legislative element of government is a unicameral Legislative Council which in 2002 consisted of 60 seats, of which 30 are indirectly elected by functional constituencies, 24 are elected by popular vote and 6 are elected by an 800-member election committee. Members of the legislative council serve terms lasting four years. On 10th September 2000 the election resulted in the following seats being awarded: - Democratic Party 12, Democratic Alliance for the Betterment of Hong Kong 10, Liberal Party 7, Frontier Party 5, Hong Kong Progressive Alliance 4, New Century Forum 2, Hong Kong Association for Democracy and People's Livelihood 1, Independents 19.

Hong Kong has a large number of political parties all worthy of note and these include: Association for Democracy and People's Livelihood, Citizens Party, Democratic Alliance for the Betterment of Hong Kong, Democratic Party, Frontier Party, Hong Kong Association for Democracy and People's Livelihood, Hong Kong Progressive Alliance, Liberal Party and New Century Forum. Political pressure groups include: the Chinese General Chamber of Commerce, Chinese Manufacturers Association of Hong Kong, Confederation of Trade Unions, Federation of Hong Kong Industries, Federation of Trade Unions, Hong Kong Alliance in Support of the Patriotic Democratic Movement in China, Hong Kong and Kowloon Trade Union Council, Hong Kong General Chamber of Commerce and the Hong Kong Professional Teachers Union.

During colonial days, prior to the handover of sovereignty, there was without doubt political stability because power was vested in the appointed governor and his team. This was definitely one of the reasons for Hong Kong's rapid growth as a manufacturing centre from the 1950s to the 1970s. The territory did mildly attempt to introduce some aspect of democracy in the 1940s after the second world war, but this received extremely little public support due to the public being so engrossed in earning a living in what were particularly hard times. The idea of introducing aspects of democracy was later shelved due to what happened in China and the communist takeover. It wasn't until the last governor, Chris Patten, arrived in Hong Kong in 1992 that aspects of democracy were finally introduced and the general public was able to democratically elect representatives to councils. However, this was not full democracy, because a certain percentage of representatives were still appointed, but it was a move in the direction of democracy that was welcomed by the whole community. Unfortunately China did not welcome the move, but naturally regarded it with suspicion, because it was a structural change in the politics of the society just prior to the handover of sovereignty and as such represented what they regarded as an unwarranted change in Hong Kong. However, it has nevertheless resulted in a very politically stable society.

The Hong Kong flag, which officially came into existence at the time of the handover of sovereignty in 1997, is a stylized white five petal Bauhinia flower in the centre of the flag with a red background. The Bauhinia is a perennial flower that continues to bloom even though the weather may be atrocious. As such this flower is particularly appropriate and representative of Hong Kong which as an economy and society has always bloomed even though the economic climate has been atrocious. Since the handover of sovereignty, the economic climate has to a large extent been very bad with Hong Kong suffering a number of very unfavourable events.

These unfavourable events have included the Asian Financial Crisis of 1997-98, the botched opening of Chek Lap Kok airport, chicken flu, SARS, the sinking Japanese Yen and its effect in 1998, the decline in the value of the USA dollar and its effect on the Hong Kong dollar and the economy due to the linked exchange rate system, the fall in stock market values with the heavy speculative stock market attack of 1998 and the double play of stock market prices and currency, unprecedented levels of unemployment and underemployment, the collapse of the property market and the halving of property values creating considerable negative equity, plummeting stock market values in 1998 which in 2006 have only just now fully regained their lost value, falling GDP growth, recession, deflation, capital flight to a certain extent, a tremendous fall in retail sales from 1997-1999, the lowering of Hong Kong's credit rating by Standard & Poor's, a growth in provision for bad and doubtful debts between 1997 and 2000, the botched introduction of a security bill, the freezing of salaries by many companies and non payment of annual bonuses which inevitably created social unease and an increased desire for greater government intervention in contrast to the rule of 'benign neglect' pioneered by the previous colonial administration. The chief executive, Tung Chee Hwa, has not had an easy ride during his time as head of the Hong Kong government, but Hong Kong has been flexible under the circumstances and the Bauhinia still blooms.

On 10th March 2005, the Chief Executive, Tung Chee Hwa, resigned just over two years before the expiry of his second term of office. The stated reason for the resignation was due to health problems primarily as a result of age and workload. Since the third quarter of 2004, the Chief Executive had experienced a steady decline in health which due to long working hours impaired performance. During his term of office since July 1997, the Chief Executive experienced a number of difficult and very unfortunate events as mentioned in the previous paragraph.

The economic effect of these events led to a general unhappiness amongst the population with regard to the Chief Executive. It is a fairly natural human response to seek to blame somebody for any calamity that befalls the general population and the Chief Executive as the head of the economy was the obvious and natural target. Therefore during his term of office there were a number of protest marches that enabled people to vent their frustration and dissatisfaction. Even so, it should be remembered that these kinds of protest and action are acceptable under a democratic and free society and that Hong Kong since the transfer of sovereignty has remained and no doubt further developed as a free, democratic and pluralistic society where the rule of law is supreme and freedom of expression, speech and association are a civil right.

As a result of the resignation, the Chief Secretary of Administration, Donald Tsang, assumed the position of Acting Chief Executive and in June 2005 was formally elected as Chief Executive. According to Article 53 of the Basic Law, a new Chief Executive appointed under these circumstances would serve a term of office to complete the remaining term of office of the resigned Chief Executive, i.e. until 30th June 2007. The Chief Executive Ordinance states that the election of the new Chief Executive must be on the 120th day after the Chief Executive office becomes vacant which must also be a Sunday. If this day is not a Sunday, then the election must be on the Sunday immediately after this day and can be no sooner or later. Therefore Donald Tsang was elected on 11th July 2005 and will serve as Chief Executive until 30th June 2007.

It is the objective of the government that the election of the third term Chief Executive in 2007 will be by means of an Election Committee that is much more representative of a broader based electorate than was the case with previous elections. Developments on this constitutional aspect of the government are of course being watched carefully with much international interest and will no doubt have a possible bearing on the future growth of the territory.

Hong Kong's growth over the last 165 years has been quite dramatic when compared with that of other cities and countries. The developments of the territory's economy, constitution, legal system, political system and business links have resulted in a very stable and prosperous society that is admired worldwide. Hong Kong has been transformed from a tiny and insignificant fishing village in 1840 to what is now in 2005 regarded as a World City with international links stretching around the globe. It was in 1841 that the British took control of Hong Kong and the territory was ceded to Britain in 1842. One of the primary reasons why the British took Hong Kong in 1841 was the territory's deep water harbour.

Hong Kong: The World City and International Business Centre

Hong Kong has one of the best natural harbours in the world and provides a natural safe haven in times of severe inclement weather such as typhoons. Its exceptional deep water harbour has been a critical advantage to cargo vessels both now and in the past, and will remain an advantage for the future. Surrounding cities do not have comparable harbour advantages like Hong Kong.

Hong Kong has a very active economy that has always been totally dependent on international trade. The territory has very few natural resources and food and raw materials are heavily imported. It has been argued that Hong Kong's major natural resource is its harbour, which is one of the best in the world. When the British traders invaded in the 1830s it was the harbour that was regarded as the major asset due to its natural sheltered landing facility. This facilitated Hong Kong being used as a staging post for further regional development. It was on this basis that British traders developed warehousing and strategic landing quarters as well as garrisoning for their regional trading exploits. 170 years later many multinational companies are using Hong Kong in a very similar manner even though the state of technology has dramatically advanced.

Hong Kong has a number of unique advantages. It has one of the best deep water harbours in the world and has been recognised for such since the early 19th century. Hong Kong has the world's busiest container port and is one of the world's major shipping centres. Hong Kong's growth and status as a premier shipping centre has been due to its strategic location on the doorstep of China. The territory has thrived as an entrepôt due to its close relationship with China, but its entrepôt function has not just been for products despatched from China and then re-exported by Hong Kong, but also for products despatched by overseas countries and then re-exported by Hong Kong to China as the final destination. Hong Kong offers unparalleled maritime services covering virtually the entire world.

The import/export trade is the lifeblood of Hong Kong and in the last 10 to 15 years re-exports have burgeoned in conjunction with this trade. The growth in re-exports has of course been due to the growth in relations between Hong Kong and China. Nevertheless it must be remembered that the growth in re-exports has been of a two way nature. Products from China have been exported to Hong Kong and then re-exported to other countries around the world. Also products from around the world have been exported to Hong Kong and then re-exported to China. As such Hong Kong has featured and functioned as a very important middleman connecting the various sources of supply and demand. This line of development clearly links into Hong Kong's objective of developing into an information society where knowledge and the expertise to use that knowledge are extremely important. Hong Kong's days as a manufacturing base are now firmly in the past. From the 1950s to 1980s Hong Kong was an important manufacturing base not only for Hong Kong companies, but also for multinational companies from around the world. From the end of the 1970s onward manufacturing moved offshore primarily for cost reasons. The vast majority of manufacturing moved into Southern China with Shenzhen being a very important location. However, due to rising costs in Shenzhen, many Hong Kong manufacturers have decided to move further north in order to reduce overall costs. Hong Kong has therefore developed into a strategic control centre and headquarters for many companies and industries with operations on a regional and global basis.

Hong Kong's links with China predate its colonial years although when the British took control in 1842 after the first opium war it was essentially a small fishing village with a very small population. For near on a century its population growth was slow with the territory largely being used as a transition point as people passed through but did not settle. Much of the trade up until 1950 was largely on a re-export basis of product coming from China. However, 1949 to 1951 was a period of major events in the region. After defeating the corrupt Kuomintang, the Communists took control of China in 1949. The Communist forces could have marched further south and easily taken control of Hong Kong. The Communists have always regarded the treaties under which Hong Kong, Kowloon and the New Territories came under British control as being unequal treaties imposed by an imperialistic force. However, the Communist forces stopped at the Shenzhen border, it now being considered that they probably thought that a British administered Hong Kong would have been more preferable than an American controlled Hong Kong.

The Americans had already demonstrated their opposition to the Chinese Communists by their clear support for Chiang Kai Shek and his Kuomintang forces. Nevertheless, in 1949, when the Communists took control of China, there was a tremendous influx of refugees from China into Hong Kong seeking to escape the Communist takeover. These refugees brought with them considerable wealth not just in money, but also in skills and knowledge. Hong Kong's population grew at an unprecedented rate with the result that there was much hardship and suffering. It was then in 1951 that the United Nations, which was to a very large extent under the control of the United States of America, because Europe was still trying to recover from the second world war, imposed an embargo on goods from China. It was not just an American embargo, it was a full United Nations embargo against China and all which that entailed. This was due to China then having a communist government and American fear of communism, as well as China's support for North Korea in the Korean War. This had the effect of literally decimating Hong Kong's economy because so much of it was based on the export of products from China. Hong Kong found that the vast majority of its exports were no longer feasible. Products from Hong Kong then had to have a certificate of origin and likewise goods destined for Commonwealth countries also required a certificate of origin. This further added to the hardship that the territory was already suffering.

It was this embargo on products from China coupled with the influx of refugees from China, together with their knowledge and financial capital, notably from Shanghai, that led to the first real seeds of Hong Kong developing its own manufacturing base. The textiles industry was one of the first developed in Hong Kong. Materials were imported so that product could be processed and manufactured, and then exported at a profit. Hong Kong has developed a number of industries including textiles, clothing, tourism, banking and investment, shipping, electronics, plastics, toys, watches and clocks, etc.

Many of the older generation in Hong Kong have tended to regard a social welfare system as an impediment to development, because it undermines the determination of society to persevere and succeed. Whilst Hong Kong industry was developing from 1950 onwards there was no social welfare system and the endemic philosophy during the 1950s, 1960s and much of the 1970s was that 'if you didn't work, you didn't eat'. It was also the case in this burgeoning capitalist enclave that one did not question the authority of one's employer for fear of losing one's job. Hong Kong had a very distinct business advantage at this point in time, because labour was very cheap and in plentiful supply, and work opportunities were also plentiful with unemployment being negligible. As such Hong Kong products were much cheaper than the same things being produced in other parts of the world.

This cheap manufacturing cost coupled with quick supply led to Hong Kong becoming the OEM centre of the East. Many western companies saw the opportunity of moving production to the East in order to reduce their costs and thereby increase their profit margins. This led to considerable growth in unemployment in the Western world as their jobs migrated East. After the jobs had gone East, Western companies then designed products to be made in Hong Kong with the western company's label. Hong Kong was an OEM centre, profits were good and Hong Kong companies gained considerable experience in product manufacture, product design and production technology. However, since 1978 and Deng Xiao Ping's open door policy, production has, in the vast majority of cases, moved north into China. Hong Kong wages have increased, profit margins have become tight, particularly on OEM projects, and Hong Kong companies have sought to develop their businesses by moving production. Hong Kong companies have in effect expanded their manufacturing base into China and reaped the benefits of low cost labour and land.

However, since the handover of sovereignty the economy has experienced some difficult times. In 1999 GDP growth contracted as a result of the Asian Financial

Crisis, but nevertheless rebounded in 2000 to reach 10%. Over the last 40 years GDP growth has been at a particularly impressive level. Hong Kong was regarded as being one of the four tiger economies of the East due to its impressive GDP growth. In 1997 at the time of the handover of sovereignty the per capita GDP of Hong Kong was higher than the per capita GDP of Britain, the colonial power. However, as already stated the Hong Kong economy is particularly dependent upon the global economy due to its reliance on the import/export trade, and the global downturn in 2000-2001 badly hurt Hong Kong exports and GDP growth, and led to an unprecedented level of unemployment in Hong Kong which was estimated at 5.2% in 2001.

The 2001 estimate of purchasing power parity was US$180 billion whilst the 2001 estimate of per capita GDP purchasing power parity was US$25,000. In 2002 Hong Kong was suffering deflation due to falling prices. This was however reinvigorating the territory's image as a place for bargain hunting.

Hong Kong no longer accounts for the bulk of manufacturing conducted by Hong Kong companies, however, it still does conduct a relatively small proportion of high value expensive product manufacture. The bulk of manufacture is now done in China, which has become the workshop of the world, or in other regional South East Asian countries such as Indonesia, Thailand, Vietnam, Taiwan, Malaysia, etc. Hong Kong is now a service orientated economy, although there is still some high value manufacturing taking place, such as expensive watches manufacture.

Between 1990 and 2000 the labour force grew from 2.75 million to 3.37 million. However, because of the declining birth rate any further expansion in the work force will have to be as a result of labour importation. Unemployment in 1990 was 1.3%, which also included an element of those changing job or between jobs thereby making the unemployment figure negligible. However, by 2000 unemployment had risen to 4.9% which by Hong Kong standards was high when considering the unemployment rate over the last 50 years. In 1999 unemployment peaked at 6.2% due to the aftermath of the Asian Financial Crisis. Also recession in the USA and Europe led to recession and deflation in Hong Kong. With regard to unemployment this was probably one of the worst years Hong Kong has ever experienced.

The current labour force was estimated as being 3.44 million in 2001 with wholesale and retail trade, restaurants and hotels accounting for 31% of the labour force; financing, insurance and real estate 13%; community and social services 11%; manufacturing 7%; transport and communications 6%; construction 2% and others 30%. The economy was running a deficit budget in 2001 with revenues being $22.9 billion and expenditures being $24.6 billion with capital expenditures being $465 million. External debt in 2001 was estimated as being $58.8 billion and the industrial production growth rate was -9% indicating a contraction.

From 1985 onwards Hong Kong experienced a very rapid and significant structural change in employment. Manufacturing industry has virtually all moved offshore with the majority of it going into China. This resulted in a continuous shift in personnel employment from the manufacturing sector into the service sector comprising wholesale, retail and import/export trades; restaurants and hotels; financing; insurance; real estate; business services; community, social and personal services; etc.

Between 1990 and 2000 the nominal wage index experienced an 83.9% increase in money terms for all industry sectors collectively. This represents an average annual increase of 6.3%, which is considerably higher than for many other developed economies. The real wage index for this period showed an increase of 12.6%. Hong Kong is a cash rich society with money being easily available to those who are prepared to work.

Gross Domestic Product (GDP) in 2000 was HK$1,267.2 billion which was more than double the GDP figure of HK$582.5 billion in 1990, or ignoring inflation and taking constant 1990 market prices, the GDP for 2000 was HK$893.5 billion which was 1.5 times the GDP for 1990. Hong Kong therefore experienced an average annual growth rate of 4.4% in real terms for the 1990s decade. The implicit price deflator of GDP, which is a broad measure of inflation in the economy, experienced an average annual rate of increase of 3.6% between 1990 and 2000, but recorded a decrease of 6.6% in 2000 due to cost and price adjustments as a result of recession and deflation due to external economic influences. The GDP growth rate in 2002 was 2.3% and in 2003 it was 3.3%, whilst the trend growth rate of nominal GDP was 4.5%. Hong Kong's GDP grew by 10.5% in real terms in 2000 reflecting the fact that the economy had recovered from the negative effects of the regional financial crisis of 1997 to 1999. Per capita GDP between 1990 and 2000 increased from HK$102,100 to HK$134,100 representing an average annual growth rate of 2.6%. Private consumption expenditure between 1990 and 2000 experienced an average annual growth rate of 4.1% showing considerable improvement in the standard of living for the population.

During the 1990s, trade in services became much more important for Hong Kong and the number of people employed in the services sector burgeoned. Production based GDP figures show a change in the economic structure of the territory. In 1990 manufacturing represented 17.6% of GDP whereas in 1999 it represented 5.8%. Financing, insurance, real estate and business services represented 20.2% in 1990 and 23.4% in 1999, whereas community, social and personal services represented 14.5% in 1990 and 21.6% in 1999. Thus services has continued to grow in importance for the economy.

Income flows between Hong Kong and the rest of the world during the period of 1993 to 2000 were enormous because Hong Kong is a major international financial centre. Factor income inflow and outflow was very high. Factor income inflow in 2000 was divided into 39% direct investment income, 23% portfolio investment income and 38% other investment income. Whereas factor income outflow in 2000 was divided into 70% direct investment income, 7% portfolio investment income and 23% other investment income. The banking sector between 1993 and 2000 accounted for more than 40% of income inflow and outflow thereby demonstrating Hong Kong's important role as an international banking centre. Hong Kong has tended to experience a greater net factor income inflow than outflow due to overseas multinationals investing in the territory. However, nowadays money is passing through Hong Kong as overseas multinationals seek to invest in China by channelling their money through Hong Kong.

In 2000 Hong Kong recorded a balance of payments surplus of $76.8 billion which was equal to 6.1% of GDP. In 2000, the territory recorded a current account surplus of HK$68.8 billion. This was made up of a visible trade deficit of HK$64.00 billion, an invisible trade surplus of HK$124.00 billion, a net factor income inflow of HK$21.50 billion and a net factor outflow of HK$12.70 billion. Added together this was equal to 5.4% of GDP. An increase in reserve assets on the balance of payments was recorded for both 1999 and 2000.

The opening up of China has resulted in Hong Kong manufacturing being moved offshore and as a result the number of people employed in manufacturing in Hong Kong has declined dramatically. During the 1990s this decline was 70.73%, but the structural changes in employment have resulted in the value added per person in the whole production process rising by 144%. This rise in value added per person is not just due to moving manufacturing offshore, but is also attributable to a number of other factors such as changes in the product mix, upgrading of product quality, improvements in labour productivity, mechanisation of the production processes, etc. In the 1990s various industrial sectors gained in prominence including the electrical and electronics sector, optical goods, paper products, printing and publishing, food and beverage, and tobacco. The move of manufacturing to China has not just been because of the low labour costs, but also because of the low land costs.

Over the 1990s many industries have experienced an increase in value added per person employed as industries have become more streamlined and efficient and cost per employee has become an important consideration in company expansion. Overall trade has continued to increase with the odd hiccup such as in 1998 and 1999 due to the Asian Financial Crisis and associated economic disturbance. Most manufacturers that have relocated production to China maintain a Hong Kong office to act effectively as a control centre and to facilitate import and export of components and product to their relative destinations. Sub-contract processing arrangements have become popular amongst import/export firms seeking to use China's manufacturing capacity.

The communications industry saw a 149% increase in its number of establishments during the 1990s from 395 to 985. Business services experienced an 86% increase in the number of its establishments and the transport and related services sector also saw a general increase in its income due to increased activity in its sector.

Hong Kong is a very externally orientated economy with its success and prosperity being totally dependent upon the prosperity or otherwise of the world economy. The economic performance of Hong Kong is dependent upon the performance of its external trade. The value of external merchandise trade between 1990 and 2000 rose at an average annual rate of 9.7% increasing its total value from HK$1,282.4 billion to HK$3,230.7 billion. The average annual growth rate of imports between 1990 and 2000 was slightly higher than the average annual growth rate of exports, being 9.9% and 9.4% respectively. The growth in total exports of goods in 2003 was 14.2% whilst the growth in total offshore trade in 2003 was 16.5%. Due to Hong Kong's position as an entrepôt and the moving of manufacturing offshore into China over the last 20 to 25 years, Hong Kong has seen a substantial growth in its re-exports primarily from China. The value of re-exports increased at an average annual rate of 12.9% between 1990 and 2000 whilst the value of domestic exports declined by 2.2% on an average annual basis. The share of re-exports in Hong Kong's trade rose from 64.7% in 1990 to 88.5% in 2000. Every year in the 1990s saw continuous expansion in re-exports except during the 1998 to 1999 Asian Financial Crisis hiccup, but 2000 saw robust growth and economic recovery.

Due to the rapid economic growth in China, it has become an important destination for Hong Kong's domestic exports. China and the USA accounted for 60% of Hong Kong's total domestic export value. These domestic exports included clothing, electrical machinery, electrical parts, textiles, office machinery parts and accessories, automatic data processing machines, jewellery, goldsmiths' and silversmiths' wares, articles of precious and semi-precious materials, and printed matter. Hong Kong's two way re-export trade has benefited very considerably from China's open door policy. China has been the main market for Hong Kong's re-exports accounting for 26.8% of re-exports in 1990 and 35.1% in 2000.

The main commodities re-exported by Hong Kong include clothing; toys; games; sporting goods; electrical machinery, electrical parts, apparatus and appliances; baby carriages; telecommunications equipment; textiles; automatic data processing machines and parts for office machines. The increase in outward processing operations in China has led to the increase in Hong Kong's imports from China with nearly all the outward processed product being for export from Hong Kong. The value of this outward processed product has been rising constantly since 1985.

Exports in 2001, including re-exports, were $191 billion whilst imports were $203 billion representing a deficit of $12 billion. Hong Kong's main export partners in 2000 were China 34%, USA 23%, Japan 6%, Germany 4%, UK 4%, Taiwan 3% and Singapore 2%. Hong Kong's main import partners were China 43%, Japan 12%, Taiwan 8%, USA 7%, South Korea 5% and Singapore 3%. The main export commodities were clothing, textiles, footwear, electrical appliances, watches and clocks, toys, plastics and precious stones. The main import commodities were foodstuffs, transport equipment, raw materials, semi-manufactures, petroleum, plastics, machinery and electrical equipment. A large share of the imported commodities were re-exported.

Communication is one of Hong Kong's main strengths. According to 1999 figures Hong Kong had 3.839 million main line telephones and with regard to mobile telephones it was one of the most highly penetrated areas in the world. The telephone system in Hong Kong is very modern and provides both domestic and international services. The territory has microwave radio relay links with extensive fibre optic network and combines microwave radio relay links and extensive floor optic network. The territory has satellite connections and coaxial cable connections making communication worldwide very fast and highly efficient.

Hong Kong currently has four television channels, two English and two Cantonese operating on analogue transmission. Many other channels are available on cable and satellite. The territory had 17 Internet Service Providers (ISPs) in 2000 with an estimated Internet use in 2001 of 3.93 million users which is approximately 54% of the population.

Hong Kong since the 1840s has been a free port and this has been one of the main aspects of its spectacular development. Most cargo is free to enter and leave Hong Kong territorial waters without incurring customs duties. Hong Kong is an important shipping port with an extensive range and variety of ships registered at the port. Ship voyages originating in Hong Kong are bound for ports on a worldwide basis, transporting cargo from Hong Kong all over the world. Larger vessels arriving at Hong Kong are very often guided into port by means of tugs and smaller vessels.

In 1997 Hong Kong had a recorded 1,831 km of highways, but this has since then seen further considerable development, particularly in the New Territories. This has facilitated rapid expansion of the passenger transport network.

The territory has 34 km of railway linking Hung Hom in Kowloon with the border of China at Lo Wu and then on to Guangzhou (Canton). This railway track is meticulously maintained and has not been subject to any problems.

The new airport at Chek Lap Kok which opened in 1998 is one of the largest airports in the world and certainly one of the best and largest in South East Asia. It is currently undergoing further expansion scheduled to be completed in 2008. The airport is one of the busiest in the world with a tremendous throughput of both passengers and cargo. The old airport, Kai Tak, used to be located in Kowloon City and was considered one of the most difficult for pilots regarding landing and takeoff. Although this airport had been a major asset in the development of Hong Kong, by 1998 it had reached the point where the amount of cargo and the number of passengers using the airport as a means of transport was just too much.

By 1998 Kai Tak was experiencing full capacity difficulties and there was a clear need for a new and larger airport facility. Due to this need for expansion the new airport of Chek Lap Kok was built on reclaimed land off Lantau island, which is the biggest island in the archipelago. The airport has a purpose built rail link connecting it with Hong Kong island, Kowloon and the New Territories. This also incorporates connections with the underground mass transit railway network. It has a purpose built road network system with an extensive number of bus services and taxis. There is also a hydrofoil system connecting the airport to Tuen Mun pier with tram links to Yuen Long in the New Territories and buses to other locations. Passengers do not encounter any problems getting to and from the airport and can very quickly move to their final destinations. The airport operates flights to destinations all over the world and is fully integrated into the international network of airports and airport services.

Hong Kong's old airport, Kai Tak, in 1995 was the second busiest airport in the world for international air cargo and the third busiest for international passenger traffic with 1.46 million tonnes of cargo and 27.4 million passengers. The new Chek Lap Kok airport was built because Kai Tak was already operating at full capacity and further expansion was urgently required. Chek Lap Kok airport has been designed to handle up to 35 million passengers and 3 million tonnes of cargo per year and with further scheduled expansion it will be able to handle 87 million passengers and 9 million tonnes of cargo per year. These projections are an indication of the expected growth in demand for these facilities to be experienced in the coming years, but will of course be influenced by movements and growth in the global economy. Hong Kong has the world's busiest container port and the world's busiest airport for international cargo. It is also one of the biggest and busiest airports in the world regarding international passenger traffic. The opening of the new Chek Lap Kok airport in 1998 has resulted in an expansion of the dense network of airline routes serving the territory and due to the airport now being removed from the populated areas it has enabled flights into and out of the territory to be on a 24 hour basis thereby further enhancing the attractiveness of the territory as a place for business location.

In 1997 Hong Kong was the world's second leading centre for international air cargo after Narita Airport in Japan. In 1995 cargo throughput was 1.46 million tonnes which at that time accounted for 20 percent of the value of the territory's external trade. Hong Kong is an air hub for South China and the new airport at Chek Lap Kok has the largest air cargo handling capability in the world. The territory has a dense route network that is serviced by many airlines and the territory has developed skills and expertise coupled with supporting services that make it the centre for air cargo in the South China region.

Hong Kong also had two heliports in 2001 for those seeking to have a bird's eye view of the territory.

Hong Kong's transport network is probably one of the best in the world. The MTR (underground) links Hong Kong island, Kowloon and the New Territories. Passengers rarely have to wait more than 3 minutes for the next train.

The city has three bus companies operating an extensive network of bus routes with a very high frequency of buses. Passengers rarely have to wait more than ten minutes for the next bus, although in some remoter parts of the New Territories the bus frequency is not as high, but in the populated urban areas buses are extremely frequent. Most buses are double decker, although single decker are available.

Hong Kong has a plethora of taxis that can pick up and drop off passengers almost anywhere within reason. Most taxi drivers are also able to speak English to varying degrees of fluency and will always assist with directions.

The city also has an extensive range of mini buses that are able to pick up and drop off passengers anywhere within reason and are an ideal quick way of getting around the territory. Mini buses are cheaper than taxis. However, in order to easily use the mini buses it is advisable to speak in Cantonese. In order to let the driver know that you want to get off, you have to say 'Lok Chair', which basically translates as 'get off vehicle'. This should ideally be prefixed with the word 'mgoy' meaning please. Mini buses are very popular in the populated urban areas.

Hong Kong has a large number of ferry services with some being local domestic services for just getting across the harbour or to an outlying island, whilst others are of an international nature travelling to China, Macau, etc. Ferry services include standard boat ferries, hydrofoils, jetfoils, etc.

Hong Kong does not have its own army, but instead a garrison of the People's Liberation Army (PLA) is stationed at various points within the territory. Defence of Hong Kong is the responsibility of China and as such the stationing of PLA troops in Hong Kong is a fundamental requirement. These forces include army, navy and air force personnel and are under the direct leadership of the Central Military Commission in Beijing and under the administrative control of the adjacent Guangzhou Military Region. Further troops if required can easily be called in from China. Military personnel are on a much lower pay scale than Hong Kong residents and have always kept a very low profile.

Geographically Hong Kong is situated at the centre of what is at present probably the most economically active area of the world. With its highly developed sea and air transport systems, Hong Kong is well situated as a hub for trade and investment into and out of China and South East Asia. The territory has consistently been rated as having one of the busiest container port operations in the world. In 1995 it had a throughput of 12.6 million TEUs (20-foot equivalent units). In 1999 Hong Kong handled 16.2 million TEU of container sea cargo making it the busiest container port in the world. In 1999, 37,500 ocean going vessels from over 200 shipping lines and over 115,000 river trade vessels visited Hong Kong.

In the 1950s and 1960s products despatched in containers from Hong Kong were actually produced in Hong Kong, now the vast majority of containers are of products produced by Hong Kong companies in China with the containers being transported by road from China, across the border into Hong Kong and then shipped from Hong Kong. Although there is an increasing number of shipments being made direct from China, the vast majority of shipments are still made via Hong Kong with its deep water harbour still being a natural advantage.

There have been many land reclamation projects along the harbour front in Hong Kong. Originally Queen's Road, Hong Kong side, was along the waterfront, but now it is a good walk from the harbour front with many roads to cross. Land reclamation has taken place on both Hong Kong island side as well as the Kowloon peninsula side of the harbour. It has thus led to a certain narrowing of the harbour. In 1842 the harbour was much wider than it is today, but in 2005 it is still nevertheless well suited for deep water cargo vessels.

One of the main reasons for the land reclamation projects has been the fact that Hong Kong has so little useable land. Hong Kong is the most densely populated city in the world and office rents and housing costs have nearly always been considered expensive when compared to other cities. This shortage of land has meant that land has had to be used very efficiently and as such developers have had to build upwards rather than outwards. Hong Kong's skyline is dominated by high rise office towers and apartment blocks. It is very common for people to live in apartment blocks that are 30 or 40 storeys high. Office towers are also 20, 30 or 40 storeys high. Factory buildings in Hong Kong developed on a multi storey basis prior to relocation into China and South East Asia. This concept of multi storey factory building aided the development of clustering of industries within Hong Kong.

Hong Kong's rise as a trading post and emergence as a major entrepôt was due to its natural location and the geographic advantages that it offered in connecting with the surrounding territories. Hong Kong has very quick and easy connection with all of China, Japan, Taiwan, Malaysia, Singapore, India, the Philippines, Indonesia, Thailand, Vietnam, Australia, etc. The natural locational advantages that Hong Kong offers have led to the development of an important sea cargo industry as well as air cargo industry. This has also facilitated developments in tourism, investment and financial management, clustering of industry support structures and services, corporate strategies on a regional and global basis, institutional arrangements to ensure a level playing field in business, etc.

Being based in Hong Kong is not like being in another world, instead the individual is at the heart of a dynamic and aggressively proactive society that has its finger on the pulse of world economic order and demand. Hong Kong has always been very responsive in the immediate sense of the word to the needs and desires of other regions around the world. That is why its import and export business is so prolific. Hong Kong has depended on world demand for its livelihood and as such has had to keep in very close contact with the rest of the world. Therefore its communications industry has developed at a prolific pace that has far surpassed other cities around the world. As such being based in Hong Kong gives the individual very easy and quick communication access to virtually all societies around the world.

Hong Kong's rise to fame as a trading post and its emergence as an entrepôt were primarily based on the geographical advantages of its location. In 1998 sea cargo into and out of Hong Kong and China accounted for approximately 85 percent of all cargo passing through the port of Hong Kong. The key competitive advantages of the port include its location, access to deep water, advanced container terminal infrastructure and transportation to and from the port as well as a very fast turnaround time in port. Also the route density (how many other ports can be reached from a given port), efficiency and reliability of service, ability to track containers at any point in their journey and low cost are key advantages offered by Hong Kong. The competitive efficiency of a port depends upon the extent of investment in its infrastructure, management skills and sophisticated software to optimize throughput. Hong Kong has invested heavily in these features thereby making it the busiest container port in the world and also one of the most efficient ports in the world. On a regional basis there are few potential competitors that could be compared with Hong Kong. Yantian and Ningbo in China, Kaohsiung in Taiwan and Pusan in Korea are a few of the competitors, but lack the infrastructure that Hong Kong possesses. Singapore is too far away to serve the same market that Hong Kong serves.

Hong Kong has the best natural harbour for hundreds of kilometres up or down the coast of China. It currently has eight large container terminals built and operated by the private sector with other terminals due to be operating soon. Container terminals 10 and 11 may be operating before terminal 9 due to China's opposition to the large stake to be held by Jardine's in container terminal 9. Land access to and from the port has been developed by the government thereby giving the port a superior physical infrastructure. Hong Kong possesses extremely advanced port management skills that facilitate optimization of the flow of containers through its terminals. The port development has been facilitated by easier access to capital in the territory and it has a far superior communications system than relevant competitors.

The Hong Kong economy is more dependent upon international trade than any other economy in the world and as such is susceptible to adverse movements in international markets. Between 1985 and 1995 annual growth in container throughput was 13 percent. A large percentage of production in Southern China is geared towards export markets and is controlled by Hong Kong firms. As the Chinese economy keeps expanding and demand in the North American and European markets remains buoyant, demand for Hong Kong's port facilities will remain high. China and North America are Hong Kong's main markets with Europe being a close third. However, in 2004 there were doubts regarding the growth of the Chinese economy in the short term and Europe was exhibiting sluggish growth. Nevertheless the North American market appeared to be very buoyant.

The port of Hong Kong is different from other ports due to it being privately operated and controlled by franchisees which has led to the private development of facilities and management for profitability, whereas most Asian ports are operated as a government service with other goals besides profitability. Hence there has been aggressive investment strategies in Hong Kong using hundreds of millions of dollars in order to expand the TEU throughput. The port has three major terminal operators and many smaller midstream operators and this has created a level of internal competition between the operators that has maintained price competitiveness. In Hong Kong it is believed that private firms with profit motives will provide a more efficient and price competitive service than the public sector.

A strong cluster of industries has developed in the territory in relation to sea cargo. Hong Kong is unmatched in its expertise and services with regard to marine insurance, evaluation and assessment of marine damages, trade finance, letters of credit, trade documentation and logistical support. As an arbitration centre Hong Kong has also developed great legal expertise in the resolution of marine disputes. Also the territory's position as a hub for international telecommunications has provided additional support to the sea cargo cluster and added to the efficiency of the territory.

The Hong Kong government attempts to track demand for cargo facilities and ensure that private sector firms can make a reasonable profit on investments.

Hong Kong's freeport status means that there are no lengthy customs procedures. The strong legal system means that firms can have greater confidence that papers and documents issued by Hong Kong banks and shippers are legitimate and that contracts will be enforced. However, the principal challenge for Hong Kong is managing growth and costs. Fluctuations in consumer demand, possible business slowdown, changes in national economic fortunes, etc. may encourage some shippers to consider re-routing their cargoes in order to cut costs to an absolute minimum. However, this would mean using lower grade services from other ports rather than Hong Kong's highly efficient top grade services.

Hong Kong skyline as seen from the Peak showing Victoria Harbour, Central, Wan Chai, Causeway Bay and the Eastern side of Kowloon Peninsula

An aerial view of Victoria Harbour

2. Strategic Advantages of Hong Kong

Over the past six decades Hong Kong has developed from being a small trading post to a leading world city economy and this development has been clearly linked with the globalisation of trade. Hong Kong has for a long time been used by world leading companies seeking to gain access to the mainland Chinese and Asian markets. This has greatly helped the city gain recognition around the globe for its status as a world class international business centre in finance and trade which has at the same time attracted many world renowned large companies and many SMEs. Hong Kong now serves as a strategic base point for overseas companies seeking access to mainland China and the Asia Pacific, but at the same time as a strategic base point for mainland Chinese companies seeking access to international markets. Hence it is a two way platform with Hong Kong benefiting from both flows. In 2006 there were approximately 3,800 overseas and mainland Chinese companies with regional headquarters or regional offices in Hong Kong and this figure is continuing to grow.

The territory offers many advantages for overseas and Chinese firms seeking to establish a regional office or headquarters. Attributes that many overseas and Chinese companies regard as locational advantages in Hong Kong include the excellent geographical location, the well established and fair legal system, the efficient communication and transportation infrastructures, the professional and impartial administration of the territory, the free and open trade structure, and the liberal taxation policies of the government. When these attributes are combined with the free flow of capital, information and people that has always been a way of life in Hong Kong, together with the fact that the city is one of the easiest places in the world to set up in business, Hong Kong becomes a very advantageous location for overseas and Chinese multinationals. Hong Kong has often been described as a jewel in the East, or as the jewel in the British empire. The British empire has now gone, but Hong Kong still shines like a jewel because of its commercial advantages and strategic location.

Even though many forecasters predicted the demise of Hong Kong in 1978 when China started to open its markets to trade and investment, the 1980s and 1990s were golden years for Hong Kong with the territory experiencing considerable economic growth at a rate far higher than most Western nations. The stock market boomed, employment prospered, property prices rose and the territory enjoyed a very healthy feel good factor. This happened even though British and Chinese politicians bickered and accused each other of insincerity regarding the handover of sovereignty. Nevertheless it was in the interests of both the British and Chinese governments to achieve a successful handover of sovereignty for Hong Kong in order to protect their own national reputations.

Hong Kong is now one of the world's leading forces in outward foreign direct investment. In 1994 and 1995 it was the fourth largest supplier of outward foreign direct investment in the world with US$21 billion and US$25 billion respectively. Hong Kong has been the leading investor in the ASEAN region and invests more in APEC than the USA does. If Japan is excluded, Hong Kong is responsible for more foreign direct investment in Asia than all of the other Asian economies put together. The territory is a key player in large infrastructure projects throughout the region and has emerged as an instigator and initiator of economic activity with activities being on a local, regional and global basis.

Hong Kong is now one of the largest foreign investors in the region due to the size and liquidity of its capital market, its policy of freedom of movement of capital into and out of the economy, and the extraordinary number of leading world banks from Europe, America, Japan and Asia that coordinate and control regional operations and activities from their bases in the territory. Hong Kong is also being used as a logistical hub for China and regional operations by thousands of multinationals and regional trans-national companies, which also helps to perpetuate Hong Kong's outward investment position. This scenario is also helped by the favourable tax regime operated in the territory. These factors in conjunction with the territory's industrial output from local and dispersed operations have made Hong Kong a cash rich economy.

An important characteristic of outward investment from Hong Kong is that it is on a business-to-business basis rather than government-to-government and therefore the investments are judged a success or failure on the basis of commercial criteria alone. This aspect of the economy is again indicative of the free spirit that is part of the fundamental nature of Hong Kong. An interesting feature that has arisen with regard to China is the 'round trip' investment in that money from China is moved to Hong Kong for investment in China to take advantage of tax breaks. The fact that investors use Hong Kong as a place from which to make investments throughout the region is testament to the strength of the Hong Kong economy and its position as a business and financial services centre.

Since 1979 and the opening up of China to foreign investment and trade, Hong Kong has become a lure for overseas firms interested in China trade and investment in the region and as such the territory has benefited substantially from the inward flow of capital. This flow has been supported and helped by the territory's strong legal system, sophisticated communications and transportation infrastructures and professional services. Companies from around the world have been attracted to Hong Kong because of its closeness and strong trade connections with China. The territory's business hub reputation and central position in the Asia Pacific are also strong and attractive features for overseas multinationals. The successful handover of sovereignty to China in 1997 and the establishment of the Basic Law as the territory's mini constitution have helped to maintain the territory's position as a business and financial centre provided that the provisions of the Basic Law are properly and fairly implemented and the autonomy of Hong Kong is respected.

Hong Kong has developed a competitive advantage as a trade intermediary due to its position as a trading hub for China and the world. Its strategic location and extensive transport links with China and the world, together with its professionalism and efficiency in trade relations has enabled it to offer multinationals an ideal business base. A significant amount of China's imports and exports are via Hong Kong. Many trading firms act as agents for overseas companies in order to sell product into China.

The unique combinations present in Hong Kong together with the superior business infrastructure are a decisive strength for overseas companies seeking to locate in the territory. Many of the world's leading civil engineering consulting firms, international corporate law firms, accounting firms and insurance firms have offices in the territory. The world's leading luxury hotel chains are also firmly represented in the territory. Over 50 percent of the overseas firms already established in Hong Kong are serving a geographic region that extends beyond Hong Kong and China. The local operations of overseas multinationals in the field of wholesale/retail and import/export activities highlights the importance of Hong Kong as a regional hub for sales, marketing, logistics and procurement functions. The Asian Financial Crisis in 1998 had an obvious effect upon the territory's level of business with the economies of South East Asia due to their suffering a serious drop in demand and currency devaluation. Nevertheless the basic infrastructure in Hong Kong is still very sound even though the territory has suffered from a record high level of unemployment, a halving of property prices with consequent negative equity, negative growth in GDP of 5.1 percent in 1998 and resulting deflation.

The strong economic performance of Hong Kong has been due to an advantageous combination of several factors, such as its location in one of the most economically dynamic areas of the world, its efficient and extensive infrastructures, its sound and strong financial markets and the growth of clusters of related industries. These advantages are supported by favourable institutions that promote a business philosophy of equality and a level playing field for all, a hardworking and highly motivated population and a strong prevailing business character that has stimulated economic development. These advantages have given rise to the development of a uniquely enterprising economy and culture.

At the time of its founding in 1843 the territory was regarded merely as a strategic point for the purposes of trade supported by military posting. The single important natural resource of the territory was its harbour, which is probably one of the best natural harbours in the world. The territory is short of any other natural resources and has had to essentially import all its raw materials and energy, capital goods and components. Hence one of its original functions was as an entrepôt under a free port system. However, the territory has now developed into a sea and air hub with extensive trade into and out of South China and South East Asia. Hong Kong is the most densely populated city in the world and due to the shortage of usable land space, office rents and housing costs are very expensive by world standards. The cost of land has had a direct effect upon industrial development strategies with the use of multi storey factories and relocation of production facilities to external lower cost areas being very common. The cost of land has also led to emphasis upon its cost efficient use. For example Hong Kong Air Cargo Terminals Ltd.'s (HACTL) second terminal is not the traditional horizontal structure of many air cargo terminals, but instead is a vertical structure that is regarded as one of the most efficient cargo handling terminals, if not the most efficient system in the world.

Hong Kong's superb telecommunications infrastructure facilitates international business and has developed primarily for that purpose in response to market demand. The cost of international calls is lower in Hong Kong than many other cities and more international telephone usage is made in Hong Kong than other cities. Hong Kong has one of the highest levels of cellular telephone service penetration. Excluding Japan, Hong Kong has the highest rate of telephone penetration in Asia and it is second to Japan worldwide in the level of facsimile usage. Hong Kong's sophisticated telecommunications and broadcasting infrastructure plays a very important part in supporting the territory's position as a regional headquarters hub for many multinationals. Hong Kong has an all digital telecommunications infrastructure with a larger capacity than many other important cities. The territory is Asia's optical fibre hub and as such possesses considerable regional advantages in terms of capacity. Recent liberalization of the telecommunications sector has led to increased competition and lower prices.

The Hong Kong stock market had 567 listed companies with a market capitalization of US$383 billion as at 30th September 1996 making it the second largest in Asia and the eighth largest in the world. Hong Kong's volume of external banking transactions is the fifth largest in the world making it a leading location for raising funds for ventures across the region and worldwide. Thomson BankWatch, the United States bank rating agency, in a 1995 survey proclaimed that Hong Kong was the regional base for the ten best performing banks in the Asia Pacific region. The World Competitiveness Yearbook of IMD International in 1996 rated Hong Kong second, after the United States of America, regarding venture capital availability for business development; second, after Switzerland, regarding favourable costs of capital; and second, after Luxembourg, regarding the positive influence of the banking sector on industry. Excluding Japan, Hong Kong is probably Asia's leading centre for raising venture capital with assets under management of more than US$8 billion as at mid 1996. Low tax rates have made it easier to accumulate retained earnings to finance new venture business than perhaps anywhere else in the world. Also Hong Kong's foreign exchange market in 1995 was ranked fifth in the world with an average daily turnover of US$91 billion.

Hong Kong's business acumen and ingenuity has been the prime reason for the Pearl River Delta (PRD) developing into what is one of the world's most important manufacturing and production centres for a vast array of industries. It is Hong Kong investment that has been a prime driving force behind the manufacturing development and expansion in Southern China. This development is now supplying product that is shipped all over the world.

Multinationals considering investment, expansion and market opportunities cannot fail to note the growth levels being achieved in the Asian economies. In 2003 the total value of trade of the Asian economies was US$3,587 billion which was approximately one quarter of the total world trade. Intra-Asian trade grew by a staggering 23% in 2003 and amounted to a total of US$1,863 billion. The momentum being experienced in East Asia is set to show further growth this year and represents ideal opportunities for the appropriate multinationals. Exports, fixed asset investment and private consumption are all experiencing a sustainable momentum. However, it is China that is experiencing prodigious growth and expansion, and is regarded by many as being Asia's brightest development, a shooting star – or golden dragon.

The Boston Consulting Group Business Matrix portrays Stars as high growth areas/units that generally require high financial investment in order to develop their perceived potential. Stars generally have the potential to develop into rich money generating Cash Cows enabling companies to recuperate expenses and earn substantial long term profit. Otherwise they may slip into becoming Question Marks due to unforeseen hazardous development or lack of correct financially targeted investment when positioned as a Star. Nevertheless, eventually the growth of a Star will inevitably slow down due to maturity. It is therefore imperative that investors and multinationals target their investment strategies correctly taking into account all the forms of competition and external market influences so as to protect the development of their market investments in order to generate the expected long term profit that can be earned from the particular market.

In 2003 the Chinese economy grew by 9% in real terms and in 2002 by 8%. In 2003 Chinese imports increased by a staggering 40% in financial terms whilst its exports increased by 35%. These are regarded as remarkable growth levels considering the country has such a substantial amount of trade with the world. China is now ranked in third place in the list of the world's merchandise importers with the USA in first place and Germany second. With regard to the level of imports China has in one year surpassed France, Britain and Japan. It can therefore be seen that China and South East Asia are very rich pickings for multinationals and must be included in global strategies and expansion plans. However, multinationals must consider the best, most cost effective and most appropriate means of reaching these markets, in order to properly enter the markets where it would be best to locate a regional headquarters or regional office. Due to its location and range of unique advantages as described in this book, Hong Kong is an ideal choice.

China's recent rapid growth has led to a substantial increase in demand for maritime transport to and from China. As a consequence this has led to a boom in the maritime industry on a global basis. There has been increased ship building particularly in Asia and increased demand for ship management. According to the United Nations review of Maritime Transport 2003 six Asian economies are now ranked amongst the 10 most important maritime economies. These six Asian economies are China, Hong Kong, Japan, Taiwan, Singapore and South Korea, and shipowners in these countries now control 38% of world total tonnage. It is expected that China's continued expansion at rates of 7% or 8% increases in GDP will continue to give rise to further expansion in demand for maritime transport and transport management.

China is importing a vast amount of raw materials and exporting a vast amount of finished product. There is an increased demand for all types of ship, both bulk and container of various sizes. This has also led to an increase in demand for maritime services such as insurance, brokerage, ship management and arbitration. As an international maritime centre at the heart of Asia, Hong Kong has experienced a considerable boom in maritime activity. Also its strategic location at the mouth of the Pearl River Delta has been of considerable benefit. The Pearl River Delta is the largest manufacturer in the world of consumer products producing more than

US$300 million worth of consumer products and 80% of the Pearl River Delta's imports and exports are handled by Hong Kong.

Hong Kong's strategic location in the centre of Asia has been a prime reason for its development as a dynamic economic city. It has led to its development as a financial and business centre, development as a leading international maritime centre due to its wonderful deep water harbour and also to the development of an extensive range of associated business activity. Hong Kong is a well established internationally reputable maritime centre with its own autonomous maritime administration and shipping register. Hong Kong has the busiest international air cargo centre in the world and it is a regional transport and logistics hub coordinating activity throughout the region. The territory has strong geographical, economic, business and cultural ties with mainland China giving it first mover advantage over any emerging business opportunities in China. This makes Hong Kong companies ideal business partners for overseas companies seeking to develop business relations with China. It also adds to the advantage of multinationals establishing a regional headquarters or regional office in Hong Kong.

Hong Kong maintains its own legal and judicial systems separate from China, it is a separate customs territory and negotiates its own air services agreements. The territory has a long history of operating under the rule of law, it has a clean and corruption free government, there is free flow of information within the territory so that business decisions can be made knowledgeably to the best effect and the government operates a simple low tax system. These aspects when taken together have made Hong Kong one of the freest and most business friendly economic environments in the world. This position has been consistently recognised by international rating organisations and is without doubt to the credit of Hong Kong and its population.

a) Freeport Status

Ever since Hong Kong was ceded to Britain in 1842 under the terms of the first Opium War, Hong Kong has been a freeport. There are no customs duties on imports or exports of merchandise to and from Hong Kong with a few exceptions. Cargo may freely enter, pass through and leave Hong Kong without imposition of duty. This situation no doubt arose because the development of Hong Kong in its initial days was not due to any form of government intervention or assistance, but instead was solely due to the commercial interests of the companies that used Hong Kong primarily as a transit point. As such these commercial interests did not seek to impose what could only have been construed as an impediment regarding their commercial aspirations.

In the early days there was serious concern regarding the cost of maintaining the territory with all its attendant problems of law and order and in 1847 a Select Committee of the House of Commons proclaimed that "we think it right that the burden of maintaining that which is rather a post for general influence and the protection of the general trade in the China Seas than a colony in the ordinary sense, should be thrown in any great degree on the merchants or other persons who may be resident upon it" (Welsh, 1997, P.187). In other words the British government decided that it did not want to pay the cost of developing and maintaining Hong Kong and that such cost should be the responsibility of those companies and organisations seeking to use Hong Kong for their own benefit. The attitude of the British government with regard to Hong Kong during this time was further displayed when the Foreign Secretary of the day, Lord Palmerston, infamously dismissed the territory as 'a barren rock'. In the 1840s serious doubts did arise regarding Hong Kong and whether or not the territory should be relinquished due to the fact that trade with Canton (Guangzhou) and Shanghai was developing at a much quicker pace. However, due to the investment that companies had already made in Hong Kong, the British decided to continue with the territory.

Hence it can be seen that the prevailing attitude was that Hong Kong had to stand on its own two feet and there would be little if any government assistance in its development. As such the territory was largely independent and had to fight for itself. It was this attitude towards Hong Kong in its early days that led to the foundation of the 'free spirit' that has been the fundamental nature of Hong Kong and one of the reasons for its success.

It is interesting to note that even in 1847 Hong Kong was not regarded as a colony in the true sense of the word, most likely due to its size, lack of resources and apparent potential at that point in time. Instead it was seen merely as a trading post for greater operations in the Far East and as such tended to be regarded as relatively insignificant and not worthy of government investment. Many overseas companies now established in Hong Kong are using Hong Kong as a base for regional operations covering South East Asia and China, and in most cases have chosen Hong Kong as a base because of the benefits of its geographical location, its freeport status and its financial and communications infrastructures, etc. Even though in 1847 Sir James Urmston described Hong Kong as an "utterly useless island" (Welsh, 1997, P.125) from a commercial point of view, it was Captain Elliot, who was primarily responsible for taking Hong Kong, who had the vision to see Hong Kong as a good strategic position for trade and military operations with considerable potential for development. It was over the next 150 years that this development was to be fully realised.

b) Intellectual Property Protection

Hong Kong now has its own Patents and Registered Designs Ordinance and Copyright Ordinance that was enacted and came into effect on 27th June 1997, thereby creating an independent registration system. Previously all registration and enforcement had to be done through the UK due to the territory being a colony. The Copyright Ordinance has been enacted to protect the interests of copyright owners as well as raise the image of Hong Kong's copyright legislation and enforcement in order to meet international standards. Previously this aspect appears to have been somewhat neglected under the British colonial administration. Also the territory is seeking to distance itself from China's lack of copyright protection which has been a frequent cause of complaint from the USA.

Under the Patents Ordinance there are two types of patent. A standard patent offers protection for a maximum of 20 years subject to renewal fees and a short-term patent offers protection for a maximum of 8 years. There are two stages in the registration system when applying for a standard patent application. Firstly, a request has to be filed regarding the recording of a patent application within 6 months of the publication of the application in a patent office. The State Intellectual Property Office in China, the United Kingdom Patent Office as well as the European Patent Office are designated patent offices. Secondly, the patent applicant has to apply for registration and grant within 6 months of the date of grant of the patent or publication of request to record, depending on whichever is the later.

A short-term patent would apply to products or processes after a required formality examination and requires that the applicant file a search report at a prescribed searching authority. Hong Kong's patent law is of a territorial nature and will only protect those patents that have been registered in Hong Kong.

A trade mark can be a variety of items including designs, letters, numerals, indications, characters, figures, the shape of goods or items, the packaging design or style of a product, the colour, sound or smell of a product or a combination of any of these items. The trade mark has of course to be unique and distinguishable and hence representative of some aspect of the product or service which in most cases is the quality and fashion of the product or service. Trade marks are used to build the image and reputation of the owner and in many cases are the distinctive item that consumers remember. On 4th April 2003, Hong Kong's Trade Marks Ordinance came into effect and clearly set out the rights attached to a registered trade mark as well as the basis and criteria for registering trade marks. It is essential that the trade mark can be graphically represented for it to be registered thereby giving the owner exclusive right and legal capability. Fraudulent use of a trade mark is a criminal offence under the Trade Descriptions Ordinance.

Under the Hong Kong Copyright Ordinance, copyright protection for work or performances originating anywhere in the world is automatic where copyright is capable of existing in the subject matter. Copyright does not need to be registered in order to exist and legal action can be taken where an infringement is found.

Hong Kong has an independent design registry under the Registered Designs Ordinance. The shape, pattern, ornamentation or configuration of a design can be registered provided it is used on an article in an industrial process. Only the outward appearance of the article is protected by registration and it must have an aesthetic appeal as well as be new. Design registration lasts for 25 years with renewal being required every five years. Registered designs are protected under copyright law for 25 years commencing from the date they are first marketed to the general public. Designs which are not registered, but capable of being registered, are protected for up to 15 years under copyright law. Infringement of a design registration can result in legal action against the infringer. Layout designs of integrated circuits are automatically protected without registration.

The Patents Ordinance, Registered Designs Ordinance and Copyright Ordinance all came into effect in Hong Kong on 27th June 1997 just prior to the handover of sovereignty as a result of the change in legal status due to the handing over of sovereignty. These ordinances together with the Trade Marks Ordinance and Trade Descriptions Ordinance comply with the Intellectual Property (World Trade Organisation Amendments) Ordinance of 1996 and are also in full compliance with the rules and regulations as well as standards of the Trade Related Aspects of Intellectual Property Rights (TRIPS) legislation.

It is the responsibility of the Customs & Excise Department to enforce the law regarding intellectual property rights. The department works closely with overseas and mainland Chinese enforcement authorities and owners of trade marks and copyright. The department has extensive powers regarding search and seizure in its investigative actions covering infringement of trade marks and copyright and false trade descriptions.

c) Property Market

The Hong Kong government owns all the land in Hong Kong and grants leases regarding the right to occupy, develop and use the land. There are no restrictions on foreign companies regarding the use of land and leasing procedures are very straightforward.

The main office areas are Central, Wan Chai, Causeway Bay, Tsim Sha Tsui and

Quarry Bay. Office occupancy costs will include rent, security deposit, property agency fee, management service charges, government rates, land rent, legal fees, etc. Occupancy leases are normally for periods of 2 to 3 years with option to renew. Tenancy agreements between landlords and tenants are registered at the Land Registry by the landlord. When the terms of a lease have been agreed, the landlord issues a Letter of Offer to be countersigned by the leasee and returned within a specified period together with security deposit, estimated rates and management service charge.

There are three types of industrial building - flatted factories, industrial/office premises and specialized factories. Approximately 80 per cent of the specialized factories are located in the New Territories whilst most of the flatted factories and industrial/office buildings are located in Kwun Tong, Tsuen Wan, Kwai Chung and Kowloon Bay.

There is a wide variety of residential accommodation in Hong Kong from detached villas with private gardens to high rise apartments.

d) Industrial Clustering and Economic Sectors

Hong Kong has evolved a number of dynamic clusters or groups of industries that symbiotically feed off and enhance each other. The clusters include the property, infrastructure and development cluster; the financial and business services cluster; the transport and logistics cluster; the light manufacturing and trading cluster; and the tourism cluster.

Hong Kong has become a leader on a global and regional basis in many aspects of real estate and infrastructure development due to the professional experience it has built up in recent decades. Property development and construction organisations are linked with engineers, surveyors, architects and interior designers in what has become a dynamic professional and highly experienced property, construction and infrastructure cluster. Developers in Hong Kong have had to contend with intense cost pressures that have created a need to complete buildings at speed and at minimum cost whilst the territory's very difficult building conditions have created the impetus for technical rigour and innovation.

In conjunction with this technical professionalism, many Hong Kong contractors have achieved full certification under the ISO 9000 quality management system. Since 1980 the property and construction sectors have annually contributed over 24 percent of GDP and as a result of escalating property values up until 1997, property assets have been very important as collateral for the expansion and diversification programmes of many Hong Kong companies. With the opening up of China, many property companies have become significant developers on the mainland and this aspect of the sector is expected to experience continued growth in both the short term and long term. The government does recognise the importance of this sector to the well being of the economy and part of its reasoning for entry into the stock market in August 1998 was to counteract the precipitous fall in both property prices and the share prices of property developers.

The financial and business services cluster accounts for more than 26 percent of GDP and is a powerful source of competitive advantage. It includes legal and accounting services as well as a dynamic financial services sector that encompasses private banking, fund management, corporate finance, currency trading, insurance, venture capital finance, direct corporate investment and stockbroking. The competitiveness of Hong Kong's economy is enhanced by the internal synergies that exist between the various parts of this cluster. For example law firms have expertise in international taxation which benefits the local banking sector; the legal, financial and accounting sector helps promote stock market transparency; etc. This cluster of successful services makes Hong Kong an attractive and highly efficient place for overseas firms to locate their regional operations.

The transport and logistics cluster incorporates air cargo, sea cargo, tourism, freight forwarders and logistics related services. The world's largest and probably most technologically sophisticated sourcing companies, freight forwarders and trade financiers are located in Hong Kong. The advanced communications infrastructure is an important source of advantage for the transport and logistics cluster because shippers and customers require up to the minute information in order to enhance their market positions. The Hong Kong Shipowners Association controls a significant proportion of the world's cargo fleet.

The light manufacturing and trading cluster comprises companies engaged in various industries including clothing, electronics, textiles, watches and clocks, plastics, toys, footwear, jewellery, etc. The cluster derives a powerful advantage from its critical mass and demonstrates competent design skills in its ability to understand and anticipate consumption trends in major foreign markets. The cluster also has the ability to integrate sources of demand and supply worldwide in order to produce successful consumer products with world class packaging. This entails the creation of logistical solutions incorporating detailed sourcing, production and distribution. The cluster also benefits from its ability to organize flexible and efficient production based on what has developed into very efficient subcontracting and parts manufacture networks comprised mainly of small and medium sized firms operating in all industries found in this cluster. The manufacturing sector remains export oriented with approximately 80 percent of the products manufactured being exported.

The garment industry in Hong Kong has been shaped to a very large extent by international quota arrangements and because Hong Kong was an early leader in the garment industry it has obtained some of the largest quotas. The third largest clothing exporter in the world is Hong Kong, and if re-exports from China were added, the territory would become the first in the world. The territory has developed a dominant position in the world's garment trade due to a number of key competitive variables that includes flexibility in design and manufacture, rapid response capabilities to speedily meet tight delivery deadlines in a fast changing fashion driven demanding market, reliable product quality, and knowledge of markets and merchandise. Hong Kong factories in this manufacturing sector are dispersed over an extensive area including China, Africa, Europe, Latin America and the Caribbean, but with management control, headquarters and logistics based in Hong Kong. The garment industry has for a long time been one of the main industrial sectors of the Hong Kong economy. However, the sector is now experiencing a number of changes that include rising costs, stagnant world prices, problems of obtaining and retaining skilled staff, the dismantling of global quota arrangements that were scheduled to take effect in 2005, and more restrictive USA rules of origin. As a result the industry is experiencing a decline in low value product, but high value product is currently stable.

The removal of quota restrictions in accordance with international agreements means that Chinese textiles and clothing products will no longer be subject to quantitative restrictions. The removal of clothing quotas will reduce costs and make Hong Kong products more cost competitive. Quota restrictions on Chinese textile exports were scheduled to be abolished in 2005. However, as a safeguard to prevent a sudden surge in imports of textiles, WTO members will be able to impose bilateral trade restraints after 2005 for an additional four years as and when they deem it necessary. The World Bank has estimated that because China has acceded to the WTO, its total share of the world market for apparel will exceed 47% in 2005, whereas had it not acceded to the WTO its share would have been approximately 19%.

The electronics industry in Hong Kong has focused primarily on OEM customers and hence has operated as a product development and manufacturing base for many overseas companies mainly from North America and Europe. As such the sector has developed skills in product development, design, marketing of services and other high value added activities in Hong Kong whilst manufacturing is conducted off shore. Strategies in the sector have mainly been developed on a cost basis as OEM customers have sought to reduce their landed costs to an absolute minimum by playing one manufacturer off against another in order to reduce prices. This sector is now finding that as a result of margins being squeezed to an excessive level and an increasing number of OEM customers trying to go direct to manufacturers in China, Hong Kong electronics manufacturers are having to develop their own product lines and start to develop their own brandnames. Most components are imported and the sector is sometimes subject to cost fluctuations as a result of shortages in key components such as microchips. Also in 1994-1995 as a result of downturns in demand overseas together with price competition between and price reductions by high profile Japanese brandname electronics manufacturers, Hong Kong manufacturers suffered considerably with profit margins disappearing in some instances. Also the sector has suffered from a lack of technological support by the government prior to the handover of sovereignty, whereas manufacturers in Taiwan and Singapore have had the benefit of government support for technological development.

Manufacturers in the territory have concentrated on OEM strategies with little attention being paid to the development of own brandnames. Hence Hong Kong has concentrated upon marketing its services, order processing, sourcing, design, product development, prototyping and quality control. These aspects have also been the main areas of concentration in other industrial sectors due to the dispersal of manufacturing processes to other low cost areas. Hong Kong is now a high cost environment and hence has to concentrate on high value added capabilities. The territory can no longer afford to compete properly in low cost activities due to developments in other regional economies.

In the civil and construction engineering sector many of the leading firms in Hong Kong are offices of overseas firms from the United Kingdom, Australia, the United States and elsewhere. The sector has not developed export markets to the same extent as other sectors in the economy due to the enormous regional demand in Hong Kong, China and South East Asia, but it is expected that further attention will be paid to export development in this sector.

The export trading sector is an important part of the economy and in 1994 generated US$23 billion or 18 percent of GDP. The sector is highly cosmopolitan, but nevertheless dominated by indigenous companies. Services offered by this sector are extensive and include trade financing; sourcing of products, raw materials and components; planning and managing production processes including product design, prototyping, certification, packaging, quality control and monitoring delivery; as well as logistical support services that encompass shipping, consolidation, scheduling, documentation and customs clearance. Hong Kong traders generally operate through a network of contacts and are able to match job requirements with costs, specifications and delivery requirements in a very efficient manner. The sector has developed a critical mass of strategic knowledge, manufacturing expertise and information networks that has resulted in it being an integral part of the larger light manufacturing and trading cluster that is firmly rooted in Hong Kong. A two way dynamic has evolved whereby the supporting services generate advantages for the export traders due to the comprehensive nature of the services they provide whilst the export traders provide a strong and sophisticated demand that drives the service providers forward.

The tourism cluster has for many years been an important sector of the economy. In 1995 tourism earnings were US$9.6 billion or 6.7 percent of GDP. Hong Kong is the world's eighth leading tourism destination on a receipts basis with 10.2 million visitors in 1995 making it Asia's leading tourist destination. The territory is often the starting or finishing point in regional travels. It has an extremely dense concentration of hotels, restaurants and retail shopping facilities that very few cities in the world can match. It is also a trade fair and exhibition hub that also helps in the further generation of income from visitor expenditure. Hong Kong's restaurant sector is rated as being amongst the best in the world. A trend that has arisen in recent years is the move by hotels to integrate into retail shopping operations and amenities in order to broaden their market to include the local population as well as hotel guests. The Hong Kong population is seen as being cash rich due to salaries within the territory being considerably higher than many other areas in the region.

In 2004 there were 12 million visits to Hong Kong from mainland China with 4 million of those visits being under the Individual Visit Scheme. The government in 2006 is seeking to extend the scheme in order to broaden the number and type of visitors. In the first two months of 2005 there were 3.64 million visitors to Hong Kong and in the first two months of 2006 this number had risen to 4.12 million. Arrivals from Europe, Africa and the Middle East were the main growth markets. On 1st May 2006 five more cities were added to the Individual Visit Scheme raising the total number of eligible cities under the scheme from 48 to 53. Tourism is a growth sector in mainland China and worldwide, and it is expected that in 2010 Hong Kong will receive 35 million visitors.

Hong Kong is currently seen as the prime tourist destination in Asia. According to a recent survey by the Hong Kong Tourism Board approximately 90 per cent of visitors stated that shopping was the main purpose of the visit. This is confirmation that Hong Kong still has a reputation as the shopping centre of the East due to its enormous range of good quality merchandise at fair prices. The Quality Tourism Services Scheme of the Hong Kong Tourism Board is aimed at raising the level and reputation of Hong Kong as a tourist destination and ensuring that companies operate at an acceptable international level. This in itself is a form of consumer protection for visitors and is supported by the Travel Industry Council.

Hong Kong: The World City and International Business Centre

During the 1970s, 1980s and early 1990s Hong Kong was regarded as offering very competitive retail prices on many of the consumer products that were available in its shops. However, from the mid 1990s onwards Hong Kong tended to lose this reputation due to rising costs and the growth in tourist competitiveness of other regional locations. Nevertheless the territory has one of the greatest concentrations of luxury hotels in the world. The Peninsula and Mandarin hotels are frequently ranked amongst the world's best hotels. Hong Kong is often regarded as the travel gateway to China and also offers a number of strong advantages with regard to tourism, such as, its central location within Asia, its status as a major international business centre, well developed communications and transportation infrastructures, an extensive airline route network making the territory a central stopping point for many airlines, one of the largest airports in the world, and its position as a place for international exhibitions and trade fairs.

The average visitor normally spends more on shopping in the territory than on the hotel. Between 1986 and 1995 arrivals increased by more than 150 percent. This trend peaked in 1997 just prior to the handover of sovereignty, but collapsed in 1998 as a result of the Asian Financial Crisis. Rich Japanese tourists had been seen as a good source of tourism income, but as a result of the Financial Crisis this sector disappeared from the market. In 1996 Hong Kong received 2.3 million Japanese visitors representing more than one fifth of the tourists visiting the city. This was more than from any other country and they spent more on each visit than anyone else except for the few rich Arabs that visited the city. Also room rates were finally realised as being excessively high and whereas previously room occupancy rates had been well above 85 percent all year round, occupancy rates plummeted to below 50 percent in some cases in 1998. This led to there being a substantially larger percentage of visitors to Hong Kong for business purposes rather than tourism. However, in recent years the regional changes in economic circumstances together with lower room rates as a result of increased sectorial competition has led to a resurgence in tourism in Hong Kong with the number of visitors reaching new highs.

Hong Kong's clusters interact and intersect each other giving rise to considerable competitive strength and in the process make individual industries much stronger than they would be individually. This interaction and intersection of the clusters has been supported by a solid legal system that has facilitated smooth and rapid development where individuals are free and protected, and firms are able to pursue their business without interruption.

Industrial clustering is a source of advantage providing knowledge spillovers, complementary products and services as well as help in building a strong supplier base due to the similar requirements of firms. Competition between local firms and the local operations of overseas firms as well as competition in the international markets have all created a pressure on firms to invest, innovate and improve their products and services so as to maintain and develop their market positions.

Hong Kong: The World City and International Business Centre

3. Hong Kong's Service Industries & Business Sectors

What does Hong Kong have to offer multinationals and companies seeking a presence in South East Asia?

a)   Business and Professional Services

Hong Kong is now a services economy and has achieved a level of services orientation that is the envy of the world. In 1997 approximately 84% of GDP was due to services making Hong Kong the most services oriented economy in the world. It is a major exporter of commercial services and rated 2nd largest in Asia after Japan. A large number of professional and business services companies are based in Hong Kong and have collectively made Hong Kong such a successful services centre. It is expected that as China integrates further into the world economy there will be an increase in demand for the services provided by Hong Kong companies. Hong Kong is expected to benefit greatly due to its strong cluster of professional services companies and unrivalled knowledge and experience of business in China. However, the scale of business opportunities that will emerge will inevitably vary from sector to sector.

Hong Kong is one of the leading banking centres in the world and certainly one of the largest in Asia. It is a major location for syndicated loans. Hong Kong has the highest concentration of fund managers in Asia, the 2nd largest stock market in Asia and is a major centre for financial derivatives. Hong Kong has one of the largest foreign exchange markets in the world, it has the largest gold bullion market in Asia, the largest number of authorised insurance companies in Asia and it is the largest venture capital centre in Asia. Hong Kong's supremacy in the financial services industry is very unlikely to be challenged on a regional basis. The legal system and institutional structures in Hong Kong are of international standing. Currency convertibility together with freedom of information and movement of capital makes business and financial activity very fluent and easy. The territory has well established supervisory institutions, a concentrated mass of institutional investors and world renowned capital markets that together make its resources unrivalled.

Hong Kong has experienced one of the world's fastest growth rates in its services sector with the annual growth rate between 1984 and 1997 being 16%. At the end of 1998, 85.9% of the working population were employed in the services sector. Growth in Asia and in particular China, combined with Hong Kong moving its manufacturing industries offshore as well as expanding them, have led to a considerable increase in demand for shipping, financing, trading and professional services which in turn has further developed Hong Kong's position as a regional trading hub and an all inclusive services centre. Hong Kong's strong services sector is pivotal in China's modernisation and expansion. Hong Kong is now a world leader in many individual service industries, but one of its outstanding features is that services can be packaged in such a way as to meet the individual requirements of any particular business.

For a long time Hong Kong has been Asia's services capital. Its strong legal framework and multitude of international institutions has led to a good growth in the territory's multinational service sectors which has made them the most advanced and most competitive in Asia. As China continues its dramatic growth trajectory and integrates more into the global economy in line with its WTO accession requirements, Hong Kong will experience exponential growth in demand for its many international business services.

b) Accounting and Auditing

In March 2003 Hong Kong had 3,607 accounting, auditing and bookkeeping firms with all the recognised international accounting firms having a presence in Hong Kong. The main service offered by these accounting firms included statutory and in-house audits, company formation, corporate finance, tax advice, listings and IPOs, company secretarial services and liquidation. Audit work is the main service offered by these companies, but the general trend is towards offering a full range of business advisory services. Most accountants in Hong Kong are full members of the Hong Kong Society of Accountants (HKSA), which is a self regulating organisation that governs and controls the professional conduct of accounts personnel in Hong Kong.

Most of the big international accounting firms have set up regional headquarters in Hong Kong due to the regional business opportunities and inevitable demand for good accounting services. The accounting industry is dominated by a few major international companies and all of these operate in Hong Kong providing the majority of services to Hong Kong's listed companies. Accounting firms are tending to become more global in their operations in order to match the global operations and aspirations of their clients. An increasing number of accounting firms, both local Hong Kong and major international firms, are seeking to enter the Chinese market. China is a major market for Hong Kong's accounting services with clients comprising Hong Kong companies and multinational organisations that have invested or intend to invest in the Chinese mainland as well as Hong Kong listed mainland Chinese enterprises. The Chinese accounting market opened in 1981 and since that date many of the top international accounting companies in the world have established a position in China, with the headquarters of most of these firms being based in Hong Kong.

Globally there is an increasing tendency towards harmonization of international accounting practices, standards and disclosure requirements which helps to facilitate capital movements as required in global business and as a result accounting firms are becoming more global. Hence size is important and major players are tending to dominate markets. Global activity now means that companies must have a presence in China and this normally requires associated activities in Hong Kong.

From 1st January 2005, the Hong Kong Society of Accountants will have a new mandatory requirement that members must pass a new competency based framework with regard to practical experience. Also people from overseas applying for membership, due to membership of counterpart institutions overseas will be required to pass an aptitude test in order to ensure that accountants working in Hong Kong are fully familiar with the local law and practice.

Many multinationals have a regional presence in Hong Kong because of the territory's well established and trusted business practices. Hong Kong is a strong adherent of international accounting practices. The accounting professionals in Hong Kong are of the highest world class standard and together with their language ability, they are perfectly positioned to assist international companies seeking a presence in the Chinese market. As a leading financial centre, Hong Kong has to date been the largest source of capital inflow for mainland China and as of July 2004 has been responsible for US$206 billion inflow into China. Its position as a liquid overseas fund raising centre has significantly helped mainland companies, which in turn has created a greater demand for its services.

In 2001 Hong Kong exported HK$232 million worth of accounting services. Hong Kong's biggest export market for accounting services is mainland China and the main exported services were statutory audit services, tax advisory services, corporate services, investment related advisory services, and computer assurance. The main types of client have been European and USA multinationals seeking a full range of professional advisory services. Other accounting services have included Chinese-foreign joint ventures seeking statutory audit services; contract related accounting services; corporate restructuring and investment advisory services; mainland companies listed in Hong Kong seeking initial public offering (IPO) services; and Chinese mainland companies in the process of expanding overseas seeking advice on establishing offices overseas including Hong Kong as well as arranging credit facilities overseas and listing services.

China's accession to the WTO represents a major opportunity for Hong Kong based accounting firms. Chinese companies must now abide by international rules and regulations regarding business practices. Previous restrictions are being phased out so that China is in full compliance with WTO requirements. This will lead to a substantial increase in the number of overseas firms seeking entry into China commercially and with that a substantial increase in demand for accounting services. Many, if not most, of the local and international firms in Hong Kong will expand their business services into China.

Hong Kong, due to its unique position, will serve as a bridge between international organisations and China giving rise to a substantial increase in demand for professional accounting services. Also the Closer Economic Partnership Arrangement (CEPA) very recently entered into by Hong Kong and China will further assist in the growing demand for Hong Kong's services. The lengthening of the Temporary Audit Business Permit under the CEPA agreement will also help Hong Kong accounting firms in their business in mainland China.

c) Advertising and Market Research

The Asian capital for advertising is Hong Kong with a per capita advertising spend that is the highest in the world. Advertising and market research are fast growing service sectors with the advertising market being dominated by multinational agencies. A handful of multinational companies handle the bulk of market research although there are consultants that specialise in various industry studies. Most of the multinationals in market research have a regional network for broader studies. China is regarded as a good potential growth market for advertising and market research. Therefore in recent years there has been a growing allegiance between companies in Hong Kong and China so as to overcome any possible constraints regarding advertising and market research work, and China's WTO membership should remove any restrictions in due course.

Hong Kong's advertising sector is set to benefit greatly from China's WTO accession. Currently there is a lack of professional advertising expertise in China and therefore many international agencies in China are forced to rely on services support from Hong Kong. It is expected that the demand for good quality advertising services will increase substantially, especially from Chinese companies as well as from Hong Kong companies and multinationals based in Hong Kong as the effects of China's WTO accession are fully realised.

Television is the main advertising medium in Hong Kong with 2003 seeing a growth rate of 26% compared to 2002. Hong Kong's total advertising expenditure covering television, print, etc. in 2003 was HK$35.8 billion representing a growth rate of 8%. In March 2003 there were 4,529 firms in Hong Kong engaged in advertising and related services generating business receipts and income of US$818 million. Hong Kong has seen a growth in advertising agencies offering account management, creative services and media planning. Some multinational agencies also offer sales promotion and public relations. The industry has two associations, the Association of Accredited Advertising Agencies and the Hong Kong Independent Advertising Agents Association.

Hong Kong exports advertising and market research services including creative advertising, direct marketing, marketing consultancy, graphic design, media buying, customised market research and the sale of research data.

An interesting and relatively new development in the realm of advertising in Hong Kong is the incorporation of flat screen televisions in many of the buses. The buses in Hong Kong are a very important means of public transportation used by the vast majority of the population. As such the buses are in most cases at most times of the day carrying many passengers. Therefore these passengers for the length of their journeys represent an almost captive market for advertisers. Many of the buses now have three Samsung flat screen televisions with two upstairs and one downstairs. Advertising is constantly being shown on these screens and represents an ideal means of reminding consumers about products and services currently available. All of the screens are equipped with audio transmission so that passengers can both see and hear the advertising. In many cases the advertising can be quite entertaining if not captivating, therefore passengers must remain alert as to when they need to get off the bus.

According to Nielsen Media Research, in the first month of 2004 Hong Kong's advertising expenditure was HK$3.2 billion representing a 14% growth on the same period in the previous year. As more overseas companies seek to enter the mainland Chinese market there will be an inevitable growth in advertising and marketing expenditure. There will be an increased emphasis on sales and distribution, brand building, corporate identity building and promotion. Increased competition will raise the level of importance of market intelligence and make advertising more critical in achieving corporate objectives. Public relations will also become much more important as a means of raising corporate and brand image.

Overseas companies entering China will have to seek to persuade the population to buy product that is not indigenously Chinese. They will also have to overcome cultural differences in their sales promotion and realise that a product that sells well in the western world based on a western style of advertising campaign with innuendos accepted in the western world, will not sell well in the Chinese and Eastern world with the same style of advertising. The advertising will have to be reformulated to take into account the cultural differences in order to achieve sales response and corporate objectives. The style of communication and product image will be critical to achieving the desired response and therefore market research into buyer response and motivation will be very important.

In the same way mainland Chinese companies seeking to move through Hong Kong in order to sell to the rest of the world, will also have to reformulate their advertising, marketing strategies and plans in order to appeal properly to the rest of the world. It should also be noted that under the CEPA agreement Hong Kong advertising companies will be able to set up offices in China two years before overseas companies can set up offices based on China's WTO accession timetable. This gives Hong Kong companies a distinct first mover advantage and is therefore a very good reason for overseas companies to consider partnership arrangements with Hong Kong companies in order to avoid this potential delay.

d) Design Services

As a regional design centre Hong Kong has world class facilities. The territory has traditional design and printing techniques coexisting closely with the most advanced computer-aided design facilities in the world. Hong Kong's design capabilities have been well recognised at international level. At the centre of Asia, Hong Kong is ideally located to help companies of all sizes and all nationalities in their design requirements at product, advertising and promotional levels in order to promote their products and services in the region.

Hong Kong's design industry incorporates a wide range of disciplines including product design, interior design, graphics design, fashion design, etc. This has led to the creation of a number of professional associations including the Hong Kong Designers Association (HKDA), the Interior Design Association (IDA), the Chartered Society of Designers (CSD), and the Hong Kong Fashion Designers Association (HKFDA).

Hong Kong is very strong in graphic design for the print media, which is backed by a well established printing and publishing industry. The industry comprises a few large design houses, many small local firms and some freelance designers. Product design capabilities are supported by the territory's shift away from traditional OEM production and move towards ODM production with design taking place in Hong Kong and manufacturing in China.

In Hong Kong there are over 1,700 design companies covering a broad range of activities. Its fashion design sector supports recognised international names and the territory has local design schools turning out graduates every year. Hong Kong's strength in fashion design is also supported by the fact that the territory is probably the leading garment exporter in the world. The general trend within the design industry is to cover the entire design project from conceptualisation to production. As a leading regional design centre, Hong Kong's support services for designers are rated as being of the best quality and include output centres, post production houses and printers, etc.

An increasing amount of Hong Kong's design work is for export with design services experiencing a growth in demand from China and South East Asia. Due to the wealth of international experience of the territory, Hong Kong designers are able to draw upon a vast array of international influences in order to meet the needs of a vast array of international customers from around the world. Hong Kong designers are ideally positioned to assist companies in the promotion of their products on a regional basis in Asia and China.

Hong Kong's design and multimedia capabilities are the best in the region. The Hong Kong government has recently established the Hong Kong Design Centre in order to promote the design capabilities of the territory. The centre is a multi-disciplinary facility promoting design standards, providing design education and raising the profile of Hong Kong as an innovative and creative design centre in Asia. Hong Kong's design services are thriving and China's accession to the WTO together with the CEPA agreement has given Hong Kong designers a clear advantage over others regarding business in China. Also Hong Kong's development of the Pearl River Delta region has enabled Hong Kong design companies to thrive and develop their competitiveness.

Hong Kong has also developed an awards system for design excellence in order to promote the industry. A new Promotion of Innovation and Design Steering Group is spearheading activities regarding the promotion of the innovation and design industry. In conjunction with Hong Kong's emphasis on design creativity, the government has also strengthened its intellectual property rights regime in full compliance with international standards. This incorporates a design registration service thereby protecting designs.

Design in Hong Kong is now recognised as being a high value added activity because of its sales function and what it provides to business. Design can also be critical to the success or failure of products as well as businesses. In order to further strengthen Hong Kong's design capabilities, the government has assisted in the establishment of a Science Park for integrated circuit (IC) design and development, as well as a Cyberport that is a digital media and wireless development centre.

e) Building and Construction

Due to the geography of the terrain, Hong Kong has developed as a leading expert in design and construction. High-rise design, high density design, slope design and space constraint design are all part of Hong Kong's expertise. It has developed this expertise due to the difficult constraints of its land mass. The quality of its architectural design expertise based on an extensive range of building types and projects is amongst the best in the world. Due to time constraints building is very efficient and cost effective with developers seeking to recuperate financial outlays as quickly and effectively as possible.

Hong Kong also exports its professional architectural services by playing a prominent role in residential development projects, commercial centres, hotels and urban planning and infrastructure projects throughout the region. All practising architects have to register with the Hong Kong Institute of Architects (HKIA). In July 1999 there were over 1,400 registered members and 130 registered architectural firms with many foreign nationals working as architects in Hong Kong. China and South East Asia are the main export markets for Hong Kong's architectural services.

Building and construction companies have developed a good reputation for quick construction of high quality office and residential blocks. Land reclamation together with specialised design and building methods have led to Hong Kong being recognised as the regional leader in the building and construction industry sector. The construction industry in Hong Kong comprises a small number of large scale local contractors, much subcontracting, and many companies that are both developers and contractors. These local contractors are using sophisticated technology and have strong financial backgrounds giving them a powerful position in this industry sector.

Foreign and local contractors in this sector as in all other sectors are treated equally and are free to tender for projects which will be awarded based on ability, track record and financial capability. China is a definite growth area for this sector with an increasing number of projects becoming available as the country maintains its impressive GDP growth rate and Hong Kong contractors have a definite first mover advantage. Therefore overseas multinationals should consider the possibility of partnership arrangements with Hong Kong contractors as a means of market entry.

Hong Kong's experience and technical expertise in the surveying sector makes it the region's leader. The buoyant construction market and the rush to build high rise offices and residences has provided invaluable experience to Hong Kong's surveying industry giving rise to good expansion. Most surveying companies now offer a one-stop shop approach to surveying services providing a comprehensive consultancy service to clients including development consultancy, property consultancy, project management, interior design and fitting out work. China is now the main export market for the surveying profession with an increasing number of construction projects in the region being led by Hong Kong investors.

f) Engineering and Producer Services

Hong Kong's engineers are noted as being hardworking, efficient, flexible and business minded. The territory has a very active engineering sector with the qualifications of its engineers being recognised internationally. The Hong Kong Institution of Engineers is a local professional body originally inaugurated in 1947, but incorporated by government ordinance in 1975 with the objective of setting professional standards and encouraging professional development.

China is the largest market for Hong Kong's engineering service exports and is currently exhibiting a great demand for high-tech equipment and engineering services. This is primarily due to Hong Kong's active investment strategy regarding mainland China together with the fact that Hong Kong is now officially part of China. An increasing number of overseas manufacturers are seeking to form partnerships with Hong Kong's engineering companies in order to develop product engineering design services so as to benefit from the close proximity with manufacturing bases in China and South East Asia.

Hong Kong's producer services in 1980 represented 20 per cent of GDP. In 2004 this figure had risen to 40 per cent and accounted for more than 70 per cent of external earnings. Trade with China has grown at an average annual rate of 7.9%. The Hong Kong government is seeking to promote the territory's producer services by encouraging companies to make a greater use of technology applications and innovation by strengthening the territory's design, research and development capabilities and emphasizing the idea of building brandnames. Part of the government's promotion is the recognition that Hong Kong now plays a vital role in what is a two way trade flow between China and the rest of the world.

g) Management Consultancy

Many of the leading consultancy companies in the world have a presence in Hong Kong including names such as McKinsey & Company, PricewaterhouseCoopers, Deloitte Touche Tohmatsu, etc. There are over 1,000 banks, investment houses and related services in the finance industry generating many opportunities for management consulting companies, many of which are in the six core disciplines of organisational management and structure, public sector management, product development, corporate strategy, finance management and information technology. The fact that there is such an abundance of management consultancy talent in Hong Kong effectively makes the territory the management consultancy centre of Asia and hence a superb location for conducting business on a regional basis. The support and infrastructure in Hong Kong is excellent for the management consultancy industry. Companies have a number of features in their favour including:

- simple and minimal licensing requirements,
- highly developed electronic and telecommunications technology,
- the free movement of capital and information,
- a clean corruption free government with a pro business attitude,
- an independent and fair judiciary,
- strong business links with China,
- a large pool of experienced management consulting professionals,
- a low, simple and predictable corporate tax system, and
- strategic location at the heart of South East Asia.

The prospects for management consultancy companies in Hong Kong are very good for a number of reasons, including China's accession to the WTO and its inevitable business expansion, government expenditure regarding the public infrastructure, banking deregulation, government outsourcing, as well as the new CEPA agreement between Hong Kong and China and the business opportunities that it will create. Under the CEPA agreement Hong Kong management consultancy companies can establish operations regarding general management, marketing management, financial management, human resources management, production management, public relations services, etc., before overseas companies will have a chance to establish companies covering these operations in China.

h) Corporate and Investment Banking

Due to its well developed financial markets and financial infrastructure, Hong Kong receives a tremendous amount of foreign direct investment with a large percentage of it being re-directed to China and South East Asia. Banks and deposit-taking companies are the main recipients of foreign direct investment. At the end of 1997, foreign direct investment amounted to US$94 billion with 93% of this figure being in the services sector. As a leading international financial centre with massive and liquid capital markets, a well developed and extremely efficient financial infrastructure, a highly talented pool of workers and many institutional investors, Hong Kong is ready to benefit greatly from China's market liberalisation.

Hong Kong is now the third largest capital raising market in the world. Stock market capitalisation is now more than 50 per cent higher than prior to 1997 and trading volume is at a record level. The stock market is extremely active. Hong Kong's financial services sector is now in the process of developing opportunities in mainland China with regard to the huge potential offered by business. It is also developing its bond markets and asset management services in China.

Hong Kong has more international banks than most other cities in the world. The territory has an extensive banking industry that includes 85 of the world's top 100 banks. This further strengthens Hong Kong's position as an international banking and finance centre. As an international banking centre, it has one of the highest volumes of external transactions in the world. This links in very clearly with its premier position as a loan syndication centre and foreign exchange market with a daily turnover in 1999 of US$80 billion. The overall quality of Hong Kong's banking system is the best in Asia with its institutions being prudentially supervised and having a high standard of market transparency and disclosure. The prominent size of Hong Kong's banking sector enables it to play a very important role on a regional basis. Hong Kong has a three tier banking system consisting of licensed banks, restricted licensed banks and deposit taking companies. The banking sector has a worldwide network of operations which in 1999 covered more than 70 countries. Hong Kong is one of the largest investors in mainland China's banking sector being one of the first to move into that sector. The Hong Kong and Shanghai Banking Corporation has recently in 2004 bought a major share interest in China's Bank of Communications which is one of the four major banks in China.

In March 2004 it was reported that Hong Kong had 136 licensed banks, 42 restricted licensed banks, 39 deposit taking companies and 89 representative offices of foreign banks from 30 economies. Hong Kong is the seventh largest foreign exchange centre in the world and is one of the three largest international banking centres in Asia with external transactions in the third quarter of 2003 amounting to US$648.2 billion.

Corporate and Investment Banking is closely monitored by the HKMA which oversees the monetary and banking system by means of continuous supervision with on-site and off-site examination and review, prudential meetings, close links with external auditors and information sharing. The Hong Kong banking system is the primary source for fund raising within the region. The Hong Kong dollar is freely convertible and will remain so in the future. All major currencies can be bought and sold in Hong Kong at market rates. There are no restrictions on currency trading or the international movement of funds as well as the repatriation of dividends and capital by foreign investors located in Hong Kong. Real time USA dollar and Euro gross settlement systems are already firmly in place in Hong Kong which is indicative of the security of the system.

Asset requirements for foreign banks seeking to establish operations in Hong Kong have been lowered recently from US$16 billion to US$510 million making such establishment much easier. China's accession to the WTO will result in a growth in global trade for China and the region with a consequent increase in demand for trade related financial services from banks in Hong Kong. Therefore growth prospects for Hong Kong based banks, both local and overseas incorporated, are extremely good.

i) The Venture Capital Market

The Hong Kong Venture Capital Association came into existence in 1987 in order to promote, protect and develop Hong Kong's venture capital industry. Hong Kong manages a large percentage of the venture capital in the region, and at present it is Asia's largest venture capital centre. The territory is to a large extent an administrative centre serving the whole region with the vast majority of venture funds being sourced from countries overseas and then distributed to companies overseas. Hong Kong is only to a minor extent an investment target. China is an important theme in Hong Kong's venture capital fund raising operations.

In 1997, 94% of venture capital funds in Hong Kong came from outside of Asia, and 92% of the funds went to overseas companies with 89% going to companies operating in the region. Hong Kong's world class financial system and low tax base make it a very attractive location for venture capitalists. The Asian Venture Capital Journal recently stated that, excluding Japan, Hong Kong and China represented the largest venture capital base in Asia. Hong Kong currently has a total capital pool of over US$14 billion.

The mission statement of the Venture Capital Association is as follows:

- To encourage a healthy venture capital industry and equity market in Hong Kong and China.

- To raise the level of awareness in Hong Kong and China regarding venture capital and equity.

- To raise the level of understanding of the benefits of venture capital and private equity in developing value in the business environment.

- To promote active investment in Hong Kong and China.

- To create an influential force through the Venture Capital Association that can influence government and other regulatory authorities.

- To provide a forum for members to exchange views and ideas as well as create a platform for interactions on a local, regional and international basis.

- To maintain a high standard of ethics within the industry.

- To ensure that personnel in the industry are of a high quality and well trained.

- To enable members to develop information resources.

- To help create investor confidence within the venture capital industry and increase the level of investment within the industry.

- To ensure that service providers can help in raising the professional level within the industry.

j) The Debt Market

Hong Kong's debt market is one of the most liberal in the world. International investors can freely invest in all kinds of debt instruments and foreign borrowers can freely draw on the domestic debt market. Overseas companies based in Hong Kong can finance their business activities by issuing various kinds of debt instruments in either Hong Kong dollars or other currencies in order to raise capital. Hong Kong has a very sizeable debt market that in March 1999 was HK$402 billion with 76% being private sector bonds. The private sector bond market is one of the largest and most liquid in the region and the secondary debt market is also one of the most active in Asia.

Hong Kong does not have any local credit rating agencies. Instead, international rating agencies have to be relied upon. In June 1994 Moody's Investor Services set up a regional office in Hong Kong and at the end of 1994 Standard & Poor also set up an office in the territory. A substantial proportion of Hong Kong dollar debt securities are now rated issues. The debt market has added greatly to the territory's position as the regional prime finance raising centre particularly for operations in China. Due to the liberality of the debt market together with its openness and variety of choices, international institutions and companies have been prompted to issue bonds thereby enabling the territory to develop further as the region's debt financing centre. Hong Kong is also one of the main proponents in developing a regional bond clearing and settlement system comprising a network of debt markets in the region. This system is called Asiaclear and will enable the settlement of Asian and international bonds in the Asian time zone thereby further facilitating the development of a regional debt market to meet regional business requirements.

At the end of 2002 the Hong Kong dollar debt securities market totalled HK$532 billion. There were a wide variety of debt instruments available including retail bonds, mortgage backed securities, floating rate notes, notes with a retail tranche, etc. Private sector bond trading is very popular and many debt instruments are listed on the stock exchange. A number of institutions are currently issuing private sector bonds including banks, corporate bodies, multinational agencies such as the World Bank and Asian Development Bank, as well as statutory bodies or government owned corporations such as the Hong Kong Mortgage Corporation (HKMC), and the Airport Authority (AA). The HKMA's Central Moneymarkets Unit (CMU) has developed extensive links with global and regional clearing and settlement systems in order to enable cross border trade in debt securities. The HKMA is active in the development of a debt market on a regional basis and is in the process of developing links with other authorities in the region.

There are many factors helping in the development of Hong Kong's debt market including:

- [ ] The openness of the market structure.

- [ ] Foreign borrowers can actively draw on the debt market without restriction.

- [ ] Debt instruments can be issued in any currency.

- [ ] Excluding Japan, Hong Kong has one of the most liquid markets in Asia.

- [ ] There is no profit tax on Exchange Fund Bills and Notes.

- [ ] Price guidance is provided by a benchmark yield curve with maturity of up to 10 years.

- [ ] Exchange Fund Paper can be used as security when trading on the margins in stock options and futures, and

- [ ] The use of Exchange Fund Paper as security in transactions enhances the liquidity of the Hong Kong dollar fixed income market.

Hong Kong is the premier regional finance raising centre and competition in the debt market is intense. The growth in the number of mainland Chinese companies listing in Hong Kong is leading to growth in the 'H-bond' market. Hong Kong is developing a multi-currency capital market and debt market, and with this the USA dollar clearing system and Euro clearing system will be integral parts because they facilitate efficient delivery and payment settlement of transactions thereby encouraging investors to be more active. The HKMA is keenly involved in this development work. Also the growth in the Mandatory Provident Fund (MPF) is forecast to boost the fund management industry and in turn the debt market due to the accrued asset value.

k) Securities

Hong Kong's securities market, like the debt market, is very liberal and liquid. The territory allows the free movement of capital into and out of the economy and there are no capital gains or dividend income taxes. Money is free to enter and leave the territory without being subject to troublesome exchange controls that only impinge on business activity. The territory has the second largest securities market in Asia with efficiency and risk management systems that are one of the best in the world. Its securities market is very internationalised with trading by investors from around the world. The securities market had 299 listed companies in 1990 and 688 in June 1999 with a total market capitalization of HK$3,590 billion. Due to the liberal and liquid nature of Hong Kong's securities market, it has attracted many international investment banks and securities organisations. The increasing listing of overseas incorporated companies on Hong Kong's securities market does not just benefit the securities industry, it also benefits associated service industries such as accounting and legal services.

The Hong Kong Stock Exchange is the second largest in Asia and the ninth largest in the world on the basis of capitalisation. However, it is the main source of foreign capital for mainland China. There are no restrictions on stock ownership, no tax on dividend income, no capital gains tax and no controls on capital movements. Many companies listed in Hong Kong are also listed overseas and all of the world's main multinational brokerage firms are active in Hong Kong. At the end of 2002 the Stock Exchange of Hong Kong had 812 companies listed on its main board with a market capitalisation of US$456.3 billion and the GEM had 166 companies listed with a market capitalisation of US$6.69 billion. GEM is the Growth Enterprise Market index. The Hong Kong Securities and Futures Commission regulates trading activities on the stock exchange which are governed by Hong Kong law and exchange rules. The blue chip indicator of the Hang Seng Index has 33 counters. The H share index which is the Hang Seng China Enterprises Index consists of companies incorporated in China and listed in Hong Kong. The Red Chip index which is the Hang Seng China - Affiliated Corporations Index consists of Hong Kong and overseas incorporated companies that are at least 30% owned or controlled by official mainland China entities.

Hong Kong has in recent years experienced an increase in the number of international investors entering the market with many initial public offerings being made globally. An increasing number of mainland Chinese companies are also listing in Hong Kong for fund raising activities. Equity finance is important for many mainland Chinese companies. Also China's accession to the WTO has made foreign investment in China more easier for foreign enterprises and this will result in a greater flow of investment capital through Hong Kong with many overseas companies seeking the guidance and assurance of Hong Kong investors because of their knowledge and expertise.

l) Fund Management

Hong Kong is the leading fund management centre in Asia having the largest number of fund managers. Its fund management industry is mainly international and offshore with a high percentage of funds coming from overseas clients. In 1999, 95% of authorised funds were domiciled abroad and approximately half the funds were managed offshore. Hong Kong is now playing a leading role in the development of China's fund management industry. The international orientation in its fund management industry is largely due to the presence of many leading investment management companies from around the world together with the very wide range of investment choices open to investors. Investors have the choice of equity funds from all of the world's equity markets plus also bonds, warrants, futures, options, money market instruments, etc.

At the end of 2002 Hong Kong had 192 companies providing fund management and advisory services with a total of HK$1,491 billion under management. By March 2003 the territory had 1,965 authorised unit trusts and mutual funds, with equity funds accounting for 57%, bonds 17% and guaranteed funds 10%. Many Hong Kong people buy stocks, shares, bonds, etc. and by 2001 approximately 9% of the adult population had invested in some form of investment fund. The MPF scheme has created another source of fund management activities and by June 2003 the MPF had created 296 approved constituent funds. It is the responsibility of the Securities and Futures Commission to properly regulate and supervise investment funds including unit trusts, investment linked assurance schemes, immigration linked investment schemes, mutual funds, pooled retirement funds as well as other forms of investment funds and schemes.

Hong Kong has more fund managers than anywhere else in the region and as such is recognised as Asia's leading fund management centre. Many of the world's largest fund management companies are operating in Hong Kong together with independent specialists. A substantial percentage of the funds under management are international and offshore, and many of the funds are managed outside Hong Kong. China is now experiencing a growing market demand for fund management experience due to its massive savings pool. This is leading to a strong growth in interest in the China fund management market by overseas fund houses and this is leading to more fund managers establishing a strategic presence in Hong Kong. The Securities and Futures Commission (SFC) is also stimulating growth in the industry by launching new fund management products such as hedge funds, guaranteed funds, index trading funds, REITs and ETFs.

Hong Kong is the leading Asian centre for international fund management and is very often regarded as a base from which to manage business across the Asia

Pacific region. In 1995 Hong Kong's fund managers managed assets totalling US$94.2 billion whilst Singapore, one of the main regional competitors had a total of US$46.8 billion under management. The United States of America and Europe are the main drivers of fund management activity in Hong Kong with local demand only playing a small role.

The freedom of movement of information, people and capital into and out of Hong Kong is seen within the industry as a critical source of competitive advantage. Hong Kong's freedom in this respect is a distinct advantage over Singapore. Stock market capitalization is higher in Hong Kong than anywhere else in Asia with the exception of Japan, and the depth of trading in individual stocks is greater than in any other market. Also Hong Kong is seen as having a deeper pool of skilled staff than elsewhere in Asia with the critical mass of fund managers and associated industries found in Hong Kong being unmatched anywhere in the region.

m) Insurance

Hong Kong has been the leading insurance centre in Asia since the 19th century. At the end of 2001, the insurance industry accounted for foreign direct investment of US$9 billion and in March 2003 there were 129 general business insurers, 19 composite insurers and 46 long term business insurers making a total of 194 authorised insurers operating in Hong Kong. Of these 95 were incorporated in Hong Kong whilst 99 were incorporated in a total of 25 other economies. The leading centre for marine insurance in Asia is Hong Kong and all of the main Protection and Indemnity Clubs operate in Hong Kong.

Due to Hong Kong being a leading insurance centre in Asia, many of the top insurance companies in the world have been attracted to set up operations in the territory. Hong Kong is number one in Asia for authorised insurance companies with many being incorporated overseas. Over the last 25 years, Hong Kong has built up a large number of professionals in the insurance industry. Hong Kong is also one of the leading markets in the region for reinsurance. The territory has the second highest critical mass of reinsurers in the region after Singapore. It is forecast that in the coming years China will have the fastest growth rate in the insurance market. In recent years China's insurance market has experienced an average annual growth rate of nearly 40%. The mainland Chinese insurance market plus Hong Kong's MPF means that foreign insurers and reinsurers are taking positions in Hong Kong.

In recent years there has been a growth in the insurance market in Hong Kong with companies seeking regional expansion. More new investment insurance products have been introduced particularly in view of the MPF launch in Hong

Kong and China's accession to the WTO.

Most insurers operate in the general business sector with the top 10 general insurers accounting for 38% of the general insurance market in 2001. In the past, life insurance has never been popular in Hong Kong because of the culture, with the market penetration rate being relatively low. However, the culture in Hong Kong is now changing and becoming more open to the concept of life insurance particularly with people tending to live longer and seeking to build a nest egg. Therefore market prospects are regarded as being good.

The service sector is seen as a good growth area for insurance products such as profession indemnity insurance, property title, etc. However, due to growth in the mainland Chinese economy, China is now seen as a major insurance market prospect. Current life insurance penetration in China is extremely low even though GDP growth of the economy is very high. Geographic restrictions are being phased out in China, which will enable insurers to develop branching operations within the country. Developments in the type of insurance product that can be offered are also taking place and good market growth is forecast.

n) Information Technology

Hong Kong is one of the most developed information technology (IT) markets in the region. Hong Kong's excellent telecommunications infrastructure is a great benefit to the IT services industry. The territory's financial sector uses some of the world's largest and most sophisticated computer applications. Hong Kong software companies have served predominantly Asian clients in designing web sites and developing electronic trading software. The Hong Kong government Digital 21 - Information Technology Strategy comprises an Applied Science and Technology Research Institute together with an Innovation and Technology Fund. Hong Kong is striving to become an innovation and technology centre for South China and the region and as such has a Commission on Innovation and Technology.

A world class Cyberport is also being developed housing large, medium and small companies specialising in the development of innovative technological services and multimedia content aimed at supporting a variety of industries. One of the objectives of the Cyberport is to raise Hong Kong's profile as a hi-tech multimedia hub. Hong Kong's world class optical fibre communications network means that Hong Kong is very favourably positioned for developing software relating to a wide variety of web based applications, EDI, e-commerce, intranet solutions, multimedia, video on demand and training. IT is becoming increasingly important in business relations because of the demand for quick response and efficiency in communication. Therefore this sector is expected to see continued growth in the coming years as Hong Kong further develops itself as the communications and control centre in Asia, and as Asia's World City.

Hong Kong spent over HK$24 billion on IT in 2000, which was one of the highest in Asia on a per capita basis. Hong Kong is currently investing in the development of a Cyberport which is a hi-tech information technology and multimedia hub designed to attract research and development teams from major hi-tech companies involved in information services, multimedia and IT applications. The investment cost is US$2 billion and many well known names are already present including Microsoft, GE Information Services and Sonera. The objective of the Cyberport development is to bring together leading IT companies in a strategic cluster and create a critical mass of professional capability in the territory thereby raising the IT profile of Hong Kong. The idea is to develop advanced IT facilities and services for all types of business and industry including trading, finance, advertising, communications, entertainment, etc. The Cyberport is regarded as Hong Kong's IT flagship and will be a world class environment ideal for overseas companies to use as a regional base.

Hong Kong's Cyberport has been designed with many shared facilities and services under a single campus and includes:

- a telecommunications and information infrastructure of world class standard with global connectivity on a broadband basis,

- a multimedia laboratory,

- a cyber library,

- office facilties with full commercial support services,

- tenants of the Cyberport are able to use the shared facilities and services as and when required,

- facilties for exhibitions and trade shows,

- a Cyber Centre capable of providing interface with the general public on an educational and entertainment basis,

- connection with universities and research organisations,

- [ ] local and international connection with venture capitalists,
- [ ] state of the art equipment and facilities with continuous upgrading,
- [ ] etc.

Business usage of information technology is substantial and increasing annually, for example, 37.2% of businesses had Internet connections; 10.7% of businesses had a website; HK$7.6 billion was spent on obtaining goods, services or information via electronic means; etc. Information technology penetration in the household market is also significant with 60.6% of households having a personal computer at home; 48.7% of households being connected to the Internet; and 39.4% of households being connected to the Internet using broadband. It is estimated that there are approximately 2.3 million personal computers in Hong Kong.

The Hong Kong government is firmly committed to the development of an information technology infrastructure in Hong Kong in both the public and private sector. The Electronic Service Delivery Scheme of December 2000 facilitates electronic interaction with the government 24 hours per day via computers at home or at work, via pay telephones and via interactive television. The Digital 21 IT Strategy of November 1998 that was revised in 2001 is a comprehensive strategy geared to developing Hong Kong into a leading digital city in the region. Its objectives and initiatives include:

- [ ] the enhancement and further development of Hong Kong's e-business environment on a world class basis,
- [ ] development and education of the workforce to a level capable of functioning in an information centred economy,
- [ ] furthering the concept of digital exploitation,
- [ ] developing the territory's strength regarding the use of enabling technologies,
- [ ] ensuring that the government is a leading force by setting a good example in e-business and the digital development of the economy.

In Hong Kong, information technology applications are increasingly being found in a wide range of sectors including banking and finance; shipping, freight forwarding and logistics; trading; wholesale and retail; manufacturing; graphic design and multimedia. CAD/CAM design systems are now very common as is computer generated imaging. Bar coding with point of sale inventory control systems facilitating just-in-time delivery systems are commonplace. Electronic billing and payment coupled with message checking, matching, validation and authentication is increasingly being used and regarded as a further move towards a cashless society. Most banks now provide on-line banking services as well as investment transactions via the Internet, mobile telephone and other electronic channels which have become increasingly popular. Electronic data interchange has grown substantially since its introduction in the early 1980s.

The growth in IT throughout the economy is creating a greater demand for highly trained IT personnel, which was projected to rise to 98,000 employees by 2005. Therefore the government has a long term commitment to implementing IT education in schools as well as seeking to attract IT professionals from overseas. Most hardware suppliers are distributors and vendors for major international computer companies, many of which have manufacturing sites in China. Software suppliers comprise a variety of custom software developers, software houses, value added resellers, system and network integrators, information system consultants and electronic data processing units.

A recent report by Forrester Research predicted that the value of e-commerce in Hong Kong would rise from US$2 billion in 2000 to a tremendous US$70 billion in 2004. Developments in the Internet, e-commerce and mobile commerce sectors are seen as being prime growth areas in Hong Kong. Due to Hong Kong having a world-class fibre optic communications network and broadband Internet being very popular, Hong Kong is seen as a very favourable location for software development regarding web based applications, multimedia, intranet solutions, e-commerce and training. The market growth potential looks very exciting.

The China market is seen as offering a huge potential for IT development with the prime software areas being telecommunications, multimedia, controlling software and networking software, on-line database services via the Internet, automation simulation systems and brokerage software. Due to Hong Kong being a bilingual centre it is in a good position to act as the interface for this development. China's projected investment in IT over the coming years is expected to exceed US$120 billion meaning that business opportunities are going to be extremely good for the correctly positioned companies with the correct product and capabilities. Hong Kong companies are very experienced at dealing with the Chinese market either through joint venture operations, branch office locations or mediating between Chinese companies and international IT firms and as such Hong Kong stands to benefit considerably.

o) Television Broadcasting & Multimedia

Television Broadcasts Limited (TVB) and Asia Television Limited (ATV) both broadcast free-to-air television channels and Hong Kong Cable Television Limited (HKCTV) broadcasts a domestic pay television programme service with over 30 channels. In Hong Kong there is no such thing as a television licence. The four analogue channels are broadcast free of charge with the television companies making their revenue from advertising and sponsorship.

There are also six non-domestic television programme services including Hutchvision Hong Kong Ltd., Galaxy Satellite Broadcasting Ltd., APT Satellite Glory Ltd., Starbucks (HK) Ltd., Asia Plus Broadcasting Ltd. and MATV Ltd. Over 90% of households in Hong Kong have fibre or broadband access due to the high penetration of the fibre optic network in Hong Kong and therefore the city is a good market for multimedia services. More pay television channels are in the process of being created and will be operational very soon.

One of the Hong Kong government policies is to promote the city as a regional publishing, communications and broadcasting hub. In his policy address in 1998, the Chief Executive explained his plan for Hong Kong to be an Internet hub, an information gateway to China, a leading World City regarding information technology and a regional base for entertainment and multimedia based information services. The Broadcasting Ordinance of July 2000 and the Digital 21 Strategy of 2001 incorporate the policy, strategy and regulations needed to make the city a business friendly environment that is open and fair, as well as encouraging investment, technological developments and innovation regarding television and all forms of broadcasting. Other organisations involved in the broadcasting and multimedia industry include the Film Services Advisory Committee (FSAC), the Film Services Office, the Film Archive Library, Filmart and Supportive Infrastructure and Funds.

Hong Kong has world class telecommunications services, including submarine optic, satellite and broadband Internet giving very low costs for information transmission to and from anywhere in the world. This gives Hong Kong a very clear and positive price advantage. Hong Kong has a well educated multi lingual workforce that is ideal for journalism and broadcasting. Hong Kong's television broadcasting and multimedia organisations also have extensive business networks across the border in China. Digital television and satellite are set to expand operations in the coming years in Hong Kong. China is also seen as a good growth market for media and multimedia as well as the Internet. China is starting to slowly liberalise its TV broadcasting business and therefore Hong Kong is the best location for foreign companies seeking to enter the Chinese market.

p) Publishing

Hong Kong has a highly developed print industry and functions as a regional publishing hub. It is one of the largest printing centres in Asia and well recognised throughout the world. The city is the Asian headquarters for many renowned major international publishers of books, magazines and newspapers including Oxford University Press, Longman, Macmillan, Readers' Digest, Financial Times, Far Eastern Economic Review, Bloomberg, The Economist, Reuters, USA Today, Agence France-Presse, etc. The city is a major news hub with over 45 international and regional media players. Press freedom and the concept of freedom of expression have been very important factors in creating the concentration of renowned international publications in Hong Kong, which has also led to considerable inward investment in the sector.

The territory's excellent communications network has greatly benefited the publishing industry because satellite communications allow international publishers to transmit text and images to and from Hong Kong in order to create exciting publications. Hong Kong has become the main choice as a regional headquarters for publishers from around the world, due to it being recognised as the advertising capital of Asia with such a high per capita advertising expense. Advertising sales are an important source of income for the printed media sector. In 1999, the Hong Kong print media had 43 newspapers of which 27 were Chinese, 9 English, 1 bilingual and 6 in other languages. Also in 1999 the Hong Kong print media had 693 registered periodicals of which 424 were Chinese, 146 English, 112 bilingual and 11 in other languages.

Editing, printing, production, marketing and distribution for the Hong Kong market as well as export to affiliated companies in other parts of the world is all conducted from Hong Kong. Many publishers have books and materials printed in Hong Kong and then exported back to their own country as well as to other markets. This has made Hong Kong a major supplier of printed materials to many markets. Many international media organisations have their offices in Hong Kong which is a base for several regional publications. Asiaweek, Readers' Digest, Asian Wall Street Journal, Far Eastern Economic Review, Financial Times, International Herald Tribune and the Economist are all printed in Hong Kong. An increasing number of titles are being translated into Chinese for the mainland Chinese market and this has resulted in Hong Kong being used as a marketing and distribution centre.

China is a market with huge potential for the publishing industry. Hong Kong publishers are now in the advantageous position of being able to market publications to the western world regarding China and market publications to China regarding the western world. Both of these worlds are eager to understand and learn about each other and Hong Kong has a wealth of knowledge about both. Newswires are a relatively new phenomenon with on-line publishing 24 hours per day. The leading newswires in Hong Kong include Reuters, Dow Jones, Bloomberg and Kyodo News.

As a regional publishing centre, Hong Kong has a very well developed publishing industry incorporating printing, typesetting, colour separation, binding and distribution of newspapers, magazines, periodicals and books of all types. There is no government censorship in Hong Kong and freedom of the press and expression is guaranteed by the constitution of Hong Kong. There is also a new Copyright Ordinance protecting the copyright of prints and CD-Rom. Hong Kong's fully digitised world-class low-cost telecommunications network, satellite connections, Internet broadband connections and extensive air route connections mean that Hong Kong is highly connected for very quick transmission of information and copy.

Due to the extensive level of its advertising expenditure, Hong Kong is a very attractive market for media and advertising companies. It is closely connected with China and has an in-depth knowledge of the Chinese market, an excellent and well supported printing industry, the world's largest air cargo facility and an educated bilingual pool of writers, journalists and technicians. All these factors have greatly helped in the development of Hong Kong's publishing industry.

Market growth is expected in China as a result of the rising educational level of the population, rising income levels, one-child policy, rising living standards, faster economic growth, a greater level of international trade and WTO accession. There is a greater demand in China for information and entertainment, which is creating business opportunities in the media and multimedia industry. Also the Chinese government is slowly liberalising the media industry and relaxing its control. Huge growth can be expected in the media industry as a result of changes taking place in the Chinese market. Hong Kong is seen as a very strategic location because of its focus on China. Many Western companies seeking a knowledge of China represent a good market for trade journals concerning China, and Hong Kong is in the best position to satisfy that need.

q) Technology

The technological state of Hong Kong has changed dramatically when comparing today with the 1950s and 1960s. The days of the sweat shop have long disappeared. Hong Kong has always prided itself on its ability to respond quickly to market demand, to spot emerging trends and to re-tool quickly so as to meet changing market conditions and ship product on time. Now many Hong Kong companies are using computer aided design, computerised production process planning and control systems, and real time data collection and management information systems in order to increase response and production times. This investment in technological advances in Hong Kong is supported by a vast production network in China.

Hong Kong has now moved away from simple original equipment manufacture (OEM) to custom OEM and also original design manufacture (ODM) for major world renowned brandnames. Under OEM terms the buyer provides complete specifications, drawings and instructions and the manufacturer merely performs the directed production operation. However, under ODM the buyer provides the concept or idea possibly with sketches and the manufacturer designs the product from start, develops, tests, certifies and manufactures the product under pre-agreed quality control systems and standards so as to satisfy the original concept. Hong Kong is now responsible for much of the added value operations within the manufacturing and sales process, including product design and development, mechanical and electrical or electronic drawing, prototyping, sampling, tool design and manufacture, product production, packaging design and manufacture, certification and approval through recognised institutes and organisations, and delivery to stated destinations.

Hong Kong has developed a biotechnology capability in recent years that has shown significant growth prospects. The industry is supported by a number of organisations including the Hong Kong Institute of Biotechnology, the Biotechnology Research Institute, the Applied Science & Technology Research Institute Company Limited, the Hong Kong Jockey Club Institute of Chinese Medicine, and the Science Park. Hong Kong's biotechnology industry is supported by a very comprehensive professional services sector, world class communications technology, extremely conscientious intellectual property protection, and an environment that is geared to being business friendly.

Approximately 72% of the production of the biotechnology industry is exported to China, with Macau, Malaysia and Singapore also receiving important amounts. The Hong Kong Pharmaceutical Technology Centre was set up in 1997 to assist in the manufacturing processes of the biotechnology industry. Companies in this industry are seeking to use Hong Kong as a springboard for activities in China and the region because Hong Kong is a central location and an ideal base for development.

The Hong Kong electronics industry has broadened and expanded considerably over the last 30 years. The territory is using state-of-the-art equipment producing high value added goods at component level and finished product level. Many

Hong Kong companies are now using surface mount technology, chip-on-glass technology, fine-pitch technology, chip scale packaging, etc. Whereas in the 1960s Hong Kong produced low grade electronic product, much of which was under OEM terms, this section of the industry has now been taken up by Chinese companies and Hong Kong companies have had to upgrade their products and develop products of a more advanced nature.

Hong Kong is an important procurement and sourcing centre in Asia for electronic parts and components. Many parts and components suppliers have offices in Hong Kong. Parts and components like semiconductors are an important part of the hi-tech industries and much of the production base of the hi-tech industries is now shifting to the Asia Pacific. This will increase demand in Hong Kong and Hong Kong's position as an effective manufacturing management control centre will give rise to an increase in the number of international investors seeking to locate regional operations in Hong Kong.

In 2000 the Applied Science and Technology Research Institute Co. Ltd. (ASTRI) was established with the objective of providing a research capability geared towards increasing the productivity and value added content of Hong Kong's industrial sector. It is expected that China's accession to the WTO is going to lead to a substantial increase in demand within the parts and components sector of the electronics industry with Hong Kong obtaining a major share of this demand. Hong Kong companies are expected to be influential in facilitating the new technologies and investment targeted at mainland China.

In the consumer electronic finished product sector digitalisation is the general trend with a good growth in demand for digital products such as television sets, set top boxes, DVD players, cameras, personal digital assistants, etc. Digital products are expected to replace analogue products in the near future. Product life cycles in the electronics sector are also becoming shorter with an increasing demand for changes in product features. This is an aspect that many Hong Kong companies are incorporating into their product development strategies so as to prolong the general product lifecycle and maximise the return on product investment. Adaptability and responsiveness are therefore key features.

In the Information Technology sector, Hong Kong companies produce many computer parts and accessories including system boards, add-on cards, computer peripherals, data storage units and computer sets. Labour intensive production is conducted in China with production planning and quality assurance being controlled from Hong Kong. Hong Kong companies have developed a niche market in TV set-top boxes, fax-to-e-mail apparatus and e-mail readers.

However, product lifecycles for IT products are generally short and therefore Hong Kong companies have been keen to access market intelligence regarding product trends so as to guide product development in what is a fast changing market. Hong Kong companies in this sector have operated in a variety of ways including OEM and ODM for major brandnames in the USA and Europe. Some Hong Kong companies have sold directly to the Hong Kong purchasing offices of European, USA and Japanese computer companies. However, others have sold to subsidiaries and sales offices in Europe and the USA, or to importers/distributors possibly on a private label basis. Hong Kong companies have also appointed agents and exclusive distributors in Asian markets to deal with distribution, technical support and after sales service.

r) Tourism and Entertainment

Hong Kong is Asia's most popular city with more arrivals than any other city in the region. Approximately 11% of the workforce are either directly or indirectly involved with the tourism industry. In 2003 there were 15,536,839 arrivals in Hong Kong, which was 6.2% less than 2002. 54.5% of arrivals were from China which is now the largest source of visitors to Hong Kong and is set to keep on expanding in demand.

The government, in 2005, was scheduled to invest US$2 billion by 2007 on tourism projects including the Tung Chung Cable Car System on Lantau Island, the Disneyland Park project on Lantau Island, a new performing arts venue, an international wetland park to be located at Mai Po Marshes in the New Territories which is a popular bird wildlife sanctuary, etc. The Disneyland Park is a major joint venture project with the Walt Disney Company and will include a theme park, hotel, shopping complex, dining and entertainment centre, as well as other facilities. The project is expected to generate considerable income and is regarded as an indication of confidence in the future of Hong Kong.

Hong Kong has been an Associate Member of the World Tourism Organisation since October 1999 and its Quality Tourism Services Scheme is aimed at maintaining and improving the quality of services particularly in the retail and restaurant sectors. The Tourism Commission established in May 1999 is responsible for tourism policies and planning. The Hong Kong Tourism Board is responsible for marketing Hong Kong as a tourist destination. The recent promotion campaign, 'Discover Hong Kong, The City of Life', focuses on five distinct aspects - sightseeing, cuisine, heritage, shopping and events. The Hong Kong Tourism Board has been active in promoting Hong Kong as a cruise destination, planning itineraries and featuring Hong Kong at trade shows. Joint promotions with airlines and hotels have also been conducted in a variety of locations. The government has also been assisting the Hong Kong Tourism Board in promoting Hong Kong as the 'Events Capital of

Asia' - in other words it is happening in Hong Kong.

The Hong Kong film industry is one of the most dynamic in the world. The territory is a major producer and exporter of films and television programmes. The growth in Asian cable and satellite channels in recent years represents good market opportunities for film and television producers. The Movie Producers and Distributors Association of Hong Kong Ltd. (MPDA) and the Motion Picture Industry Association (MPIA) are the two major associations in the film industry. The industry is highly geared towards export and in recent years has gained significant international acceptance due to the action films of renowned performers like Bruce Lee and Jackie Chan. Since 1997 there has been an annual film market in Hong Kong promoting the territory as a film distribution centre for the region.

According to a recent Hong Kong Trade Development Council report, Hong Kong could be a main player in the regional film industry. In 2001 the number of film exhibitors at Hong Kong's Filmart increased by 20 per cent to 1,190 and the number of foreign buyers increased by 30 per cent to 130. Exports of the local film industry generated over HK$400 million (US$51.3 million) in that year. Trade Development Council services promotion senior management stated in the report that as the second largest film export centre in the world, Hong Kong is recognised as having the potential of becoming the biggest film trading centre in Asia.

Hong Kong is now increasingly on the circuit for international performers due to the size and quality of its venues. An increasing number of annual events are now taking place in Hong Kong. Most major hotel chains have a presence in Hong Kong and there are 38,000 hotel rooms as well as 4,800 guesthouse rooms. Hong Kong has one of the busiest airports in the world with 550 flights each day to 140 cities around the world on a 24 hour basis. Very few cities can match that kind of airport facility.

Hong Kong was successful in its bid to host the East Asian Games in 2009, whilst Beijing is hosting the 2008 Olympic Games and in 2010 Shanghai will be hosting the World Expo. These events are of course expected to lead to a surge in tourism demand for Hong Kong as well as a surge in tourism demand for China with many of the tourists to China passing through Hong Kong. As such the city is preparing for this surge in demand with committed government assistance as required.

The exhibition and convention sector is an important part of the tourism industry and Hong Kong is now recognised as the exhibition centre of Asia due to its high profile and professional facilities which are world renowned. In 2001 the city hosted over 1,700 international events, which attracted over 506,000 overseas delegates and participants. Many exhibitions staged at the Hong Kong Convention and Exhibition Centre are now annual events regularly attracting full capacity audiences, making the events a success not only for the participants, but also for the visitors.

s) Trading and Procurement

According to a Census and Statistics Department report of June 2001, there were 3,237 foreign companies with either regional headquarters or regional offices in Hong Kong and 1,005 of these foreign companies were trade related service firms. Approximately 20% of Hong Kong's total workforce is in some way involved in the role of trading and procurement and this represents a substantial pool of qualified and experienced workers. As a result of Hong Kong's close proximity to the factories of Southern China, together with the territory's independent and fair legal system and the abundance of very well connected entrepreneurs and traders, over 75 per cent of consumer product buyers around the world now source and purchase China made merchandise through Hong Kong traders. This clearly endorses Hong Kong's position as the world's main source for consumer products due to its close and natural link with China. According to WTO trade statistics in 2000 Hong Kong was the 9th largest trading economy in the world and in 2001 its merchandise trade reached US$391 billion.

Fortune magazine has 17 international trading companies listed in its Fortune 500 global firms and 16 of these are well established in Hong Kong. Many leading trade and procurement companies and buying offices from around the world have offices in Hong Kong with the result that Hong Kong is the trading and procurement capital of Asia and indeed the world. The trading and procurement companies in Hong Kong now enjoy tremendous support and infrastructure advantages including:

- now being a part of China, the manufacturing centre of the world,

- having many skilled trade professionals with an expert knowledge and experience of consumer product sourcing and sales,

- having free port status,

- a modern and very sophisticated logistics support system,

- having a low and predictable corporate tax system,

- [ ] a fair and independent judiciary,

- [ ] free and unrestrained flow of capital and information,

- [ ] world class telecommunications system,

- [ ] the city had the world's busiest container port in 2001 handling 17.8 million TEU of cargo with 80 international shipping lines travelling to over 500 destinations in approximately 170 countries,

- [ ] Hong Kong's Chek Lap Kok airport had one of the busiest air cargo facilities in the world in 2000, handling 2.24 million tons of cargo. The airport served 64 scheduled airlines each week with 3,000 flights to over 130 destinations worldwide.

China's accession to the WTO represents a very interesting time for Hong Kong with excellent growth in business opportunities. China is now recognised as the manufacturing centre of the world and an increasing number of companies in the USA, Europe and elsewhere are seeking to relocate their production to China in order to reduce costs and increase their competitiveness. By 2005 China will in compliance with WTO requirements have reduced its tariffs from an average of 25% to an average of 8.9% creating a good increase in business opportunities for trading and procurement, sourcing and distribution. Under WTO regulations the Chinese market will gradually be opened to international trade which will give Hong Kong trading and procurement companies a tremendous opportunity to sell and distribute product throughout China. This is expected to be a very profitable opportunity for Hong Kong companies.

Also over the next five years it is envisaged that Chinese manufacturers will not only improve the quality of their manufacturing, but also increase the quantity thereby enabling them to develop and supply higher quality products not only throughout China, but also around the world. Therefore there will be an increase in the two way flow of goods with an increased amount of product flowing out of China to the rest of the world, and an increased amount of product flowing from the rest of the world into China, and Hong Kong will be in the middle, at the centre, controlling and coordinating much of this increased trade. Therefore over the next five years Hong Kong companies can expect a very profitable increase in business.

Regarding the future prospects of trade and procurement companies, readers should contact any or all of the following organisations:

Hong Kong Trade Development Council
Head Office
38/F, Office Tower, Convention Plaza
1 Harbour Road
Wan Chai
Hong Kong
T: (852) 2584 4333
F (852) 2824 0249
E: hktdc@tdc.org.hk
W: http://www.tdctrade.com

Hong Kong Exporters Association
Rm 825, Star House
3 Salisbury Road
Tsim Sha Tsui
Kowloon
Hong Kong
T: (852) 2730 9851
F: (852) 2730 1869
E: exporter@exporters.org.hk
W: http://www.exporters.org.hk

Hong Kong Shippers' Council
Rm 2407, Hopewell Centre
183 Queen's Road East
Wan Chai
Hong Kong
T: (852) 2834 0010
F: (852) 2891 9787
E: shippers@hkshippers.org.hk
W: http://www.hkshippers.org.hk

t) Retail

The Hong Kong retail sector is very active. The recent deflation experienced by the economy has led to a general reduction in retail prices. From the 1960s to the 1980s Hong Kong was known as the shopping centre of the East due to its low prices, abundance of products on sale and millions of enthusiastic shoppers prepared to haggle over bargains. However, in the 1990s prices tended to rise gradually as was evident throughout the economy with many prices peaking in 1997, in particular in the housing market. Nevertheless deflation in recent years has led to price reductions making Hong Kong much more attractive as a retail centre. In 2001 Hong Kong received a record number of 13.7 million tourists, which was an increase of 5.1% compared to the previous year. These tourists in 2001 spent US$8 billion in Hong Kong of which US$4 billion was just on shopping. 58,000 retail outlets surveyed in 2001 collectively reported retail sales totalling US$24 billion. Therefore the retail market in Hong Kong is still very active.

Many of the world's leading retailers have a presence in Hong Kong. Hong Kong offers luxury, mass market and discount retailing. The city has often been regarded as the retail capital of Asia, if not the world, and as such is an ideal location for retail business. Hong Kong had the highest purchasing power in Asia, after Japan, according to the World Bank in 2001.

Hong Kong, with a population of nearly 7 million, is the most densely populated city in the world with 6,250 people per square kilometre. This density is higher in certain urban localities such as Mong Kok, Sham Shui Po, Kwun Tong, Choi Hung, Wong Tai Sin, etc. This density enables retailers to very quickly reach a receptive market and make a profit. Hong Kong does not have a sales tax or VAT system. As a freeport there are no import duties or tariffs on most merchandise on sale in Hong Kong. Shops are generally open 7 days per week and normally for at least 12 hours per day, although some stores such as 7-11 are open 24 hours per day. Shops are always open on public holidays such as Easter and Christmas although many will close at the time of the Chinese New Year. Hong Kong offers both indoor and outdoor shopping facilities. The air conditioning for much of the indoor shopping is enjoyed by most when it is hot outside in the summer. The street markets outside in the evenings are very popular, particularly Temple Street and Tung Choi Street where one can find a vast array of all types of merchandise on sale.

The pegging of the Hong Kong dollar with the USA dollar since October 1983 has to a large extent helped to maintain price stability. Hong Kong's superb and highly efficient transport system with airport, railway, underground, buses, mini buses, ferries, taxis, cross harbour tunnels, etc. has helped the retail industry tremendously because it has enabled shoppers to move quickly and freely from one location to another without hassle. The level of advertising in Hong Kong, whether its television, radio, street hoardings, billboards, etc., is excessive and a very high stimulus to shoppers and therefore helps to maintain the level of shopping activity amongst the population. Also Hong Kong's location on the doorstep of China, the world's manufacturing centre, has greatly assisted in the flow of goods to Hong

Kong, the majority of which are manufactured in China. Hong Kong is also only a short flight from anywhere else in Asia and hence half of the world's population has relatively quick and easy access to Hong Kong's retail experience.

Hong Kong's position as an international tourist destination and the growth in China's own retail market and manufacturing capability have heightened the prospects for Hong Kong retailers. It was forecast that in 2005 Hong Kong would receive 18.3 million tourist arrivals with approximately one third being from China. According to the Hong Kong Tourism Commission, Hong Kong Disneyland which opened in 2005 was expected to attract an additional 1.4 million tourists that year, and by 2020 it is projected that it will attract 2.9 million additional visitors. It was planned that by 2005 Hong Kong would have more shopping malls with around 4 million square feet of retail area, much of which will be located in prime commercial space.

China's WTO accession will inevitably lead to a surge in the Chinese retail market providing many business opportunities for Hong Kong companies seeking to expand their retail operations. As mentioned previously the quality of China's manufactured product is expected to increase giving rise to Hong Kong companies under the CEPA agreement being able to source the best quality products at the best prices before foreign competitors enter the market. The increasing retail business opportunities that are expected to emerge as a result of China's accession to the WTO will mean that multinational retailers based in Hong Kong will be uniquely positioned to take advantage of market opportunities in order to market and distribute their products directly to China and the region.

Hong Kong has for many years been a base for test marketing products for sale throughout the region. The regional changes that are now taking place particularly with regard to China's accession to the WTO will make Hong Kong even more important as a location for test marketing products and therefore more activity in this area can be expected particularly from multinational companies seeking to develop their positions within the market and the region. For further news regarding retail prospects readers should contact :

The Hong Kong Retail Management Association
Unit B, 22/F, United Centre
95 Queensway
Admiralty
Hong Kong
T: (852) 2866 8311
F: (852) 2866 8380

u) Hong Kong's Manufacturing Capabilities

Hong Kong has during the last 50 years developed a strong business base. It has a strong presence in many sectors and types of business that complement and support each other thereby creating a clustering effect which in turn helps to attract more high value added business to the territory. The clustering effect is a kind of symbiosis that benefits all those involved in the cluster and enriches Hong Kong society.

Nevertheless, Hong Kong like all major cities is confronted with challenges that need to be overcome for the city to prosper and survive. When compared to other regional locations Hong Kong is a relatively high cost environment and as such needs to emphasize development of high value-added business. Like all cities Hong Kong has to continually seek to upgrade the quality and capability of its manpower and talented individuals particularly in the light of technological developments. Hong Kong must also continually develop and enhance not just its regional ties, but also its global ties so as to maintain its position and reputation as a financial and commercial business centre with global capabilities.

Three important events in Hong Kong's manufacturing history happened around 1970. First, Hong Kong joined the General Agreement of Tariffs and Trade (GATT) whilst China remained outside the organisation. Second, trade barriers against Hong Kong products were removed. In 1971, the USA stopped the requirement of a certificate of origin for Hong Kong products, and Japan together with the European Economic Community (EEC) and Commonwealth countries decided to grant preferential tariff rates to Hong Kong as a developing economy. Third, Canada, the USA and the EEC adopted import quotas for Hong Kong clothing and textiles.

In 1999, it was estimated that in southern China, Hong Kong companies owned and operated approximately 400,000 factories and employed over 5 million workers and this figure is continually expanding. Due to Hong Kong's very close links with China and the extent of its investments in China, many importers from Japan, the USA and Europe have preferred to source and import products from China by cooperating with a Hong Kong company often under some form of partnership arrangement instead of going direct to China. This has no doubt been due to Hong Kong's established international reputation, its legal system, its history of trade and extensive knowledge of and connections with China.

As Hong Kong companies have expanded their manufacturing facilities to various locations throughout South East Asia including China, companies interested in importing from these locations have turned to Hong Kong companies due to their ability to guarantee quality and on time delivery, and this has further raised Hong

Kong's profile in the international market. At the time of the handover of sovereignty in 1997, Hong Kong owned and operated a vast network of manufacturing facilities in many countries. In Hong Kong itself there were high skill, high value added factories manufacturing designer clothes and very high value watches. In southern China many thousands of Hong Kong owned factories, many of which had less than 50 workers, collectively employed millions of workers manufacturing a vast array of products. In South East Asia and Asia in general a smaller network of Hong Kong owned and operated factories existed.

Production facilities have also been set up in other countries such as Brazil, the Czech Republic, Mexico, South Africa, Poland, Zimbabwe, Honduras, etc. So it can be seen that Hong Kong's manufacturing facilities and capabilities are very extensive and yet Hong Kong remains the centre of control for all these operations. It is this centre of control capability that makes Hong Kong an ideal location for multinational regional headquarters or regional offices. Hong Kong's manufacturers are using their knowledge and financial resources to control a very wide manufacturing network many times greater than their operations in the HKSAR.

Due to Hong Kong's manufacturing sector being dominated by small companies there tends to be a lack of R & D together with a lack of real financial commitment towards R & D. This is an area that multinationals should consider for possible exploitation.

Hong Kong is noted as a place where it is exceptionally easy to start a business. Any person of any nationality can start a business by simply submitting the relevant forms and paying the registration fee. These forms comprise a memorandum of association detailing company objectives, an articles of association detailing company regulations and a statutory declaration of compliance with the company ordinance. The total fees were less than HK$3,000 in 2004. Hong Kong therefore has many small companies literally numbering tens of thousands.

Due to there being so many small manufacturers in Hong Kong, overseas buyers have a very large pool of manufacturers to choose from and so encourage them to compete and undercut one another on a price basis. However, collectively Hong Kong's many manufacturers possess an extensive knowledge and experience regarding manufacturing in Asia that is not available anywhere else in the world. Multinationals should be well aware of the ease with which businesses can be established in Hong Kong as well as the ease with which they can disappear.

A distinctive feature of Hong Kong's manufacturing companies particularly in the early years was the dominance of family-based companies. In September 1997, the proportion of Hong Kong domestic manufacturers employing less than 10 people was 78.7 per cent and over 96 per cent of manufacturers employed fewer than 50 people. Many Hong Kong companies have tended to have a somewhat paternalistic corporate culture due to being owner-managed and in many cases employing members of the family. This has led to a certain conservative tendency in corporate activities and a reliance on traditional business practices. It has also led to a blurring of the employer employee relationship with the development of the corporate family mentality.

From its very early days as a manufacturer, most Hong Kong manufacturing companies have primarily focused on export. In line with Porter's theory regarding the five forces, a small domestic market can easily become saturated forcing manufacturers to look overseas for sales growth thereby benefiting industrial development. This can be encouraged by a buoyant overseas market. Hong Kong consumers soon found themselves in a saturated market for many consumer goods and the speed with which new varieties were introduced was quite dramatic. This made Hong Kong consumers very sophisticated and well informed. The Hong Kong market is regarded as being very discerning and as such many companies use the city as a place for test marketing their new product releases. In many instances some consumer products have already become commonplace in Hong Kong before they are introduced into western markets.

It has been reported that Hong Kong has a relatively narrow export product mix with over two-thirds of exports in 1997 coming from just 10 product categories. Also Hong Kong has relatively few export markets with nearly 70% of exports in 1997 going to just five markets. China has been the main market for over 10 years and is expected to remain so.

The opening up of China in the late 1970s meant that Hong Kong no longer suffered from a shortage of land and labour. Hong Kong manufacturers rapidly expanded into China raising the level of their manufacturing capability as well as maintaining or even improving their cost effectiveness. This also led to extensive expansion in foreign direct investment into China much of it flowing through Hong Kong. Many Hong Kong manufacturers previously relied heavily on OEM contracts from major international brandname companies, but this sector has now become increasingly dominated by China and therefore Hong Kong manufacturers have been forced to develop their own products. Hong Kong is now a world class manufacturer of toys, textiles, clothing and consumer electronic products.

Changes in the global retail market are naturally affecting the manufacturing market. Retailers have become larger organisations with bigger networks of stores and therefore there has been a decline in the number of buyers. This has made retailers stronger and buyers more powerful in their negotiations. These buyers are more able to demand exclusivity of supply for their retail market as well as impose conditions not only on overall quality levels but also on delivery times. Many of these buyers seek to minimise their stock holdings and so demand just-in-time deliveries with penalties for late delivery. This kind of development follows Porter's Five Forces model very closely.

Manufacturing is tending to become more global with product parts and subassemblies being produced in a variety of countries prior to final assembly at one location. Improved information systems, better transportation systems, better engineering and production equipment together with improved design facilities are all helping in the globalisation of manufacturing. In conjunction with this globalisation there is a creeping regionalisation in the form of regional agreements between countries offering members preferential terms of trade. This regionalisation is against Hong Kong's open door trade philosophy.

Due to the increasing trend towards globalisation with product parts being manufactured in many different countries before being shipped to one location for final assembly, the marked country of origin is no longer a reasonable means for consumers to judge the quality of a product. Instead brandnames have now become a crucial means of consumers determining product quality and hence brandname owners are now extremely concerned regarding the quality and protection of their brandnames because of their potency and profitability. In conjunction with buyers devoting more time towards marketing, brandname development and market distribution there has been a growing move away from OEM (original equipment manufacture) towards ODM (original design manufacture) enabling Hong Kong manufacturers to devote more time and ability towards engineering development and production design work and as such be responsible for a greater part of the value added chain.

The growth in the size and power of some overseas buyers due to the size and potential of their organisations has resulted in greater demand for product quality assurances and tighter specifications, but at the same time large volume orders have resulted in reduced prices and tighter margins. Mid range buyers are generally becoming fewer, niche market buyers are increasing and hypermarket style buyers are getting more powerful.

In conjunction with this trend has also been the trend towards greater brandname development. This is affecting the relationship between Hong Kong manufacturers and overseas buyers. Production specifications including quality requirements together with contract terms have generally become much more strict. Although the size of these contracts may be very attractive, the contract terms are often onerous. However, brandnames are now a fundamental part of the retail experience and are something that consumers are increasingly aware of and expect to encounter. It is therefore essential that the owners of established brandnames take great care to ensure the protection of those brandnames so that the full marketing value of those brandnames can be achieved. Therefore manufacturing specifications are often very strict in order to ensure that product quality and delivery are as required in order to protect the brandname. The manner in which the value of a brandname is achieved will depend upon the nature of the product or service to which that brandname is applied. However, it must be borne in mind that it takes a great deal of expenditure and investment of time, energy and money to create a feasible brandname with a long term future.

Hong Kong's diverse range of industries offers many strengths with relatively few weaknesses and as such represents good investment opportunities for overseas multinationals seeking to enter Hong Kong, China and South East Asia. Buyers from around the world have often marvelled at the reputation and proficiency of Hong Kong industry. A brief look at some of these sectors can be very enlightening.

The Hong Kong clothing industry's knowledge of both national and international rules and regulations regarding clothing manufacture and export is a key strength of the industry. With its knowledge of quota restrictions, category shifts, tariff rates, rules of origin, documentation requirements, etc., Hong Kong companies are very proficient at controlling production processes in order to maintain low costs and high profit margins. Hong Kong clothing manufacturers are very well informed regarding clothing trends in western markets so that their production matches market requirements.

One of the greatest strengths of the electronics industry in Hong Kong is its ability to effectively cost and efficiently manage the manufacturing process. The industry has built a reputation for excellent organisation of production processes and has manufactured very high quality product at competitive prices. They are also very proficient at introducing new technology into their products as well as upgrading factory operations with new production techniques.

The main strengths of the plastics industry are the diversity of product manufactured and the number and variety of companies in the industry. It also has a wide range of technical skills in plastics processing together with much experience in injection moulding, blow moulding, thermoset moulding, extrusion, etc.

Hong Kong's toy manufacturers are probably the most efficient toy production managers in the world. Hong Kong's toy industry is a world leader. OEM contracts enable Hong Kong toy manufacturers to be fully informed of toy trends around the world. The top toy exports of Hong Kong are a clear sign of the industry's strength and diversity. The incorporation of technology and skills found in other industries adds to the dynamism of the toy industry.

Efficient production management with on time delivery is a key strength of Hong Kong's watch and clock industry. Companies have developed a reputation for manufacturing good quality clocks and watches at very reasonable and competitive prices whilst maintaining strict production schedules.

v) Hong Kong's Services Sectors

Hong Kong is now the most service focused economy in the world with its service sector generating a very high percentage of GDP. In 2001 the services sector generated 87% of Hong Kong's GDP. The restructuring of the economy has resulted in companies moving low value-added work out of Hong Kong and instead concentrating on high-value, technology based markets. Most of the low value-added production has moved mainly to China, but also to other countries as well, whilst high value-added production of a much smaller scale has stayed in Hong Kong.

Hong Kong's services sector is one of the most developed in Asia. During the period 1990 to 2001 the value added component of the services sector rose at an average annual rate of 8.7% reaching US$134 billion, whereas the average annual growth rate of nominal GDP was 7.3%. Therefore the services sector share of GDP rose from 74% in 1990 to 87% in 2001. Transport; storage; communications; and community, social and personal services experienced the fastest growth. The wholesale, retail and import/export trades, restaurants and hotels represented the largest sections of the services sector and accounted for 26.1% of GDP in 2001. In the first 6 months of 2001, Hong Kong exported US$20.6 billion worth of services.

Hong Kong and Singapore have consistently been exporters of services. In 2000 Hong Kong was ranked second in Asia after Japan with regard to the total value of services exported and at the same time was ranked ninth in the world for the export of services. Hong Kong's main services exports comprised transportation, trade related services and travel services, representing 36%, 30% and 18% respectively of the total value of exported services. Financial services represented 9% and insurance 7%. Hong Kong is a net exporter of services giving it a competitive advantage over other economies. Surpluses for 2000 were recorded with regard to transportation services at US$10.4 billion or 54%, financial services at US$2.4 billion or 12% and trade related services at US$10.9 billion or 57%.

Hong Kong has already established its position as one of the main centres for services both regionally in South East Asia and also globally. Hong Kong's future depends upon the competitiveness of its service industries as well as the quality of the services that it provides. As an international business centre Hong Kong provides world class services both regionally and globally. The economic philosophy of Hong Kong dictates that enterprise, free markets and competition are the best means of assuring innovation, quality and competitiveness.

As such the Hong Kong government believes that private business which has been the foundation and past source of success in the territory is the best means of developing a successful services industry now and in the future. Private enterprise will determine the pace and direction of the development of the services industry whilst the government will ensure that official policies help rather than hinder business decisions and the markets for services remain open and competitive.

The Hong Kong government put forward an eight point framework for supporting the services sector of the economy comprising :

- "promoting exports of services;

- promoting inward investment in services;

- promoting Hong Kong as an international financial centre;

- enhancing service productivity;

- providing an infrastructure of support;

- investing in education and training;

- implementing a comprehensive programme to promote Hong Kong's strengths as a global and regional services centre;

- setting up the Business and Services Promotion Unit as a dedicated Unit to co-ordinate and monitor the Government's support on various fronts"

(Hong Kong Information Services Department, 2003)

The Business and Services Promotion Unit was established in May 1997, just prior to the handover of sovereignty. Its function was to coordinate and support the work of various parts of the government in Services Promotion, help business programmes and monitor the progress of new initiatives. In July 2000 the Business and Services Promotion Unit merged with the Trade and Industry Bureau and then became part of the new Commerce and Industry Bureau, which is now known as the Commerce, Industry and Technology Bureau.

According to the Hong Kong Information Services Department, the Services Promotion Programme has the following four areas of work :

- ☐ to lead in the strategic thinking and planning for the future development of the services economy in Hong Kong,

- ☐ to invigorate and strengthen institutional support structures within the services sector of the Hong Kong economy,

- ☐ to support feasible industry initiatives ensuring that they receive the appropriate attention and priority, and

- ☐ to help develop international recognition and understanding of the services economy in Hong Kong and thereby encourage public support for it.

Trade related services exports amount to HK$100 billion each year with merchanting representing 72% and offshore merchandising transactions representing 14%. The export of trade related services experienced very fast growth in the 1990s with the average annual growth being equivalent to 13%. In 1990 it was HK$26.4 billion and in 2001 it was HK$99.3 billion, representing a considerable increase within a decade. Offshore trade income is expected to see further growth in the coming years due to China's WTO accession and good performance in Asia. Re-exports will grow as domestic exports contract and direct exports bypassing Hong Kong increase, but Hong Kong's management and control of regional business activity will continue its steady growth rate.

As China has opened up over the last 28 years, Hong Kong industries have expanded their production base and capability, and as a result increased their market competitiveness. Hong Kong industries since the 1960s have in effect now moved further up the value chain by collectively and wholeheartedly moving from a low value-added labour intensive production status to that of a high value-added and technologically based status. In recent years this has led to a rapid increase in producer and support services such as trade financing, import and export, insurance, certification and testing, transportation and warehousing, product design, research and development, market research and promotion. Due to Hong Kong's cost structures being relatively higher than surrounding regional locations, low skilled labour intensive activities are no longer competitive in Hong Kong and have already been moved offshore to cheaper environments. Hong Kong is now focusing on high value-added activities in various economic sectors. Four particularly important sectors are financial services, logistics, tourism and producer and professional services.

Steering committees have been established with the objective of promoting the development of these particular sectors. Hong Kong now has a growing range and number of professional services that are ideal for the use of multinationals. These services include legal, accounting, consultancy, public relations, advertising, engineering and design services. Hong Kong provides these services to clients from Hong Kong, China and throughout the rest of the world. As such these services are ideal for multinational requirements and help to ensure that multinationals located in Hong Kong are very well supported in conducting their businesses cost effectively and efficiently. Hong Kong is also placing greater emphasis upon the further development of its service capability and is devoting resources to become more innovative and make greater use of information technology so as to add further value to the services that it provides.

The government is currently seeking to increase Hong Kong's external connectivity for the Internet; enhance e-commerce throughout the territory; up grade Hong Kong's electronic presence in Europe and the United States of America; improve the dissemination of financial and economic news regarding Hong Kong to important trading partners; promote the digital entertainment industry; assist businesses of all sizes in their exploration of the Chinese market and its relevant business potential; promote the territory's professional services in China; adopt measures to strengthen the infrastructure in order to enhance Hong Kong's position as a leading maritime centre in Asia; enhance the Hong Kong public understanding of the importance of developing Hong Kong into a global knowledge based economy as well as building public confidence in the economic future of Hong Kong, its service centre capabilities and the need to remain competitive; and also promoting the concept of the importance of quality service in all activities of the economy.

It has been argued that the key to business success is either a competitive price for ones product or service, or product/service differentiation. Historically Hong Kong's prices have always been competitive, but now cost structures have risen in the local environment and China is more price competitive. Therefore Hong Kong has moved more towards product differentiation in line with its move to more value-added production and services. A greater emphasis is placed on quality, speed, customer orientation, market drivers and creativity. These aspects will greatly assist multinational companies that want to form partnerships with

Hong Kong companies. As a major regional financial and commercial centre, the city has become the telecommunications and broadcasting centre of the region. Due to the free flow of readily available information in Hong Kong regarding economic developments in China and the region, Hong Kong has become the best location for analysts and investors interested in market opportunities in China and the region and as such is an ideal headquarters location for multinational corporations. The growing closer economic partnership between Hong Kong and China means that there will automatically be a greater flow of goods and services between the two locations.

The Hong Kong government is continually striving to maintain and develop the territory's institutional framework to facilitate market developments. It is continually reinforcing its institutional strengths such as its low, simple and efficient tax system; the territory's rule of law and equality of individuals before the law; its concept of the level playing field for all types of business activity; law and order within the territory; and its business friendly environment. The government knows that it is these institutional strengths that are a clear asset to Hong Kong and help to attract multinationals to locate their regional headquarters or regional offices in the territory.

The Hong Kong government is also committed to investing in sections of the overall social infrastructure of the territory that the private sector is naturally reluctant in which to engage. These sections of the overall social infrastructure include the education system, the health and social security system, libraries and the environment. The government is also determined to raise the quality, capability and level of understanding of the work force in Hong Kong as well as attract talented and needed individuals from overseas. The Hong Kong government is a willing and active participant in multilateral and bilateral economic and trade negotiations and associations that have a bearing on Hong Kong's prosperity as well as world economic order.

In the 1980s public expenditure in the economy was 16% whereas by 2001-02 this had risen to 22% and with an ageing population there is an increasing demand for social security payments. From 1998 to 2002 there has been a cumulative growth in government expenditure that has not been matched or equalled by a cumulative growth in GDP. This inevitably puts pressure on the government to raise its income levels so as to meet payment demands. Under the terms of the Basic Law, the Hong Kong government must keep expenditure within the limits of revenues in order to balance its books. However, surpluses and deficits will be accepted on a temporary basis, but not as a permanent trend. A target that is often used by the government is to have sufficient fiscal reserve funds equivalent to approximately 12 months of projected government expenditure so as to meet operating and contingency requirements. On 31st March 2003 fiscal reserves were estimated to be HK$325.6 billion which is equal to 15 months government expenditure. It is the government's intention that the Exchange Fund will be used to maintain the stability and reliability of the Hong Kong Dollar and the monetary system, and that fiscal reserves will be used to support the Exchange Fund and its activities.

In recent years the property sector has declined and consolidated resulting in a reduction in income for the government from land premiums, stamp duty on property transactions and profits tax from the banking and property sectors. Up until 1997 the property market was extremely active and generated considerable income for the government, but in 1998 the market collapsed with prices being halved. It is not expected that the market will regain such activity again for at least another 10 or maybe 15 years. Growth in the property sector in the short term will be very slow and sluggish. Therefore the government has to look elsewhere for income. Also the government Consolidated Account has suffered several deficits between 1998 and 2002. It is therefore the government's target for the financial year of 2006-07 to balance the Consolidated Account, balance the Operating Account and reduce expenditure to 20% of GDP or less.

It is projected that the government will achieve operating and consolidated balances by 2006-07 when fiscal reserves are expected to be HK$271.2 billion, which would be equal to 12 months government expenditure. It is also projected that expenditure on capital works between the financial years 2003-04 and 2006-07 will be between $25 and $30 billion per year subject to the progress of individual projects. The Hong Kong government is acutely aware of its financial position and obligations and is naturally doing everything possible to ensure that income and expenditure are managed properly and efficiently in order to present Hong Kong as the jewel in the Orient and the natural magnet for multinational companies and organisations seeking to develop and expand business activities in Hong Kong, China and South East Asia.

Hong Kong is an important sourcing centre in the Asia-Pacific region with a very high percentage of the population engaged in the import/export trade. Hong Kong handles a growing percentage of China's external trade and over 95% of Hong Kong's re-export trade is product or service either from or destined to China. Hong Kong handles a tremendous amount of offshore trade. Most Hong Kong import/export companies are small with under 10 people, but there are some large companies employing over 100 people and tending to act as buying offices. There are three basic types of import/export companies -- direct traders who merely buy and sell sourced products without adding any significant value, traders with some value added services, and traders with sophisticated value added services who will even conduct design activities.

Offshore buying and selling by Hong Kong import and export traders is mainly in relation to business conducted with China. It has been argued that the idea of borderless manufacturing in Asia was pioneered by Hong Kong trading companies who are routinely sub-contracting assembly work on behalf of their customers to factories in Asia in order to obtain the most cost effective manufacturing. Hong Kong trading firms are now trying to expand their role in the value chain by undertaking such activities as design and engineering, testing, packaging, shipping, marketing and distribution.

Due to its trading history, Hong Kong has built up an extensive knowledge base making it a prime sourcing centre in the region. Hong Kong trading companies, particularly the larger ones, are increasingly acting as the control centres in charge of raw materials purchase, production site choice, manufacturing supervision, product distribution and marketing around the globe. Hong Kong's strategic location, strong legal framework and advanced infrastructure provides trade with a sense of convenience and certainty. Traders have tended to collect in the city with the result that the large number of traders in Hong Kong has given the city a comparative advantage in its role as middleman in international trade and this has tended to naturally accumulate and reinforce itself.

During the 1960s and 1970s, industrial testing and inspection services in Hong Kong expanded due to the growth in the manufacturing industry which was exporting primarily to the USA and Europe. At that time samples were regularly sent to destination countries for testing, but as the volume of trade grew, it became more practical and economic for local laboratories to perform the testing requirements in accordance with customer specifications. Hong Kong has now gained many years experience in product testing and certification, and its quality standards for product and service are now well recognised by international buyers worldwide. Over the last 25 years as Hong Kong's manufacturing industry has been moved offshore so to has its product testing and certification activities.

The Hong Kong Laboratory Accreditation Scheme (HOKLAS) was established by the Industry Department as a voluntary scheme with the objective of upgrading the testing and management standards of Hong Kong laboratories. A number of mutual recognition agreements have been established between HOKLAS and overseas countries with mutual endorsement of technical standards. In 1998, HOKLAS in conjunction with six other organisations became founding members of the Asia Pacific Laboratory Accreditation Cooperation (APLAC) Multilateral Recognition Arrangement (MRA).

The rapid growth in industrialisation in China in recent years coupled with Hong

Kong companies moving manufacturing operations into China, has made China the most important market for Hong Kong's testing laboratories. Hong Kong is ideally positioned to provide overseas buyers with the quality assurance and inspection services they require to guarantee that their products are to the correct standards. The laboratories in China are managed by headquarters in Hong Kong so that the quality control procedures can be entirely conducted in China thereby eliminating the need to ship product to Hong Kong for inspection. However, should overseas buyers require inspection and testing in Hong Kong, this can still be performed.

Hong Kong's status as a leading business centre in the world has attracted many internationally recognised consulting companies to establish a presence in Hong Kong. The sector is very active with many members also exporting services primarily into China, which is regarded as a potentially strong growth market. International consulting firms are attracted to Hong Kong because of its international skills and technology, its well established sector of experienced consultants, its rich client base and the fact that it is a recognised international business centre with many multinational corporations.

w) Taxation

When considering a base for local or regional operations, the tax structure of the city or country is a very important consideration because of its impact on corporate financial objectives. The tax structure can either be an advantage or disadvantage for the company depending upon corporate objectives. Hong Kong has always generally been regarded as an easy place to make money because this has often been the primary objective of companies and individuals over much of its history.

Hong Kong has a narrow tax base relying on direct taxes such as corporate profits tax, salaries tax and property related tax. Recent experience has shown that in an economic downturn such a narrow tax base can result in fiscal deficits. It would not be prudent or in the interests of the economic health of the community to increase direct taxes in order to increase government revenue during an economic downturn. Such action would also undermine the competitiveness of the territory. As a result Hong Kong is now considering introducing a consumption tax in the form of a goods and services tax or value added tax as has been done in more than 120 other countries. The objective of such a tax is to broaden the tax base in order to avoid fiscal deficits occurring during economic downturns. A decision on whether or not to implement a goods and services consumption tax will be made very soon. The government is also currently considering various other means of raising government finance including land and sea departure taxes, increases in rates, reductions in personal allowances under the salaries tax, etc.

The tax system in Hong Kong is a major attraction for foreign multinationals and investors. Hong Kong operates a simple tax structure that is very business friendly. The objective of this simple tax structure is to encourage more businesses to invest in establishing themselves in Hong Kong. Hong Kong has a low corporate tax rate of 17.5% and a low personal tax rate of 16%. It is believed that Hong Kong tax rates encourage productive labour as well as corporate investment. Very few countries can match Hong Kong's tax rates and according to the IMD World Competitiveness Yearbook in 1996, the fiscal policy of Hong Kong was the most favourable in the world with regard to entrepreneurial activity. Personal tax in Hong Kong was rated first in the world for promoting work initiative. The simplicity and clarity of Hong Kong's tax structure results in considerable savings for Hong Kong based companies.

Hong Kong does not impose a capital gains tax or an interest tax of any sort. Dividends are exempt from tax and there is no withholding tax, and losses incurred can be carried forward indefinitely for tax deduction purposes. Income earned through buying and selling stocks and shares or property and interest generated on bank accounts and savings is free of tax. This has been the practice in Hong Kong for a very long time, even when the territory was a British colony. Strangely this never seems to have been the case in Britain. Capital flows are free to enter and leave Hong Kong without restriction because Hong Kong's investment philosophy and regulations are open and transparent. The government in accordance with its philosophy provides a level playing field for both local and foreign investors in order to properly encourage entrepreneurship and raise the level of competition in business.

The Hong Kong government has always preferred to take a back seat and allow competitive private enterprise to be the main source of investment within the economy. This links in with the British government's statement in 1847 that it did not wish to invest in the territory like it had done in other colonies and that it should be the residents of the territory who should invest themselves and provide for their own means of support.

The Hong Kong government sees its role more as being the arbiter of business, ensuring that competition is fair and level, and helping provide education so that more individuals can participate within the dynamic competitive environment of the economy. Therefore the private sector has always been the driving force within business and economic development. Hong Kong's open economic structure exposes its resident companies to intense competition from international forces with the result that Hong Kong companies are forced to innovate and improve their products and services in order to meet international requirements. Protectionist policies are totally alien to Hong Kong and its spirit of dynamic competition.

The low, simple and predictable corporate and personal tax rates in Hong Kong enable companies and individuals to accumulate financial resources quicker than anywhere else in the world so as to invest in new business and business growth opportunities. Low tax rates have been extremely important in promoting corporate investment and growth.

Other regional competitors cannot match Hong Kong's low tax rates and the advantages that Hong Kong's tax system offers. Hong Kong's corporate profits tax rate is the lowest in the region, it is simply applied and is levied only on income that is generated in Hong Kong. As such other income that is generated outside Hong Kong, but passes through Hong Kong is not subject to tax in Hong Kong. This is generally regarded as considerably attractive to companies based in the territory or considering locating in Hong Kong with operations outside Hong Kong. The tax rates of regional competitors will vary and are often subject to additional taxes thereby making Hong Kong the cheapest location with regard to tax.

Profits tax for corporations increased from 16% to 17.5% for the year of assessment 2003/04 and 2004/05. Profits tax for unincorporated businesses increased from 15% to 15.5% for the year of assessment 2003/04 and to 16% for 2004/05.

Profits tax is charged against net profits generated in Hong Kong or produced from a profession, trade or business carried on in Hong Kong. The tax is payable on actual profits for the year of assessment. According to Government sources, profits tax is primarily calculated for the year of assessment based on the level of profits in the preceding year and then later adjusted when the actual level of profit for the year of assessment is known. All expenses incurred in the assessment year are deductible before tax.

Profits from debt instruments issued in Hong Kong are subject to a tax rate of 50% of the normal profits tax. This rate also applies to the profits generated by Hong Kong authorised reinsurance companies involved in the business of reinsuring offshore risks.

Salaries tax is charged on income in Hong Kong and its calculation is basically the same as for profits tax, but at a slightly lower rate. Tax payable is calculated on a sliding scale with the higher income incurring a higher tax rate above a certain level. Nevertheless nobody pays more than 16% of his or her total income in tax. However, due to the generous personal allowances under the tax system in Hong Kong, a large section of the community pays no tax. In 1997, 53% of the population paid no tax. Salaries tax covers income, commissions, bonuses, awards, gratuities, allowances and perks. Foreign nationals are exempt from salaries tax if they have spent less than 60 days in the territory during any year of assessment.

The standard rate of income tax for the year of assessment 2003/04 was 15.5% and for the year 2004/05 it was increased to 16%. Various deductions and allowances are applicable based on circumstances including allowances for dependants, children, married person's, self education, elderly residential care, donations, recognised occupational retirement schemes, mandatory provident fund schemes, single parent, disability, etc.

Owners of land and buildings were charged property tax before 2003 at the rate of 15% on actual rent received with a 20% allowance for repairs and maintenance. Property owned by a business in Hong Kong is exempt from property tax, but the profits derived from such ownership are charged profits tax.

The standard rate of property tax chargeable against land and/or buildings in Hong Kong is based on the net assessable value of the property and in the year of assessment 2003/04 was 15.5%. This increased to 16% for the year 2004/05.

Other taxes:

The hotel accommodation tax rate is 3% and is imposed on accommodation expenditure by guests in hotels and guest houses.

Estate duty is charged as follows:

- Nothing for estates valued at HK$7,500,000 or below.

- 5% for estates valued at HK$7,500,000 to HK$9,000,000.

- 10% for estates valued at HK$9,000,000 to HK$10,500,000.

- 15% for estates valued at HK$10,500,000 and over.

Stamp duty is charged as follows:

Fixed duties from HK$3 to HK$100 and *ad valorem* duties from 0.1% to 3.75%.

Duty Payable	HK$ Value of immovable property
HK$100	less than 1,000,000
0.75%	1,000,000 to 2,000,000
1.5%	2,000,000 to 3,000,000
2.25%	3,000,000 to 4,000,000
3%	4,000,000 to 6,000,000
3.75%	over 6,000,000

The Rating and Valuation Department is responsible for billing and collecting rates. These rates are levied at a fixed percentage of the rateable value of the property and for residential accommodation are quite low. The revenue raised from rates charges is used to finance the various public services provided by the Municipal Councils and provides a reliable revenue for the government. When assessing the billing charge for rates, the Rating and Valuation Department will estimate the annual rent that a property might be expected to generate at a designated date in order to determine the rateable value of a property. General revaluations are performed at regular intervals in order to keep rateable values of properties up to date.

Hong Kong does have an airport departure tax imposed on all persons leaving the territory. This is a very small nominal sum that for the vast majority of persons is insignificant and is nothing about which to be really concerned. In 2002 the departure tax was HK$80.

The Dutiable Commodities Ordinance imposes levies on only four types of commodities which are alcoholic beverages, tobacco, hydrocarbon oil and methyl alcohol, and the Customs and Excise Department collects duties on these products irrespective of their geographical origin.

A First Registration Tax in accordance with the Motor Vehicle (First Registration Tax) Ordinance is imposed on all motor vehicles used on the roads in Hong Kong. This is assessed based on the published retail price, or purchase price plus insurance, freight fees and brokerage or agency fees related to purchase and importation.

The major sources of revenue for the government are profits tax; salaries tax; land sales; stamp duty; betting duty; fees & charges; properties & investment; duties; utilities; rates; loans and reimbursements; Capital Works Reserve Fund (excluding land premium transferred from Suspense Account); motor vehicle first registration tax; personal assessment; royalties and concessions; property tax; fines, forfeitures and penalties; loan fund; estate duty; air passenger departure tax; hotel accommodation tax; civil service pension reserve fund; cross-harbour tunnel passage tax and disaster relief fund. Service income in Hong Kong and pension income are also subject to tax.

Hong Kong operates generous allowance schemes whereby an initial allowance of 20% is made for capital expenditure in construction of industrial buildings and structures in the year of expenditure together with a 4% annual allowance until the total expenditure is written off. Depreciation allowance on commercial buildings is 4% annually. Refurbishment and decoration of buildings capital expenditure is amortised over 5 years at 20% annually straight line method.

A 100% write off of expenditure on plant and machinery for manufacturing or computer hardware or software is allowed where it is owned by the end user. Capital expenditure on market research, feasibility studies and other research activities regarding business and management science are also deductible items.

Other deductions allowed include interest on borrowed funds, rent for buildings and land occupied, trademark and patent registration fees, payments for acquisition of patent rights, bad debts incurred, scientific research expenditure, contributions to employee retirement schemes and payments for technical education.

There is an understanding with Mainland China regarding tax relief for Hong Kong airlines and shipping companies. Hong Kong and China already have arrangements in place to avoid double taxation on shipping, aviation, land transport, personal tax and other business areas.

With regard to double taxation, Hong Kong has arrangements with the United States of America, the United Kingdom, Germany and the Netherlands concerning shipping profits. The territory also has arrangements regarding airline profits with Bangladesh, Belgium, Canada, Denmark, Estonia, Germany, Israel, Korea, Mauritius, New Zealand, Norway, Russia, the Netherlands, Sweden and the United Kingdom.

4. Why Hong Kong is a Business Paradise
Why Choose Hong Kong as a Base?

In many western countries it is only possible to conduct maybe 2 or 3 meetings in a day, but in Hong Kong it is possible to conduct many more, maybe 10, 12 or 20 in one day. It is very common for overseas companies with a buying office in Hong Kong to arrange a series of meetings for a visiting executive and have all the meetings conducted within a very short time frame. This is easily done by arranging for local suppliers to meet the visiting executive at a hotel or office in an orderly manner in order to present their products and ideas.

It has often been stated that Hong Kong is the easiest place in the world in which to set up a company. It is very easy to rent premises with a telephone line, install a fax machine and a computer or laptop, devise a company name and letterhead and then commence trading as an unlimited company. This requires a small nominal payment to the customs and excise department. If trading as a limited company, it is very easy to appoint a solicitor to complete the necessary paperwork for a small fee.

Another reason for Hong Kong often being regarded as a business paradise is the communication facilities available in the territory. It is possible to quickly and cheaply as well as very conveniently have contact with anywhere in the world by means of telephone, fax, cable, satellite, e-mail, etc.

Due to the international nature of the economy and its dependence on trade with the world, the Hong Kong population has much more of a business mentality than virtually anywhere else in the world. The population pays much more attention to stock market levels and stock prices as well as currency exchange rates. A large percentage of the population have investments in stocks and shares as well as currencies, and this is much more than in most other economies.

Another feature that conveniently lends itself to the notion of being a business paradise is that it is very easy to get a wide variety of cuisine to satisfy many different tastes. There is an abundance of restaurants and fast food retail stores working considerably longer hours than in many western countries. Also there is a plethora of hotels in the territory with some of these hotels being recognised as of world class quality. As such it is extremely easy to entertain business guests and clients. This all facilitates the smooth wheels of business, which is one of Hong Kong's regional objectives and advantages. The plethora of hotels also makes it very easy for overseas executives to visit and stay in the territory in order to negotiate contracts, agreements and orders with local companies. It also facilitates Hong Kong being used as a staging post for other regional activities and this is further enhanced by the geographical location of Hong Kong in the centre of South East Asia.

Also, due to the economic history of Hong Kong since 1950 and its work ethic mentality, attitudes have been fostered within the society leading to an eagerness for efficiency, attention to detail and a desire to meet the challenges of being successful in business. This mentality within the local population has further enhanced the concept of Hong Kong as a business man's paradise.

The Hong Kong Chinese are renowned for their optimistic business mentality that has been emboldened by a can-do spirit, a strong work ethic and a keen approach to bargaining. Upward mobility has been a very strong driving force in all sectors as individuals seek to better themselves and this has been supported and fostered by a very favourable tax regime that promotes this can-do-spirit. In the 1950s and 1960s as the population increased dramatically due to immigration and industries started to flourish, the workforce had no safety net in the form of social security and could easily be replaced by others. Therefore the ethics that developed were to follow instructions and work as hard as it took to get the job done.

This spirit has become the social foundation that has underpinned much of the territory's expansion during the last two decades. As a result of this spirit the territory has developed a sense of self reliance and responsibility for its own endeavours and this independence of action is also reflected in its early history in the 1840s when the British government clearly stated its intent not to support the development of Hong Kong as a colony in the ordinary sense, but instead that the responsibility for the development of Hong Kong should rest upon its inhabitants. Due to the strong work ethic of the population combined with open markets for its products, unemployment in Hong Kong has normally been well below three percent, but unfortunately due to the Asian Financial Crisis it soared to 6.5 percent by the end of 1998. However, the long term forecast is that it will decline back to a more normal level in the coming years.

Hong Kong has developed as a business paradise and is considered to be one of the most entrepreneur friendly societies in the world. Hong Kong was ranked first in the 1995 IMD World Competitiveness Report regarding entrepreneurial attitude to risk taking support and reward, and individual initiative. With regard to sense of entrepreneurship and innovation, the World Competitiveness Yearbook by IMD International in 1996 ranked managers in Hong Kong second in the world.

Due to the nature of the society and its dependence on international trade,

Hong Kong has a more international outlook than most other cities. The news media on television and in the press have a much greater level of international content than in other countries such as Britain.

The concentration of overseas multinationals together with the international activities of Hong Kong companies both greatly contribute to the depth of Hong Kong's international experience in business. The society is very much business orientated with the vast majority of people regarding business as an important part of everyday life. Wealth and prosperity are regarded as being created by individual effort rather than the fortune of natural resources, competition is seen as a force producing improvement and essential for economic and personal prosperity, and government is seen as a referee setting clear rules for business activity as well as providing basic infrastructure and indirect support in the form of education and training.

As such the general social attitude is noticeably different from that of many other countries and is a source of powerful competitive advantage. This social ethos combined with the industrial clusterings and economic institutions of Hong Kong has enabled entrepreneurship to thrive in a dynamic manner that has led to the economic success of the territory.

5. Unique Combinations

The Hong Kong economy exhibits a variety of unique combinations that are not normally seen in other economies. These combinations manifest themselves in the relationship between government activity and business activity, the relationship between local Hong Kong firms and overseas multinationals, the relationship between business entrepreneurship and corporate management, and the relationship between the different business strategies of hustle and commitment which together have contributed to the development of a vibrant and robust economic system.

The Hong Kong government has as far as possible maintained a policy of non intervention in the business sector. The Hong Kong Monetary Authority (HKMA) effectively operates as a central bank and oversees all monetary activities within the economy. The government tends to act more as a referee and lay down the ground rules for the way in which business is allowed to be conducted in the territory. It is then up to the private sector companies to manage their own affairs within the economy and develop their own strategic advantages so as to maximize the benefit that can be obtained from economic opportunities. Business decisions are generally left to the private sector and the allocation of economic resources is left to market forces.

Many infrastructure projects such as the Mass Transit Railway, the Kowloon Canton Railway, the building of roads and highways, the gas and electricity supplies, etc. are left to the private sector to develop, finance, build and operate with the government merely overseeing fair play and ensuring that the consumer is not overcharged. The government has consistently maintained a fair and open trading environment for all with emphasis being on a level playing field. Capital is free to enter and exit the economy as companies wish, and corporate and individual tax rates are kept low in order to motivate people. Together with the government policy of 'positive non-intervention', it has resulted in a society where companies and individuals are free to either succeed or fail subject to their own individual efforts and capabilities.

This independent philosophy and free spirit has been fundamental to the territory since Hong Kong was established and has often been regarded as a source of competitive advantage. In Hong Kong there is a clear distinction between the government as referee in the economy and private companies as commercially active units in the economy. The government does not take an active role in business, but instead leaves such activity to the private sector. This situation is rare in the world and unique in Asia.

In Singapore, the government has a direct hand in the economy and through its holding company, Temasek, has substantial stakes in many leading companies in the Singapore economy.

In Malaysia, the United Malays National Organization run by the government holds stakes in many of Malaysia's local companies. In China, the giant state trading corporations are government controlled. In Korea, the government has supported the chaebol by means of state controlled banks and maintained protected markets in order to ensure their profits and domestic development. In Japan, the Ministry of Finance conducted foreign exchange rationing to preferred companies and industries.

When compared to the other Asian tiger economies (Singapore, South Korea and Taiwan), Hong Kong has recorded the largest gains in TFP (total factor productivity) even though its micro economic affairs have been subject to the least amount of government intervention. Many of Hong Kong's competitors do not operate in the same open and free manner that has been a fundamental characteristic of the Hong Kong economy. Hong Kong maintains a simple tax structure with low corporate and personal tax rates that promote productive labour initiative and investment. The 1996 version of the IMD World Competitiveness Yearbook recorded that the fiscal policies in Hong Kong were more favourable to entrepreneurial activity than any other fiscal policies in the world, and the personal tax rates in Hong Kong were rated as the best in the world for encouraging individuals to work. Hong Kong's investment policy is open and transparent allowing the free flow of inward and outward capital without special regulation or restriction.

Nevertheless in certain areas of the economy the government has played a much more active role. Extensive government provision has been made in education, healthcare and medical services. The government has also been permanently involved in the property market due to the fact that the government owns all the land in Hong Kong and sells land leases to developers as an important means of raising government revenue.

In 1998 as a result of the Asian Financial Crisis and speculation by hedge funds the Hong Kong Monetary Authority (HKMA) had to take the unprecedented action of entering the stock market in order to counteract speculative activity designed to profit from forced movements in the currency board mechanism and short positions on the stock exchange. As a result this made the Hong Kong Monetary Authority a major shareholder in some of the territory's major companies. Although the HKMA's action was designed to protect the market and hence the economy, its action was criticized as counter to the fundamental spirit of the economy.

Hong Kong's mixture and balance of overseas multinationals and local companies is unique in Asia and possibly not found anywhere else in the world. Singapore is dominated by overseas firms and state holding companies. Korea does not have a comparable contingent of overseas firms. Taiwan is close but does not have the international cosmopolitan character of Hong Kong. In Japan, overseas firms do not play as important a role as in Hong Kong. In 1997 Hong Kong was the regional base for the largest community of multinational firms in Asia with more than 2000 multinational companies having regional offices and headquarters in the territory. Over 200 of the Fortune 500 companies have a presence in Hong Kong and the American Chamber of Commerce and British consulate are the largest American chamber and British consulate outside their respective countries.

Due to the nature of the society, overseas firms can draw upon a wealth of infrastructure, knowledge and capabilities from an unusually large, integrated, cosmopolitan local and expatriate business community. Also as a result of the expansion in trade and investment over the last 20 years many local firms have become increasingly trans-national in their structure and operations and have benefited from the influence of overseas firms settled in the territory. This combination between local and overseas firms has given the territory a unique balance that is dynamic and symbiotically productive.

Hong Kong primarily exhibits two types of business cultures, the entrepreneurial culture and the managerial culture. The territory has a vast number of privately owned small and medium sized entrepreneurial companies, many of which employ fewer than 50 people. Many of these small establishments are linked with larger factories through an efficient and flexible sub-contracting network that enables the manufacturing sector to respond swiftly to changes in demand. The structure within many of these companies is often patriarchal with decision making power highly concentrated at the centre of the company particularly in the small family owned companies.

This situation often persists even when companies expand and as a result enables these companies to respond very quickly and flexibly to market movements and fashion trends. However, such structures often lack detailed long term planning for market strategies and business investment.

Nevertheless this entrepreneurial sector has given rise to many professional merchants that have become role models for others and are highly respected individuals within society. One such model would be Mr. Li Ka Shing who came to Hong Kong in 1939 penniless and is now one of the richest people in the world. The entrepreneurial sector thrives on intuitive management and social mobility.

The managerial culture has evolved from the colonial hongs who established themselves in the earlier days of the territory and is now predominant in many of the large organizations that often provide various key infrastructure services and include companies such as Jardine Matheson, Swire Group, Hongkong Telecom, HSBC, etc. The management structures operated by these organizations are similar to those found in North America and Western Europe, where decision making is more distributed with greater delegation by top management and long range planning is an important feature.

The number of managerial style firms in the territory has expanded over the past decades as an increasing number of multinationals have settled in the territory. However, it is the influence upon each other and the interaction between entrepreneurial and managerial companies in Hong Kong that is unique. Entrepreneurial firms have learned from the management systems of the managerial firms and obtained talented individuals who have been through the training systems of larger managerial firms, whilst the managerial firms have been influenced by and benefited from the fast pace of the entrepreneurial firms.

Hong Kong firms have predominantly exhibited two types of strategies, either hustle strategies where the emphasis is upon speed and flexibility combined with reliable quality, delivery and competitive pricing, or commitment strategies where the emphasis is upon the employment of large fixed investments intended over time to change the shape of competition in an industry in a manner that is beneficial to the company. Commitment strategies are often found in the activities of the large infrastructure and utilities operators and in industries in which cash flow is relatively stable. These are also a common feature of the managerial type firms. Hustle strategies are often found in the activities of the entrepreneurial type firms and have led to agility in product development moving from low end to high end products within the same company and also the ability to move quickly from one market sector to another market sector. Hustle strategies and the emphasis upon speed of delivery have also helped to foster and promote efficiency within the vast subcontracting and parts manufacture networks that are characteristic of the Hong Kong economy.

Hong Kong has demonstrated versatility and flexibility in its manufacturing. Producers have found that the versatility offered by the many small factories linked together by means of an extensive sub-contracting network has been the best means of dealing with the frequent and somewhat troublesome changes in overseas market demand. The use of outward processing plants in China has helped to maintain flexibility in productive capacity as well as to maintain the price competitiveness of products. These two types of strategies support each other within the economy. The commitment strategies of the infrastructure developers and operators provide a relatively stable set of support structures and the hustle strategies of firms provide a dynamism and customer base that benefits the commitment strategists. Hong Kong's combination of hustle and commitment strategies and activities are unique in Asia.

The unique combinations between government and business, local and overseas firms, entrepreneurship and management, and strategies of hustle and commitment found in the Hong Kong economy has given rise to a strong, resourceful and balanced economy where different types of companies and organisations with different strategies and managerial approaches thrive together and interact as well as support each other thereby strengthening the whole economy.

Unique Combinations

6. Non Government Organisations - NGOs

a) The Commerce, Industry and Technology Bureau

The Commerce, Industry and Technology Bureau incorporates the following three branches:

- ☐ **The Commerce and Industry Branch** which is responsible for all policy matters regarding Hong Kong's external trade relations, promotion of inward investment into Hong Kong, protection of intellectual property and support activities for business and industry;

- ☐ **The Communications and Technology Branch** which is responsible for innovation and technology, developments within the telecommunications sector, all policy matters regarding broadcasting, issues regarding film related subjects, as well as control of obscene and indecent materials; and

- ☐ **The Office of the Government Chief Information Officer** which is responsible for all matters relating to policy, strategy and implementation of programmes and initiatives regarding information technology.

The Commerce, Industry and Technology Bureau oversees seven executive divisions in the government organisational structure and these include:

- ☐ the Trade and Industry Department
- ☐ Invest Hong Kong
- ☐ Intellectual Property Department
- ☐ Innovation and Technology Commission
- ☐ Radio Television Hong Kong
- ☐ Television and Entertainment Licensing Authority

☐   Office of the Telecommunications Authority

The mission of the Commerce, Industry and Technology Bureau comprises a number of aspects including the promotion and enhancement of Hong Kong as a leading international business centre; the development of a business friendly environment in Hong Kong with many support services that is guaranteed to attract investment into Hong Kong; the promotion and positioning of Hong Kong as a World City and as a premier digital city that also functions as the telecommunications hub of Asia; the further development and utilisation of the growing economic links between Hong Kong and the Pearl River Delta of Guangdong province in China further enabling Hong Kong to be recognised as the leading city in what is fast becoming an economically fully integrated Greater Pearl River Delta; and promotion of the high value added, creative and advanced technological activities taking place in Hong Kong thereby leveraging the power of the very strong service sectors in Hong Kong and the very strong manufacturing sectors in the Pearl River Delta, much of which are owned and controlled by Hong Kong companies.

The Commerce, Industry and Technology Bureau in Hong Kong has developed a number of mission strategies with the objective of enhancing the economy. The bureau will seek to promote Hong Kong's position as a leading international business and trade centre. In doing this it will seek to further develop Hong Kong's efficient business friendly environment and in the process attract further international investment into Hong Kong.

The bureau will support Hong Kong's position as Asia's telecommunications hub and the premier digital city in the region. It will be involved in the promotion of high technology inputs into Hong Kong that are not only creative, but also high value added. This will be done by making full use of the highly developed manufacturing and services sectors in both Hong Kong and the Pearl River Delta (PRD). Hong Kong and the Pearl River Delta are currently in the process of economically integrating due to the level of investment flowing from Hong Kong into the PRD. The bureau will use the developing economic links between Hong Kong and the PRD to further promote the advantages of the whole region in order to attract international investment.

External Commercial Relations

The Commerce and Industry Branch of the Commerce, Industry and Technology Bureau has administrative responsibility for Hong Kong's external commercial relations. The Basic Law stipulates that Hong Kong and China are separate customs territories and Hong Kong has full autonomy with regard to its external commercial relations and may independently join international organisations and trade agreements. The bureau has been actively involved in the Closer Economic Partnership Arrangement (CEPA) signed in June 2003 by Hong Kong and China.

It works closely with the Trade and Industry Department and the Hong Kong Trade Development Council to monitor changes and developments in China's commercial trade laws and regulations. The Joint Commission on Commerce and Trade for China and Hong Kong was established by the Bureau and China's Ministry of Commerce with the objective of developing cooperation and communication regarding commerce and trade. The bureau is also active in the Asia-Pacific Economic Cooperation (APEC) with regard to the development of open and free trade as well as investment. It is also actively involved in the activities of the overseas Economic and Trade Offices around the world.

Supporting Business and Industry

The Commerce and Industry Branch of the Commerce, Industry and Technology Bureau has complete responsibility for policies in the following areas:

a) Promoting Hong Kong's Service Industry

The department is continually organising publicity programmes to promote Hong Kong's services sector and to raise the quality of the sector. The department has a HK$100 million Professional Services Development Assistance Scheme that is used to support services industries in order to raise their competitiveness.

b) Raising the Competitiveness of Hong Kong Industry

All efforts are made to encourage companies to make full use of innovative technology in order to improve productivity and raise the level of added value in products. Industrial development is supported by a world class infrastructure. The Commerce and Industry Branch also works very closely with the Trade and Industry Department to network with all sections of industry.

c) Small and Medium size Enterprise Support

The Commerce and Industry Branch has full responsibility for policies regarding SMEs and provides a vast range of services geared towards supporting SMEs.

The Trade and Industry Department also has a Small and Medium Enterprises Office providing support services including:

i) provision of information, business advisory services and seminars via the Support and Consultation Centre for SMEs,

ii) provision of loans via the SME Loan Guarantee Scheme, the SME Export Marketing Fund, the SME Training Fund and the SME Development Fund in order to support efforts regarding market expansion, installation of equipment, working capital needs, training, etc. in order to raise company competitiveness,

iii) providing a Mentorship Programme whereby SMEs are given the guidance of experienced professionals, business executives and entrepreneurs,

iv) providing the Small and Medium Enterprises Committee with secretariat support.

d) **Promoting Trade**

The Commerce and Industry Branch is responsible for the Government Electronic Trading Services (GETS) programme designed to increase the level of submission and processing of trade related documentation by electronic means. The objective of this programme is to reduce the amount of paperwork and increase the level of efficiency. Under the branch policy, the Hong Kong Trade Development Council has responsibility for external trade promotion, and the Hong Kong Export Credit Insurance Corporation has responsibility for insurance protection of exporters regarding non payment by overseas customers due to commercial and political risks.

Promotion of Inward Investment

The Commerce and Industry Branch has day-to-day responsibility regarding policy formulation and work coordination concerning inward investment strategies. It is assisted by Invest Hong Kong and the overseas Economic and Trade Offices. Also other organisations such as the HKTDC contribute to investment promotion activities. This aspect of the work done by the Commerce and Industry Branch is regarded as being very important, because inward investment is a source of new technology, it creates more employment and leads to improvement and diversification in management culture as well as enriching the cosmopolitan character of the city.

Intellectual Property Protection

The Commerce and Industry Branch has full policy responsibility for intellectual property protection in Hong Kong. The department has the assistance of the Intellectual Property Department regarding registration of patents, designs and trade marks, and the assistance of the Customs and Excise department regarding policy enforcement.

b) The Hong Kong Productivity Council

The Hong Kong Productivity Council (HKPC) was established by statute in 1967 with the objective of increasing the productivity as well as material and labour efficiency of the various business sectors in Hong Kong. The organisation is a multi-disciplinary force with a vast range of knowledge and experience in many business sectors. The organisation is governed by a council composed of 22 members plus a chairman. Council members are drawn from a wide range of fields including managerial, labour, academic, professional and government departments.

The HKPC organisation employs many highly trained and skilled staff and consultants in order that it can provide business with a vast range of services. These services are provided for a reasonable fee as the organisation is also government sponsored. The HKPC services include consultancy, product development, technology transfer and various forms of training in industrial and commercial sectors. The Hong Kong economy has experienced radical changes during the last 30 years and has moved from being a mass production and assembly economy to that of the most services oriented economy in the world.

The Hong Kong economy has moved from being a low value added production base to a higher value added production base and with this a greatly increased level of creativity in applied technology has taken place. This is an essential move for Hong Kong to remain at a competitive level in the global market place. As such the HKPC has invested in new technologies and upgraded training to fully utilise the latest technology so as to enhance the overall performance of the companies and organisations that employ its services.

It is the HKPC's mission to promote and increase the productivity of Hong Kong companies by providing a form of integrated support in order to enhance the effective use of resources and raise the value added content of products and services thereby increasing the territory's international competitiveness. It is via this mission together with the essential teamwork of highly educated and skilled professionals that the HKPC contributes greatly to Hong Kong's satisfactory development and performance in the competitive global economy.

A company's or country's productivity is a primary source of competitive advantage. Productivity has often been described as the relationship between input and output. To raise the level of productivity in a relationship means to achieve a higher level of output from the same or lower level of input. When a company is able to do this it raises its level of competitiveness. The raising of the level of productivity can be achieved in many forms be it reduction in cost, increase in production volume, increase in the level of innovation, quicker delivery or more on time delivery, increase in the level of quality, etc. Increases in the level of productivity basically amount to increasing the value added content of the product or service in some form or other. It has been argued that increasing productivity is in effect a form of wealth creation and therefore raises the standard of living.

Productivity can be raised by increasing the level of knowledge of the community and the level of understanding and usage of technology. According to Professor Michael Porter of Harvard Business School, USA, real competitive advantage is derived from productivity and in the long term is critical to the economic viability of a company or economy. Companies must seek to enhance their competitiveness by increasing their productivity in order to raise the value added content of their products or services to a higher level than their competitors. A company can raise its productivity by means of its corporate strategy based upon the markets that it seeks to enter or needs to enter in order to remain a viable competitor in its particular market sector.

It is now well recognised that China will probably be the largest market in the world by 2020-2025. This prospect has been seriously put forward in a CIA report and is widely accepted particularly when one considers the dramatic growth rate in GDP of China in recent years. Therefore multinationals cannot afford to ignore this market both from a sales point of view and a production point of view. China is now recognised as the workshop of the world because of its low production costs and many companies have moved their production and manufacturing facilities into China so as to lower their production costs and in effect raise their level of productivity. China's accession to the WTO also represents a further opening of this market to business interests from around the world.

In order to properly enter this market and so raise corporate productivity and company competitiveness, multinationals must seek to locate themselves either in the market or very close to the market, and preferably in a location that offers very efficient, effective and competitive services. This is one of the reasons why many multinationals from around the world are locating themselves in Hong Kong because of its obvious strategic position and abundant business resources that multinationals obviously need. For many multinational corporations Hong Kong is the ideal business location because it enables companies to cover both China and South East Asia and hence maximise the opportunity to raise productivity.

Companies involved in manufacture can locate their production plant in China, but keep operational control and marketing as well as sourcing in Hong Kong. Companies seeking to sell product to China can use Hong Kong as a platform from which to operate or they can form a partnership with a Hong Kong company and allow the Hong Kong company to penetrate deeper into the Chinese market based on its deeper cultural, economic and geographic experience.

It must be borne in mind that a company that does not seek to raise its productivity will inevitably be left behind by the competition and as a result will start to dwindle and contract. It will find that its employees will seek opportunities elsewhere in more competitive companies, it will find its level of investment will decline, it will experience difficulty in raising finance within the market, and it will not be able to create better value for its customers. Therefore companies must strive to raise productivity in order to remain competitive. With China being such a major rapidly emerging market, both from a production point of view and increasingly from a sales point of view, due to the country merging further into the global economy, multinationals must develop strategic competitive positions with regard to this market in order to remain competitive in their relevant business sectors. Hong Kong is ideally placed to meet these competitive productivity requirements.

Higher productivity leads to business expansion which attracts new investment giving rise to greater employment opportunities and increased cashflow within the economy and hence a higher standard of living. Productivity is created by utilising labour, capital and knowledge as inputs to improve operational efficiency and create customer value by producing new products, services, applications, technology, markets, lower costs, better quality, quicker cycle times, etc. The HKPC helps industry by providing an extensive range of services including research and development; innovation; effective marketing for brandname development; new product development; design; new services development; upgrading the quality of products and services; time compression in various forms such as cycle time reduction, reducing production lead times, and reducing time to market for products and services; environmental management; component production; etc. A relationship with this organisation can be very rewarding for multinationals with offices strategically located in Hong Kong.

c) The Hong Kong International Arbitration Centre

The Hong Kong International Arbitration Centre (HKIAC) provides a comprehensive range of support services dealing with arbitration and the mediation of disputes. It will assist parties in deciding on the best means to resolve the dispute based on the available options. A number of options are available including negotiation, conciliation and mediation, arbitration or litigation.

Negotiation is the most common form of dispute resolution and most disputants opt for this means of resolution. However, if negotiations fail, it then becomes necessary to seek one or several neutral third parties to assist in the negotiation.

Conciliation and mediation take place when a third party is appointed to assist in the dispute resolution. The mediator does not have the power to impose a resolution, but instead attempts to overcome any impasse or deadlock by encouraging the parties towards an amicable resolution. A deadlock may arise due to a lack of trust or genuine difference of opinion or interpretation of the facts. The mediator acts as a communication channel between the parties and can filter out unwelcome emotions so that the parties concentrate on the underlying facts and objectives of the case. Mediation has generally been a very efficient and successful means of dispute resolution.

For disputing parties to take their case to arbitration, there must be agreement between the parties to use arbitration as a means of settling the dispute. It is very common for commercial agreements to include an arbitration clause so that any disputes arising during the conduct of the agreement may be settled by means of arbitration. Arbitration means that the dispute will be heard by an individual or panel of individuals rather than be referred to a court. Arbitration is a legal procedure that normally results in the arbitrator issuing an award in favour of one of the parties to the dispute. The award is final and binding on both parties to the dispute, but may be challenged in exceptional circumstances. An arbitration award is very similar to a court judgement and like a court judgement it is enforceable. Arbitration awards that are made in Hong Kong are enforceable through court action in virtually all trading nations throughout the world.

Where there is not an arbitration agreement between the parties or any other means of settling the dispute, litigation may be commenced through the courts in Hong Kong. Litigation is regarded as the last chance of resolving a dispute due to resorting to the legal processes of a court. Both parties will appoint their chosen legal counsel and the dispute will be competently resolved in the courts.

The dispute will normally go to the Court of First Instance for a decision. However, the decision of the Court of First Instance may not be final because the aggrieved party may appeal to the Court of Appeal. If the financial amount involved in the dispute is more than HK$1,000,000 the aggrieved party has an automatic right of appeal against any decision of the Court of Appeal and may take the case to the Court of Final Appeal in Hong Kong.

Hong Kong is a prime centre for dispute resolution in Asia due to its unique location and history. It has a great understanding of Asian traditions regarding mediation and dispute resolution as well as a great knowledge and understanding of western principles of dispute resolution. Hong Kong offers all the necessary requirements for arbitration including facilities, expertise, law and enforcement. Hong Kong's facilities are probably the best in Asia. It is geographically very convenient due to being in the centre of Asia, it has superb communications networks, its transport infrastructure is probably the best in Asia and its accommodation facilities are second to none. Hong Kong is also the international financial and commercial capital of Asia making it a highly respected and regarded city.

Hong Kong has a wealth of knowledge and expertise in a vast array of sectors including business law, commerce, information technology, shipping, finance, construction, etc. and can easily draw upon this vast array of knowledge and expertise in dispute resolution via arbitration. Hong Kong has many architects, accountants, engineers, bankers, lawyers and insurance experts, plus many other specialists in a vast range of areas. It also has many lawyers capable of advising on Hong Kong law and the law in other countries and as such the city is capable of drawing on an international source of specialist knowledge.

Due to the history of the territory, Hong Kong law is largely based on English common law and its continuance in its current form is guaranteed by China under the Joint Declaration on the Question of Hong Kong signed on 19th December 1984 by the Chinese and British Governments. It is also protected under the Basic Law issued by the National People's Congress of China in April 1990. The Hong Kong Arbitration Ordinance, which is listed as Chapter 341 of the Laws of Hong Kong, provides for the legislative support of mediation and arbitration conducted in Hong Kong. This law provides that there are two very distinct arbitration regimes. The first regime is for domestic arbitration whilst the second regime is for international arbitration. The UNCITRAL Model Law has been applied in international arbitration cases conducted in Hong Kong since April 1990. Most arbitration cases in Hong Kong are now international arbitration cases where the parties are not resident in Hong Kong.

With regard to enforcement of arbitration awards, Hong Kong is a signatory to the New York Convention on the Recognition and Enforcement of Foreign Arbitral Awards, which gives a detailed framework regarding the recognition and enforcement of arbitration awards. Over 100 countries are signatories to this convention and Hong Kong adopted the convention on 21st April 1977 when the UK accepted the convention. Hong Kong's acceptance of the convention was due to it being a colony of the UK at that point in time and therefore unable to formulate its own terms of acceptance. China is a signatory to the convention and applied the convention to Hong Kong after the handover of sovereignty on 1st July 1997. Arbitration awards made in countries that are signatories to the convention are recognised and enforced in Hong Kong. The Hong Kong Arbitration Ordinance also enables Hong Kong courts to enforce domestic arbitration awards as well as arbitration awards made in non-convention countries. Hong Kong's arbitration awards are also enforced in the countries of other signatories to the convention.

The Hong Kong International Arbitration Centre (HKIAC) was established in 1985 to assist disputing parties to resolve their disputes either by arbitration or by other means of dispute resolution. It was established by a group of leading business and professional people in Hong Kong to be the focus for dispute resolution in Asia. It has been generously funded by the business community and by the Hong Kong Government, but it is totally independent of both and it is financially self sufficient.

HKIAC is a non-profit making company limited by guarantee. It operates under a Council composed of business and professional people of many different nationalities and with a wide diversity of skills and experience. Administration of HKIAC arbitration activities is conducted by the Council through the Centre's Secretary-General who is its chief executive and registrar.

The contact address is as follows:

Hong Kong International Arbitration Centre
38/F, Two Exchange Square
8 Connaught Place
Central
Hong Kong Special Administrative Region
T: (852) 2525 2381
F: (852) 2524 2171
E: adr@hkiac.org
W: http://www.hkiac.org/main.html

The Hong Kong Mediation Council (HKMC) was set up within HKIAC in January 1994 to promote the development and use of mediation as a method of resolving disputes. HKMC is a division of HKIAC.

Hong Kong is now a very popular place for arbitrating international cases of dispute. The city is seen as safe and the legal system as fair and impartial. In conjunction with its strong legal system and excellent arbitration system, Hong Kong has developed considerable expertise in arbitration at an international level. In 2001, Hong Kong dealt with 307 international arbitration cases several of which were where both sides were Chinese companies using Hong Kong to resolve their dispute. The Hong Kong International Arbitration Centre is an independent organisation with no affiliation to the government and is now recognised as being a leading dispute resolution centre in Asia.

Since Hong Kong established its International Arbitration Centre in 1985, it has developed into one of the world's leading arbitration jurisdictions. Hong Kong has three major advantages as a place for arbitration and mediation.

1. Hong Kong has a well established legal system based on the rule of law. It has an independent judiciary. Under the principle of 'One Country, Two Systems', China's legal system does not apply in Hong Kong, instead English common law prevails. Therefore business people have confidence that contracts will be honoured and enforced as has been the case since 1985 and the territory's establishment as an International Arbitration Centre.

2. Hong Kong has a long history of experience in dealing with both Asian and Western traditions and as such has a unique ability in settling cross-cultural disputes. Hong Kong probably handles the largest number of cases in which neither party is local when compared to other arbitration venues in Asia.

3. Hong Kong has an enormous number of experienced professionals to deal with dispute settlements. These include lawyers, insurance experts, accountants, architects, bankers, engineers, etc.

As a leading Asian business centre, Hong Kong is a prime location for resolving commercial disputes. The Hong Kong Arbitration Ordinance is one of the best arbitration statutes in the world. Hong Kong probably handles more cases where neither party is local than any other arbitration centre in Asia. The providers of arbitration services are normally taken from various professional services throughout the economy including lawyers, engineers, accountants, quantity surveyors, architects, etc. and therefore the prime centres for arbitration are usually established and renowned commercial centres.

Hong Kong has four institutions for arbitration and mediation including the Hong Kong International Arbitration Centre (HKIAC), the Hong Kong International

Arbitration Centre Mediation Council, the Hong Kong Institute of Arbitrators (HKIArb) and the Chartered Institute of Arbitrators. Hong Kong and China have recently signed the Memorandum of Understanding for Reciprocal Enforcement of Arbitral Awards in 1999, so that arbitration awards made in China are also enforced in Hong Kong and arbitration awards made in Hong Kong are also enforced in China. It is expected that there will be a growth in demand for arbitration services in the coming years particularly with regard to China. In 1999, it was reported that the International Chamber of Commerce (ICC) established its first regional office in Hong Kong. The International Court of Arbitration which is a leading international arbitration institution is a part of, and operates under, the International Chamber of Commerce.

7. The Hong Kong Monetary Authority

The Hong Kong Monetary Authority was established on 1st April 1993 and acts as Hong Kong's central banking institution. The merging of the Office of the Exchange Fund and the office of the Commissioner of Banking led to the creation of the Hong Kong Monetary Authority (HKMA). The HKMA reports to the Financial Secretary and its functions and responsibilities are laid out in the Exchange Fund Ordinance and Banking Ordinance. A prime responsibility of the HKMA is the maintenance of monetary and banking stability within Hong Kong. The functions of the HKMA have been listed as:

- maintaining the stability of the Hong Kong dollar,

- ensuring the sound and effective management of Hong Kong's official reserves under the Exchange Fund,

- promoting and ensuring the safety of the banking system in Hong Kong,

- developing the financial infrastructure in Hong Kong in order to ensure that money is able to flow smoothly and freely throughout Hong Kong without any form of obstruction.

The policy objectives of the HKMA are:

- to maintain and ensure currency stability under the linked exchange rate system with the USA dollar by means of careful management of the Exchange Fund, monetary policy activities and operations, and any other activities deemed necessary or expedient with regard to currency stability,

- regulation of banking business and banking activities including the business of taking deposits, and careful supervision of all authorised institutions in order to promote the stability and safety of the banking system in Hong Kong,

- to promote and enhance the integrity, efficiency and careful development of the financial system in Hong Kong including payment and settlement arrangements.

The Financial Secretary and Monetary Authority each have specific monetary and financial functions and responsibilities and these have been clearly agreed and outlined in an Exchange of Letters between the two. The Exchange of Letters also clarifies the powers of delegation possessed by the Financial Secretary with regard to the workings of the Monetary Authority under the relevant Ordinances. These Letters of Exchange are public documents that can easily be perused by anybody merely by visiting the HKMA website.

The Exchange Fund Ordinance places the Exchange Fund under the Financial Secretary's control and according to the ordinance, the Exchange Fund is to be used for affecting the exchange value of the Hong Kong dollar. It can also be used to maintain the stability and integrity of Hong Kong's financial systems in order that Hong Kong can maintain its position as an international financial centre. The HKMA assists the Financial Secretary under the Exchange Fund Ordinance in the performance of his functions.

Under the Banking Ordinance, the HKMA is responsible for regulating and supervising all banking business and bank activities including the taking of deposits. The HKMA is responsible for the authorisation of licensed banks, restricted licence banks and deposit taking institutions that are active in Hong Kong.

The HKMA is officially the lender of last resort to the banking sector in the Hong Kong economy and will assist major institutions in times of need. It is also involved in ensuring that the financial disclosure framework is properly implemented for large companies and institutions in order to ensure that financial viability is properly maintained. The HKMA facilitates, but does not direct, the development of the banking sector which is extremely competitive both locally and globally. It has also been involved in developing the infrastructure of financial markets by developing overseas links with countries such as Australia, New Zealand, USA, etc. This has been with the objective of developing the regional debt market and facilitating investment in stocks and shares overseas. The Hong Kong Stock Exchange is now linked with the Nasdaq exchange in the USA. The accession of China to the WTO presents growth opportunities for Hong Kong's financial markets that will definitely materialise over the next ten years.

The HKMA's five main principles practised in its work are stability, transparency, safety, integrity and efficiency. These are the qualities and attitudes that the HKMA believes are a necessity for Hong Kong's position as an international financial centre.

The HKMA has a number of advisory committees to help administer its duties including the Exchange Fund Advisory Committee, Sub-Committee on Currency

Board Operations, the Banking Advisory Committee and the Deposit-Taking Companies Advisory Committee. There is also a Chief Executive's Committee which reports to the Chief Executive on the progress being made with various major assigned tasks of the various departments as well as advising the Chief Executive on policy matters regarding the operation and function of the Monetary Authority.

The HKMA monitors the performance of the economy and GDP growth in order to attempt to predict future growth and determine where action will need to be taken in order to ensure the smooth running and function of the economy. The HKMA monitors the effect of external factors on the Hong Kong economy and the extent of external trade as well as the demand factors in the economy. The level of investment within the economy, both local and overseas, is closely watched in order to determine growth patterns. The main economic indicators followed by the HKMA include: Gross Domestic Product (real and nominal); external trade (merchandise and services); fiscal expenditure and revenue; consumer prices; labour market movements; money supply at all levels; interest rates; exchange rate movements; foreign currency assets; stock market indices; banking sector profitability; banking sector asset quality and types; capital adequacy ratios (local and overseas); liquidity; loans and advances for use in Hong Kong and outside Hong Kong; as well as the number, nature and type of overseas banks with branches in Hong Kong.

The HKMA will also monitor risk premiums within the economy. The exchange value of the Hong Kong dollar is normally measured by the trade weighted Effective Exchange Rate Index which is predominantly affected by the exchange rate of the USA dollar with other major currencies. The HKMA attempts to predict future economic activity and the growth or decline in imports, exports and re-exports based on previous performance, current market conditions and expected future market conditions. The banking sector is closely monitored and analysed to determine its stability, asset quality, bad debts likelihood, performance, profitability, deposit level and lending, etc. The growth in the credit card business and electronic business activity is an area also receiving very careful attention. Bankruptcies both personal and corporate is another area that the HKMA will monitor very carefully in order to minimise its effect on the economy.

On 17th October 1983, the Hong Kong dollar was linked with the United States dollar and this link has been in place ever since. This has resulted in currency stability because exchange rates been the Hong Kong dollar and other foreign currencies are determined by movements of the United States dollar against those other foreign currencies. Prior to the linked exchange rate system, Hong

Kong operated a floating exchange rate system that caused serious currency fluctuations and was generally regarded as problematic. The exchange rate has been linked at US$1 = HK$7.8 and most traders have found the linked rate to be particularly advantageous because they generally quote in United States dollars due to it being a freely convertible currency. However, the recent weakness of the US dollar during 2001 – 03 made Hong Kong a very attractive proposition because of the linked currency exchange rate. It also helped boost Hong Kong's export potential.

It has often been argued that the linked exchange rate system, whereby the Hong Kong dollar is linked to the USA dollar is the lynchpin of financial stability in Hong Kong and as such the government and the HKMA will do all that is necessary to protect the link. The financial markets have often been compared to a turbulent sea where the only thing that is constant is change. Therefore the linked exchange rate system between the Hong Kong dollar and the USA dollar has served as a solid anchor for Hong Kong's highly externally oriented economy and as a solid base for monetary and financial stability. The linked exchange rate system is really a currency board mechanism that incorporates the full backing of the monetary base with the reserve currency as well as convertibility between the monetary base and the reserve currency at a predetermined fixed exchange rate.

The entire monetary base in Hong Kong is fully backed by foreign reserves and any change in the size of the monetary base must be fully matched by an equal change in the foreign currency reserves that back the monetary base. Exchange rate stability is maintained by means of the currency board system having an automatic interest rate adjustment mechanism. When the demand for Hong Kong dollar assets declines causing a weakening of the Hong Kong dollar exchange rate towards the convertibility rate, the Hong Kong Monetary Authority will purchase the Hong Kong dollar currency from banks causing a contraction in the monetary base of the economy. This causes interest rates to rise which in turn creates the monetary conditions that lead to capital inflows thereby maintaining the exchange rate stability. Likewise if demand for Hong Kong dollar assets increases causing a strengthening of the exchange rate, the Hong Kong Monetary Authority will exchange Hong Kong dollars for USA dollars (i.e. use Hong Kong dollars to buy USA dollars) thereby resulting in an expansion of the monetary base and downward pressure on interest rates which automatically discourages capital inflows. However, it must be borne in mind that a reduction in USA dollar interest rates automatically leads to a reduction in Hong Kong dollar interest rates purely because of the linked exchange rate system.

During the decline in USA dollar interest rates from 2001 to 2003 this had a dramatic effect on Hong Kong dollar interest rates basically eliminating bank interest on Hong Kong dollar savings accounts. Also external market turbulence will affect the currency board mechanism to varying degrees creating different types of pressure, but in recent years it has led to automatic adjustments to counteract the turbulence. Market perceptions have a very significant effect on demand for Hong Kong assets and China's accession to the WTO is a positive effect on demand for Hong Kong assets.

As part of its currency board operations, the HKMA has enhanced the transparency of currency board operations by regularly publishing the Currency Board Account ever since March 1999. This clearly shows the monetary base on the liabilities side of the account with the assets side of the account showing the backing assets of the currency board. This has enabled the public and investors to see that any change in the monetary base is equally matched by a corresponding change in the foreign reserves. The Monetary base is composed of certificates of indebtedness, coins in circulation, exchange fund bills and notes issued, interest payable on exchange fund notes, balance of the banking system and net accounts receivable/payable.

The Backing assets are composed of investment in designated USA dollar assets, interest receivable on investments and net accounts receivable/payable.

At 31st December 1999 this was:

$$\frac{\text{backing assets}}{\text{monetary base}} = \text{backing ratio} \qquad \frac{\$257.0 \text{ billion}}{\$234.4 \text{ billion}} = 109.6\%$$

The convertibility undertaking of the currency board mechanism is monitored very carefully with the objective of maintaining convertibility at HK\$7.8 = US\$1.00. In 1998, the Exchange Fund Advisory Committee Sub-Committee on Currency Board Operations was established to supervise the operations of the currency board arrangements in Hong Kong.

Since 1st April 1999, the issue and withdrawal of coins in circulation has been based on the fixed exchange rate. Also since 1st April 1999, interest payments on Exchange Fund Bills and Notes on the monetary base have not been neutralised, but instead the increase in the Aggregate Balance due to interest payments has been absorbed by the issue of additional Exchange Fund paper. This has enabled non-discretionary growth of the Exchange Fund Bills and Notes programme.

The linking of the USA dollar and the Hong Kong dollar naturally affects the price competitiveness of Hong Kong products. As the US dollar appreciates it raises the value of the Hong Kong dollar thereby making Hong Kong products more expensive as was the case in 1997. However, when the US dollar depreciates the

Hong Kong dollar automatically depreciates thereby making Hong Kong products cheaper as was the case in 2001-2003.

The HKMA has had an office in New York since 1996 and an office in London since September 1999. These offices have enabled the HKMA to have unconditional convertibility 24 hours per day. These offices have also enabled the HKMA to have 24 hour coverage of market developments in foreign exchange and financial markets around the world.

The promotion of the safety and stability of the banking system in Hong Kong is one of the main responsibilities of the HKMA. As part of its supervisory role the HKMA will monitor the quality of local bank assets and seek to ensure that banks and authorised institutions can operate competitively and on a commercial basis. The HKMA monitors the banking institutions in accordance with the Banking Ordinance and ensures that the liquidity ratio and capital ratio of these institutions is acceptable. A guiding principle of the HKMA's activities is to ensure that depositors and creditors are not put at any risk. Off site and On site reviews are conducted of institutions to ensure that they are operating correctly.

The HKMA operates a risk based supervisory framework where comprehensive well-defined risk profiles are developed and supervisory plans formulated. The quality of the risk management practices as well as the internal controls of the institution are assessed by means of a risk based evaluation process. This results in a risk management rating for the institution that is then assigned and formally incorporated into what is known as the CAMEL rating of the institution. CAMEL is an internationally recognised framework covering Capital adequacy, Asset quality, Management, Earnings and Liquidity of banks.

As a result of the Asian Financial Crisis of 1997-1999 there was a surge in the level of bad debts within the economy and therefore nowadays there is an increased level of attention to loan recovery requirements and procedures which prior to the Asian Financial Crisis had always been at a very low level. This is an area that has received careful attention from the HKMA. The HKMA operates a broad scope for loan classification based on the Basel Committee recommendations and regularly conducts examinations of local bank loan classification and provisioning.

Hong Kong is recognised by the IMF for the accuracy of its statistics and has been listed on the Dissemination Standard Bulletin Board (DSBB) as from 25th April 1997. The HKMA is an active participant in regional and international forums of banking supervisors including the SEANZA Forum of Banking Supervisors, the Offshore Group of Banking Supervisors and the Core Principles Liaison Group established under the auspices of the Basel Committee on Banking Supervision. Regular contacts are also maintained with important overseas regulators in the USA, the UK, Japan, South Korea, Macau, Canada, Denmark, etc. The HKMA in conjunction with the Mandatory Provident Fund Authority, Securities and

Futures Commission and the Insurance Authority is active in the supervision and regulation of Mandatory Provident Fund (MPF) intermediaries and their selling of MPF contracts.

It has been considered by the HKMA that for Hong Kong to maintain and consolidate its position as an international financial centre there is a need for a greater liberalisation of banking markets. This would raise the level of competitiveness within the industry, but should be clearly supervised to ensure the safety and soundness of the industry. In order to promote greater competition within the industry, in 1999 the one branch policy for foreign banks in Hong Kong was relaxed in order to allow such banks to be able to operate from three separate buildings rather than just one. This has increased the flexibility of operations for foreign banks and enhanced Hong Kong's renowned position as a free and open financial centre.

In June 1999, the HKMA introduced the Interim Financial Disclosure package. Under this package it was recommended that all authorised institutions incorporated in Hong Kong, that satisfy a specified size criteria, should disclose information regarding their published profit and loss statement, off balance sheet exposures and loan quality. The information that was expected to be obtained by means of this disclosure included details of key components regarding the profit and loss of the company, clear information regarding the loan structures of the company, analysis of loans that are overdue and rescheduled as well as details of the contractual and notional amounts relating to off balance sheet exposures. This type of disclosure makes for a more open and freer economy where investors and clients have a much clearer view of performance.

As Hong Kong's central bank, the HKMA seeks to ensure that there are no regulatory impediments affecting the role of banks in the financial growth of the economy. Nevertheless, the HKMA seeks to ensure that the growth in banking institution balance sheets is conducted in a safe and secure manner. Therefore the HKMA closely reviews lending policies and credit risk management in order to ensure that it is prudent and that suitable control systems are operated.

Electronic banking via the Internet and mobile telephones is a new phenomenon in Hong Kong that is receiving considerable attention and activity. Mobile telephone banking and transactional websites have already been launched by a number of banks in Hong Kong and many other banks are currently in the planning and development process of this facility. Public acceptance of electronic transactions is rising very quickly. The HKMA is providing a secure regulatory environment to properly manage risks arising as a result of electronic banking activities. Offshore banking activities over the Internet are also monitored by the

HKMA using specialist teams with the necessary skills and information technology knowledge so that relevant controls can be maintained.

Hong Kong's position as an international financial centre is largely due to its strong and highly advanced market infrastructure. The enhancement and further development of this infrastructure is a very important mandate of the HKMA. Hong Kong's Real Time Gross Settlement (RTGS) system is a highly efficient and extremely reliable means of settlement of interbank payments. The processing time is four minutes for stock market transactions, nine minutes for cheque clearance, four minutes for low value bulk electronic payment items and three minutes for Joint Electronic Teller Company Limited (JETCO) items.

Banking is the fundamental part of financial activities in Hong Kong. At the end of the 20th century there were approximately 285 authorised institutions and representative offices of banks from 41 countries operating in Hong Kong. Many of the top 100 banks in the world have offices in Hong Kong and much of the banking business is conducted in foreign currencies. Hong Kong's position as a major international financial centre is due to a number of factors including its established legal system, strategic geographical location, advanced and very active business infrastructure, liberal economic policies, open and corruption free governmental system, free flow of information, transparent supervisory framework, adherence to recognised international standards, and a well established business mentality amongst the workforce and population. These factors have enabled financial institutions to prosper in a very competitive environment. In 1999 Hong Kong was the 7th largest foreign exchange trading centre in the world with a daily turnover of US$79 billion. Hong Kong is also one of the largest gold bullion markets in the world. Its stock market is the second largest in Asia serving Hong Kong and overseas investors, as well as being a source of funding for the region, particularly China.

The HKMA maintains close contact with other regional and international financial authorities and forums. This enables Hong Kong to maintain its competitiveness as an international financial centre as well as helping to promote itself. These contacts help to promote international understanding of Hong Kong's monetary and banking policies, share financial information with other central banks so as to enhance oversight of financial markets, develop more effective policies based on better understanding of economic and financial trends, enhance access to technical expertise and assist other central banks and institutions in developing a better understanding of Hong Kong's economic development.

The HKMA has been very active in the development of regional bond markets, it being realised that globalisation of financial markets has led to a tremendous increase in cross border capital flows which can be very disruptive in financial markets. Deep and liquid bond markets are seen as a means of recycling the substantial savings of the region. The HKMA has also been active in developing contacts and cooperation with multilateral organisations and regional central banks.

At the end of 1999, Hong Kong's foreign currency reserves were US$96.3 billion, which was the fourth largest in the world. The official reserves stood at HK$748.3 billion representing a significant store of value. Hong Kong is therefore a very cash rich society with a substantial reserve backing. The HKMA manages the official reserves through the Exchange Fund in a consistent and conservative manner in line with international best practices. The long term strategic investment of the Exchange Fund is based upon the HKMA's investment objectives which include:

1. the preservation of its capital base,

2. ensuring that highly liquid short-term USA dollar denominated securities are used to support and preserve the entire monetary base,

3. ensuring that monetary and financial stability is maintained with sufficient liquidity in the economy, and

4. maintaining the purchasing power of the assets and achieving a suitable return on capital investment.

At the end of 1999, the Exchange Fund's assets were HK$1,014 billion. The Exchange Fund is divided into two portfolios - the Banking Portfolio and the Investment Portfolio. Under the Banking Portfolio, the monetary base of the economy is fully backed by interest bearing short-term highly liquid USA dollar denominated securities. The remaining part of the Exchange Fund which is the Investment Portfolio is invested in equity markets and OECD bonds in order to maintain the long-term purchasing power of the assets. According to 1999 data regarding the investment benchmark of the Exchange Fund, investments can be made in 20 bond markets, 10 equity markets and 18 currency markets.

The Reserves Management Department of the HKMA is responsible for everyday management of the Exchange Fund whilst strategic investment is the responsibility of the Exchange Fund Advisory Committee. External managers in overseas major financial centres are employed by the Exchange Fund in order to invest a sizeable percentage of the total assets because these external managers possess expertise and skill as well as geographical coverage of chosen markets.

It is possible to book a tour of the HKMA in order to see the workings of the organisation and its structure as well as learn more about its function and philosophy. Tours last approximately 30 minutes and are conducted twice a day on Mondays to Fridays and once on Saturday morning. A tour is highly recommended because of its educational value. It is also free of charge.

Hong Kong has developed a three tier system of deposit taking institutions comprising licensed banks, restricted licensed banks and deposit taking companies. Total customer deposits with these institutions between 1990 and 2000 grew at an average annual rate of 11%. Hong Kong dollar deposits grew at a faster rate than foreign currency deposits. Between 1990 and 2000 loans and advances increased at an average annual rate of 10.4% with property related loans being the most important type of bank lending activity. Broad money supply between 1990 and 2000 grew at an average annual rate of 13.3%.

The Hong Kong government's finances are through fund accounts. The main account covering departmental expenditure and revenue collection is the General Revenue Account. Other funds exist to finance capital investment and expenditure as well as government loans. These funds are the Capital Works Reserve Fund, Civil Service Pension Reserve Fund, Disaster Relief Fund, Land Fund, Loan Fund, Capital Investment Fund, Innovation and Technology Fund and the Lotteries Fund.

Revenue from direct taxes and indirect taxes as a percentage of government revenue have both declined during the period from 1990 to 2001. Direct taxes have declined from 41% to 33% and indirect taxes have declined from 28% to 23%. Other sources of government revenue include fines, land premia, interest, dividends, fees and charges, forfeiture and penalties, and repayment of loans. Public expenditure by the government is from a number of sources including the Housing Authority, trading funds, statutory funds (with the exception of the Capital Investment Fund) and all types of expenditure that is charged to the General Revenue Account. Some of the major policy areas for public expenditure have been education, housing, infrastructure and security. Government reserves at the end of the 2000-2001 financial year stood at HK$430.3 billion.

On 13th August 1998, the Hang Seng Index fell to what was at that point in time a five year low of 6660. The territory suffered a very serious attack on its stock market as hedge funds sort to influence stock prices and interest rates. This resulted in the HKMA having to enter the stock market in order to beat the hedge funds at their own game and so counteract the aggressive and disruptive speculation that was taking place. The final result of this action was that the HKMA became the largest stock holder of some of the leading stocks in Hong Kong, but the speculators were comprehensively beaten and normality returned to the market. Subsequently stock market rules and requirements were tightened so as to prevent such speculation happening again. The HKMA later disposed of these holdings in a very careful and coordinated manner so as not to disturb the market, which has subsequently risen to a more appropriate level of over 16, 000 by July 2006. At the beginning of August 2006, the Hong Kong Stock Market breached the 17, 000 level, its highest ever.

On 25th October 1999 the Hong Kong Monetary Authority (HKMA) established its Tracker Fund. This started trading on the Hong Kong Stock Exchange on 12th November 1999 with the objective of disposing of the stocks bought by the HKMA during the 1998 stock market entry to combat speculation. This fund has been very well received and the HKMA's disposal of its purchased stock holding has been done very effectively without disturbing the market.

Hong Kong is renowned for its business acumen in foreign exchange, securities and banking. However, it is considered by relevant authorities that the territory needs to increase its liquidity so as to attract more financial product users to Hong Kong and also attract more capital and investors from China and overseas. The Hong Kong government is currently working with the Hong Kong Monetary Authority, Securities and Futures Commission, Hong Kong Exchanges and Clearing Limited and the financial services sector so as to facilitate increased liquidity within the economy.

It has also been suggested that Hong Kong needs to enhance its market system in financial services to make it more user friendly for investors, issuers and intermediaries. Further debate on this aspect of the economy can always be expected.

Contact details for the HKMA are as follows:

Hong Kong Monetary Authority
55/F, Two International Finance Centre
8 Finance Street
Central
Hong Kong
T: (852) 2878 8222
F: (852) 2878 2010
Telex: 74776 XFUND HX
E: hkma@hkma.gov.hk also info.centre@hkma.gov.hk
W: http://www.info.gov.hk/hkma

Hong Kong: The World City and International Business Centre

8. The Mandatory Provident Fund

Hong Kong has always been a very self-reliant society ever since its inception. Very soon after the British took control of Hong Kong in 1842, the British government decided very clearly that it did not want to invest in developing Hong Kong and that such expenditure should be the responsibility of those living and working in Hong Kong. As mentioned previously regarding the city's development as a free port, a clearly recorded pronouncement by a Birtish government committee stated that the burden of maintaining Hong Kong and protecting the general trade in the China Seas was to be the responsibility of the merchants and those persons residing in Hong Kong, because Hong Kong was not regarded as a colony in the traditional sense.

This refusal of the government to invest in the territory was the original source of the free and independent spirit of Hong Kong and an inspiration for private enterprise. Therefore Hong Kong has very little if any publicly owned industry. It is instead owned by corporations that work with the government.

Nevertheless like many cities around the world, Hong Kong has an ageing population that needs financial support. In order to address this situation the legislative council of the government enacted the Mandatory Provident Fund (MPF) Schemes Ordinance in 1995 which came into effect on 1st December 2000. The Mandatory Provident Fund (MPF) covers approximately 3.4 million workers aged between 18 and 65. Under the scheme, both employers and employees each have to pay 5% of the employees monthly income into an MPF approved investment scheme.

For employees earning less than HK$5,000 per month they do not have to contribute, but only the employer pays 5% of the employees income into the scheme. MPF monthly contributions are subject to a maximum of HK$1,000 (i.e. 5% of HK$20,000). The Mandatory Provident Fund has been designed to offer financial protection during retirement. It is the biggest ever social scheme introduced into Hong Kong and has been widely accepted by both employers and employees. In 2004 97% of employers and 96% of employees had joined MPF schemes.

Prior to 2000 only one third of employees in Hong Kong were covered by a retirement scheme. Now 84% of the workforce in Hong Kong are protected by a retirement scheme as a result of the MPF. The success of the MPF schemes has been due to the partnership participation of both employers and employees and their willingness to make joint contributions under what is a mandatory system. The financial scale of the MPF schemes is huge and in 2004 the total net asset value was almost HK$100 billion. As a result of contributions under the scheme HK$2 billion is added to the MPF accounts every month. Although the primary objective of the MPF was to provide retirement protection, this huge and growing asset fund has also served to further develop the financial markets.

The debt market has seen growth due to the accumulation of funds under the MPF schemes with demand for debt instruments of longer maturity, larger size and capable of producing a steady stream of income. Demand for good quality rated bonds has also added to greater market liquidity helping the development of both primary and secondary debt markets. Also due to the size of the MPF asset value much investment has been made in the local stock market. In 2004 approximately 52% of MPF assets were invested in equity markets. It has been estimated that the Mandatory Provident Fund Scheme (MPFS) will experience a growth in the size of its assets from HK$146 billion (US$19 billion) in 2000 to an estimated HK$2,954 billion (US$279 billion) in 2030.

The introduction of the MPF schemes has to a certain extent caused something of a social change within society. People have become more aware of the need to save and plan for their retirement and well being. No longer are extended families living under the same roof as was the case 50 to 100 years previously. The family structure is tending more to a nucleus as happened in western societies during the 1950s to 1970s. It has become much more important for individual members of society to provide for their own well being by saving and investing for their future retirement. This has given rise to a demand for service providers in the form of trustees, scheme administrators, fund managers, actuaries, etc. Like most cities Hong Kong has an ageing population and it is predicted that in 2031 there will be over two million people aged 65 and over. The elderly dependency ratio will then be 380 per 1000 individuals meaning that there will be one elderly person for every 2.6 people of working age.

The mission of the MPF Scheme Authority (MPFA) is to ensure the provision of retirement protection for Hong Kong's workforce through an effective and efficient system of prudential regulation and supervision of privately managed provident fund schemes under the MPF system.

The MPF scheme is monitored by a committee covering operational and administrative aspects. This committee includes members from employers associations, labour unions, the retirement scheme industry and the government. The objective of the committee is to ensure that the MPF is effective and efficient as well as prudent in its investments.

In conjunction with the MPF there is also the Comprehensive Social Service Assistance (CSSA) Scheme which is publicly managed and is a social safety net for the elderly. The MPF scheme is a mandatory privately managed fully funded contribution scheme with the objective of protecting individual retirement security. These two publicly managed and privately managed schemes together are a real source of security in retirement for the population.

Due to the MPF scheme being a mandatory system which requires members to save and invest for life after the age of retirement, the Mandatory Provident Fund Authority (MPFA) and the government have a moral obligation to guarantee that the system remains stable and safe, and that risks are managed prudently while the market remains flexible. Safety and stability are essential conditions for maintaining investor confidence as well as developing future product of scheme providers. The MPFA has the duty of protecting the rights of scheme members whilst ensuring that service providers have the flexibility to maximise investment returns. It can be seen that the Mandatory Provident Fund system is a collective investment by the Hong Kong population in the sustainability and overall stability of Hong Kong society. As such Hong Kong will benefit greatly from the MPF system because of the reassurance that it offers to the general population. People will feel more content with their future.

The MPFA was established in September 1998 with the objective of regulating and monitoring the operation and function of the MPF system. The Mandatory Provident Fund Schemes Ordinance (MPFSO) details the responsibilities of the MPFA and these include:

- ensuring that all relevant people and organisations comply with the MPFSO;

- ensuring that persons and companies approved to act as trustees administer all relevant registered schemes in an acceptably prudent manner;

- registering all acceptable provident fund schemes;

- overseeing the correct payment of mandatory contributions and ensuring that the correct rules and guidelines are in place in order to appropriately administer all registered schemes;

- performing all other functions and duties required by the MPFSO or other ordinances;

☐ proposing any appropriate and considered reforms of the law in relation to retirement schemes and provident fund schemes; and

☐ promoting the further development of provident fund schemes and retirement schemes in Hong Kong whilst ensuring that all schemes are administered in the most prudent and efficient manner possible by all trustees and service providers.

The MPFA has clear overriding authority over the whole MPF system thereby guaranteeing its complete and precise efficacious function and fulfilment of its objectives.

The MPF system covers full time and part time employees aged between 18 and 65 who are employed under an employment contract for not less that 60 days; and self employed persons aged below 65.

During June 2004, there were 48 approved MPF schemes with 321 constituent funds. An MPF scheme may comprise one or more constituent funds and each constituent fund will have its own investment policy. A constituent fund may be comprised of a portfolio of investment in equities, bonds or other forms of investment such as unit trusts or insurance policies.

People contributing to their chosen MPF scheme are known as members and have the right to choose the investment funds of the MPF scheme in which they wish to invest. These investment funds have different levels of risk. For example, the capital preservation fund and guaranteed fund have a low risk, bond and stable or balanced funds have a medium risk and equity funds have a high risk. In other words the return on investment varies and funds can rise as well as fall. Everytime a contribution is made to the scheme, the MPF service provider invests the money in the chosen fund(s).

A Capital Preservation Fund is in every scheme because it is a statutory requirement under the MPF Ordinance. It is a low risk fund that invests in Hong Kong dollar assets such as short term bank deposits or high quality debt securities of a type permitted by the MPFA.

A Money Market Fund invests in short term high quality interest bearing securities with the objective of achieving higher interest rates than those obtained on large deposits.

A Guaranteed Fund is a low investment risk fund, and in June 2004, there were approximately 40 Guaranteed Funds in the MPF market. These will either be a Capital guarantee of the net total amount of the MPF contributions after deduction of administrative fees, or a Return guarantee of a minimum rate of return on the investment. The Guaranteed Fund may be investment linked or non-investment linked, but a minimum investment period normally applies.

A Bond Fund invests in bonds or debt instruments which may be issued in different countries by many different organisations including governments, public utilities, banks, commercial organisations and even supranational agencies like the World Bank. These bonds or debt instruments must meet the credit rating requirements stipulated by the MPF legislation. A Bond Fund earns its income from interest generated by the bonds held by the fund, which may be held to maturity or traded on the market.

A Stable or Balanced Fund is an investment mix of bonds and equities (stocks). There are many stable funds in the MPF market. A typical stable fund invests in both stock markets and bond markets, either globally or regionally in order to reduce the overall risk as well as to take advantage of investment opportunities in different markets and economies. The risk level is between that of a Bond Fund and an Equity Fund, and the expected return is usually higher than a Bond Fund, but lower than an Equity Fund.

An Equity Fund invests in equities (stocks) traded on recognised stock exchanges and aims to achieve a high rate of return through capital appreciation over a period of time. Nevertheless stocks can be volatile and go up as well as down thereby affecting returns. Equity Funds may be global funds investing in global equity markets or country funds investing in single countries.

An Index-Tracking Fund has the single objective of tracking the performance of a particular stock market index. It is normally passively managed as stocks of the index are traded within the fund based on their respective weight within the index. This results in the fund moving in close accordance with the tracked market index. An index tracking fund generally trades less frequently compared to an actively managed fund resulting in lower administrative and management costs for fund holders.

Hong Kong: The World City and International Business Centre

9. The Legal System

Hong Kong's legal system is based largely upon English common law. Since the handover of sovereignty there has been a move to develop a written constitution. The territory now has a bill of rights as well as the Basic Law from the National People's Congress. These constitutional papers together with common law rulings have enshrined the fact that the rule of law is paramount in Hong Kong and applies equally and fairly to all individuals without exception. The concept of the rule of law has been part of Hong Kong's legal system since the founding of the territory back in the 1840s. Hong Kong has an independent judiciary and the courts make their own judgements.

The judiciary is independent of both the executive and legislative branches of government and will remain so. This independence is enshrined in the Sino-British Joint Declaration on the Question of Hong Kong signed by the British and Chinese governments in 1984 and also in the Basic Law. The Court of Final Appeal is the highest court in Hong Kong and is constituted by the Chief Justice, who is head of the judiciary, three permanent judges and one non-permanent judge.

The High Court comprises the Court of Appeal and Court of First Instance. The Court of First Instance has an unlimited jurisdiction regarding both civil and criminal cases. Civil and criminal appeals from the District Court and the Court of First Instance are heard in the Court of Appeal. The District Court is the next rung down in the judicial system and deals with both civil and criminal cases up to a certain level. Murder, manslaughter and rape are above the District Court and require a higher level of the judiciary. Also the District Court can only deal with monetary cases up to a certain level. The lowest rung in the judicial system is the Magistrates Court, which has the highest volume of cases accounting for 90% or more of all cases. Hong Kong has 10 magistracies and magistrates have jurisdiction over a wide range of offences, which are below that of the District Court.

In addition to the courts there are tribunals including the Lands Tribunal covering ratings and valuation, and compensation for land resumption; the Labour Tribunal covering civil claims regarding contracts of employment; the Small Claims Tribunal covering minor civil claims; the Obscene Articles Tribunal covering the acceptability or otherwise of articles; and the Coroner's Court covering death due to unusual circumstances.

In accordance with Article 9 of the Basic Law, Hong Kong now has a bilingual court system where both English and Cantonese can be used thereby ensuring that nobody is disadvantaged due to lack of ability or understanding of a language. The comprehensive legal aid system in Hong Kong has been developed so as to ensure that any person seeking to pursue or defend a legal action is not prevented from doing so due to a lack of resources. The legal profession is very well established in Hong Kong with many solicitors and barristers available.

Hong Kong is generally regarded as having a corruption free government because of its structure and the checks and balances in place to ensure that corruption is not allowed to develop.

a) Legal Services

Many of the world's leading legal firms have a presence in Hong Kong. There is a concentration of legal capability in Hong Kong with over 650 registered foreign lawyers, and many of the world's largest legal firms have an office in Hong Kong, thereby making Hong Kong the Asian international law centre. The legal services support and infrastructure in Hong Kong is very comprehensive and includes:

- ☐ An independent judiciary founded on English Common Law.
- ☐ A regulatory system that is very well structured and transparent.
- ☐ An abundance of professionally qualified legal counsel.
- ☐ An open jurisdiction with regard to foreign lawyers.
- ☐ A corruption free pro-business government structure.
- ☐ Low and easy to understand corporate tax system.
- ☐ Free flow of capital and information.
- ☐ Convenient and quick access to China and Asia.

Hong Kong has the highest number of corporate headquarters of multinationals in the region and is also the leading financial centre in Asia. In 2003 there were 966 multinationals with regional headquarters and 2,241 multinationals with regional offices in Hong Kong, representing a good demand for legal services.

The Chinese mainland is the most important export market for legal services due to the number of foreign and Hong Kong companies investing or seeking to invest in China. Hong Kong to date has been the largest source of direct investment in China with contracted capital inflow by the end of 2003 being US$414.5 billion and utilized capital inflow by the end of 2003 being US$222.6 billion which respectively represent 44% and 44.4% of the national total. It should also be remembered that China is one of the main investors in Hong Kong with direct investment being US$76.2 billion or 22.6% of total inward direct investment at the end of 2002.

There are over 2,000 Chinese enterprises registered in Hong Kong with assets of over US$220 billion, and Hong Kong is probably the main offshore fund raising centre for Chinese companies. Also Hong Kong is Asia's main international arbitration centre resolving many international business disputes over trade, joint ventures, shipping, construction, etc. All of these above factors give rise to a substantial demand for legal services in a wide variety of capacities and hence help emphasize Hong Kong's position as a well established and renowned legal centre.

A number of factors represent new business opportunities for the legal sector. Hong Kong's position as an international finance and business centre, China's accession to the WTO, the recently signed CEPA agreement between Hong Kong and China, Hong Kong's position as the leading arbitration centre in Asia, the increasing number of both foreign and Chinese firms seeking to locate in and use Hong Kong as a regional base and springboard for regional operations, the restructuring of the Chinese economy in line with WTO requirements and the ever increasing number of new companies seeking to establish themselves both in Hong Kong, China and other parts of the region all present new opportunities and rich pickings for the legal sector.

The legal profession in Hong Kong is self regulatory. The Law Society of Hong Kong and the Hong Kong Bar Association are responsible for regulating the legal profession. There is a clear separation between barristers and solicitors. Barristers are to be found in the higher courts dealing with cases regarding intellectual property, criminal cases, landlord/tenant disputes, personal injury cases, etc., whereas the range of services provided by solicitors dealing with civil law cases can be classified as follows:

- ☐ Commercial law regarding joint venture agreements, partnership formation and incorporation, mergers and acquisitions, company administration and secretarial services.

- ☐ Banking and finance law relating to capital market transactions, debt issues, finance of projects, bank security and related collateral, loans, equipment leases, hire purchase, corporate finance activities, etc.

- ☐ Securities law relating to the issue of shares, derivatives, debt, and initial public offerings (IPOs).

- ☐ Intellectual property law covering ownership, protection, enforcement and licensing.

- ☐ Conveyancing law regarding property transactions including property development and financing, property litigation, landlord and tenant agreements, and commercial as well as residential sales and purchases.

- ☐ Admiralty law and its investigations.

- ☐ All forms of litigation and arbitration both domestic and international.

- ☐ Legal matters relating to China and business in China. Many legal firms now have dedicated units to deal with matters relating to China.

In order to practice foreign law in Hong Kong, foreign lawyers and foreign law firms must be registered with the Hong Kong Law Society.

Hong Kong has a very liberal jurisdiction where foreign (i.e. non-Chinese) lawyers may practice. Due to the export oriented and global nature of the economy with its many multinational regional headquarters and regional offices, many international legal firms now serve their clients in the region from offices based in Hong Kong. China is an important market for Hong Kong's legal services and as restrictions are lifted in China, particularly with regard to WTO requirements, Hong Kong is ideally set to take advantage of the situation and expand further into China's legal market.

Hong Kong lawyers also have an advantage over other nationalities because of their understanding of China and its customs and laws, as well as the fact that Hong Kong is a major investor in China. The export of legal services from Hong Kong is primarily to the regional offices of overseas multinationals, construction companies, investment banks, industrialists and developers, etc. that have considerable business interests in the region and require legal advice on a fairly regular basis. Chinese enterprises seeking listing in Hong Kong as well as overseas have to comply with listing rules and automatically seek legal advice from Hong Kong lawyers on how to comply.

b) Dispute Settlement

The legal system in Hong Kong has been built on the concept of the rule of law together with judicial independence.

Hong Kong's courts and jurisdiction are as follows:

Court	Jurisdiction
High Court	Unlimited
District Court	Up to HK$600,000
Small Claims Tribunal	Up to HK$50,000

Hong Kong has a highly externally orientated economy due to its dependence on trade relations with the rest of the world. Therefore trade regulations are of necessity kept to an absolute minimum.

c) Customs Regulations

The customs authorities in Hong Kong observe very strict regulations regarding the temporary importation or exportation of controlled items. Controlled items include firearms and ammunition, narcotics, medications, ivory, sensitive high technology, military products, animals and plants, meat and poultry, and textiles. If any of these items are brought into Hong Kong without a licence, the goods will be seized and a prosecution enforced. Trafficking in dangerous drugs will receive a penalty of life in prison and a heavy fine.

Visitors to Hong Kong are required to declare liquors, tobacco, cigarettes, cigars, and methyl alcohol which will all be subject to maximum limits. Merchandise imported for commercial purposes will also be subject to import declaration. Hong Kong has no currency restrictions and therefore visitors will be able to carry any currency, in any amount, into Hong Kong. However, excessive currency loads will obviously arouse suspicion.

Importation of animals such as cats and dogs will be subject to quarantine requirements and will require a special permit to be issued by the Hong Kong Agriculture, Fisheries and Conservation Department.

Hong Kong is a free port with no customs tariffs on imported product except for four specific categories - tobacco, hydrocarbon oil, alcoholic beverages and methyl alcohol. The Customs and Excise Department will collect duties on these categories of product irrespective of their geographical origin, i.e. whether imported or locally manufactured. Duty rates are governed by the Schedule to the Dutiable Commodities Ordinance.

The following prohibited articles require an import or export licence prior to importation or exportation: arms and ammunition, radioactive substances, radio transmitting equipment, pesticides, animals and plants, dangerous drugs, pharmaceutical products, endangered species, medicines, irradiating apparatus, acetylating substances, ozone depleting substances, textiles and certain foodstuffs.

An import/export declaration must be submitted to the Commissioner of Customs & Excise within 14 days of the import or export of any goods together with payment of the relevant declaration charges.

The Legal System

10. Exhibitions, Trade Fairs and Conventions

Hong Kong is now a major player on the convention and exhibition network. The convention and exhibition facilities in Hong Kong are the best in Asia and every year Hong Kong hosts a number of major international exhibitions and conferences. The main exhibition and convention facility in Hong Kong is a major investment located on the harbour side of Wan Chai district, Hong Kong island. However, another new international exhibition and convention centre, Asia World-Expo, has recently been opened next door to Chek Lap Kok airport.

Hong Kong is Asia's premier trade fair, convention and exhibition centre. The Hong Kong Convention and Exhibition Centre is one of the largest convention and exhibition facilities in the region and has been recognised as one of the best convention and exhibition centres in the world. Hong Kong hosts many international exhibitions with exhibitors from around the world and these like other local exhibitions attract an extensive range of visitors from all over the world. Hong Kong has a distinct advantage compared to other cities in the region due to its strategic location in Asia and its position as the best gateway to China. Coupled with its top quality facilities, Hong Kong is an ideal location for an exhibition or convention visit before moving on to visit other cities and possible clients.

Hong Kong has often been ranked as one of the most popular, if not the most popular, city for international meetings. The exhibition and trade fair industry also contribute substantially to the economy of Hong Kong. The Hong Kong Convention and Exhibition Centre, (HKCEC), has a floor space capacity of 63,580 sq. m. making it one of the biggest convention and exhibition facilities in Asia, as well as one of the best and most modern facilities in Asia, if not the world. Other first class exhibition facilities in Hong Kong include the Hong Kong Exhibition Centre and the International Trademart.

A number of very important international commercial event organisers have now established regional headquarters in Hong Kong and some also have offices in China. These offices are part of a worldwide network geared towards organising events more efficiently. A variety of service companies are involved in convention and exhibition activities and these include stand constructors, insurance companies, travel agents, freight forwarders and hotels. All of these service companies together with the event organisers help facilitate the smooth preparation and function of the exhibitions and conventions. As China develops it is experiencing an increasing demand for exhibition and convention services and facilities, which in turn creates demand for support from Hong Kong.

Exhibitions, Trade Fairs and Conventions

Many exhibitions and conventions are held at the HKCEC throughout the year. The centre is owned and run by the Hong Kong Trade Development Council, which has in effect been a very strong marketing unit for Hong Kong for many years.

The centre is a stylish and imaginative design that captures a sleek modern appeal and is a symbol of Hong Kong's modern success. Hong Kong is now recognised as the trade fair and exhibition capital of Asia due to the extent of its facilities and the extensive number of exhibitions that it stages.

The HKSAR offers top quality infrastructure geared to presenting the best exhibitions together with the necessary expertise for staging and running exhibitions. Hong Kong is a natural location for major international exhibitions because of the dynamic international commercial environment of the city. The city is noted for an extensive range of exhibitions including the world's largest leather fair as well as electronics, gifts and housewares, watches and clocks, jewellery, toys and games, optical goods and cosmetics exhibitions which are held every year. Many of these exhibitions are international with exhibitors from around the world taking part and the number of visitors from around the world is also extensive. Joining an international exhibition in Hong Kong enables exhibitors to build networks with suppliers and buyers from major international markets.

The HKCEC is one of the most technologically advanced exhibition centres in the world and is recognised worldwide for it's outstanding features. Between 1994 and 1999 it was consistently voted as the 'Best Overseas Centre'. The centre has a full range of facilities enabling exhibitions to be staged efficiently and cost effectively whatever the size of the exhibition. The centre also has support amenities and services including business and catering thereby offering exhibitors maximum convenience and value. The business facilities offered at the HKCEC include computers, e-mail, Internet and multimedia services enabling exhibitors to keep in total contact with offices and clients around the world. This is supported by Hong Kong's all digital telecommunications network.

The Hong Kong government is renowned for its pro-business position and the level playing field that it offers for both international and domestic companies. The territory's world class business structures and high level of efficiency and speed make Hong Kong a truly dynamic environment that totally promotes business. The business culture and philosophy of the society make Hong Kong a perfect environment for international exhibitions and the business that naturally flows from such exhibitions.

Hong Kong's extensive links with the Asia Pacific region and the world, its strategic location on key trade and transport routes, its highly developed world class telecommunications infrastructure and its entrepreneurial efficiency make it the meeting place for Asia and the world. Hong Kong is ideally positioned for exhibitions and conventions because it is within 6 hours flying time for approximately half of the world's population and is therefore easily accessible particularly with a world class airport operating 24 hours per day with flights to and from so many destinations.

The many multinational corporations with regional headquarters or regional offices in Hong Kong, more than any other Asian city, is testament to Hong Kong's importance as a regional, if not global, trade city that is the ideal stage for international exhibitions. Many mainland Chinese companies have also demonstrated that Hong Kong is their preferred trade show location in Asia due to its international appeal.

Some would argue, quite rightly, that Hong Kong due to its location and history has emerged as a crossroads for the meeting of cultures and exchange of ideas and that this has led to it becoming a very cosmopolitan city. Hong Kong is one of the most cosmopolitan cities in Asia. There are an extensive number of nationalities living and working in the territory. The cultural mix, interchange and exchange makes the city an extremely vibrant, dynamic and exciting place to live and work. It is this richness in its character that is particularly appealing to many people and it is this richness that shines like a beacon for other cities to emulate.

This cosmopolitanism has added to Hong Kong's status and reputation as the trade fair capital of Asia. Hong Kong is a world leader in the organisation of conventions, exhibitions, trade fairs and corporate events. The city offers many advantages for this type of function. Hong Kong's policies have made the movement of product and people for exhibition purposes very convenient and cost efficient. As a free port Hong Kong does not impose any trade licence or tariff requirements, so merchandise to be exhibited at an exhibition or trade fair can be brought into the territory freely without restriction. There are no taxes or currency restrictions that could hinder or irritate exhibitors. Hong Kong has a very liberal visa policy for many countries that enables individuals to enter the territory freely without restriction except upon the length of stay which may vary up to 6 months. It is recognised by the Hong Kong authorities that successful international exhibition and trade fairs require easy entry and passage for people and products.

Hong Kong's highly efficient airport and seaport facilities operate on a fully integrated advanced transport network that enables people and product to be efficiently moved to their desired destination. This system is linked to a very efficient and comfortable urban transport network, which enables people to get about Hong Kong quickly.

Overseas visitors making use of Hong Kong's exhibition and conference facilities have an extensive range of hotels, hostels and guest houses at which to reside whilst in Hong Kong. Many of the hotels are internationally recognised and provide a world class standard of service. The range of available accommodation is designed to meet all tastes and budgets.

The HKCEC is centrally located along the harbour front in Wan Chai district and is easily reached from all the major hotels. Other exhibition sites are also available in Hong Kong including the nearby Hong Kong Exhibition Centre and the Hong Kong International Trade and Exhibition Centre in Kowloon Bay. Other venues would include the Hong Kong Coliseum and the Hong Kong Stadium subject to what is actually being promoted.

Hong Kong is the preferred location for many exhibitions and conventions and as such has developed a very sophisticated, experienced and innovative industry around its exhibitions. Many leading international exhibition organisers and service companies have representative offices in Hong Kong providing a full range of services covering all requirements for exhibitions including planning, stand design and construction, logistics, marketing and office support, etc. Hong Kong's exhibitions industry is dynamic and lively, and geared to making its exhibitions not only a success but also an enjoyable event.

According to the Hong Kong Tourism Board, 42 international exhibitions attracting 295,261 visitors and 130 international conventions attracting 17,535 visitors were held during 2003 in Hong Kong. The annual survey conducted by CEI Asia Pacific magazine in 2002 voted Hong Kong as the 'Best Exhibition City' for the second consecutive year. In 2003 the Gifts, Premium and Houseware Fair held in Hong Kong had 3,790 exhibitors from 31 countries. This is an international fair held every year and is one of the largest gift, premium and houseware fairs in the world.

The Asia Pacific Leather Fair which is a bi-annual event and one of the largest in the world for this type of product was held in Hong Kong in 2003 with 3,092 international exhibitors from around the world. The Hong Kong Electronics Fair, which is the second largest electronics fair in the world and held annually, in 2003 attracted 1,950 exhibitors from Hong Kong and overseas and received 48,291 visitors.

The Hong Kong Jewellery and Watch Fair is the biggest pearl fair in the world, the second biggest diamond and gemstone fair in the world and one of the three largest jewellery fairs in the world. The 2003 fair had 1,852 exhibitors and attracted 35,890 visitors from around the world. The Hong Kong government is currently negotiating with the International Telecommunication Union (ITU) regarding the hosting of the ITU Telecom World exhibition in 2006. This exhibition has always been held in Geneva and would be a major exhibition if held in Hong Kong.

Hong Kong: The World City and International Business Centre

An aerial view of Victoria Harbour with the distinctive Convention and Exhibition Centre

Exhibitions, Trade Fairs and Conventions

A daytime view of the Hong Kong Convention and Exhibition Centre, which is one of the largest exibition facilities in Asia

Night-time view of the Hong Kong Convention and Exhibition Centre

In 2003 Skytrax Research named Hong Kong International Airport as the world's 'Best Airport' for the third consecutive year with it offering many flights every day from Hong Kong to many destinations around the world. In 2002 the Hong Kong Convention and Exhibition centre was voted the 'Best Overseas Centre' for the 9th consecutive year by the United Kingdom's Meetings & Incentive Travel magazine. The centre is hosting many exhibitions and conventions every year with remarkable attendance figures.

Hong Kong has many experienced convention and exhibition experts involved in booth design, contractor services, marketing professionals and freight forwarders who all facilitate the smooth running and performance of exhibitions. Hong Kong is also one of the best cities, if not the best, in Asia for hotels. Most of the major hotel chains have a presence in Hong Kong and room rates are very competitive with room service being of the best quality. Hong Kong's local transport network is amongst the best in the world with a wide range of types of transport all coordinated to facilitate the easy movement of people about the city. The city also has a broad range of cultural and entertainment facilities.

The demand for exhibition and convention facilities in Hong Kong has experienced good growth in recent years. China's accession to the WTO, construction of the new AsiaWorld-Expo exhibition centre next to the airport, the continued growth in integration of Hong Kong and the Pearl River Delta, the relaxation of visa requirements for visitors to Hong Kong from mainland China, the Closer Economic Partnership Arrangement between Hong Kong and China etc., have all added to the demand for convention and exhibition services.

The AsiaWorld-Expo exhibition centre next to the Hong Kong International Airport will function as a complimentary exhibition facility to the HKCEC. The Closer Economic Partnership Agreement enables Hong Kong companies to supply exhibition and convention services in China. China's accession to the WTO is expected to lead to Chinese companies and international multinationals attempting to develop joint venture partnerships and business opportunities in China via trade fairs and conventions held in Hong Kong with Hong Kong being used as the window of opportunity.

Many Chinese are now visiting Hong Kong and in 2003, there were 86,317 visitors from China to Hong Kong as either participants, exhibitors or buyers at conventions and trade fairs held in Hong Kong. Hong Kong has performed the role of East-West convention and exhibition centre in Asia and this function is now growing in importance because of Hong Kong's integration with Guangdong province. There has been an obvious growth in the number of international multinationals, acting as buyers and exhibitors, taking part in trade fairs and exhibitions in Hong Kong. These organisations are seeking easy access through Hong Kong to

Chinese manufacturers and buyers and hence to the potential market of 90 million consumers just over the border from Hong Kong in Guangdong province.

On 21st December 2005 Hong Kong's AsiaWorld-Expo opened to the public. The centre is the largest exhibition and convention facility in Hong Kong and has over 70,000 square metres of rentable space. AsiaWorld-Expo is classified as a world class state-of-the-art facility that has been built with a budget of HK$2.35 billion by a public private partnership that includes the Hong Kong Special Administrative Region Government and a business consortium that includes Dragages Hong Kong Ltd. and Yu Ming Investments Ltd. together with land contribution by the Hong Kong Airport Authority.

The centre has ten ground level exhibition halls with each hall having an organiser's office, modular size meeting rooms and catering facilities. It has been designed for exhibitions, trade fairs, conventions, conferences, concerts, entertainment and sports functions and events. The facility includes AsiaWorld-Arena which is a multipurpose 13,500 seated arena incorporating the highest quality acoustic sound system, modular seating systems as well as backstage facilities. This Arena is ideal for conferences, concerts and events. The meeting and conference centre on level 2 of the facility also includes a seaview restaurant together with banquet and hospitality services.

AsiaWorld-Expo incorporates the highest level information technology and telecommunications services. It has Asia's largest indoor access of wireless broadband internet enabling thousands of exhibitors and visitors to simultaneously access broadband internet services. This type of technological facility will be greatly welcomed and increasingly used by the many people taking part in exhibitions and events. The broadband facilities at AsiaWorld-Expo also enable the multimedia shows and broadcasts within the facility to be of extremely high quality. The centre has the latest IP telephony communications systems that are of the best quality and highly efficient. The facility is also equipped with a high quality PA system and all meeting rooms in the centre have their own servicing facilities, telecommunications and wireless LAN.

AsiaWorld-Expo has been built with the emphasis being upon accessibility. It is fully integrated into an extensive multi-modal and highly efficient transport network. It is the only exhibition and conference centre in the world to be located and fully integrated with one of the busiest international airports in the world. It only takes a few minutes walk from Hong Kong International Airport to AsiaWorld-Expo by means of a direct footpath. Therefore businessmen can fly into Hong Kong in the morning and go straight to AsiaWorld-Expo for an exhibition, conference or function and then fly out of Hong Kong later the same day without having to travel to the centre of Hong Kong.

AsiaWorld-Expo can also be reached by a 25 minute train ride from Hong Kong Station on Hong Kong Island and this train line is fully connected with the MTR underground system to reach many other parts of Hong Kong and Kowloon with further connections for the New Territories. The facility is well connected by bus routes and high speed ferries can reach locations such as Macau within 40 minutes or cities such as Shenzhen, Zhuhai, Guangzhou and the Pearl River Delta within 90 minutes. The centre is also within very easy reach of many hotel facilities as well.

AsiaWorld-Expo is one of the largest and most technologically advanced exhibition and conference centres in the world. It is yet another reason why Hong Kong is very definitely the trade fair capital of Asia. The venue is a global platform for exhibitions and events attracting visitors from all around the world. The centre is already developing an impressive calendar of international exhibitions and events which are expected to generate estimated economic benefits for Hong Kong of HK$4 billion in the first year of operation.

A major event to be staged at AsiaWorld-Expo in September 2007 will be the Asian Aerospace exhibition. For the last 25 years this has been Asia's main international aerospace event which has been rated as one of the top three in the world. This event has in recent years been staged in Singapore and its move to Hong Kong further demonstrates Hong Kong's influence, role and position as a major gateway to China and the Asia Pacific.

The following organisations are very useful contacts regarding trade fairs, conventions and exhibitions:

Hong Kong Trade Development Council
Head Office
38/F, Office Tower, Convention Plaza
1 Harbour Road
Wan Chai
Hong Kong
T: (852) 2584 4333
F: (852) 2824 0249
E: hktdc@tdc.org.hk
W: http://www.tdctrade.com

Hong Kong Convention and Exhibition Centre (HKCEC)
1 Expo Drive
Wan Chai
Hong Kong
T: (852) 2582 8888
F: (852) 2802 7284
E: info@hkcec.com.hk
W: http://www.hkcec.com

Hong Kong Exhibition & Convention Industry Association (HKECIA)
16/F, Wayson Commercial House
70 Lockhart Road
Wan Chai
Hong Kong
T: (852) 2878 1368
F: (852) 2869 6103
E: enquiry@exhibitions.org.hk
W: http://www.exhibitions.org.hk

Hong Kong Exhibition Centre
3-4/F, Low Block
China Resources Building
26 Harbour Road
Wan Chai
Hong Kong
T: (852) 2827 9908
F: (852) 2827 5776
E: hkec@crchkec.com.hk
W: http://www.crchkec.com.hk

AsiaWorld-Expo
Hong Kong International Airport
Lantau
Hong Kong
T: (852) 2838 8808
F: (852) 2561 2822
E: info@asiaworld-expo.com
W: http://www.asiaworld-expo.com

Hong Kong International Trade and Exhibition Centre (HITEC)
1 Trademart Drive
Kowloon Bay
Kowloon
Hong Kong
T: (852) 2620 2838
F: (852) 2620 2307
E: enquiry@hitec.com.hk
W: http://www.hitec.com.hk

Hong Kong Tourism Board
9-11/F, Citicorp Centre
18 Whitfield Road
North Point
Hong Kong
T: (852) 2807 6543
F: (852) 2806 0303
E: info@hktb.com
W: http://www.discoverhongkong.com

Hong Kong Hotels Association
Rm 508-511, Silvercord Tower II
30 Canton Road
Tsim Sha Tsui
Kowloon
Hong Kong
T: (852) 2375 3838
F: (852) 2375 7676
E: info@hkha.org
W: http://www.hkha.org

Hong Kong: The World City and International Business Centre

11. Hong Kong Science and Technology Park

The Hong Kong Science and Technology Park (HKSTP) is a Hong Kong government inaugurated statutory body that was established on 7th May 2001 with the objective of developing the physical and intellectual infrastructure needed to assist in the development of high technology companies. It is the objective of the Hong Kong Science and Technology Park to transform Hong Kong into the leading technology innovation centre in Asia.

The HKSTP offers the latest advanced facilities and support services for high technology companies choosing to locate in Hong Kong. These services include IC design and development support services, a photonics development support centre and access to a vast range of scientific and business minds from across the world. The HKSTP currently incorporates a Science Park located in the New Territories; a Tech Centre located in Kowloon Tong; industrial estates located in Tai Po, Yuen Long and Tseung Kwan O; and a head office located in Tsim Sha Tsui, Kowloon.

The relevant contact details are as follows:

Head Office: Suite 1905-13
Tower 6, The Gateway
9 Canton Road, Tsim Sha Tsui
Kowloon
Hong Kong
T: (852) 2629 1818
F: (852) 2629 1833

Tech Centre Office: 1/F, Tech Centre
72 Tat Chee Avenue
Kowloon Tong
Kowloon
Hong Kong
T: (852) 2788 4433
F: (852) 2788 4261

Science Park Office: Unit 301-2, Innovation Centre
6 Science Park West Avenue
Hong Kong Science Park
Pak Shek Kok
New Territories
Hong Kong
W: http://www.hkstp.org

The HKSTP's vision of its business role is to lead Hong Kong towards becoming Asia's major international centre of innovation and technological development with particular focus on what are regarded as very strong industrial clusters. These clusters include the electronics, biotechnology, precision engineering, information technology and telecommunications industries. The HKSTP also places great emphasis upon the development of Hong Kong as a place for high value, skill intensive manufacturing and service industries.

The HKSTP has developed a mission programme with the objective of providing high quality infrastructure and support services and facilities for all types of innovation and technological development in the aforementioned industrial clusters. It will continually seek to upgrade manufacturing and service capabilities in all industries. It will provide a full service programme for all technology start-ups. It will also attempt to foster partnerships and forms of collaboration between industrial sectors, universities and research institutes through training, consultation and research programmes with the objective that innovative ideas and thinking can be brought together to enhance developments.

The HKSTP has been very active in its worldwide international promotion of itself, its capabilities and its facilities. During the last 3 years it has conducted overseas campaigns in a great many countries including Australia, Malaysia, China, the USA, the UK, Japan, Ireland, Denmark, Finland, etc. It has also sent many delegations overseas and has had numerous contacts with science and technology parks overseas including Sweden's Kista Science City, Denmark's Micro Technology Centre, the USA's Silicon Valley, etc. This type of high level promotion has on many occasions been jointly conducted with Invest Hong Kong and the Hong Kong Cyberport.

Seminars, conventions, company visits and media interviews are the normal scope of events for these delegations visiting overseas countries with the objective of promoting Hong Kong's capabilities and facilities, attracting overseas companies to visit Hong Kong and use the facilities as well as invest in establishing themselves in Hong Kong and generally raising the technological profile of Hong

Kong. This type of activity has attracted considerable attention from companies around the world and has helped to enhance Hong Kong's position as the Asian hub for innovative and advanced technological capability.

The HKSTP has a total of sixteen buildings with a total floor space of 169,700 square metres, plus a nine storey car park building and five hectares of landscape space. The total area of Hong Kong Science Park is 22 hectares and the land and premises in the three industrial estates totals 239 hectares. The construction of the Science Park is being conducted in phases. The grand opening of phase 1 was carried out on 27th June 2002. Construction of the Science Park is government funded under the Public Works Programme.

The HKSTP welcomes enquiries from companies regarding technological development and innovation particularly in the chosen sectors of electronics, biotechnology, information technology, telecommunications and precision engineering. Hong Kong regards itself as being particularly strong in these sectors and therefore able to offer companies a strong support service for their desired technological development and innovation.

The Science and Technology Park in Hong Kong has been designed as a technology cluster of world class standard with the objective of encouraging suppliers, customers, service providers and business partners to form a high technology collaboration.

HKSTP has signed a memorandum with China's Ministry of Science and Technology whereby the seven IC design bases of the Mainland will cooperate with HKSTP in IC design and development thereby helping Hong Kong raise its profile as a high-tech product design and innovation centre. The cooperation will involve the exchange of information, sharing of various design and development resources and the joint participation in project developments.

Under the 2004 Digital 21 Strategy, the government is geared towards making Hong Kong a leading digital city with emphasis being on the benefit for the whole community. Consideration is now being given to the possibility of merging the Information Technology Services Department with the Communications and Technology Branch of the Commerce, Industry and Technology Bureau (CITB).

Hong Kong's Cyberport has recently added a highly innovative Digital Media Centre to its facility providing state of the art equipment for digital media content developers and multimedia professionals. The Digital Media Centre will be of great benefit to smaller companies in the production of computer generated images.

Another new facility at Hong Kong's Cyberport is the Wireless Development Centre which offers connectivity to wireless networks including GSM, GPRS, 802.11, EDGE and 3G. The facility is a multi operator and multi vendor platform and is generally impartial to all commercial considerations. Developers will be able to reduce their costs and development times by building and testing their applications across different operators and devices.

Hong Kong Science and Technology Park

12. Telecommunications

Hong Kong is the telecommunications hub of Asia. It has one of the most technically advanced telecommunications infrastructures in the world.

Hong Kong's telecommunications sector per capita revenues are amongst the highest in the world. The sector in 1996 was estimated to have generated US$4 billion in revenue excluding Internet services. Hong Kong has four fixed network services operators, four cellular network operators, and 50 paging network services. The Hong Kong telecommunications system is one of the best in the world due to the heavy investments it has received over many years. Cable and Wireless developed an extensive network of submarine cables centred on Hong Kong thereby giving the territory a distinct advantage as a regional communications hub.

Due to the strong trans-national orientation of firms in the territory there has been substantial demand for international services with the result that Hong Kong is noted for its high quality and low cost of international communications. Singapore and Sydney are seen as competitors offering a similar range and quality of services, but Hong Kong can handle a higher volume due to its investment in all digital technology. Deregulation in the industry has intensified competition and led to lower prices thereby enhancing the competitive position of the territory with demand forecast to grow substantially in the short and long terms.

Up until 1995, Cable & Wireless Hong Kong Telecom had a local telephone monopoly as well as an exclusive licence for external telecommunication. However, since 1995 onwards the local telephone market has been open to competition and more players are now active in the market with the result that competition has led to lower prices. Since early 2000, the external telecommunications market has been open to competition with the result that by June 2002 there were 213 external telecommunications service operators. By June 2002 the office of the Telecommunications Authority had also issued 8 satellite based and 16 cable based External Fixed Telecommunications Network Service licences.

As at April 2002 there were approximately 2.65 million Internet users in Hong Kong which represented a market penetration rate of 39% with 256 Internet Service Providers (ISPs). More than 98% of households and over 95% of business buildings are equipped for broadband Internet connections. Hong Kong was also the first city in the world to introduce to its population broadband-based interactive television, which is regarded as a key requirement for video-on-demand functions.

Hong Kong has over 400,000 km of fibre-optic cable so that the telephone network completely covers 100% of Hong Kong even though the geography of Hong Kong has hilly terrain. A major advantage for Hong Kong is that it is geographically compact and its many high rise buildings are easy to wire up.

The Hong Kong government has been active in promoting the telecommunications industry even though it is fully privatised. As a world class city offering many business advantages for both local and international multinational companies, a world class telecommunications infrastructure is vital. Also as a leading finance, trading and transportation centre with very active markets, the telecommunications facilities are a vital part for many companies. The Hong Kong government has enacted the Electronic Transactions Ordinance and the Telecommunications Ordinance, which have created the legal framework for electronic transactions as well as the necessary provisions for its safe implementation. The government's Digital 21 IT strategy enhances and promotes Hong Kong's information infrastructure and services. The Electronic Service Delivery Scheme is another aspect of the government's promotion of telecommunications services.

Business opportunities in the telecommunications sector are abundant. China's accession to the WTO will see China's vast telecommunications market open up slowly, but steadily, with the result that there will be a surge in joint venture operations and business partnerships between Chinese, Hong Kong and foreign companies. More licences for ISPs are readily available. The government is actively helping to create a suitable environment for further developments in the telecommunications industry with its Science Park, Cyberport, Innovation and Technology Support Funds and on-line government, and hence helping to create more investment and business opportunities for local and multinational firms.

As a telecommunications hub, Hong Kong can expect to experience a growth in the amount of telecommunication traffic between China and the rest of the world via Hong Kong. The city may very well become the e-commerce hub of mainland China, due to the growth in e-commerce. China is set to become one of the most important Internet markets in the World with a quoted 33 million users by 2004 according to International Data Corp. (IDC).

Hong Kong telecom operators can expect to see themselves as the partners of global telecom giants with regard to mainland investments due to their knowledge and expertise in dealing with China.

The role of telecommunications is vital to Hong Kong's competitiveness in electronic commerce. Hong Kong's position as a leading business centre in the Asia Pacific region is due to its advanced telecommunications infrastructure that has enabled a vast amount of domestic and international communication and interchange by both voice and data transmission. Hong Kong is the regional leader in terms of international call time, penetration of telephone lines, mobile telephone usage and facsimile machine usage. Mobile telephone, paging, telepoint and value added network services are provided at very competitive prices by a number of operators in the market.

As the first major city in the world to fully digitise its fixed telephone line network system this helped to create the environment for its leading position regarding international call time as well as support its position as the leading regional business centre and World City. In Hong Kong, telephone numbers are classified as fully portable. In other words when the telephone user changes location by moving office or residence, the telephone number can be transferred to the new location thereby avoiding having to notify contacts, business associates and friends of a new telephone number due to having moved. Multinationals very often choose Hong Kong as their telecommunications hub for services covering the region because of the quality of the services provided by the city as well as its advanced technological status.

Hong Kong's telecommunications is also a strong factor in the decisions of many multinationals to locate in Hong Kong because of the advantages that it offers. Hong Kong's telecommunications industry is privately owned without restriction on foreign investment and is therefore a very liberal market. Also many Hong Kong operators have gained a position in mobile telephone markets overseas as telecommunications markets have opened up. A good example of this would be Hutchison Whampoa's involvement in the Orange mobile telephone network in the UK.

Hong Kong has become the centre for re-routing of international telephone calls. Surveys have revealed that Hong Kong has the lowest average cost for international telephone calls and that the leasing of a fibre circuit international data line is cheaper in Hong Kong than anywhere else in the Asia Pacific. The largest teleport in Asia is Hong Kong. Multinational companies, television channels and international press agencies can downlink as well as uplink their satellite signals from all over the Asia Pacific region using Hong Kong's dedicated relay services. Hong Kong also has at least 8 submarine cable system connections.

The Hong Kong telecommunications services market is open to competition so that any company can set up business provided it meets the necessary requirements. Therefore Hong Kong is ahead of most countries in the region regarding liberalisation of the market. Operators offer many services including electronic mail box, store-and-forward facsimile as well as electronic data interchange. Many multinational companies have now set up their own internal communication systems for ease of business communication within their company structures in order to avoid having to use external communication systems. This has involved obtaining international leased circuits from various telecommunications operators. This type of activity has grown quickly in Hong Kong in recent years. Such multinationals are mainly from the USA, Europe and Japan.

Five companies currently operate local telephone services - Hutchison Global Communications Limited, New World Telecommunications Limited, PCCW HKT Limited, Hong Kong Broadband Network Limited and Wharf T & T Hong Kong Limited.

It takes less than one week to install a telephone line. In 2004, the basic business telephone line charge (flat rate) was HK$128.80 per month whilst a residential telephone line cost HK$110.00 per month and the installation fee was HK$475.00. Local telephone calls in Hong Kong are free. Therefore the user can make any number of local telephone calls and only pay the monthly rental charge. Also due to the level of competition within the industry, international calls are much cheaper than in other cities around the world. Liberalisation of the IDD service market in recent years has resulted in call charges becoming even cheaper. Hong Kong's IDD service is one of the most economical in the world.

Hong Kong has one of the highest telephone densities in the world with there being 59 telephone exchange lines per 100 population in 2000. The number of telephone exchange lines rose 61.2% from 2.42 million in 1990 to 3.90 million in 2000. In April 1999, Hong Kong had 3.26 million mobile telephone subscribers representing a penetration rate of 48%, which was the highest in Asia. The mobile telephone market has six operators and in 2000 there were 79 mobile telephone service subscribers per 100 population. However, in 2005 there were approximately 85 mobile telephone service subscribers per 100 inhabitants in Hong Kong, which is one of the highest penetration rates in the world. This shows just how popular the product has become in what has so far been a relatively short product lifecycle.

It would appear that the mobile telephone market is saturated in Hong Kong and therefore for further development manufacturers will have to concentrate on product diversification and invention upgrading. By October 2001 there were four companies with licences for third generation (3G) mobile telephone services and by June 2002 there were six companies offering Mobile Virtual Network Operator services. The Hong Kong telecommunications market is extremely active and very competitive.

With regard to standard telephone usage, in 2000 there were 4.9 billion minutes external telephone usage which was more than three times the volume of 1990.

Facsimile usage also grew by 300% during the period of 1990 to 2000 with there being a recorded 400,000 facsimile lines at the end of 2000. In 2000, there were 230,000 Internet customer accounts with dial-up access, and Internet traffic volume was 15 billion minutes.

Also in 2000 there were over 390,000 customer accounts for broadband Internet. Since 2000 these figures have obviously risen, but it goes to show how important and well used is Hong Kong's communications infrastructure. It is this communications infrastructure that is one of the fundamental assets of Hong Kong as an international business centre that makes it ideal for regional corporate headquarters and/or regional offices of multinationals.

Telecommunications

13. Miscellaneous Points - Social Aspects

Up until the early 1960s Hong Kong had always been viewed as a transitory point with very few people making the place their home. Now there is a growing number of private property owner occupiers that have made Hong Kong their home. They were born in Hong Kong, grew up in Hong Kong and intend to remain in Hong Kong. They are Hong Kong's work force. The proportion of owner occupier households in Hong Kong increased significantly from 42.6% in 1990 to 51.1% in 2000. In the mid 1990s many potential first time buyers dreaded the property market because of its spiralling property prices. They generally thought that it would take many years for them to be able to raise the necessary deposit to purchase a home.

At that point in time the required deposit was 30%, which on a property costing 2 million dollars would amount to HK$600,000 which seemed exorbitant and out of reach for many first time buyers. However, the property market crash and slump of 1997-98 has more than halved property prices making it much more affordable for the vast majority of the population, but unfortunately leaving some property owners with negative equity. Anybody of any nationality can buy property in Hong Kong at market prices, but only Hong Kong permanent residents can buy property under the government home ownership housing schemes designed to sell property at slightly reduced prices, but with the condition that the property cannot be sold for a stated period of time thereby eliminating profiteering. Nevertheless there are an increasing number of people living in private permanent housing as owner occupiers thereby confirming the growing permanency of the population.

a)   Identity Cards

Identity cards (ID cards) were introduced into Hong Kong in 1949 due to the sudden growth in the population as a result of the surge in migrants leaving China after the communists took power following the civil war in China. The original ID cards were made of stiff paper with the reverse side having a photograph and thumbprint. The first laminated ID cards appeared in 1960 followed by juvenile ID cards, which were smaller and only showed the holder's surname as well as place and date of birth.

A revision of the laminated ID card took place in 1973 with changes including textual modification, removal of the thumbprint and addition of the place of birth. At this time adult and juvenile ID cards were of the same format. The first secure computerised ID card was introduced in 1983 and this ID card was made up of an advanced security paper with anti forgery watermark and was encased in a clear plastic cover. A revised computerised ID card was issued in 1987 in two formats. One format stated that it was a Hong Kong Permanent ID card and the holder had the right of abode in Hong Kong. The other format stated that it was a Hong Kong ID card, but did not entitle the holder to the right of abode.

The identity card has now been a part of Hong Kong society for over 50 years and the vast majority of the population have grown up and been fully accustomed to having and carrying an ID card. Therefore the majority of the population now regard the ID card as a part of their identity.

Since June 2003 Hong Kong has been in the process of introducing a new Smart ID card. This Smart ID card incorporates a microchip that will hold an increased amount of data regarding the holder of the ID card. It will also incorporate functions that were not available with previous ID cards. The Smart ID card will have immigration applications and the holder will have the option of including non-immigration applications. With regard to immigration applications the Smart ID card will be a proof of identity in a very secure form. The microchip will hold basic personal data together with templates of two thumbprints and will enable very quick immigration clearance through control points. If the ID card holder is not a permanent resident the microchip will also be able to hold information regarding conditions or even restrictions of residence in Hong Kong.

With regard to optional non-immigration applications the Smart ID card can be used for e-Cert, as a library card and also for driving licence related functions. E-Cert is issued by Hongkong Post and enables cardholders to conduct electronic transactions, like ESD applications, very securely over the Internet. The Hongkong Post e-Cert is in effect an online identity card that enables authentication of the user. It provides integrity, confidentiality as well as non-repudiation of transmitted data during an electronic transaction. E-Cert means that the Hongkong Post Certification Authority verifies the e-Cert applicant's identity. E-Cert enables cardholders to prove their identity including digital signature as well as send encrypted messages.

The validity period of the e-Cert on Smart ID cards is three years with the first year being free and subsequent years incurring an annual charge. Incorporation of e-Cert into the Smart ID card microchip offers many benefits to the cardholder. Hongkong Post e-Cert can be used for both public and commercial purposes including e-mail communication, electronic government services, online entertainment, trading stocks and shares, online shopping, making payments and also for electronic banking services. It is expected that the use of e-Cert with the Smart ID card will encourage further industry initiatives leading to the development of new business applications and services. This will further stimulate the development of e-commerce and e-government in Hong Kong leading to further growth in the Hong Kong economy.

Another optional non-immigration application that can be incorporated into the Smart ID card microchip is the ability to use the Smart ID card as a library card. After a simple registration process at any public library, the Smart ID cardholder will be able to take advantage of the various services that the public libraries provide.

Under Hong Kong law anybody driving a vehicle in Hong Kong must carry their driving licence whilst driving. It is projected that from 2006, the Smart ID card will be able to hold driving licence details and therefore Smart ID card holders with this application will not need to also carry their driving licence when driving in Hong Kong.

b)   Electronic Services

Hong Kong is developing into an information society with advanced technology leading to the greater dissemination of information throughout society. The percentage of households with a personal computer connected to the Internet rose from 36.4% in 2000 to 48.7% in 2001. Of these households, the percentage with broadband connection rose from 5.7% in 2000 to 39.4% in 2001. The number of computer users within the general population has increased in recent years with further increases expected as computers and associated technology become more engrained in the society.

Over the past few years the Hong Kong government has been actively pursuing the task of developing an e-government infrastructure. The objective of this is to provide business and the general public with easily accessible and user friendly government services by electronic means. Many government bureaux and departments have been incorporated into the government's electronic plans so as to deliver fast and accurate services. The focus of the government 2004 Digital 21 Strategy is to improve service quality and effectiveness thereby creating value for customers and government.

The government seeks to increase utilisation of e-government services by making the customer the centre of attention and reducing departmental boundaries. Attention will be paid to customer relationship management and price, so the customers will be more willing to use the service. Customer segmentation will be applied to help rationalise channel services and improve cost effectiveness.

Miscellaneous Points - Social Aspects

A number of initiatives have already been put into effect with more expected in due course. These include:

- ☐ The Electronic Service Delivery (ESD) Scheme that enables the government and the private sector to provide integrated online public and private services.

- ☐ The Smart Identity Card in conjunction with other applications facilitates the development of an information infrastructure that enables the government and private sector to introduce other innovative and valuable e-applications.

- ☐ The Electronic Tendering System (ETS) enables suppliers worldwide to conduct business with the Hong Kong government. In 2003 the Government Logistics Department recorded a total of 3,000 suppliers from over 30 countries as registered to use the ETS system.

- ☐ The Government Electronic Trading Service (GETS) Scheme enables traders to electronically submit trade related documents to the government thereby speeding up the operational process and efficiency. This system is also experiencing expansion by commercial service providers offering other services to the trading community which is creating further opportunities for business development.

- ☐ The HKedCity is a community wide educational platform that developed from a particular e-government initiative. It has over 1.4 million registered users.

- ☐ The 1823 Citizens Easy Link is an easy use telephone number system for handling enquiries and complaints covering an extensive range of services. In 2003 it recorded over 1.1 million calls to this service. The service is currently being expanded to incorporate more government departments and areas of work.

- ☐ The Interoperability Framework facilitates the flow of information from individual government agencies and enhances the effective communication between government and the private sector.

In order to ensure reliable and secure e-government applications, comprehensive information security policies have been implemented. The Electronic Transactions

Ordinance together with its amendments has created a legal environment facilitating the secure and extensive use of e-government facilities and transactions.

The Hong Kong government is committed to further developing its e-government facilities regarding it as required technological development that will greatly enhance business and social interactions. Customer relations management is seen as a key area for e-government development in order that the general public becomes familiar with and accepts the facilities that are being developed. The government is continually trying to identify new areas where utilisation of its e-government facilities can be enhanced and new facilities developed. The government seeks to be more accessible to its public and more focused on efficiency and cost effectiveness in performing its duties. Further developments in e-government activities are to be expected soon.

On 9th December 2000, the Electronic Service Delivery (ESD) scheme was launched by the Hong Kong government with the objective of providing the community with public services via the Internet and other electronic means. With this scheme the government was providing over 60 types of public service on-line. Recent surveys have indicated that E-mail was the most commonly used Internet function with 93.6% of companies surveyed and having Internet connection in 2001 using E-mail. On-line sourcing of information was the second most commonly used Internet function with 87.5% of the companies surveyed and having Internet connection in 2001 using on-line sourcing of information as a business requirement.

The Electronic Service Delivery Scheme (ESD) is operated as a joint venture between the government and the private sector. The private sector operator develops, finances, operates and maintains the ESD system whilst the government pays the operator transactions fees once a pre-agreed volume of transactions has been reached. As part of the agreement between the government and the private sector operator, the private sector operator can use the ESD information infrastructure for advertisements and e-commerce services thereby generating additional income.

This business structure encourages the private sector operator to continually promote the greater use of ESD services amongst business and the public as well as introduce new services thereby broadening the facility. It also minimises the government's business risk. This innovative facility is very customer focused and enables users to draw together a diverse range of facilities and services that may be required for a particular function. As such value is added and speed is enhanced, and information is generated. Nevertheless it is planned that during the middle of 2006, the government will commence a new electronic one-stop access portal (OSP) facility with the objective that it becomes the main means of

Miscellaneous Points - Social Aspects

accessing online information and services from the government. The new OSP facility will eventually absorb the current Government Information Centre and lead to the repositioning of e-government services currently being supplied under the Electronic Service Delivery Scheme.

Other government bureaux and departments are also working in partnership with private sector companies to develop e-government services. The Government Electronic Trading Service (GETS) is a government/private sector venture for the electronic submission and processing of trade related documents. The Government Logistics Department is working with the private sector in the Electronic Tendering System with management and operations being by the private sector. The HKedCity is an e-government service that is a partnership between the government funded Hong Kong Education City Ltd. and the private sector, social service agencies, education groups and Internet portals with the objective of providing educational hardware and software, information, resources and activities to teachers and students. It can be seen that the development of e-government services is totally dependent upon the government's relationship with private sector companies.

This is totally akin to much of the economic development in Hong Kong whereby the government is very much a background figure providing a level playing field and fair regulations with the investment and development work being done by private sector companies. This has been the case in the development of Hong Kong's seaport facilities, its airport and airport facilities, its railway and public transport network, etc.

The Hong Kong government in its attempts to increase the use of its e-government services has devised a common look and feel website design initiative that has been widely accepted and is viewed as a means of improving accessibility and aiding website navigation procedures for users. One of the objectives of this initiative is to improve the search function and strengthen the role of the Government News Bulletin. A further development in this sector is the increased use of m-government services via mobile telephones due to Hong Kong having one of the highest penetration rates in the world for mobile telephones. There is also a move towards making greater use of wireless technology in service delivery.

Authentication is an area that demands careful consideration due to the requirements for security and privacy as well as user friendliness. The Electronic Transactions Ordinance of January 2000 provides a legislative framework under which certification authorities can be recognised. This is geared towards presenting a highly secure facility that supports transactions requiring authentication, confidentiality, integrity and non-repudiation. The Smart ID card uses this technology by offering the capability to store a digital certificate for secure e-transactions. The e-Cert capability that can be included on the Smart ID card is helping to build up a mass of digital certificate users that will in time give rise to the creation of more new, secure and innovative e-services.

The Inland Revenue Department has introduced a taxpayer identification number (TIN) for tax filing purposes as well as interactive tax enquiry services and this also uses a secure authentication mode. On 31st January 2000 the Hong Kong Post Certification Authority established the Public Key Infrastructure with the objective of providing Hong Kong with electronic authentication services so as to facilitate the further development of e-commerce in Hong Kong.

There is without doubt a growing demand for e-government services in Hong Kong. In 2004 the average number of page views each month on all government websites was 155 million, representing an 80% increase compared with 2002. Over 90% of government services that can support an electronic means of delivery are provided with an e-option enabling the user to decide whether or not to opt for the e-option of the particular service. All government bills now have an e-payment option to facilitate speed of payment.

Over 1,500 government forms of various types can be downloaded online and 400 e-forms can be completed and submitted online. Much government information can now be accessed online. Also as part of the government's drive towards increasing the level of electronic service and activities within government, over 80% of procurement tenders are now being conducted via electronic means and this automatically means that suppliers must be able to reciprocate by the same electronic means.

Statistics show that Hong Kong had 259 licensed Internet Service Providers (ISPs) at the end of 2001 with 2 million dial-up access registered customer accounts and 7000 leased line access accounts. Internet related services in 2000 generated a total of HK$3.3 billion for Internet Service Providers (ISPs) according to the annual survey regarding Storage, Communication, Financing, Insurance and Business Services. Basic connection charges in 2000 accounted for 45.8% of total Internet related services receipts, with it being the main line of business receipts for ISPs.

The government's enthusiasm for IT is demonstrated by the fact that since the early 1990s government spending on IT has increased very significantly. In 2001/02 government spending on IT was HK$2.5 billion, which represented a 307% increase on the HK$0.6 billion spent in 1992/93. There has also been a marked increase in the use of technology with only 77 workers per 1000 having access and using a workstation in 1992 whereas in 2001 this figure had risen to 586 per 1000 workers.

With regard to the IT & T sector the territory is experiencing continued expansion. In 1998 there were 5,800 organisations and 66,500 people employed in the sector. However, by 2000 there were 8,100 organisations representing a 41.6% increase and 78,800 employees representing an 18.5% increase. The rapid growth in the telecommunications industry in the 1990s successfully strengthened Hong Kong's status as a regional telecommunications and Internet hub. The telecommunications infrastructure has greatly contributed to the success of the Hong Kong economy and this sector comprises companies providing a wide range of telecommunication services including fixed telephone and telegraph, radio paging, mobile telephones, etc.

At the end of 2001 there were 5.7 million mobile telephone subscribers in Hong Kong with the year having experienced an 8.9% increase in the number of subscribers. For every 100 members of the population there were on average 84.4 mobile telephone service subscribers thereby confirming Hong Kong as having one of the highest levels of mobile telephone service market penetration in the world. It should be remembered that Hong Kong had a population of 7.3 million in July 2002 and therefore a subscription total of 5.7 million at the end of 2001 indicates a very high penetration rate for this product line.

Hong Kong is a major import/export centre for computer hardware and software between overseas firms and China as well as other Asian countries. During the 1990s there was remarkable growth in the value of trading activities in computer products. Imports of computer hardware in 1992 were HK$27.2 billion whereas in 2001 imports were HK$128.9 billion representing a 374% increase. Exports of computer hardware in 1992 were HK$34.3 billion whereas in 2001 exports were HK$114.6 billion representing a 234% increase. Imports of computer software in 1992 were HK$1.1 billion whereas imports in 2001 were HK$2.2 billion representing a 100% increase. Exports of computer software in 1992 were HK$0.6 billion whereas exports in 2001 were HK$3.0 billion representing a 371% increase.

Computer hardware imports were from China, the USA, Singapore, Malaysia and Taiwan whereas hardware exports were primarily to China and the USA which together represented 57% of computer hardware exports. Computer software imports were from Singapore, the USA, China, Taiwan and Canada whereas software exports were primarily to China and the USA which together represented 61% of computer software exports. It can therefore be seen that computer hardware and software import and export is a thriving business for Hong Kong which is totally in line with the Hong Kong government's idea of making Hong Kong an information society. This business sector can be expected to further expand and develop in the coming years.

Trading in telecommunications equipment also displayed remarkable growth during the 1990s. Imports of telecommunications equipment in 1992 were HK$14.5 billion whereas imports in 2001 were HK$67.7 billion representing an increase of 368%. Exports of telecommunications equipment in 1992 were HK$12.6 billion whereas exports in 2001 were HK$41.4 billion representing an increase of 228%. Imports of telecommunications equipment were from China, Republic of Korea, Singapore, the USA and the UK. Exports of telecommunications equipment were primarily to China and the USA, which together represented 52% of exports. Again it can be seen that this business sector is also expanding quickly and further expansion is expected in the coming years.

The Hong Kong government has increased its emphasis on incorporating information technology teaching into the education curriculum so as to raise the level of understanding and usage of information technology in the general public in the coming years. It is the government's keen objective that information technology will play a greater part in the economy of Hong Kong and in the lives of its citizens. Under the 'Digital 21' Information Technology Strategy launched by the government, a key initiative of the strategy is the Electronic Service Delivery Scheme with the objective of providing over 100 types of public service to the community via the Internet and other electronic means. The number of services provided is in the process of being built up and currently includes services such as filing tax returns, paying government bills, applications for business registration certificates by sole proprietors, registration of job vacancies, searching for job applicants, etc.

A recent survey in 2001 regarding the use of electronic business services amongst the general public found that the ATM (Automatic Teller Machine) was very popular for withdrawing, depositing, transferring money and checking account balances. It is very common to find people queuing to use an ATM in busy places. The use of e-cash/EPS (Easy Pay System) is generally regarded as a very convenient way of paying bills. Also using the telephone to settle payments by PPS (Payment by Phone Service) is another popular way of settling bills. However, probably one of the most commonly used electronic business services is the Octopus card. This is a special type of card that incorporates a microchip against which a stored dollar value can be made. The Octopus card is used as a very convenient means of immediate payment primarily on transport such as buses, trams, trains, ferries, etc. In 2000, there was a total of 10.8 million daily passenger journeys on the Hong Kong public transport system with all modes of transport being used. As such this demonstrates the enormous potential use of the Octopus card thereby making the idea feasible and profitable. Most people in Hong Kong over 15 years of age use an Octopus card every day. The card

Miscellaneous Points - Social Aspects

can be purchased from any MTR underground station or KCR station by paying a deposit which in 2004 was HK$50 and specifying the required amount of value for the card to hold which may be HK$50, HK$100, HK$200, etc. Further value can be purchased from MTR and KCR stations as well as at many stores such as 7/11 or Circle K.

When boarding a means of transport the card carrier merely holds the card next to an electronic reader, which automatically deducts the amount of the fare. It is not even necessary to take the card out of one's wallet, but merely hold the wallet next to the electronic reader and it will beep to indicate that it has deducted the appropriate fare and recorded the fact that a passenger has boarded. The Octopus card can also be used in some restaurants and fast food outlets when ordering and paying for a meal. As such the Octopus card is a step forward towards a cashless society. It is highly recommended that visitors to Hong Kong, that are going to live in Hong Kong or possibly stay for a period of time, should make full use of the Octopus Card. It greatly relieves the user of the necessity of carrying many coins when using public transport. Its convenience also lends it an element of fun.

c) Public Utilities

Hong Kong's distribution of gas, electricity and water is as good as any other developed economy in the world.

Hong Kong has two electricity companies, Hong Kong Electric Company Ltd. and China Light and Power Company Ltd. which both provide a world class standard of electricity supply. These companies also provide a technical advisory service on a range of matters including power quality, application and connection of new supplies, etc.

Hong Kong Electric Company Limited supplies electricity to Hong Kong Island and Lamma Island. China Light and Power Company Limited supplies electricity to Kowloon, the New Territories and outlying islands except Lamma Island.

In Hong Kong, fuel gas is extremely popular for domestic, industrial and commercial purposes with town gas and industrial gases being the most common types. Town gas is the most common source of gas supply for residential usage.

Water is billed on a four months in arrears basis. Water charges also include sewage service charges.

d) Medical Services

Hong Kong's medical and health facilities have improved considerably over the past two decades. At the end of 2000, the territory was recorded as having 35,100 beds in 44 hospitals and institutions. These hospitals and institutions were under the control of the Hospital Authority and included 23 hospitals in correctional institutions, 21 nursing homes, 5 government clinics and maternity homes, and 12 private hospitals. The number of doctors and nurses in the territory has increased significantly and the number of out-patient facilities has also increased.

Apart from old age, cancer, heart disease and pneumonia remain the dominant causes of death in Hong Kong. Nevertheless these ailments all showed decreases during the decade from 1989 to 1999. This trend is probably due to the improved socioeconomic situation in Hong Kong, the availability of higher quality medical services as well as a greater awareness and concern for health issues.

Hong Kong has good medical facilities with highly qualified doctors and staff. Clinics are available and require a minimum payment of approximately HK$20.00 in order to see a doctor and obtain medication. However, private doctors will charge more and also provide the medicine. There is no need to take a prescription to a pharmacist.

e) Social Security

Hong Kong does have a social security system and social security payments are made to individuals, but only in dire need. The social security system in Hong Kong is not comparable to the social security systems in western countries. Due to the independent nature of Hong Kong, social security has generally been regarded as a drain on society. However, since the end of the 1990s and the economic changes Hong Kong has experienced, people have become more socially conscious and concerned regarding general public welfare. The previous philosophy of 'if you don't work, you don't eat' has now been discarded as economic circumstances have changed. In the financial year 2000-2001, HK$18.7 billion was paid out under the Comprehensive Social Security Assistance (CSSA) Scheme and the Social Security Allowance (SSA) Scheme. The main recipients were the elderly. Other schemes include the Criminal and Law Enforcement Injuries Compensation Scheme, the Traffic Accident Victims Assistance Scheme and Emergency Relief.

f) Postal Services

The postal service in Hong Kong is very efficient, fast and reliable with letters being delivered to addresses or air carriers the next working day. The service is very inexpensive by world standards with a local letter to a Hong Kong destination in 2004 costing HK$1.40 for the first 30 grams, an airmail letter costing HK$2.40 for the first 20 grams and an aerogramme costing HK$2.30.

The post office has an Inland Parcel Post service for packages up to 20 kg, an Air Parcel Post service with the destination determining the maximum acceptable weight and a Speedpost service for small items. A number of international courier services are available in Hong Kong. Companies such as DHL, Federal Express and UPS provide a very quick and efficient delivery service at very competitive prices.

g) Labour Conditions

Wage levels are determined by supply and demand, with no minimum wage level. Wages are calculated on the basis of hourly, daily, monthly or piece rates. Working times vary from 5 days to 5 1/2 or 6 days per week.

Fringe benefits that employers may provide may include Lunar New Year bonus (1 month's salary), medical allowances, good attendance bonus, subsidised meals, annual leave (paid), subsidised transport to and from work, and free or subsidised accommodation. The Hong Kong Employment Ordinance also provides for statutory holidays, sick and maternity leave, severance payments, and long term service payments.

The Labour Department provides a conciliation service to settle employment disputes. In 2002 there were no disputes.

There are two types of holidays in Hong Kong:

1) General holidays for banks, schools, public offices and government departments.
2) Statutory holidays under the Employment Ordinance for employees plus banks and schools. In 2004 there were 12 statutory holidays.

h) Visa Requirements

People may visit Hong Kong in most cases as a tourist without visa, but in some cases a visa is required. Generally a passport is sufficient for entry into Hong Kong although in certain cases there may also be a requirement to provide evidence of onward/return transportation by sea or air. The length of stay under a visitor visa will vary depending upon the country of origin of the visitor. However, extension of stay may be obtained upon correct application and provision of a reason for the required extended stay. Visitors will require at least four months validity on their passports. A visa is also required for work or study in Hong Kong.

When applying for a Hong Kong employment visa, the applicant is required to submit the following information:

a) the name, address and telephone number of the employer for which the applicant is proposing to work. It must also be clarified whether or not the employer is the applicant's sponsor;

b) a photocopy of the letter of appointment or service contract clearly stating the employment post, salary and benefits that will be received;

c) a full description of the job which the applicant will perform;

d) photocopy proof of the academic qualifications and relevant working experience of the applicant with regard to the post; and

e) a letter, if possible, from the applicant's employer clarifying why the post cannot be filled locally.

People seeking to work or invest in Hong Kong must obtain a visa prior to entering Hong Kong unless they already have the right of abode or right to land. The employment law in Hong Kong requires that foreign nationals seeking employment must be in a position to properly contribute to the economy by providing knowledge, experience or special skills of value to the economy that are not readily available in the territory. Applications for visas should be submitted to the HKSAR or Chinese Diplomatic and Consular Mission. Foreign residents in China should submit their applications to the Beijing office of the government of the HKSAR.

When planning to invest in Hong Kong, the visa applicant must provide additional information such as:

- [ ] details of the proposed business including size, nature and financial undertakings,

- [ ] details of all partners of the business including names, addresses and telephone numbers

- [ ] details of the number of employees both local and expatriate.

The HKSAR Immigration Department issues visas.

Spouses and children may accompany applicants if they can be supported with regard to finance, accommodation, etc.

Hong Kong is also operating an admission scheme for talents and professionals from China with the objective of attracting such talents and professionals with specific knowledge and skills from China, where there is a need or shortage in Hong Kong. It is envisaged that such needed talents and professionals will increase Hong Kong's competitiveness and economic development. The admission scheme covers all sectors of the economy and is quota free, but will be regulated according to the needs of the economy.

i) Typhoons

During the summer season from June to September, Hong Kong is hit on average by two or three typhoons and typhoon signals are raised. A typhoon signal number 8 or above means that offices and businesses close and will not reopen until the signal has been lowered. If it is lowered before midday then businesses will reopen, otherwise they will remain closed for the rest of the day and open the following day when the signal should have been lowered.

Hong Kong currently has six typhoon signals, 1, 2, 3, 8, 9 and 10, all of which indicate the direction of the wind. Typhoon signals 1, 2 and 3 are preliminary signals as the typhoon is drawing near, whereas typhoon signals 8, 9 and 10 are when the typhoon is overhead and hitting Hong Kong with force. Signals 4, 5, 6 and 7 are no longer used due to being regarded as unnecessary.

j) Dual Nationality

China does not recognise dual nationality. However, there are many people living and residing in Hong Kong claiming dual nationality and legally possessing valid passports from more than one country. Hong Kong recognises dual nationality.

k) Crime

In 2000 the crime rate was 1,159 per 100,000 population, which was the third lowest recorded level over the previous 10 years. Theft and burglary are the two most common types of crime and the age group with the highest number of arrests is young persons aged between 16 and 20. The Hong Kong Special Administrative Region has an extremely low crime rate due to the excellent efficiency of the Hong Kong police force. Hong Kong is recognised as being one of the safest, if not the safest, place in Asia where the public is at liberty to go anywhere at any time without fear of crime.

l) Traffic Conditions

In Hong Kong the safety of public transportation is good, urban road conditions and maintenance as well as rural road conditions and maintenance is good. Traffic drives on the left-hand side of the road and there is often congestion in Hong Kong's urban areas during the daytime when people are travelling to and from work. The speed limit is 50 kilometres per hour in urban areas and 80 kilometres per hour on highways or else as indicated by road signs.

It is mandatory for drivers and all passengers to wear a seat belt and it is illegal to use a hand held mobile telephone whilst driving. Use of a mobile telephone whilst driving will incur a HK$2,000.00 fine. Nevertheless it is still legal to use hands free devices such as speakerphones and headphones. All vehicles must have third party liability insurance in accordance with the law.

According to 2002 information, dangerous driving that results in the death of another person carries a fine of HK$50,000.00, imprisonment for 5 years and disqualification for a minimum of 2 years. Drivers involved in a traffic accident may well be asked to undergo a simple test to detect the possible influence of alcohol. Drivers found to be exceeding the permitted level of blood alcohol will be prosecuted.

| Miscellaneous Points - Social Aspects |

At least 90 percent of the Hong Kong population use public transport, because the Hong Kong public transport network is probably one of the best in the world. There are taxis, buses, mini buses and the mass transit railway (MTR) which is the underground system. Waiting time for a bus is rarely more than 5 minutes because of the high frequency.

Due to Hong Kong being the most densely populated city in the world, the public transport system has a huge market demand and so the frequency of the transport system is very high and it is a profitable industry. Public transport is safe and very inexpensive. The MTR is a very popular means of transport and in 2002 was carrying an average of 2 million passengers each week.

m) Traffic signals

Recently nearly all traffic lights in Hong Kong at street crossing points have been equipped with an audio signal mechanism primarily to assist the blind and visually impaired people to cross the road. When the traffic lights are green for the cars to go, pedestrians will be able to see a red figure of a man and also hear a slow audio beep signal indicating that it is not safe to cross the road.

When the traffic lights turn to red for the cars to stop, pedestrians will see a green figure of a man and also hear a quick audio beep signal indicating that it is safe to cross the road. In 2005 the maximum penalty that could be imposed for crossing the road wrongly, i.e. not in accordance with the visual and audio indicators, was HK$650.00.

n) Social Life

Hong Kong is a truly cosmopolitan city. As Asia's world city, Hong Kong has developed a very international lifestyle. Multinational corporations from around the world have set up offices in the city and transferred expatriate staff from their individual countries. This has created a very diverse ethnic mix within the city and enhanced the cosmopolitan and international character of Hong Kong. However, Hong Kong is not just an international platform for global business opportunities, it has developed as a world class cultural and sports events arena.

The city is also renowned for its dinning and shopping facilities and also has some stunning natural environments. Another very special feature of a highly developed and modern city like Hong Kong is that it is a very safe place to live and work and also to raise children. The standard of living in Hong Kong is now fully recognised as being world class.

One of the reasons for Hong Kong's reputation as a superb city for dining out is its ability to attract culinary talent of an international character so as to satisfy the diverse demand for different cuisine. Hong Kong's international character coupled with its local Chinese cuisine has made Hong Kong one of the great culinary centres of the world.

Hong Kong has developed an effective network of social clubs and recreation facilities in order to meet the demands of its executive lifestyle. They provide an ideal environment for dining out with the family as well as the perfect place to meet and interact with other people, both local and international, from other companies in the various business sectors of Hong Kong. As such they offer an ideal means of developing business contacts.

Hong Kong is ideally located for quick and convenient access to many popular holiday destinations throughout Asia and South East Asia. Whether it be a family holiday, a remote beach or a cultural heritage tour, all of these are conveniently available in locations very close to Hong Kong. The new Chek Lap Kok airport offers frequent flights together with reliable high quality service making Hong Kong a great and very convenient place to be with regard to holidays.

Miscellaneous Points - Social Aspects

A fish market in Hong Kong

A street market in Mongkok

A tram stop in Central District

Traffic and Commuters in Causeway Bay

Night markets are a popular event, this is Temple Street night market in Kowloon

14. Education

Hong Kong provides nine years of basic education at primary and lower secondary level and it is a legal requirement that children in the territory attend school during these years. The percentage of the population having attained secondary education at 15 and over increased from 59.5% in 1990 to 70.2% in 2000, and the percentage of the population having attained education at degree level more than doubled from 5.1% in 1990 to 11.4% in 2000. The total number of students enrolled in higher education increased from 1990 to 2000 at an average annual growth rate of 3.5% and the number of students enrolled with the Open University doubled between 1990 and 2000.

Education is an important government expenditure projected as HK$59.5 billion for the financial year 2004-05 representing 23 per cent of government expenditure in that year. It is Hong Kong's intention to move more towards being a knowledge based economy in order to move further up the value chain in the products and services that it provides.

Hong Kong is placing a much greater emphasis on its language learning capability in order to satisfy a perceived need for language proficiency now and in the future. The increasing trend and drive towards globalization together with a more open Chinese market has made it even more important than ever before for Hong Kong to enhance both its English and Chinese language proficiency in order to fully meet the inevitable challenges of the future. English proficiency is vitally important because it is the international language of business and the preferred means of communication of the vast majority of overseas countries in the international arena. Putonghua (Mandarin) is increasingly important because it is the national language of China and Hong Kong is now a recognised city of China. As such the community must incorporate Putonghua into its educational system. Cantonese is vitally important because it is the native language (dialect) of the Hong Kong community and is spoken fluently throughout Hong Kong by the native Hong Kong Chinese.

Although in recent years there has been much debate regarding the medium of tuition to be used in schools and whether or not it would be better to use English or Cantonese, it is now one of the long term goals of the Curriculum Development Council to use Putonghua when teaching the Chinese language. This is in accordance with national requirements that the population should be able to speak the national language fluently. Nevertheless it must be realised that Hong Kong is developing a very clear competitive advantage in its language capabilities. Much of the population is bilingual speaking Cantonese and English, and a growing proportion of the population is now trilingual speaking Cantonese, English and Putonghua.

Such language capability makes Hong Kong an ideal employment source for multinationals seeking to enter and develop the Chinese market. Cantonese is the native language of the Hong Kong population, English is the international language of business and Putonghua is the national language of China which is now regarded as the workshop of the world. Therefore to be able to speak all three of these languages fluently makes Hong Kong citizens ideal employees for multinational companies locating their regional headquarters or regional offices in Hong Kong and seeking to expand into the Chinese market.

Multinational expatriates planning to move their families to live in Hong Kong for a period of time will of course be concerned regarding the education of their children. Hong Kong has more than 40 international schools as well as 15 schools in the English Schools Foundation. These schools offer curriculums from all over the world designed to meet the requirements of different nationalities from around the world. Curriculums offered by these schools are the same as those offered in Britain, America, Canada, France, Germany, Japan and Australia. The International Baccalaureate curriculum is also available. Therefore expatriate parents have no need to worry about the education of their children.

The standard of education is also very high with many Hong Kong secondary schools sending graduates to world famous universities such as Oxford and Cambridge in England. The international schools also offer different languages as the medium of tuition so that parents and children can choose their preferred medium based on those available. Also a child being educated in Hong Kong is learning in a multi-ethnic environment with a diverse range of cultures and is therefore being naturally introduced to this diverse range of cultures and variety of ethnicity.

This creates a greater level of understanding of the rich diversity of life and eliminates any tendency to insularity that may possibly arise in a single ethnic culture. This diversity of culture and ethnicity blends in very well with Hong Kong's cosmopolitan culture. Children will certainly be able to see and feel both Western and Chinese cultures because of the environment.

In Hong Kong, education on a fee-paying basis is available for expatriate children of all ages. The English Schools Foundation (ESF) is probably the primary source of education for English speaking children. It currently operates ten co-educational primary schools and five secondary schools. All of the schools follow the British educational curriculum adapted for Asia and are geared to providing an

English language education.

Primary school for 5- to 11-year-olds starts in September for children reaching 5 years of age by 31 December of that year. Secondary school is for 11- to 18-year-olds studying to GCSE and GCE Advanced levels. A requirement for entry into an ESF school is that at least one of the parents of the child should be a resident Hong Kong tax payer. Parents should contact the ESF Central Office regarding admissions. There is a strong demand for places. In 2004 the school fees were HK$47,300 per annum for primary school education and HK$78,600 per annum for secondary school education. The schools operate a zoning system, or catchment area system, with children being expected to attend the school serving their residential area. The ESF also has two kindergartens in Sheung Wan and Tsing Yi for children aged 3 to 5 at an annual fee of HK$39,500.

The five schools in the Hong Kong English Schools Foundation use a UK curriculum that has been adapted for Asia and these schools are positioned within the top 10% of schools in the UK examination system, even though they are not selective. Examination results for 2000 showed that at General Certificate of Secondary Education (GCSE) level the Hong Kong Schools Foundation had four times as many A* grades as UK schools. Also for the core subjects of English, Maths and Science, the Hong Kong English Schools Foundation had twice as many students with A* to C grades than in UK schools. Results for the GCE Advanced Level examinations were also of a very high standard. This led to many students gaining places at prestigious universities around the world such as Oxford, Cambridge, Durham, Harvard, Yale and Stanford.

The Chinese International School curriculum prepares students for the International Baccalaureate examination. The 2000 results were of such a high standard that it resulted in the Chinese International School being rated as one of the top International Baccalaureate schools in the world. Many students who have studied at the Chinese International School have gone on to study at prestigious universities throughout the world.

There are other schools for expatriate children of different nationalities including the Hong Kong International School, Canadian International School, the German Swiss International School and the French International School, all of which are fee-paying schools. These schools follow the curriculums of the various countries.

The Hong Kong International School uses a USA curriculum and in 2000 achieved results well above those of US schools. This led to many students progressing onto prestigious universities. The German Swiss International School uses either a UK or German curriculum subject to which medium of tuition is being used. Results at this particular school are again quite exceptional when compared to other leading countries. In 2000 the pass rate at GCSE was 95% for those students in the International Stream. 38% of the exam results were at

A* level whereas in the UK only 4.6% of exam results were at A* level. 68% of the exam results were at either A or A* level whereas in the UK only 15.8% of exam results were at A or A* level. At Advanced level the pass rate was 97%. The French International School uses a UK and International Baccalaureate curriculum or French curriculum subject to the language stream in which the student is studying. In 2000, 100% of the students studying at the French International School achieved an International Baccalaureate award and have progressed onto universities for tertiary studies.

Tuition fees at these International Schools ranged from HK$52,020 to HK$117,900 per annum for primary education and HK$60,360 to HK$136,700 per annum for secondary school education in 2004. In addition to paying the tuition fees, enrolment in most of these international schools also requires the purchase of debentures on a company/individual basis or the payment of annual capital contributions. At present there is a strong demand for places in these schools and as more multinationals set up offices in Hong Kong and transfer staff to Hong Kong, it can be expected that demand for places will increase.

Education

15. Transport and Logistics

a)   Sea Transport

Due to trade developments over the last 50 years, Hong Kong has evolved to become a sea transport hub in Asia. The city is strategically located along a very important sea route, it has a silt free natural deep water harbour capable of accommodating all sizes of ships and the Chinese mainland over the last 25 years has developed into an enormous cargo base. Its excellent port facilities and services are supported by trade, financial and many other services making the city one of the largest, best developed and most prosperous trading locations in the world.

It has been consistently rated as the world's busiest container port and is renowned for its efficiency with ship turnaround time being probably the fastest in the world. Container throughput in Hong Kong is expected to reach 24 million TEUs by 2006 and 33 million by 2016 representing remarkable growth rates. The rapid expansion of the cargo base in southern China will provide good long term growth for Hong Kong's port facilities.

China has become the main source and destination of transhipment business handled by Hong Kong operators. River trade vessels now carry goods between Hong Kong and China rather than ocean vessels and China has become the main cargo source for Hong Kong. Containers are handled either at Kwai Chung, Stonecutters Island or at mid-stream mooring buoys with most break bulk cargo being handled at the mooring buoys.

It is projected that China will be the largest container market in Asia by 2006 with approximately 20 million TEUs. It is expected that in 2006 Asia will account for 57% of containerised exports in the world. Hong Kong is expected to face growing competition from China's ports in the coming years primarily on a cost basis, but these ports will not be able to match Hong Kong's efficiency and support services for many years to come due to the need for infrastructure investment and development. Nevertheless Hong Kong's growth in throughput of containers can be expected to decline. In order to assist the market situation, the Hong Kong government has been making efforts to strengthen Hong Kong's reputation and position as an international shipping centre.

The government has reduced the merchant shipping registration fee, lowered annual tonnage charges by 5 per cent, simplified ship survey requirements, computerised ship registration procedures, and reduced the tax burden on shipping companies by negotiating double tax agreements with trading partners. The objective of these measures has been to build up Hong Kong's registered tonnage as well as attract overseas shipping companies to establish regional offices in Hong Kong in order to manage their ships in the region.

As a result of China's accession to the WTO, it is expected that the volume of trade will continue to grow at a healthy rate and as a consequence there will be a further development in freight forwarding and logistics services. Hong Kong can expect to obtain long term benefits from the growth and liberalisation of the logistics and freight forwarding sectors as a result of China's WTO accession.

In 2000 the total tonnage of cargo discharged and loaded reached 220 million tonnes and 80% of the total cargo throughput was transported by ocean and river. Hong Kong was again ranked as the busiest port in the world in 2000. A total of 18.1 million TEUs (20-foot equivalent units) were handled in 2000 which was approximately four times the total number of containers handled in 1990. Hong Kong was the first port in the world to handle over 1,000,000 containers in a single calendar month.

As the busiest container port in the world, in 2001 Hong Kong handled 17.8 million TEU. 116,190 river cargo vessels and 34,650 ocean going vessels called at Hong Kong in 2001. Hong Kong has many international shipping lines providing more than 380 weekly container services to more than 500 destinations located in 167 countries. At present there are eight container terminals with many berths and the ninth container terminal is in the process of being introduced. Further expansion of terminal facilities is in the process of being planned.

Hong Kong's logistics industry enjoys many advantages. It has the world's busiest container port with nearly 18 million TEUs passing through in 2001. It has the world's busiest airfreight terminal handling nearly 2.1 million tonnes of cargo in 2001. Transhipment time of cargo passing through Hong Kong waters from the rest of the world destined for the Pearl River Delta, China, has been reduced from what was previously two days to now being less than 24 hours. The Shenzhen Western Corridor which is scheduled to be completed by 2005 will increase the overall capacity of vehicular traffic on cross border trips by 44,000 vehicles to a total of approximately 80,000 vehicles per day. The Hong Kong government is also reforming the customs process in order to speed up customs clearance for cross border traffic by introducing new and quicker arrangements for trucks crossing at the Lok Ma Chau Control Point.

The Logistics Development Council is currently in the process of studying how information technology can be used to facilitate the exchange of data between participants in the logistics industry. The participants include consignors, the Customs and Excise Department, banks, transport companies and container terminal operators. Hong Kong is a transportation and logistics hub in the Asia-Pacific. The development of its transportation sector is closely intertwined with that of the logistics sector.

The competitiveness of Hong Kong's aviation and container freight services are fundamental to the success of the logistics sector. The aviation sector has been opened up recently to allow a greater number of flights to the territory and the catchment area of Chek Lap Kok airport now includes the Pearl River Delta. With regard to sea transport preparations are already in process for the construction of Container Terminal 10 to meet the growth in demand for sea freight. A Digital Trade and Transportation Network system was scheduled to be launched in 2005 to facilitate information and data exchange across various industries. This will have the effect of increasing the speed of trade and the movement of cargo. Attempts are also being made to reduce land transport costs.

b) Air Transportation and Air Cargo

1) In 2001 Hong Kong International Airport was recognised as the busiest international air cargo facility in the world. In 2002 the total amount of air cargo handled was then a record high of 2.48 million tonnes. However, in 2005 the total throughput had risen to 3.4 million tonnes.

2) In the first half of 2006 Hong Kong International Airport had 78 scheduled international airlines operating some 5,300 flights to over 140 destinations in what is one of the busiest and most extensive aviation route networks in the region.

3) The marine cargo terminal in the airport, directly linking with 17 ports in the Pearl River Delta, came into operation in March 2001.

4) Chek Lap Kok airport is being developed as a logistics centre in order to attract air cargo and value-added services through the airport.

In 2003 Hong Kong handled 27 million passengers and 2.64 million tonnes of cargo. Also on 20th January 2000 the new Passenger Terminal Northwest Concourse of Chek Lap Kok airport commenced operation. This new extension of the airport substantially raised the airport's passenger handling capacity. Hong Kong's two air cargo terminals are both privately owned. Super Terminal 1 handles 85% of the cargo including express cargo, whilst Asia Airfreight Terminal handles 15% of the overall cargo. Cargo is either carried on passenger aircraft or dedicated air cargo freighters. There is an increasing demand for air cargo due to changing consumer market demand whereby importers have to maintain low inventories, whilst business cycle times and order frequencies are much faster.

Four airlines, Cathay Pacific Airways, Jet Aviation Business Jets, Air Hong Kong and Hong Kong Dragon Airlines use Hong Kong as their base. Europe is an important market for air cargo whereas China is not, due to the majority of trade with China being by rail or river. North America accounts for approximately 20% of air cargo shipments.

The Hong Kong Special Administrative Region Civil Aviation Authority has been assessed by the USA Federal Aviation Administration and classified as being of Category 1 in full compliance with international aviation safety standards regarding the superintendence of Hong Kong's air carrier operations.

Recent statistics show the growing importance of air cargo as an increasing amount of value in Hong Kong's exports is being despatched by this means. Hong Kong currently has a dominant position in the air cargo sector because of its facilities at Chek Lap Kok airport. An increasing amount of electronic product is now being despatched by air freight and with the continuing trend towards relocating production capacity to China and other parts of Asia, Hong Kong can expect to see a continued growth in its export of electronic products to overseas markets being despatched by air freight. The territory is also seeing good growth in its component exports to other Asian production sites. This is a thriving sector that multinational companies should consider for market opportunities.

According to the Boeing World Cargo Forecast of 2003/04 more than 50% of air cargo shipments will be in the Asian markets by 2019. The policies driving airfreight include just-in-time, low inventory, rapid product changes, quick response, etc. and these ideas are being brought into business philosophy more often thereby intensifying competition. Hong Kong is attempting to encourage air freighters in order to strengthen its position as the regional air cargo hub. Incentives are being used to encourage air freighters to use the quiet time between midnight and 6.00 am.

Landing and parking fees have been reduced and an increasing number of foreign airlines are able to add Hong Kong to their flights. As part of the promotion, the Airport Authority is providing a 50% rebate to airlines on landing charges during the first year they fly to a new destination. Hong Kong has also joined with the four smaller surrounding airports of Huangtian (Shenzhen), Macau, Baiyun (Guangzhou) and Zhuhai in a collaborative move to present a unified brandname called 'PRD A5 Group'. A website has been set up for this group.

Chek Lap Kok is one of the world's leading airports. The air cargo terminal is the biggest in the world and in July 1998 when the airport opened it had an annual cargo capacity of 3 million tonnes together with a passenger capacity of

35 million. However, when further development has been completed it will have an annual cargo capacity of 9 million tonnes together with a passenger capacity of 87 million making it probably the biggest airport in Asia and one of the biggest airports in the world.

Due to its central location in East Asia, Hong Kong is an ideal location as a regional hub because it has the shortest travelling distance to all other major urban centres in the region making frequent business travel that much easier. Approximately half the world's population can be reached within 6 hours flying time from Hong Kong.

The development of Chek Lap Kok airport and its associated projects was at the time of its development one of the largest development projects in the world. The airport was built on reclaimed land off the coast of Lantau island which is the largest island in the archipelago. The associated projects with this development included the world's longest road-rail suspension bridge, a high speed railway connecting the airport to major population centres, 34 kilometres of expressways and tunnels, a new town development and a third cross harbour tunnel as well as railway stations and terminals. All of these associated projects were completed by 2005.

Hong Kong is now the air traffic centre of Asia and with the re-positioning of the airport away from population centres, it will be able to accept 24 hour traffic thereby enhancing Hong Kong's competitiveness. Hong Kong has developed an extensive network of air routes enabling passengers and cargo to get from Hong Kong to anywhere in the world at a very quick speed. Hong Kong's position as an air cargo hub is much stronger than any nearby airport because it has a strong cluster of support services, a good size local market and perfect geographic location.

Hong Kong has a very extensive network of air and sea transport links with the rest of the world and this network infrastructure is used very efficiently. In the year ending 31st March 2003, Hong Kong International Airport handled 2.55 million tonnes of cargo and 34.2 million passengers. Even though the airport is still relatively new having opened in 1998, these handling figures are already close to capacity. From 1996 to 1999 Chek Lap Kok airport in Hong Kong was the busiest in the world regarding international air cargo.

c) Express Cargo

Express cargo services are experiencing a continued growth curve as businesses demand quicker services. It has been estimated that during the 1990s Hong Kong's express cargo services experienced growth rates of around 25% annually. Due to the nature of the business and the premium rates charged this sector is very profitable. Chek Lap Kok airport has specific facilities designed to handle express cargo requirements. A few multinationals with wide ranging global air and ground level networks such as UPS, Federal Express and Speedpost now dominate Hong Kong's express cargo industry.

Speedpost is run by the Post Office and has distribution links serving over 80 countries. Larger express cargo services work on a fixed price and fixed weight basis. Mainland China is regarded as a good market with a high growth potential and Hong Kong has an advantage due to it's location. China is expected to become a major express cargo market in the early 21st century. Increasing globalisation of business structures is seen as a further reason for growth potential within the express cargo service.

The 24-hour express centre at Hong Kong International Airport has a handling capacity of 200,000 tonnes per year. Even though express cargo only represents 7% of the total cargo despatched, the revenue from express cargo is much higher than that generated by normal seafreight delivery. The air express market in Asia is forecast to grow at 18% annually for the next five years and is being driven by the need for quick response delivery, last minute orders, smaller more frequent volumes, samples, etc. The second runway at Chek Lap Kok airport and the reduced landing charges have been an encouragement for airlines. DHL Worldwide Express has recently moved its regional airfreight centre to Hong Kong. The increasing logistics facilities together with the airport's sea-air cargo links have further enhanced Hong Kong's position as a competitive air cargo hub.

The multinational companies involved in the express cargo industry in Hong Kong generally operate on hub strategies whilst seeking to fill their cargo planes. Smaller operators tend to work on niche market strategies and also tend to offer more flexible services. Competition in the industry is nevertheless intense. The main markets for express cargo are Europe and North America although there is good growth in Asia. Hong Kong's position as the gateway to China is important for the regional development of the express cargo industry. Many large operators already have joint venture arrangements in China, and the transport logistics sector in China offers good business development prospects for the express cargo industry. This industry is experiencing good growth worldwide. The Boeing forecast is that by 2019 express cargo delivery services will account for 31% of delivered products internationally. China's accession to the WTO means that foreign courier services will be able to enter the Chinese market via joint ventures upon accession and will be free of all restrictions three years after accession. The Hong Kong Customs and Excise Department recently signed a memorandum of understanding with four express carrier associations regarding cargo clearance, it being the objective of the memorandum to provide the framework for the promotion and efficient support needed in customs controls and trade facilitation.

Hong Kong: The World City and International Business Centre

Wan Chai seen from Central District

Hong Kong Container Port

Hong Kong International Airport on Chek Lap Kok

Minibuses in Mongkok, Kowloon, during rush hour

The Light Rail (LR) connects the New Territories towns of Tuen Mun and Yuen Long.

Transport and Logistics

Hong Kong International Airport on Chek Lap Kok, AEL (Airport Express Line) train.

Hong Kong's three bus companies provide an efficient network of bus routes covering Hong Kong Island, Kowloon, Lantau and the New Territories

Tsing Ma Bridge is the world's heaviest suspension bridge, with 55 000 tonnes of steel in 125 deck units

Star Ferries on Victoria Harbour

d) Freight Forwarding

In December 2002, Hong Kong had 2,172 sea cargo forwarders and 732 air cargo forwarders. Developments in the freight forwarding industry now mean that forwarders are offering a broader range of services due to vertical integration. These additional services include warehousing, distribution and logistics solutions. The range of services offered by freight forwarders differs based on the size of the organisation. Large freight forwarders sometimes offer an extensive range of services including warehousing, air express consolidation, distribution, trucking, customs clearance, tracking and monitoring, e-commerce facilities, etc., whereas smaller freight forwarders will offer a much more limited range of services.

There are two associations of note in the industry, the Hong Kong Association of Freight Forwarding and Logistics Limited (HAFFA) and the International Air Transport Association (IATA). IATA members control 80% of the market and have a global network capability. Many large operators are IATA members. The trend now is for freight forwarders, particularly the larger companies, to target large companies in order to develop exclusive arrangements and contracts by offering extensive logistics services.

A number of global trends are currently affecting the freight forwarding industry and freight forwarders are being forced to respond positively. The trends are globalisation of supply chains, shortening of product lifecycles, mass customisation, low inventory levels, frequent and quicker small orders requiring quick response times, etc. As a result manufacturers are now using third party logistics in order to deal with transport, inventory management, warehousing and order fulfilment. China's accession to the WTO will inevitably lead to a greater demand for a wider variety of freight forwarding services as the volume of trade increases. The Closer Economic Partnership Arrangement (CEPA) between Hong Kong and China is also expected to lead to an increase in demand for freight forwarding services and consequently will provide more business opportunities for Hong Kong freight forwarders. There will also be an increase in the number of companies offering supply chain management services in the near future.

Hong Kong is one of the most trade orientated economies in the world. Its history and livelihood has been built on the import/export trade. Hong Kong has placed great emphasis upon the development of its container terminal facilities so as to facilitate its position and role as the busiest container port in the world. Chek Lap Kok airport has a 24 hour cargo handling facility and the airport freight forwarding centre performs much needed consolidation work. Warehousing, distribution and total logistics solutions are all part of the Hong Kong freight forwarding service. Most Hong Kong freight forwarders are members of the Hong Kong Association of Freight Forwarding Agents (HAFFA) whereas large airfreight forwarders tend to be members of the International Air Transport Association (IATA). A trend within the freight forwarding industry is to build lasting relations with companies so that companies tend to use a particular forwarder on an exclusive basis. This means that the forwarder has to very often provide a tailor made service for customers in order to ensure regular and exclusive business.

At present the main source for cargo shipments by Hong Kong freight forwarders is the Chinese mainland and an increasing number of Hong Kong freight forwarders and logistics providers are now operating in China. Initially this was just in Shenzhen and Guangdong province, but now they are moving further northwards as an increasing number of Hong Kong manufacturers and investors have moved northwards. Hong Kong has however considered establishing a third party logistics park to strengthen and support its position and role as the logistics hub in the region.

e) Shipping and Container Services

1) In 2004, the port of Hong Kong had some 80 international shipping lines with over 400 container line services per week to over 500 destinations. Also there were over 300 daily feeder services linking Hong Kong with the Pearl River Delta area.

2) Port operators held various world records for vessel handling. One of the world records was 336 moves per vessel hour, which was set in February 2001.

3) The expansion of the Lok Ma Chau boundary crossing has increased the handling capacity of cross-boundary traffic, from 19,000 to 32,000 vehicles per day. Every day, some 26,000 goods vehicles, including 13,000 container trucks, cross the boundary.

The busiest port in the world in 2003 was Hong Kong with a throughput of 20.4 million TEUs. Hong Kong Cargo Forecasts of 2000/2001 predicted that by 2010 Hong Kong will be handling 29.7 million TEUs and by 2020 this will have reached 40.5 million TEUs. The extensive port facilities in Hong Kong are privately owned and run. The government is not involved in ownership, but merely oversees its proper use and function. Hong Kong's port operators are private companies that have purchased the right to reclaim land in order to develop and operate as port facilities. The government has supported private management of Hong Kong's port facilities believing that it engenders greater efficiency and cost savings. This arrangement is unique among the world's major ports.

The Port Development Board, which is a government agency, is empowered to develop plans in conjunction with industry experts so as to match port facilities with cargo throughput. In 1995 Hong Kong was the world's busiest container port handling approximately 12.6 million TEUs and it is projected that it will handle 31 million TEUs by 2006 and 36 million TEUs by 2011. However, the recent recession in Hong Kong in 1998-99, coupled with a slowdown in the Chinese economy at the same time, and hence a slight decline in re-exports, was just a temporary hiccup as the Asian and world economy made adjustments.

Apart from being the busiest container port, Hong Kong's shipping industry has a very dense route network and a highly efficient port turnaround time of only 12 hours. Approximately 80% of the city's total external cargo was handled by the port facility in 2003. The new container terminal number 9, over which there has been much controversy due to the involvement of Jardines in its construction, has a design capacity that will add an annual 2.6 million TEUs to the total TEU capacity of the port when it is completed.

Hong Kong is served by many shipping lines and containers dominate the liner market. Cargo tracking information is readily available with many liners. As one of the world's major ports, Hong Kong is the only one not managed by a port authority, i.e. under government control, but is instead built, owned, financed and operated by private investment. The terminals at Kwai Chung and Stonecutters Island are owned and operated by four private consortia. The largest current independent port operator in the world is the Hutchison Port Holdings Group from Hong Kong, which handles a substantial percentage of global container traffic. The company owns, manages and operates terminals in China, Panama, Indonesia, the UK, Bahamas, Myanmar, etc. Hong Kong is recognised as being a major ship owning and management centre in the shipping industry and is currently exporting its port development and management capabilities to other countries, in particular China.

Sea transport has been an essential part of Hong Kong's transport infrastructure for a long time and has experienced tremendous growth since the 1950s and 1960s. Sea borne cargo in 2002 was 192 million tonnes with approximately three quarters of it being by ocean going vessels. 54 million tonnes in 2002 was transhipment cargo with China being the main source and destination of the transhipment business. The vast majority of cargo is containerised, particularly transhipment cargo. Approximately 200 shipping lines serve Hong Kong with many of them offering door to door multi-modal services. Liners operate on planned scheduled time tables with fixed rates on routes calling at specific destinations. Many routes are conference routes where the shipping lines have agreed the tariffs and sailing schedules. The liner shipping lines mainly handle containerised cargo. Tracking systems have been installed on many routes so shippers can know exactly where their cargo is at any time.

The container terminals in Hong Kong have a total of 22 berths and these terminals are operated by private consortiums. Geared barges are used to service vessels not booked into terminal berths. These vessels will be loaded and unloaded whilst in the harbour or close by. The manufacturing centres of the Pearl River Delta and Guangdong province are the main cargo base for Hong Kong. This has led to a sharp increase in river trade, which has become the fastest growing form of external transport accounting for 54 million tonnes in 2002. River trade vessels use public cargo working areas, privately run berths and terminals, the three feeder berths located at the container terminals as well as the river trade terminal in Tuen Mun in the New Territories.

As a major ship owning and management centre, in March 2004, the Hong Kong Shipping Register had 908 vessels equivalent to 21.75 million gross tons. However, according to the Hong Kong Shipowners' Association in 2002, members owned or managed 62 million deadweight tons. Therefore Hong Kong is a very important shipping centre. Mega-containerships with a capacity of 10,000 to 12,000 TEUs are expected to be in full operation very soon and according to the Marine Department, Hong Kong can handle such enormous ships. The signing of the CEPA agreement between Hong Kong and China will also facilitate Hong Kong operators in increasing the number of shipments from China as well as the use of supporting services and facilities.

f) Logistics Development

The development of Hong Kong's trade over the last 20 years has given rise to Hong Kong's development as a logistics hub. As the amount of trade has grown Hong Kong's logistics function has become more important with regard to aiding and facilitating the smooth flow of trade. A number of factors have helped the logistics development in Hong Kong including:

1) There are warehouses in the territory offering space to enable dock cargo consolidation and distribution activities.
2) Enactment of the Electronic Transaction Ordinance and establishment of a Public Certification Authority has been done to secure 'e-commerce' transactions.

3) The Land Cargo Advance Clearance Scheme is designed to facilitate traders in the submission of manifests by fax, e-mail or in person at least one hour in advance of the arrival of goods vehicles at the boundary for customs clearance.

4) Import/export control of air transhipment cargo has been relaxed, except in the case of some sensitive products, under the Air Cargo Transhipment (Facilitation) Ordinance.

5) The Logscom and the Logscouncil were set up to support the 'Logistics Hong Kong ' initiative, which aims at enhancing Hong Kong's status as the preferred international logistics hub in Asia.

6) Formed in November 2001, the Logscom provides policy steering for logistics development in Hong Kong.

7) The Logscouncil, formed in December 2001, advises the Government on measures to promote logistics development. It implements policies set by Logscom, and also provides a forum for the public and private sectors to discuss and coordinate matters concerning the industry and to carry out joint projects.

8) There are five project groups formed under the Logscouncil to deal with different priority areas as well as to implement programmes and these are physical infrastructure, IT infrastructure, human resource development support for SMEs, and marketing and promotion.

It is expected that in the next few years the Pearl River Delta (PRD) region will experience a boom in its logistics function making it a logistics hub for Hong Kong and possibly the Asia Pacific region. At a recent meeting of the Political Consultative Committee in Guangzhou, China, it was decided that the PRD should develop into an important logistics centre for China and possibly the Southeastern region with Guangdong and Shenzhen both being an important axes for the centre. The Chinese government is intent on improving the business environment of the PRD with a clear emphasis upon logistics, infrastructure and tourism. The demand for logistics services and international freight forwarding is expected to increase as a result of the expansion in China's trade with the rest of the world.

g) Hong Kong / Mainland China Transport

The transport connections between Hong Kong and China have increased considerably in recent years. At present there are direct flights from Hong Kong to more than 40 cities in China; each day there are seven through trains both ways between Hong Kong and Guangzhou; each day there is a train from Kowloon station in Hong Kong to Zhaoqing in Guangdong province which also stops at Foshan, Guangzhou and Dongguan; there are also through trains from Hong Kong to Shanghai and Beijing on alternate days. Also there are many scheduled ferry services between Hong Kong and a number of cities in China including Shanghai, Guangzhou, Xiamen, Zhuhai, Shekou, etc.

The Guangzhou - Shenzhen superhighway will greatly improve road transport when it opens soon. To drive from Hong Kong to Guangzhou takes approximately 3 hours. A bridge is currently being constructed to link Hong Kong with Macau and Mainland China.

Hong Kong's comprehensive public transport system comprising railways, franchised buses, public light buses (mini buses), taxis, ferries, trams, & non-franchised buses (NFBs) is very well coordinated.

h) Internal Transport

Due to its geographical size Hong Kong has limited road space and in the urban city areas often suffers congestion during peak time rush hours. In accordance with transport planning policy, the underground system, railway and franchised buses have priority. It has been stated that the underground Mass Transit Railway (MTR) and Kowloon Canton Railway (KCR) form the backbone of Hong Kong's transport system with other modes of transport generally performing a supplementary role. It has always been an objective of the transport department to minimize wasteful competition as well as reduce any adverse effects on the roads and the environment.

The total number of public light buses (PLBs) has remained constant at 4,350 since 1976. The total number of taxis in the territory has remained unchanged since 1994 at 15,250 for Hong Kong Island and Kowloon, 2838 for the New Territories and since 1997 Lantau Island has had 50. Between 1998 and 2003 the total number of franchised buses increased by 5% from 6,018 to 6,319 whilst the total number of non-franchised buses (NFBs) increased by 20% from 5,868 to 7,047. NFB services include Hotel Service, Student Service, Tour Service, Contract Hire Service, Employees Service, International Passenger Service, Residents' Service, and Multiple Transport Service. These are authorised under the Passenger Service Licence (PSL) issued by the Transport Department.

Other important and popular modes of transport include the Airport Express railway service, Hong Kong Island tram service, the New Territories Light Rail Transit (LRT) tram service, cross harbour ferries and hydrofoils.

Hong Kong's transport and utilities have often been described by locals and visitors as efficient, convenient and always on time. The infrastructure in Hong Kong is probably one of the best, if not the best, in the world because of its functional efficiency and attention to detailed service.

Hong Kong's Port Master Plan 2020 is a long term study of the future of the port being conducted by the Port, Maritime and Logistics Development Unit of the Economic Development and Labour Bureau. The objective of the study is to develop a long term competitive strategy over a 20 year planning frame that will enable Hong Kong to realise growth opportunities for the port, increase port efficiency and develop better positioning of the port with regard to supply chain competition.

The transport system in Hong Kong is probably one of the most efficient in the world. Being a densely populated city, the transport is abundant meaning that there is very little waiting time for passengers particularly with regard to buses, mini buses, trams, trains, taxis, underground railway (MTR - Mass Transit Railway) and ferries. Prices on buses and Hong Kong Island trams are at a fixed rate for the journey wherever the passenger gets on and off, rather than different charges for different distances. Charges on the trains, underground railway, cross-harbour tunnel buses, New Territories trams, taxis and mini buses vary on the distance travelled.

Public transport charges in 2004 were as follows:

Means of Transport	Fare (Single Journey)
Mass Transit Railway (underground)	HK$4 - HK$23
Airport Express (connecting airport and urban areas)	HK$60 - HK$100
Kowloon Canton Railway	HK$3.5 - HK$33
Light Rail Transit (LRT) (north west tram system in New Territories)	HK$4.0 - HK$5.8

Franchised Buses	HK$2.4 - HK$45
Minibuses	HK$2.0 - HK$20
Trams (Hong Kong Island)	HK$2.0
Ferries (and Hydrofoils) (return trip to China)	HK$2.20 - HK$80
Taxis (Hong Kong & Kowloon)	HK$15 flag fall for first 2 km + HK$1.4 per 0.2 km
(New Territories)	HK$12.5 flag fall for first 2 km + HK$1.2 per 0.2 km
(Lantau Island)	HK$12.00 flag fall for first 2 km + HK$1.2 per 0.2 km

It should be noted that even though these prices were valid in 2004, they will have been subject to inflationary changes over time.

16. The China Factor

Hong Kong originally started as an entrepôt port. A landing position for traders, primarily British, with aspirations for Far Eastern trade. Product passing through Hong Kong was mainly from China with very little going through Hong Kong into China. However, in the 1830s the main product passing through Hong Kong was opium destined for China. This declined substantially after the first opium war, but was not eliminated and outlawed until the 20th century.

In the 1940s after the 2nd World War, Hong Kong was a thriving entrepôt, but then in 1949 the Communists took control of China and in 1951 the United Nations which was dominated by the United States of America imposed an embargo on products from China. This was an absolute disaster for Hong Kong that very nearly destroyed the territory. At that point in time 90% of the product exported from Hong Kong was produced in China and therefore the livelihood of Hong Kong as an entrepôt was almost eliminated.

It was at that time in 1949-1951, that there was a mass exodus of immigrants fleeing China because of the communist takeover and many of these immigrants fled to Hong Kong. These immigrants brought with them their wealth in the form of money, gold, knowledge and experience. It was these immigrants that to a large extent founded the manufacturing industry of Hong Kong. Light manufacturing industry burgeoned dramatically over the years covering textiles, garments, household items, jewellery, watches and clocks, electronics, toys, etc. Due to the low wages in Hong Kong, Hong Kong product was very price competitive and as such undermined competing industry in the western world. This created the effect of jobs migrating to the East as an increasing number of western companies went east to places like Hong Kong seeking OEM manufacturers capable of developing and manufacturing product in accordance with company specifications. Hong Kong probably became the most important OEM centre in the world, because western companies seeking OEM manufacturers felt at ease due to Hong Kong being a British colony under British law and administration. This process led to Hong Kong companies developing a wealth of knowledge and experience.

The 1960s and 1970s was a definite boom time for Hong Kong with substantial annual growth in GDP. Unemployment was virtually non-existent as manufacturing companies mushroomed throughout the territory. The strong work ethic of the community and its independent spirit led to Hong Kong being recognised as a prime manufacturing location even though product quality was sometimes not up to standard. Nevertheless as companies gained greater knowledge and experience of overseas markets, production quality did naturally improve.

Prior to the 1960s Hong Kong had always been seen as a transit point with people passing through, but not staying to live in the territory. This had been the case ever since the founding of Hong Kong back in 1842. Many people would come to Hong Kong to work and earn money, and then leave to live elsewhere. However, in the 1960s the first generation of native Hong Kong civilians emerged. Children who had been born in Hong Kong and had grown up in Hong Kong needed to be educated. These people saw Hong Kong as their home and intended to stay and live there. The government therefore decided to invest in the education structures of the territory so that all children were provided with free education at both primary and secondary level. Hong Kong was therefore developing its own labour force and with this development demands grew for improved standards of employment and production.

During the 1960s and 1970s product produced in Hong Kong was very price competitive. Companies did not seek to increase their margins by raising their prices because of the negative effect such a move would have on demand. Instead they sought to keep their prices low and make money on the basis of volume of production because it was realised that low prices increase demand. During this time Hong Kong was recognised as a shoppers paradise in the tourism industry, because of its low prices when compared to other destinations as well as its extensive range of product. However, over time production costs did rise with the effect that prices rose marginally and margins were squeezed to a certain extent.

However, in 1978 under the leadership of Deng Xiao Ping, China decided to open up to foreign investment. Many commentators then erroneously stated that Hong Kong was finished because companies would go direct to China. Some companies did and seriously regretted it because they got burnt, to coin a phrase, because they were totally ignorant of the cultural differences and the fact that China had no experience of dealing with the outside world. However, Hong Kong having a predominantly Chinese population had a greater understanding of the culture and how to proceed.

Between 1978 and 1985 many Hong Kong companies moved their manufacturing plants across the border into China under export processing agreements whereby it was agreed that the labour force would be from mainland China, components used in the manufactured product would be either from mainland China or outside China, and manufactured items would be exported from China with shipment being made through Hong Kong. Special Economic Zones were established in China with Shenzhen, just north of Hong Kong, being the main one. This export processing arrangement with China effectively meant that within 10 years Hong

Kong ceased to be a manufacturing base and instead developed into a service economy. This change in economic structure of the territory has been regarded as something quite astounding because of its speed and smoothness. At the same time the export processing arrangements with China enabled Hong Kong companies to expand their manufacturing facilities in China due to the low cost of production again enabling them to sell at low prices with increased volume. Hong Kong companies are now the main employers in the Pearl River Delta region employing over 5 million workers. This close relationship with China has enabled Hong Kong to consolidate and expand its position as the most strategic and logical gateway to China.

Hong Kong is now the number one investor in China and leads the way regarding investment analysis and decision making with regard to China. Hong Kong has acted as a source of capital for China, a guide for overseas companies seeking to invest in China and a trading partner for both overseas companies and Chinese companies. Hong Kong is now promoting itself as a partner for overseas multinationals seeking to develop relations with China because the territory has built up such an extensive knowledge of the whole of China including its approach and means of conducting business.

It is quite logical that Hong Kong should have such an advantageous position with regard to China and business relations with China. After the communists took power in China in 1949, they effectively shut themselves off from the world. Some would regard this as a serious mistake, but some would argue that after the history of the 19th and early 20th century with the imperialistic invasions of China by many countries, it was a fairly natural thing to close the door to the rest of the world. Some would also argue that the UN embargo against China in 1951 was effectively the rest of the world closing the door against China. Nevertheless Hong Kong was in a unique position because it effectively acted as China's eye on the rest of the world and the rest of the world's eye on China. Hence Hong Kong was the place where East meets West.

The commentators in 1978 who said Hong Kong was finished could not have been more wrong, because during the 1980s and 1990s up until the handover of sovereignty in 1997, Hong Kong experienced yet a further boom time with substantial annual growth in GDP even though negotiations between China and Britain regarding the handover of sovereignty were sometimes heated. The 1980s and 1990s was probably one of the most economically active times for Hong Kong with tremendous results. The territory was internationally recognised as one of the best economies in the world, Hong Kong was rated as one of the most openly competitive cities in the world, its banking sector was recognised as excellent and having a positive influence on industry, Hong Kong was seen as a prime source of capital at very favourable costs, the territory was seen as a leading centre for raising venture capital and the city was seen as a good place to live.

However, at the end of the 1990s the picture changed. The Asian Financial Crisis brought a serious problem for the majority of East Asian economies with markets collapsing and currencies being devalued. However economies like Hong Kong and Singapore weathered the storm, but nevertheless felt the effects. Unemployment which had traditionally been negligible in Hong Kong rocketed and reached 6.5% at the end of 1998. Underemployment also became a noticeable problem. Tourism was seriously affected and room occupancy rates plummeted to below 50% when they were normally between 80% and 90%.

A major concern in the territory at the end of 1997 was the collapse in property market values. At the end of 1998 residential property values were approximately half of what they had been during the middle of 1997. This left many residents in a negative equity situation as their mortgages were higher than the value of their properties. At the end of 1998 property prices were still falling. It was not until 2002-2003 that property values appeared to have reached their lowest point and it is not expected that they will rise like before in the near future. Office rents also experienced a decline in value in conjunction with residential property prices. However, some would argue that residential property prices and office rents had risen to an unsustainable level by the middle of 1997 and a property market crash was inevitable.

The 1997 level effectively made Hong Kong one of the most expensive cities in the world on a par with Tokyo, London and New York. Such high property prices were in effect detrimental to Hong Kong, because such high prices discouraged overseas companies from locating in the territory, the high hotel rates discouraged tourists and investment in general was discouraged due to cost. Therefore the decline in property prices, office rents, hotel room rates, etc. has been a hidden bonus for the territory because of its beneficial effect on business activity.

Many look upon the word deflation with fear, but this is just irrational. Deflation is merely the market mechanism working to lower prices and values to a more realistic level after they have become inflated. Market values including property, stocks portfolios and assets became inflated by the middle of 1997 to such a level that it was detrimental to the economy and therefore deflation was inevitable in order to reduce those market values back to a more realistic level. Over investment, as was the case in East Asia before 1997, leads to inflation in asset values which in turn creates market jitters as investors fear for the projected return on their investments. Deflation has the effect of lowering asset values, lowering prices, curtailing economic opportunities and increasing competition. This in turn benefits consumers as retail prices decline. The lowering of retail prices has had the effect of stimulating tourism in Hong Kong with the result that room rates have substantially improved, but hoteliers have to be wary regarding room costs.

The fall in asset values which commenced in 1998 has had the effect of making the territory more attractive from an investment point of view as overseas companies have considered potential takeovers. The British transport company Stagecoach bought the bus company Citybus and their British competitor First bought a rival bus company China Motor Bus (CMB), part of the ferry service and also the Hong Kong island tram service. Transport is a very important and active sector of the Hong Kong economy because the vast majority of people do not own cars nor even seek to own cars because the public transport network in Hong Kong is probably the most efficient in the world. It is also very competitively priced although some would argue that in recent years it has become more expensive.

In 2001 it was formally announced that China would become a member of the World Trade Organization. After negotiating for 15 years to become a member of first GATT and then the WTO, China's application was formally accepted by the current members of the WTO. When it was announced that China would be joining the WTO, Hong Kong rejoiced because of the benefits that Hong Kong would receive. Consideration needs to be given to what exactly those benefits are going to be.

Previously Hong Kong manufacturers were manufacturing product in China under export processing arrangements. This meant that materials were imported into China, Chinese labour was used to manufacture the products and then the products were exported with shipment being made through Hong Kong. Now Hong Kong manufacturers can sell the products that they manufacture in China to the people of the Chinese mainland. This means that Hong Kong manufacturers can expect to see a dramatic increase in demand for their products, because their production will now be exported as well as sold to mainland China. Hong Kong has therefore suddenly gained a vast domestic market hinterland.

Product development can be expected to flourish. Hong Kong manufacturers will not just be developing products for western markets, but will also develop products for the mainland Chinese market.

With China joining the WTO, Hong Kong can expect to see a surge in the number of overseas companies seeking to develop relations with China through Hong Kong. Hong Kong is currently promoting itself as a means of entry into China and offering the possibility of partnerships being developed between overseas companies and Hong Kong companies with the objective of developing the China market. Hong Kong as the gateway to China is becoming even more prominent and pronounced.

It has been reported that China's accession to the WTO will be regarded as an historical event that will be extremely important in transforming the global economic landscape in the 21st century. It is expected that investors from around the world will be attracted by China's WTO accession and financial markets will experience a substantial increase in capital flows. Already there is competition amongst the financial centres of the region seeking new business opportunities as a result of the accession and Hong Kong can expect to obtain a substantial proportion of these new business opportunities.

Hong Kong is not just the richest city in China, it is the most technologically advanced and the most internationally experienced city in China. However, China is seeking to develop Shanghai and is investing heavily in the city. It is planned that a national gold exchange will be developed in Shanghai soon. In due course the Renminbi will become freely convertible and investment and trade flows will become more open and smooth. It is envisaged that in 50 years time Shanghai will be the economic centre in the East of China and Hong Kong will be the economic centre in the South of China. Both of these cities will serve their respective hinterlands with investment being channelled through the appropriate economic centre dependent upon the particular objective of the investment. However, at this point in time and for at least the next two decades the Hong Kong economy will be much more advanced than the Shanghai economy and therefore there is no prospect of replacement as envisaged by wrongful doom-mongers. In fact, as an international financial centre Hong Kong faces more competition from Singapore rather than Shanghai because the financial markets of Hong Kong and Shanghai are currently at very different stages of development.

Hong Kong can therefore rest assured that it is China's economic powerhouse and will remain so for some considerable time subject to world events. China is currently Hong Kong's biggest trading partner in financial terms and as a result of this relationship more than 50% of all external investment in mainland China flowed from Hong Kong in 2001. Approximately 90% of Hong Kong's re-exports originate from or are destined for China, making Hong Kong a major entrepôt for the China trade. Hong Kong is a major primary source of funding for mainland Chinese enterprises. There are also an increasing number of mainland companies establishing themselves in Hong Kong. In 2001 this number had reached 1850 and was growing as more mainland companies seek international experience. An increasing number of Chinese companies will seek to set up operations in Hong Kong, seeking listings on the stock exchange or GEM and this will give rise to a demand for a wide range of professional services.

By February 2004 there were 260 Mainland Chinese companies listed in Hong Kong with a market capitalisation of HK$1,900 billion. There is an increasing demand from Chinese enterprises in mainland China seeking to access capital from foreign markets and the China Everbright group is just one organisation planning to expand its investment banking business in Hong Kong in order to satisfy this growing demand.

It can be seen that over the last 25 - 30 years the prosperity of Hong Kong and its stability has been greatly influenced if not dependent upon the China factor. The relationship between Hong Kong and China has been crucial to the development of Hong Kong and in the coming years this relationship will deepen and develop further to the benefit of both China and Hong Kong. It is this relationship that overseas multinationals must consider deeply when determining their investment proposals and business prospects. The business opportunities are plentiful and the prospects are bright. China has recently been recording an annual GDP growth rate of between seven and nine percent, which far outstrips the vast majority of other countries. China is now seen as a major importer and consumer of oil products because of its rapid development and some are tempted to say that this was one of the reasons for the surge in oil prices in May 2004.

Overseas multinationals must also consider their competitors objectives and aspirations in order to determine how they are going to proceed. It has been estimated that by 2020 China will be the biggest market in the world and with the current rate of development this looks like a very real prospect. Therefore multinational companies cannot afford to ignore the China factor. Depending upon the size and resources of the multinational as well as its product portfolio and corporate objectives, Hong Kong is currently offering an ideal means of entry into China as well as being an ideal base location for dealing with the rest of South East Asia.

With China joining the WTO Hong Kong's domestic market has immediately grown to a continental scale domestic market and Hong Kong is clearly in the correct position to capture first-mover advantage because of it location and very close kinship and association with China. Hong Kong companies are clearly positioned to act as guides or partners for overseas companies seeking to enter the Chinese market. This aspect will provide yet another strong stimulus for the Hong Kong economy and due to its well developed financial industry, its infrastructure and advanced communications technology, Hong Kong is well positioned to take the lead in opening and developing the China market.

Overseas multinationals must clearly see the advantages of being located properly in Hong Kong and connecting properly with the organizations that can assist in opening and developing the China market. Hong Kong has clearly been able to consolidate and expand its position as the most important strategic gateway to China by acting as an investor, a trading partner and a source of capital. The further opening up of the Chinese mainland economy will eventually in the next few years lead to it becoming a large domestic market for goods and services from Hong Kong as well as being a manufacturing base for Hong Kong manufacturers. The further opening up of China to international trade will also strengthen the advantages of Hong Kong as a regional, if not global, base for multinational corporations to conduct their business in China and other regional markets.

In 2004 China's external trade was the fourth highest in the world at over US$1,000 billion. China has in recent years emerged as the world factory due to its low production costs. As China's production capacity has developed, its demand for capital and material goods has also developed. This has further strengthened the two way flow of trade through Hong Kong. Finished product is exported from China to overseas markets to a large extent through Hong Kong and capital goods and materials are imported from overseas markets into China to a large extent through Hong Kong. Therefore Hong Kong benefits greatly from the two-way flow as its trade related services face greater demand.

This has aided Hong Kong's position as a trading and logistics hub serving both mainland China and the rest of the world. This has also led to an increase in direct investment into China being channelled through Hong Kong because of its recognised financial management expertise. Further production expansion in China is to be expected together with further increases in demand for Hong Kong trade related services and financial management services.

However, Hong Kong could possibly face some challenging issues in the near future. Although Hong Kong is much more competitively placed than other Asian manufacturing sites, because if its long and extensive production history and sourcing activities in China, Hong Kong can expect to face greater competition from indigenous mainland Chinese manufacturers striving to boost their competitiveness due to China's WTO accession and hoping to have direct relations with buyers in western countries. China's WTO accession will also lead to an increase in the number of overseas companies seeking direct access to mainland Chinese manufacturers with the objective of lowering costs to an absolute minimum. However, multinationals must realise that even though China now has WTO accession and is in the process of making structural economic changes so as to fully comply with WTO requirements, companies in China do not yet have international experience and are not yet fully aware of international trading requirements.

Hong Kong has many decades of international trading experience and was one of the first WTO members. Its history of trade relations with the rest of the world has placed it firmly and recognisably at the top with regard to open markets, financial security, etc. Therefore at present it is much more advantageous for overseas multinationals to form partnership relations with Hong Kong companies in order to develop and exploit market opportunities in China as well as product sourcing and manufacture in China. Hong Kong companies have a distinct advantage in their knowledge of the China market and how organisations function in China as well as the cultural influence in social and business relations.

China's open door policy since 1978 coupled with global trade liberalisation has speeded up the development of industry in China. Now products from China are not just price competitive, but they are also improving in quality. This has led to an increasing number of multinationals from Europe, the USA, Japan, South Korea, Taiwan, etc. relocating more sophisticated production processes to China either by means of outsourcing or direct investment. This will continue to help Hong Kong exporters because of their expertise in quality control, inspection, certification, management, marketing and logistics support. It is expected that Hong Kong will continue to see growth in its re-exports as an increasing amount of product is exported from China through Hong Kong, but at the same time see a further decline in domestic exports as even more manufacturing is finally moved offshore. Nevertheless service exports will see growth in the coming years due to the structural economic changes that have taken place.

In recent years China has grown in importance as the world factory and between 1991 and 2001 it experienced a 34% increase in inbound foreign direct investment as well as a 14% increase in total exports. This is clearly indicative of economic growth that is of benefit not only to China, but also to Hong Kong and the region. China's WTO membership is leading to foreign investors in the country gaining a greater sense of security with regard to business with overseas markets. China's investment environment is improving greatly and a huge domestic market is developing in China. As a leading trading and logistics hub, Hong Kong serves mainland China as well as the world, and will definitely benefit greatly from the increasing international location of manufacturing and sourcing activities into mainland China.

Trade flows through Hong Kong are clearly expected to grow substantially due to the increased demand from China for capital goods and materials from the rest of the world as well as the increased export of finished products from China to the rest of the world. A large part of these trade flows into and out of China will be through Hong Kong giving rise to a substantial increase in demand for Hong Kong's trade services.

The increasing availability of parts, materials and productive capacity in China is a growing attraction for overseas manufacturers considering developing a presence in China. However, at this point in time Hong Kong does still command a recognised advantageous position with regard to trade in China and therefore in order to conduct business with China, many overseas companies still prefer to deal with Hong Kong trading companies. On the basis that Hong Kong has well established trading networks; a fair, impartial and internationally recognised judicial system; a world class telecommunications system and very efficient business support services, overseas companies naturally feel more secure and at ease conducting their China trade through Hong Kong companies.

Continued growth of the Chinese economy is very important to Hong Kong because of the opportunities that it offers. Export growth will be stimulated by the continuing relocation of export production and sourcing activities to mainland China in order to compete on a worldwide basis. China is now experiencing a strong growth in domestic demand for a wide range of products. Over the last two decades China's consumer market has experienced great changes due to economic reforms that have led to the increase in income and supply of goods. Spending patterns have changed with greater emphasis upon good quality consumer goods and services, communications and education. Coupled with the reduction in tariff rates, China's accession to the WTO will help Hong Kong's exports to mainland China. Liberalisation of China's trading and distribution sectors is having the effect of opening up a vast home market for Hong Kong manufacturers and trading companies.

The growth in consumption has led to an increased demand for various types of products. Fashion jewellery is expected to experience a good growth in demand in China. There is also expected to be a growth in demand for watches with fashionable designs in which Hong Kong companies excel. The removal of restrictions regarding domestic sales in China of product manufactured by Hong Kong manufacturers based in China presents such companies with a potentially vast market opportunity. However, such sales will not be reflected in Hong Kong's trade statistics because production will be at a Hong Kong owned factory located in China with the sales then taking place in China. In other words the final product will not have passed through Hong Kong. The only thing to have possibly passed through Hong Kong may have been imported materials and components on their way to China and the manufacturing process. There again possibly the materials would be sourced in China which would effectively make the whole process totally in China, but nevertheless under Hong Kong organisation and management.

This type of scenario can be expected to see rapid growth in the coming years as China makes economic structural changes in line with its WTO accession. Hong Kong will certainly benefit, but it will not be shown in Hong Kong's trade statistics.

Hong Kong exporters and manufacturers are renowned for supplying competitively priced quality merchandise in the form of garments, toys, electronics, timepieces, jewellery, household electrical appliances and stationery items. Much of the concept behind this production is value for money for the buyer with the encouragement to place larger orders for bigger production runs at lower unit costs due to economies of scale. Simple economics in action and very effectively employed to the advantage of both seller and buyer.

Hong Kong is still dominant in sea cargo in South East Asia, but is facing growing competition from mainland China. As China trade grows so will sea cargo competition from mainland Chinese ports. However, this is not the case with air cargo. Hong Kong's regional dominance of the air cargo sector is very secure. Hong Kong's Chek Lap Kok airport has a far greater network of international connections than any other airport in the region. This is increasingly important due to the global trend now being towards short product cycles and smaller order volumes with more frequent quicker deliveries thereby allowing companies further down the distribution chain to minimise stock holdings. This trend means that there is an increasing reliance on airfreight for delivery of exports. In 2001, US$44 billion of product was exported from Hong Kong by airfreight - equivalent to 1/4 of total export revenue. Both domestic exports and re-exports were despatched by airfreight and electronic products accounted for half of the exports by air in 2001.

The top four export markets accounting for over 50% of airfreight shipments in 2001 were South Korea, Taiwan, Singapore and Malaysia. These markets are important suppliers of electronic products to developed western markets. Hong Kong was primarily exporting components to these markets.

a) China's entry into the World Trade Organisation (WTO)

The Chinese mainland is now evolving into an enormous hinterland market for Hong Kong's goods and services as well as a tremendous resource for global trade. China is heading towards a transparent rule based trading and investment system, which will inevitably attract a definite increase in foreign multinational activity.

It took 15 years of protracted negotiations for China finally to be admitted to the World Trade Organisation in December 2001. The Chinese government is now in the process of implementing changes to its laws, regulations and administrative rules so as to comply with the terms of its accession to the WTO and WTO rules and principles. This will inevitably take time to fully achieve, but the end result will be a much more open and freely accountable China that will be economically more powerful and more integrated with the rest of the world.

China's joining of the WTO will have an effect on the Hong Kong economy because of the structural changes that will inevitably take place. This will inevitably mean that companies will have to review and possibly change their business strategies and objectives. The level of competition will definitely increase not only due to the increase in the number of overseas companies seeking to enter the market, but also due to the number of Chinese companies seeking to be active in the market. Therefore a more proactive business strategy and possibly a more aggressive sales strategy will be required.

China's laws, regulations, rules, directives, decrees, etc. regarding trade in goods and services as well as intellectual property rights aspects will all be under supervision of the WTO and compliance with WTO requirements will be essential and strictly monitored. Therefore the market in China is due to become more akin to that in western countries.

Hong Kong's pre-eminent role as the many gifted business hub linking China with the outside world will inevitably face challenges with the opening of China as overseas companies seek to go direct to China for business. However, as the richest city in China with the most international business experience and contacts and relations stretching around the world, together with a unique in depth knowledge of both China and the western world, Hong Kong as a world city has much to offer overseas multinational companies and Chinese companies seeking to develop business relations. It can be expected that competition will increase sharply from both foreign companies and Chinese companies. Trade flows are expected to be easier and volumes can be expected to increase as a result. Business opportunities will increase and the fact that China is now the hinterland for Hong Kong means that Hong Kong manufacturers can expand their production and freely sell their products in China. This will lead to yet another surge in demand for Hong Kong services including finance, transport, accounting, engineering, telecommunications, design, management consultancy, etc. China's market share in various sectors will also increase due to abolition of trade barriers.

Demand for logistics services is set to increase dramatically to cope with the new environment. China's expanding trade relations with the rest of the world together with its investment activities are set to benefit Hong Kong due to the demand for the city's services. Hong Kong is now in the process of developing more value added and focused services to meet the growing demand from China. The city's well developed skills in financial services, transportation, trading, business services, communications, etc. are set to play a more active role as China develops rather than a diminished role.

A recent Trade Development Council survey found that over 75% of overseas buyers preferred to obtain China made products through Hong Kong companies. This is no doubt due to the differences in culture and understanding of the different countries. However, due to its economic history Hong Kong is very familiar with both Western and Eastern cultures and therefore can serve as a means of linking the two. China's WTO accession will definitely lead to an increase in the number of multinational corporations (MNCs) located in the region and provided that Hong Kong can maintain and upgrade the quality of its services as well as contain the costs of doing business it will still remain attractive to MNCs.

Hong Kong's global characteristics are clearly demonstrated by the tremendous number of multinational corporations with regional headquarters or regional offices based in the city. Hong Kong's pre-eminent position as the regional international financial and trade centre will not be challenged for a number of years. The territory has currency convertibility, free flow of information and capital, an excellent legal framework, tested supervisory institutions, massive liquid capital markets and superb financial services. As such demand for Hong Kong's services is set to increase in line with the increase in trade with China.

WTO membership for China means that it will have full access to markets in other WTO member countries without discrimination. It has been reported that average import tariffs in China were scheduled to decline from 14.8% to 8.9% by 2005 and that trading and distribution rights for foreign companies will be phased in slowly. Foreign investment restrictions will be relaxed enabling overseas multinationals to invest in distribution services, telecommunications, financial services, business services, tourism, etc.

Hong Kong will face major structural changes in its relations with China due to China's WTO accession because of its effect on market terms and conditions and the inevitable liberalisation that will surely follow. The benefits of China's WTO accession will affect all market sectors with long term implications. China is set to become an integral part of the global economy as production and distribution becomes increasingly globalised. Hong Kong's position as a regional hub for overseas companies seeking to enter the mainland Chinese market as well as Chinese companies seeking to use Hong Kong in order to go global is set to continue to develop strongly because of the developing trade patterns. This means that Hong Kong will move further towards a state of providing higher value-added services so as to maintain its pre-eminent position.

Due to actions during the 1980s and 1990s, China has evolved into a very competitive manufacturing base for many consumer goods and now accounts for many types of consumer goods sold around the world. Industries in China are set to benefit from China's WTO accession because of the rules based system and environment for business. The services industries are set to see an increase in competition due to liberalisation. Trade and investment barriers are being dismantled as China complies with WTO requirements and foreign direct investment is set to boom. One of China's main advantages is that it is a competitive production base for product sold both locally in China and overseas.

Accession to the WTO is leading to the removal of tariff and non-tariff protection which in time will result in Chinese domestic industries and products being more competitive due to the importation of advanced machinery and production inputs being at a lower cost.

Domestic industries are expected to experience an increase in the number of strategic alliances between foreign investors and Chinese companies due to the increased flow of foreign capital. China is also reviewing its legal and administrative structures to ensure compliance with stipulated WTO rules and principles. The WTO will be regularly reviewing such compliance of all its members including China. In January 2001 the WTO listed 116 laws and regulations that needed to be revised together with 573 that needed to be repealed. By September 2001 40% had been dealt with and the matter was progressing smoothly. Future changes in China's legal system for trade and investment will follow WTO protocol. The rule of law is becoming much more important in China as a direct result of WTO accession and adherence to its rules and regulations.

The Ministry of Foreign Trade and Economic Cooperation (MOFTEC) is primarily responsible for overseeing the implementation of WTO rules and regulations in international trade. The China-WTO Notification Enquiry Centre has been established under the auspices of MOFTEC with the objective of answering enquires regarding China's WTO agreement together with all enquires relating to relevant WTO laws and regulations. Also under MOFTEC, the Department of WTO Affairs is responsible for regular negotiations conducted within the WTO organisational framework as well as China's relationship with the WTO organisational structure.

The Fair Trade Bureau for Import and Export which is also under the auspices of MOFTEC works on matters regarding anti-dumping, anti-subsidy and protective measures as well as coordinating China's response to foreign anti-dumping accusations. The effective working and coordination of these organisations demonstrates that China is clearly moving towards a rule of law situation with regard to international trade, which is something to be greatly welcomed by the world community. It also helps China's further integration into the global community. Hong Kong will benefit greatly from these developments and companies must therefore review and mould their business and investment strategies accordingly so as to maximise their profit potential.

Hong Kong's transport and logistics cluster has developed over a number of years with a very strong competitive edge. The city's strategic location and extensive transport connections with China and the rest of the world together with its high efficiency and professional character in conducting trade relations has made this a very powerful cluster. In 2001 approximately 40% of China's imports and exports passed through Hong Kong. Many trading companies in Hong

Kong act as agents for the sale of foreign company exports into China. In 2001 approximately half of the multinational companies with regional headquarters or regional offices in Hong Kong were in the distribution trade sector with over 90% of these companies distributing product into China as well as other South East Asian countries.

Many importers in overseas markets still import Chinese product through Hong Kong trading companies. There is thus a two way flow of product, services and interests with Hong Kong clearly in the centre providing an almost specialist matching and coordinating function. However, China's entry into the WTO means that an increasing number of mainland Chinese companies will be developing a knowledge and understanding of WTO rules and regulations, and will be better able to conform to international trade practices. This will inevitably lead to a growth in direct relations between China and the rest of the world. Therefore Hong Kong's role as a trading hub will face pressure that will lead to changes in how Hong Kong provides the sort of services to satisfy the needs of both China and the rest of the world in an open and fair trading system on a globalised basis.

Hong Kong's sophisticated and diverse infrastructure and trade supporting services together with its intimate and extensive knowledge and connections with southern China will help to maintain Hong Kong's position as the pre-eminent trading hub in the region. Also as China reduces its barriers in order to comply with WTO accession requirements there will be an increase in the number of companies seeking to develop relations with China and this will inevitably lead to an increase in the number of companies seeking to rely on the services provided by Hong Kong companies. With the Chinese market now increasingly open to international trade more and more overseas companies are seeking trade opportunities with China. However, many companies, particularly the smaller companies, prefer to operate through Hong Kong trading companies. There are a number of reasons for this preference including:

- Hong Kong's well established legal system,
- the territory's knowledge and experience in China trade,
- its cultural affinity with China,
- its knowledge and experience in risk management,
- its ability in supply chain management, and
- its extensive knowledge and sourcing capability in China, etc.

Hong Kong: The World City and International Business Centre

It should also be remembered that at this point in time due to the histories of Hong Kong and China, Hong Kong companies are more professional than their mainland Chinese counterparts regarding international trade, business and distribution services.

However, when overseas buyers are not reliant on Hong Kong manufacturers as a sourcing base, there will be an increased probability that these overseas buyers may seek to go direct to China. Nevertheless recent survey information has indicated that 95% of Hong Kong based buying offices and purchasing agents source China made product from Hong Kong manufacturers. Hong Kong's sourcing role is also expected to be boosted by the anticipated growth in exports as a result of China's WTO accession.

Recent survey data has indicated that 90% of overseas importers regard Hong Kong trading companies and manufacturers as excellent when complying with required product specifications, 80% regard them as excellent regarding on time delivery and 77% consider the quality of services that Hong Kong companies provide as being much better than that provided by mainland Chinese companies. This re-affirms Hong Kong's pre-eminent position as the prime trading hub in South East Asia, the ideal location for foreign multinational regional headquarters or regional offices and a very experienced competitive business partner. Hong Kong as the World City in South East Asia is moving towards being a global integrator in international trade.

China's accession to the WTO and the further opening up of its economy will provide a wonderful environment for the economic growth of Hong Kong. Hong Kong's role as a hub will be boosted by the expansion and growth in China's trade and investment operations with the rest of the world. Hong Kong's extensive services sector including financial services, professional and business services, communications, transportation, trading, etc. will play a very important part in this expansion of the China trade.

Multinational companies with regional headquarters or offices in Hong Kong will find their positions strengthened as trade inevitably expands and China integrates more into the global economy. Nevertheless the competitive strength of Hong Kong is not just for exploitation by overseas multinationals, an increasing number of mainland Chinese companies are also seeking to exploit the strengths of Hong Kong as a means to the global market. Chinese companies have for some time now seen Hong Kong as the springboard to global activities, because of its capital raising capabilities, its management expertise and its renowned market intelligence and this can be expected to continue to grow in the future as China's WTO membership develops.

As a direct result of China's accession to the WTO it can be expected that in the coming years, Hong Kong will experience fundamental changes in its position as a trading hub for China. However, an important point to be considered is how Hong Kong will develop in order to meet the demands of China and the rest of the world as China continues to open up its economy to trade and develops an enhanced position in global manufacturing and distribution networks. This is inevitably going to affect the service provision by Hong Kong companies. Nevertheless its role as a trading hub will be reinforced by Guangdong as a manufacturing base together with its sophisticated infrastructures and trade supporting services. As a result of the continued expansion in the Chinese economy, more overseas multinationals will be attracted to the region in search of market opportunities in China and many of them will rely on the range of services provided by Hong Kong companies.

Hong Kong has not only the busiest container port in the world, it also has the busiest international air cargo terminal in the world. Hong Kong has the best location, infrastructure, expertise and services capability to meet even the strictest supply chain requirements. Its communications networks and advanced information technology systems have allowed Hong Kong to quickly develop e-logistics. Due to its location, Hong Kong dominates the regional air route networks with more flights than any other city in the region. Its air cargo handling and support services make it an ideal air cargo terminal and adds to Hong Kong's competitiveness. Further business developments and expansion in China as a result of WTO accession will lead to a growth in demand for air cargo services in Hong Kong.

Hong Kong's reputation has been built on a number of factors including its policies on the free flow of capital and information, its convertible currency, its well established impartial legal system and regulatory norms, and also its very effective and fair prudential supervision of its dynamic financial institutions. On this basis Hong Kong has emerged as a leading financial centre in Asia enjoying world ranking for its activities in banking transactions, foreign exchange trading, venture capital, stock market activities, loan syndication, insurance and fund management. Hong Kong's financial services environment is rated as excellent.

Hong Kong and Shanghai's financial markets are at present very different. The Renminbi is not yet freely convertible in international foreign exchanges and therefore Shanghai does not have the institutional and commercial setups yet to integrate properly with world markets like Hong Kong does when conducting international financial business. Hong Kong is a regional centre for Asia whereas Shanghai at present is not. Hong Kong also acts as a conduit for foreign capital flows into China. Hong Kong is also a very important centre for mainland Chinese companies seeking to raise funds for international activities.

Hong Kong's main manufacturing area is now Guangdong province and the Pearl River Delta. However, it is China's intention to re-develop the Yangtze River Delta and Shanghai. Some would argue that this poses a serious threat to

Hong Kong, particularly with the structural changes that will take place in China's economy as a result of WTO accession. However, it must be accepted that a country the size of China can very easily cope with more than one financial centre and some would argue that a country the size of China actually needs more than one financial centre. Therefore there is now a real prospect that within the next 10 to 15 years Hong Kong will be the financial centre in the south of the country whilst Shanghai will be the financial centre in the east of the country. Both of these centres will have their own developed stock exchanges, similar legal systems and will represent two different points of entry for foreign capital investment. The particular point of usage of foreign investment within the country will determine the mode of entry and the point of entry.

According to a mid-1998 survey reported by the Hong Kong Trade Development Council, managers of multinationals working in both Hong Kong and Shanghai have consistently rated Hong Kong as a more superior environment than Shanghai. It has been suggested that with China's accession to the WTO and the development of Shanghai, that more multinational corporations will seek to locate their regional headquarters or offices in Shanghai, but surveys of business attitudes when comparing Hong Kong and Shanghai have shown that there is a clear preference for Hong Kong. On points such as centrality to important markets, financial services, transportation infrastructure, communications infrastructure, rule of law, government economic policy, quality of local managers, quality of life, support and supply industries, political cleanliness, and technological environment, Hong Kong is considered to be much better than Shanghai. It is only on the costs of conducting business that Shanghai has the edge over Hong Kong.

Both Hong Kong and Shanghai are based in independent economic regions. Hong Kong has the Pearl River Delta and Shanghai has the Yangtze River Delta. However, at present with regard to overseas multinationals seeking to establish a regional base, it essentially means that if one city is chosen, it is considered to be a loss for the other city. Nevertheless the Chinese government is intent on developing Shanghai as a regional financial and trade centre and at the same time maintaining Hong Kong as a regional financial and trade centre. This is perfectly logical because a country as enormous as China can easily accommodate two financial and trade centres. In future, multinationals will choose between these centres based on their corporate objectives and the best means of achieving those objectives. The future for both cities looks bright.

Hong Kong has more multinationals with regional headquarters than any other city in Asia because its location and business services are unrivalled. Hong Kong offers many advantages due to its communications network and infrastructure. The majority of these regional headquarters are not just covering Hong Kong and China, but also South East Asia.

The number and scale of smaller size multinational companies is increasing quite quickly and their line of business tends to be more focused. Due to their size these multinationals outsource more activities and rely more heavily on the support services and business infrastructure in the locations where they are based. Hong Kong is therefore an ideal environment for this type of multinational because Hong Kong is on the doorstep of the Chinese mainland and offers a complete range of business services. Many of these smaller multinationals operate on a very well coordinated basis with offices in various locations and activities contracted out to various organisations in various localities and therefore the communications infrastructure is critically important. These newer structures are a move away from the traditional command and control centre structures of the past. Nevertheless Hong Kong companies although developing deeper roots and connections with mainland Chinese companies, are inextricably linked with western companies thereby ensuring that Hong Kong remains a global hub.

Also as China becomes more integrated into the world economy and more Chinese companies attempt to globalise, Hong Kong will grow in importance as the preferred location for these newly globalised Chinese companies conducting regional operations. This is already happening as by mid 2000 there were already 229 Chinese companies using Hong Kong as a location for their regional headquarters and regional offices.

China's accession to the WTO provides a greater level of security for Hong Kong manufacturers in China because of the improving regulatory structure of the environment and as such provides a greater level of security for existing investment as well as improved opportunities for new investment in China. Foreign investors will be treated the same as local domestic investors. WTO membership also gives China more secure access to many other overseas markets of countries that are WTO members because of the reduction or elimination of trade barriers and restrictions in accordance with WTO requirements. China is in the process of changing its trade and investment structures so that they are in full agreement with WTO requirements in many areas such as customs valuation, intellectual property rights, rules of origin, technical barriers to trade, import licensing, pre-shipment inspections, etc.

Hong Kong has invested greatly in the manufacturing and export industry in China over the last 25 years. The export platforms that Hong Kong has built up in China over these last 25 years will benefit greatly from China's WTO membership, because it will mean that the country will have more secure access to markets overseas in other WTO countries, the country's investment environment will be improved and there will be a wide open domestic market.

It is expected that China's WTO accession will lead to a growth in the level of competition within the country as more companies including Hong Kong and overseas multinationals move into the distribution sector. The distribution sector is set to become a very active sector as an increasing number of companies place a greater emphasis upon the scale of distribution for their products so as to develop their brandnames in the general market. Regional as well as national giant players will emerge soon. Hong Kong manufacturers with operations already in China will be able to expand their operations vertically in the supply chain by moving into wholesaling and retailing.

These companies will have an advantage over newcomers in the form of closeness to the market, established transportation and communications networks and proven logistics. China is no longer a closed market for sellers, but has become an open market for buyers. Product or service price cannot be the only means of strategic competition otherwise the company will fail. Instead market strategies need to be broadened to establish strong and lasting positions. Companies have to compete on the basis of distribution, brandname awareness and reliability, product mixes, sales promotions, technical proficiency, public relations, product uniqueness, etc. Competition on non-price business aspects is expected to become more intense in the very near future.

China is now a vast and diverse market with many potential business opportunities, but companies need to assess very carefully how they can most profitably take advantage of those business opportunities in the most efficient and productive manner possible. It has been considered by some that distribution channels should be kept short and as wide as possible with the development of local partnerships being particularly important so that market environments and customers can be researched deeply and properly. The objective of this approach is to facilitate the effective development of distribution networks in the most profitable and lasting manner. Short distribution channels enable retail prices to be kept low and margins to be good, whereas long distribution channels tend to raise retail prices and squeeze margins.

Companies should also consider the possibility of partnership arrangements as a means of market entry and development where the local partner has full market access and complete thorough knowledge of the market and its characteristics and the overseas partner has the financial, technical and product or service required by the market. Such a partnership when performed carefully in a coordinated manner can lead to a successful and quick market entry that is profitable and lasting.

Companies should be aware of the development of niche market opportunities which in China are likely to be quite large. Hong Kong companies generally excel at this type of market activity.

China planned to eliminate import tariffs on toys by 2005. As the distribution sector for toys opens up it can be expected that large retail chains will enter the market quickly. Major names like Wal-Mart and Toys 'R' Us will expand further into this potentially vast market. However, Hong Kong's toy companies will still be more familiar with the sourcing and distribution structures in the market than overseas companies. Nevertheless, Hong Kong companies will face competition not just from overseas multinationals, but also from local Chinese companies.

It should be noted that overseas patents must be registered again in China with the relevant Chinese authorities for the patents to be enforceable in China. Therefore multinationals concerned about patent rights must investigate this aspect so as to ensure the safety of their intellectual property.

Since 1980 China has developed into a formidable manufacturing base supplying product worldwide. In 2000 the World Bank estimated that China accounted for a quarter of all toys, a third of all suitcases and handbags, and an eighth of all footwear sold in the world. However, the development of its producer services sectors such as trading, banking and finance, professional and business services, logistics and telecommunications has been somewhat more restrained. This presents considerable opportunities for Hong Kong's services sector due to it being the most services oriented economy in the world and a regional leader in many service industries.

As the leading services centre in the region, Hong Kong excels in its provision of services and is fully capable of providing a package of services to meet any business requirements. China's entry into the WTO has led to many market opportunities in the services sector for both Hong Kong and foreign companies. It has been considered by some that the opening of China's services sector may lead to the next wave of Hong Kong investment into China in a similar manner as to the investment in manufacturing that happened when China opened it's doors in 1978.

Prior to WTO accession China's wholesale and retail distribution systems were classified as underdeveloped. However, changes take time and it was expected to be between 2005-2006 that these distribution systems would be brought into full compliance with WTO requirements, and therefore at such a level that overseas multinationals would be able to use them properly for the distribution and sale of their products. Different sized multinationals will target different market segments based on their corporate strategies and market philosophy.

It is expected that big international retail companies such as Wal-Mart from the USA may decide to concentrate on large cities and counties capable of providing the necessary market demand for such a large retail store, whereas Hong Kong retailers may decide to concentrate on localised residential areas providing a lower level of market demand that would not be sufficient for the large retail stores. In that way Hong Kong retailers avoid major competition from large players. International trading companies like many found in Hong Kong have the necessary expertise to control efficient distribution systems as will be required in the Chinese retail market and therefore substantial business opportunities are available.

Changes regarding the level of ownership in business dealings are also set to take place with foreign owned subsidiaries being allowed by 2005-2006. It is expected that the value of China's external trade will rise considerably soon leading to an increased demand for quality services in the distribution sector as well as in the logistics industry. Hong Kong has expanded noticeably into the freight forwarding and logistics services sectors in China in line with the increased level of trade. At present these services are geared to the international market, but will in due course also incorporate the domestic market. Hong Kong companies are currently ahead of foreign companies and have substantial market knowledge, information technology development and investment in China, and are therefore good partners for foreign companies seeking market entry. Companies must carefully consider the most appropriate strategy to employ and whether diversification or concentration or something in between would be the most appropriate for this market.

Due to Hong Kong's advanced telecom sector, information technology infrastructure and bilingual capability, many Hong Kong companies are ideally positioned to play an important role in the development of China's Internet sector. Hong Kong investors have a clear long term interest in China's Internet-related business even though the market conditions are generally very tough. In the telecommunications sector Hong Kong players are active in the global market, particularly in Asia, and are ready to develop the China market. A mobile telecommunications world leader like Hutchison Telecom would be an ideal partner for voice, data and m-commerce services. Hong Kong has valuable experience in broadband technology. Broadband services integrate telecommunications, interactive multimedia services, broadcasting and Internet-related services. This technology and experience is regarded as a valuable asset for developing the market in China.

China's accession to the WTO means that its financial markets will be opened presenting Hong Kong financial institutions with good investment opportunities in the short and medium term. However, long term prospects indicate an increased level of competition from global financial giants. China's WTO accession also means that Hong Kong banks as well as foreign banks can now start meaningful operations in the country with business in Renminbi local currency. Therefore competition is set to intensify. It is expected that foreign banks are more likely to work with foreign companies and will most likely concentrate on trade financing, foreign exchange, syndicated loans, settlements and capital movements for large multinational corporations as well as sizeable Chinese enterprises. Hong Kong banks will have a greater level of country expertise due to Hong Kong being a part of China and will be in a better position to deal with smaller sized companies requiring bank facilities.

It was predicted by International Data Corp. that the revenue from e-commerce in China would increase from US$43 million in 1998 to more than US$11 billion in 2004. It was also expected that most of the revenue would come from business-to-business e-commerce transactions.

China's insurance market in recent years has experienced tremendous growth at an average annual rate of more than 20% making it one of the fastest growing insurance markets in the world. Many analysts regard this growth rate as being sustainable in the short term with good business opportunities for insurers. Reform of the social security system in China is also seen as offering potential opportunities to insurers. Therefore this market sector offers tremendous business opportunity that will definitely appeal to multinationals particularly with the growth potential being so positive. In conjunction with China's obvious growth in insurance requirements, the Mandatory Provident Fund in Hong Kong has led to a number of foreign insurers strengthening their regional operations with Hong Kong being the regional insurance centre.

Companies such as the ING Group, Axa and Swiss Re have made Hong Kong their regional headquarters. The market has recently developed a two way flow position with mainland Chinese financial institutions using Hong Kong as the gateway to the rest of the world and overseas financial institutions using Hong Kong as the gateway to China. Therefore Hong Kong gains in both instances. Hong Kong has one of the largest number of reinsurers in the region backed up by sophisticated capital markets and many fund managers.

China's securities and investment fund sectors are developing rapidly and an increasing number of Chinese companies are seeking to list in Hong Kong so as to have access to overseas funds which means more business for Hong Kong. Chinese companies in Hong Kong are now an important force contributing substantially to the economy's strength. Hong Kong Stock Exchange statistics revealed that in early 2006 there were 211 mainland Chinese companies listed on the Hong Kong Stock Exchange. The total market value of these mainland Chinese companies was HK$3.36 trillion which represented approximately 38% of the total market value in Hong Kong.

Hong Kong is well recognised as the leading fund management centre in Asia and is therefore expected to have a very important role in the development of China's fund industry. Major Hong Kong based companies such as HSBC, Jardine

Fleming, Schroders, Manulife and American International Group to name but a few already have Chinese partners for joint venture investment fund management activities. Investment bankers in Hong Kong are ready for the increased demand for their services, which will inevitably flow due to China's accession to the WTO.

China is taking measures to upgrade and improve its domestic road networks in order to raise the competitiveness of the economy due to the anticipated increase in demand from the transport, distribution and logistics industries. Hong Kong companies have developed a reputation as service integrators and are major investors in China's road networks and property development projects. China's accession to the WTO presents further growth opportunities for investors and developers and will give rise to increased demand for a range of services including engineering services, architectural services, property services as well as planning and specialist consultancy services. This represents a major growth market and therefore an ideal opportunity for multinationals either to set up a regional office to work in the relevant sectors or else form a partnership with a Hong Kong company in order to operate in the relevant sectors.

One of the largest advertising markets in Asia is China. Many international advertising agencies have established their regional headquarters in Hong Kong due to its central location in Asia and well developed services and facilities. When China gained accession to the WTO it was agreed that two years after accession joint-venture advertising agencies could be majority foreign owned. It was also agreed that four years after accession there could be wholly owned subsidiaries. In other words 2003 and 2005 respectively. The top 10 advertised products in China in 2001 were all Chinese brands and local brands sell much better than foreign brands in many consumer product categories. Therefore multinationals must consider carefully how to develop a local brand that will sell on a national basis rather than impose a foreign brand on the market because people may very well react negatively to what will be regarded as a foreign and alien brand.

People prefer to buy what they consider to be their native product rather than the imported product of another land. Kong Wah Holdings Ltd., an audio, video and telecommunications manufacturer from Hong Kong, have developed their own brandname 'Konka' for products to be sold in China with considerable success. It has often been a marketing strategy of companies in their own countries to promote nationalism in their marketing campaigns so as to bolster their own native products and production.

For example, the 'Buy British' campaign in Britain together with the included image of the national flag in the product packaging was a form of nationalistic sales aimed at drawing consumers away from imported product. Linguistically it was a simple use of effective alliteration in order to jog people's memories when shopping and encourage a sense of patriotic nationalism.

Hong Kong has a well developed advertising industry with a wide range of professional capability in producer services, graphic design, creative advertising and production. As a result many international agencies based in mainland China rely on the services support of Hong Kong companies. China's WTO accession is definitely leading to a growth in demand for advertising services and all that this entails in the way of design and production. The growth rate in the advertising sector is considerable and due to China's WTO accession it is expected to continue at such a high growth rate. Likewise the market research industry is also experiencing a tremendous growth rate with it being reported in 1999 as 50% per annum.

As a leading design centre in the Asia Pacific region Hong Kong is ideally positioned to help companies in the promotion of their products and services throughout the region. The support services such as output centres, post production houses and printers that Hong Kong designers are able to call upon are excellent and highly regarded throughout the world. Hong Kong offers very advanced computer aided design facilities of a world class standard. The design industry has experienced considerable growth recently with an increasing number of Chinese companies seeking to use Hong Kong designers so as to ensure that their product presentations are more acceptable to foreign markets. This aspect can be expected to experience further growth as competition intensifies due to China's WTO accession. A particularly strong advantage for Hong Kong designers is their capability of integrating Chinese culture and Western style into their designs and this no doubt comes as a result of the different cultural influences the city has experienced both during its colonial days as well as during its development into a very cosmopolitan city.

A large number of business services companies and many types of professionals are to be found in Hong Kong, and together they have helped to build Hong Kong into a major successful services centre and the most services oriented economy in the world. It is forecast that the demand for Hong Kong's services will rise as China integrates more into the world economy. Hong Kong will benefit greatly as a result of its strong cluster of professional services companies and its extensive and unequalled knowledge and experience of business in China. Nevertheless, the number of business opportunities in China will of course vary between the different sectors.

Overseas multinationals will also be able to benefit from this growth situation in conjunction with Hong Kong companies. Law firms will see growth spurred by the expansion in investment activities and the need for legal interpretations. Hong Kong is effectively at a crossroads point with an increasing number of Chinese companies seeking to go global through Hong Kong and an increasing number of foreign companies seeking to enter China through Hong Kong. This translates into an increased demand for accounting, legal and related professional services in Hong Kong. The management consultancy sector will also benefit greatly from China's WTO accession.

In 2000 China was the fifth most popular tourist destination and according to the World Tourism Organisation by the year 2020, China is expected to be the most popular tourist destination. In 2000 China had 31 million foreign visitors, and in 2020 it is projected to receive 130 million foreign visitors. At the same time Hong Kong is projected to see its number of foreign visitors rise from 13 million in 2000 to 57 million in 2020. These projections show that the tourism market is expected to see substantial growth and with it a substantial rise in income from tourists. Many visitors to Hong Kong now also visit China as an add-on feature in their tours. Hong Kong has an extensive wealth of experience in the tourism sector and many of its hotel management companies are active in the China market giving Hong Kong a very competitive edge in China.

Hong Kong is therefore set to benefit greatly from the projected expansion in China's tourism industry. Also, the opening of Hong Kong Disneyland in 2005 was expected to cause a surge in the number of tourists to Hong Kong and China. It was expected that 3.4 million overseas tourists would have visited Hong Kong Disneyland during its first year of operation and that this figure will increase to 7.3 million by its 15th year of operation. It will also lead to an increase in the number of tourists from China to Hong Kong.

Hong Kong is currently experiencing a surge in the number of visitors from mainland China. The quota system for mainland visitors has been abolished and visa limitations have been relaxed so there has been a sharp rise in both business travellers and tourists from China visiting Hong Kong. In the first 10 months of 2002 there were 2 million tourists visiting Hong Kong, 1.8 million came from China. This represents a good rise in spending within the tourism sector and is expected to continue. Two Hong Kong travel agents, Hong Thai and Wing On, have been allowed to take part in mainland China joint-venture travel agencies and further developments along this line of business are expected in the future. Deflation in Hong Kong has helped this sector prosper. Over 80% of tourists visiting Hong Kong are from Asia.

Between 1990 and 2000 Hong Kong experienced an annual average growth rate of 7.1% in the number of visitors to the territory. In 2000 there were 13.1 million visitors. China was the main source of visitors followed by Taiwan in 2000.

Market conditions are changing as a direct result of China's accession to the WTO. The Chinese market is now clearly in the process of opening up to international trade. It was agreed at the time of China's accession that all quotas would be eliminated within five years. By January 2005 all restrictions regarding geographic location and clients were supposed to have been removed. It was also agreed that foreign banks would be free to conduct foreign currency transactions with local companies and individuals.

China will continue to reform the state of its economy by removing trade and investment barriers so as to fully comply with all WTO requirements. This process is expected to take a number of years, but good progress is being made. These changes are also expected to have an important effect on the structural transformation of the economy in Hong Kong. It was estimated that due to China's WTO accession, trade between Hong Kong and the mainland would increase by between four and six percent by 2005.

The average tariff on industrial products was scheduled to be lowered from 17% to 9.4% by 2005. The average tariff on agricultural products was scheduled to be lowered from 22% to 17% by 2004. Foreign investment restrictions on distribution services, audio-visual and tourism will be relaxed to enable greater international participation. China will fully participate in the WTO Information Technology Agreement. Majority foreign-owned and wholly foreign-owned hotels in China will now be possible due to WTO accession. Three years after WTO accession both local and foreign companies will be free to import most types of products into all of China.

Foreign companies will be able to participate in many types of distribution services over what is projected to be a phase-in period of three years commencing from the date of WTO accession. Liberalisation of market access for most service industries will be phased-in over a period of six years commencing from the date of accession.

WTO accession also means that intellectual property rights will be protected due to full implementation of the Agreement on Trade-Related Intellectual Property Rights (TRIPS Agreement) and this will be legally guaranteed. China's Patent Law as well as Copyright and Trademark Laws have also been amended to comply with WTO requirements.

Hong Kong: The World City and International Business Centre

17. Investment Flows

Hong Kong is unique in that it does not offer financial incentives to induce companies to locate in Hong Kong. Many cities that do offer incentives have seen how MNCs have accepted the incentive, whatever it may be, and when the incentive has been used up the MNC moves on to the next city prepared to tempt it with a financial incentive. Many European and American cities have used incentives in order to reduce unemployment, Hong Kong does not. Hong Kong's primary incentive is its business environment and all that this entails. Hong Kong has shown the world that financial incentives are not a necessary part of place marketing. Nevertheless under place marketing activities cities are sold as different things to different audiences.

As a highly externally oriented economy, Hong Kong has developed into a very important regional business centre accounting for a substantial volume of cross-boundary investment. As such inward and outward direct investment is very important. Direct investment comprises equity capital, reinvested earnings and other capital. In 2004 foreign direct investment into Hong Kong was US$34 billion which was the second highest in Asia and seventh in the world. In 2005 this figure increased to US$35.9 billion. This investment was in a variety of business sectors including transportation, logistics, financial services, information technology, tourism, business and professional services, trade related services and entertainment.

In 2001 Hong Kong's largest source of inward direct investment (DI) was China with 29.3% and the second most important source was the British Virgin Islands (BVI) with 28.9%. The main recipients of outward direct investment from Hong Kong in 2001 were China and the British Virgin Islands. The close economic links between Hong Kong and China account for a substantial amount of the cross boundary investment made by Hong Kong. The investment flow is of course two ways because China is also investing in the territory. Hong Kong's external direct investment (DI) statistics show that the British Virgin Islands and Bermuda are important offshore financial centres for Hong Kong funds. This is due to Hong Kong companies establishing non-operating companies in those territories in order to channel DI funds through those centres back to Hong Kong or to other places. Foreign companies also use these centres to channel funds to Hong Kong.

The most important suppliers of inward direct investment in 2001 were China, the British Virgin Islands, the USA and Singapore. The major recipients of inward direct investment were investment holdings; real estate; various business services, wholesale, retail and import/export trades; banks and deposit taking companies; and the communications sector. A significant amount of this inward direct investment were funds originally from Hong Kong that were being indirectly channelled through these offshore financial centres on the way back to Hong Kong.

Offshore financial centres accounted for 60% of the total outward direct investment from Hong Kong. The British Virgin Islands was the most popular offshore financial centre for indirect channelling of direct investment funds. 80% of outward direct investment from Hong Kong was related to equity capital with the rest comprising loans and trade credits. China received 30.7% (or HK$844 billion) of Hong Kong's outward direct investment in 2001 of which Guangdong received 48.1% (or HK$405.7 billion).

The British Virgin Islands was the main source of direct investment income inflow to Hong Kong whilst China was the second most important source of DI income inflow. The main outward direct investment economic activities in 2001 were investment holding, real estate and various business services accounting for 62.5% of outward DI; wholesale, retail and import/export trades accounting for 9.8%; manufacturing accounting for 5.3% and the communications sector accounting for 3.5%. The main inward direct investment economic activities in 2001 were investment holding, real estate and various business services accounting for 32.6% of inward DI; banks and deposit taking companies accounting for 23.1% and the communications sector accounting for 20%. China is an important destination for Hong Kong outward direct investment. In 2001 Hong Kong's direct investment in China covered a wide range of business activities with the communications sector accounting for 37.2%, manufacturing 26% and investment holding, real estate and various business services 25.1%.

The overall investment environment in Hong Kong is generally regarded as very favourable. Companies have stated that the banking and financial services in Hong Kong, the tax regime, currency stability, rule of law and telecommunications services are all very positive factors with regard to investment flows. Multinational companies and organisations when considering investing in Hong Kong or moving investment funds to Hong Kong will find that the environment and services for dealing with their investment funds are far better than in many other locations and as such the money can be employed much more efficiently and productively.

In 2001 it was reported that approximately half of Hong Kong's outward DI goes to companies based in offshore financial centres such as in the Cayman Islands, Bermuda and the British Virgin Islands. However, these funds are not used in these offshore financial centres, but are instead channelled to places such as China and other developing countries. A substantial amount of these funds even go back to Hong Kong. Hong Kong companies are conducting these activities for strategic reasons.

18. Integration of Hong Kong and China

Since China opened its doors in 1978, Hong Kong and China have grown together. A very strong partnership now exists as the economies of the two locations are inextricably linked. China is the production base whilst Hong Kong is the highly proficient service base. China excels in manufacturing and production whilst Hong Kong excels in financial, transportation, business, logistics and high value-added services. The combination of the two locations and all their advantages presents a very attractive broad based business environment that is ideal for multinationals. In 2004:

- approximately 30 per cent of China's export trade was via Hong Kong,
- approximately 43 per cent of Hong Kong's foreign trade was with China,
- the main source of inward direct investment into China was from Hong Kong,
- China was the main source of direct investment into Hong Kong (excluding tax haven economies),
- Hong Kong companies with manufacturing facilities in Guangdong province employed over 5 million workers,
- in Hong Kong approximately one million workers were employed in services related to manufacturing operations in China.

According to a Hong Kong Trade Development Council report in September 2004, Hong Kong is a World City and also a leading commercial and financial centre in Asia. The strong economic and commercial links between Hong Kong and China have enabled a growing number of mainland Chinese companies to establish representative offices or regional headquarters in Hong Kong. This has enabled many Chinese companies to expand their global operations by using Hong Kong as a platform because of its well established international trade links and financial services. It has also enhanced Hong Kong's position and competitiveness as a location for regional headquarters or regional offices. An increasing number of Chinese companies are seeking to establish global operations by using Hong

Kong. Hong Kong is also a very important gateway to the Chinese market due to the well established China trade and investment services in the territory.

Under a ruling on 31st August 2004, the Chinese authorities in the form of the Ministry of Commerce (MOFCOM) and the State Council's Hong Kong and Macau Affairs Office have made it a great deal easier for mainland Chinese enterprises to establish offices in Hong Kong. China is encouraging such investment in a wide range of business activity because of the benefits that it will produce not just for China, but also for the region in general. It has also helped highlight Hong Kong's economic competitiveness and attraction as a regional location for corporate offices as well as its position as an international commercial and financial business centre. The now open Chinese market is another good reason for Hong Kong so often being chosen as a regional location by both Chinese and overseas companies.

Many mainland Chinese companies see distinct advantages in Hong Kong in the form of the many foreign chambers of commerce and multinational corporation headquarters and offices in the city making liaisons particularly appropriate. The comprehensive range of trade related services and the free flow of extensive market information regarding potential markets, consumer demands and consumption trends facilitates product development and marketing aspirations. Hong Kong's position as the trade fair capital of Asia facilitates meetings with overseas buyers and the extensive number of overseas buying offices in Hong Kong makes trade negotiations much easier. The increasing number of mainland Chinese companies establishing headquarters in Hong Kong for global operations is automatically helping Hong Kong upgrade from a regional base for headquarters to a global base for headquarters.

The increasing number of mainland Chinese companies and overseas multinational corporations investing and establishing themselves in Hong Kong is enhancing the development of clusters within the Hong Kong economy which in turn enhances its competitiveness and attraction as a regional base.

At present Hong Kong:

- ☐ has the greatest concentration of fund managers in Asia,

- ☐ has the largest and most developed venture capital market in Asia,

- ☐ has a stock market that is Asia's second largest and the world's eighth largest,

- ☐ has an insurance market that is the second most developed in Asia,

- [ ] has a loan syndication centre that is the second largest in Asia,
- [ ] has the third largest banking centre in the world, and
- [ ] has a foreign exchange market that is the seventh largest in the world.

As the 11th largest trading entity in 2003, Hong Kong's external trade amounted to US$223.4 billion with over 50% of it being of Chinese origin. Approximately 88% of Hong Kong's GDP is due to services, with 33% of this being import-export and trade related services.

Hong Kong's position as a regional hub for transportation and warehousing services can be expected to grow as China develops because product is not just flowing out of China to western markets, it is also flowing from overseas markets through Hong Kong into China. It is a two way flow of merchandise and produce that will greatly enhance the Hong Kong economy.

Hong Kong is a leading financial centre with a worldwide reputation. The territory provides very efficient and sophisticated banking and financial services to its customers worldwide. Hong Kong's banking sector offers a very wide range of banking services. It is normal practice for companies in Hong Kong both local and overseas multinational offices to remain with the same banks when arranging trade finance facilities. This is because trade finance is generally regarded as a relationship banking service and the good practice and high calibre of banks in Hong Kong coupled with the territory's worldwide reputation has given both buyers and sellers great confidence that payments will be made on time and documentation will be processed efficiently.

The close and long term relationship between banks and traders underpins Hong Kong's comparative advantage with regard to international trade and trade finance. Hong Kong's banks are further strengthened by their ability to assess and accept risks regarding trade with China.

Hong Kong has been a leading insurance centre in Asia for a long time. The thriving international trade and shipping activities in Hong Kong have attracted a great many underwriters and brokers to conduct their business in Hong Kong. These underwriters and brokers provide a comprehensive range of insurance services covering all the parties involved in all forms of trading and shipping activities. Insurance is available not just for domestic exports and re-exports, but also for transhipments and direct shipments.

Direct shipments are those shipments made direct from one source, such as China, to a buyer overseas without passing through Hong Kong, but the shipper will be based in Hong Kong. The insurance sector is closely related to the banking sector and applications for trade finance usually involve insurance cover, and banks often act as agents for insurance companies.

Hong Kong's industrial testing and inspection services are well recognised internationally by many trade buyers for their quality and efficiency. In 2002 there were 106 accredited testing laboratories in Hong Kong. However, quality assurance and inspection services are never the sole responsibility of the accredited testing laboratories. Many traders provide in-house quality inspection in accordance with ISO regulations for their customers to ensure that quality requirements are satisfied. Due to the growth in the China trade, there has been a corresponding growth in testing and inspection services, and the majority of testing and certification companies as well as the quality inspection sections of many traders have established their operations in China so as to provide on-site services.

On 17th December 1999, the government instituted the Admission of Talents Scheme with the aim of attracting talented people from China and overseas to work in Hong Kong. Under the scheme, applicants must possess good qualifications, knowledge or skills that are not readily available in Hong Kong. The objective of the scheme is to enhance the economy as a manufacturing and services centre with particular emphasis on technology, knowledge and high value added functions.

Since the opening up of China in 1978, Hong Kong companies utilising the low costs there have greatly expanded their scale of manufacture and enhanced their competitiveness. As a result South China has evolved into one of the world's most important production bases. The trend towards globalization coupled with Hong Kong's integration with China has led to economic restructuring at a very rapid pace. The process of economic integration between Hong Kong and China is leading to factor price equalisation whereby the price of tradable products changes quickly due to free trade between the two places. Price differentials between Hong Kong and China will narrow gradually. However, adjustments in non-tradable factors like land and labour will be negligible. Prices in Hong Kong will remain higher than in China just as prices in New York, London and Tokyo are higher then in their surrounding areas.

Hong Kong offers multinationals a number of distinct advantages due to its strengths. Four of these strengths are geographic location, institutional strengths, high calibre talent and a strong business base. Hong Kong's geographic location is particularly advantageous due to it being in the centre of East Asia, which is currently the most economically active area in the world. China is the fastest growing economy in the world with annual GDP growth rates that far outstrip other countries. For Hong Kong it is now a continental size domestic market with immense business and investment opportunities and as such it represents a market opportunity that multinationals cannot afford to miss. Hong Kong is without doubt the prime gateway to China and current promotional activity regarding the available support services being marketed by the InvestHK organisation are a testament to the richness of the market opportunities.

Hong Kong has deep rooted institutional strengths at its core that have been developed and fine tuned over many years. These institutional strengths include the rule of law which is fundamental to the Hong Kong system of justice; a level playing field for all business activity ensuring that competition is free and fair so that the best and most suited company wins the contract; clean and corruption free government ensuring that administration of the territory is performed without prejudice to any section of the society; free flow of information thereby enabling companies to be freely informed of all relevant facts in their business activities; simple and low tax regime for both corporate and personal tax; as well as efficient and effective market regulatory systems designed to facilitate smooth, cost effective and efficient business. These institutional strengths have now, since the time of Deng Xiao Ping, been combined with the philosophy of 'one country, two systems' for the betterment of both Hong Kong and China.

Hong Kong has a very wide range of talented individuals in its society. The territory has highly proficient business, management, professional services, scientific research and educational staff at all levels ensuring that activities in their relevant sectors are conducted in the most appropriate and efficient manner. The population is to a large extent bi-literate in both Cantonese and English, and an increasing number of people are also capable of speaking Putonghua (Mandarin), which due to integration with China is becoming more and more in demand. The population is to a large extent familiar with both Chinese and Western culture, management, business operations, mindset and social practices. Hong Kong has a very cosmopolitan society and therefore language and cultural interchange is very common and beneficial to the society as well as helping to develop business understanding on an international level.

CEPA and Regional Development

Hong Kong is the natural partner for foreign companies and investors seeking to enter China's vast market. According to the latest data Hong Kong is responsible for a substantial and growing volume of China's total trade with the rest of the world. In 2003 26% of trade between China and Europe passed through Hong Kong.

In 2004 Hong Kong entered into a Closer Economic Partnership Arrangement

(CEPA) with China that gives Hong Kong service providers unparalleled access into 18 service sectors in China, including maritime and road transport, freight forwarding, logistics and storage services. This gives Hong Kong companies another distinct advantage over foreign counterparts and will lead to yet further development of Hong Kong's service sector.

CEPA, the Individual Visit Scheme and Renminbi business initiative have helped the flow of capital, goods and people between Hong Kong and China thereby speeding up economic integration.

Approximately 98% of Hong Kong's businesses are classified as small and medium sized enterprises (SMEs). Many of these SMEs will benefit greatly from the CEPA liberalisation of sectors. Logistics is a pillar industry in Hong Kong and Hong Kong SMEs will gain first mover advantage through CEPA because China's third party logistics market has enormous business potential. CEPA has resulted in the lowering of threshold requirements for distributors and these were scheduled to be completely removed in 2004. Hong Kong has the advantage because under CEPA Hong Kong companies will be able to establish wholly owned enterprises at least six months before foreign companies can establish such enterprises.

Under CEPA there will be no tariffs imposed on Hong Kong exports to China, which means that Hong Kong product will automatically become more competitively priced. The zero tariff rate for Hong Kong exports to mainland China under CEPA ensures that Hong Kong has a distinct competitive advantage over products from other countries. CEPA has made access to the Chinese market extremely favourable for many service sector companies and this will in turn attract greater investment to Hong Kong as overseas organisations seek to exploit the opportunities. CEPA has therefore strengthened Hong Kong's unique position as the best entry point into China.

Companies that use Hong Kong in order to access the Chinese market will benefit greatly from the CEPA agreement, because no other location can offer such advantages. This in turn enhances Hong Kong's position as a major business centre in Asia. The rapid economic growth of China together with its accession to the WTO and opening up of the country represents a golden opportunity for economic growth in Hong Kong. Coupled with CEPA, it is expected that Hong Kong will experience substantial growth in the short and medium term. It is forecast that the annual GDP growth rate in real terms over the next four years will be 3.8 per cent.

In the banking sector the asset requirement for non-mainland Chinese banks has now been lowered from US$20 billion to US$6 billion making the sector more attractive for smaller banks.

The Individual Visit Scheme, which commenced in October 2003, has had the effect of boosting mainland visitors to Hong Kong from a figure of 600,000 per month to more than 1 million. This has resulted in a greater level of spending within the economy, which has generally benefited SMEs.

Hong Kong and China have now signed agreements recognising the qualifications of its surveyors, architects and structural engineers under the CEPA agreement. This has further helped the integration of Hong Kong and China and given greater support to its industrial structures. CEPA also enables Hong Kong companies to establish wholly owned consulting organisations several years ahead of competing foreign owned companies thereby further strengthening Hong Kong's first mover advantage. CEPA is without doubt a definite advantage for Hong Kong companies in the China market and one from which overseas multinational companies seeking to form partnership arrangements with Hong Kong companies would do well to bear in mind when negotiating such partnership arrangements.

Hong Kong is also included in the Pan-Pearl River Delta Cooperation and Development agreement that will lead to further business activity by Hong Kong investors and service providers thereby developing and expanding business within nine selected provinces in China covering an area of 2 million square kilometres with a population of 450 million. The Pan-Pearl River Delta region represents a huge market due to the size of its population and is a strong and growing production base offering a wide range of resources. The provinces included in this region are all set to make full use of Hong Kong, Asia's World City, in order to enhance the overall competitiveness of the region in global markets. This development is set to make Hong Kong an even more significant player in the global market due to what can be expected to be a significant increase in business activity in various sectors throughout the economy. Multinationals cannot afford to miss the opportunities that this development will present.

The Pan Pearl River Delta development will further strengthen Hong Kong's role as the preferred international and regional transport and logistics hub. The multimodal transportation network of the region is set to receive further economic and industrial development thereby presenting further business opportunities. Hong Kong's main shipping services are international maritime services and container port services. Hong Kong shipowners and ship managers control over 8% of world tonnage. Hong Kong offers a comprehensive and high quality maritime service and has at least 900 companies involved in shipping activities covering financing, marine insurance, ship registration, broking, arbitration, ship management, repair and replenishment, and surveying, etc.

Hong Kong has a preferential port dues agreement with China and double taxation agreements with 11 trading partners. In 1999 the Hong Kong Shipping Register grew to 9.3 million tonnes, however by 2004 this had risen to 23 million tonnes and further expansion is expected. The Hong Kong Maritime Industry Council is currently implementing new initiatives designed to enhance the territory's position as a base for international maritime companies, business and services.

Hong Kong has consistently been rated as the world's busiest container port for 11 years out of the 12 years from 1991 to 2002, and in 2003 had a throughput of 20.4 million TEUs (twenty-foot equivalent units). Hong Kong is probably the most important commercial gateway to China and therefore has to ensure efficient and fast port facilities to ensure quick vessel turnaround times. Hong Kong has formulated a further development strategy for its port facilities in order to ensure that it maintains its competitive position. This development strategy is laid out in the Hong Kong Port -- Master Plan 2020 document.

Further container terminal facilities are scheduled for development not just in Hong Kong, but also along the Chinese coast in order to deal with the continued growth in trade with South China. These terminal developments will also be able to accommodate even larger super vessels. Hong Kong is not just a recognised international maritime centre offering an extensive range of services, it is a pre-eminent logistics centre and natural gateway to what is projected to become the largest market in the world.

Multinational organisations must understand the strategic importance of a Hong Kong location and the advantages as well as benefits that being located in Hong Kong can offer to overall corporate structure and function. The profitability of a regional headquarters or regional office in Hong Kong speaks for itself because of the control centre function that such an office can have for corporate activities and functions throughout not just Hong Kong and China, but also South East Asia and Asia in general.

19. Invest Hong Kong

Hong Kong is the World City that means business. This is the message from Invest Hong Kong (InvestHK).

Its role is to promote Hong Kong's many advantages as an investment and business hub in Asia. It provides assistance to corporations looking for direct investment opportunities in the territory and aims to ensure that companies have all the support they need to establish operations in Hong Kong - Asia's World City.

The InvestHK Vision is to clearly affirm and embolden Hong Kong's position as the leading international business centre in Asia and its Mission is to attract as well as retain important investment in Hong Kong that is economically and strategically advantageous for Hong Kong as well as overseas investors. InvestHK provides various types of assistance to investors seeking direct investment opportunities in Hong Kong.

InvestHK is the Hong Kong Government agency promoting Hong Kong's advantages, facilities and services as a business base that multinationals can fully utilise when based in Hong Kong. The organisation assists foreign investors in setting up their offices and developing a presence in Hong Kong. It also provides an aftercare service in order to ensure that everything is progressing as expected and objectives are being achieved.

InvestHK is a government department that was established on 1st July 2000 with the objective of attracting foreign inward direct investment into Hong Kong. The organisation offers a very comprehensive range of investment services with a clear emphasis upon solutions. InvestHK not only facilitates investment, but also provides a continuous service to ensure that investments are proceeding as planned. This approach is designed to ensure that companies seeking to invest in Hong Kong are fully supported when establishing or expanding their operations in the dynamic economy of Hong Kong.

InvestHK provides an all inclusive support service regarding inward investment for prospective and existing overseas investors in Hong Kong. Hong Kong is a leading financial and commercial centre in Asia with worldwide links and as such it is a prime destination for overseas businesses and investors of all types and sizes. Hong Kong offers investors a strong list of advantages including the fact that it is the number one location in Asia for multinational regional headquarters, it is centrally located in Asia on established trade routes with extensive air and sea connections to locations around the globe, it has been consistently classified by recognised agencies as the freest market in the world, it has a unique position as the best and most developed gateway to China and as such is ideally located for conducting business with China, it has a well recognised and long established legal system where the rule of law is paramount, it has the free flow of information which is requisite for business, and it has a highly educated population with a strong business mentality. These features of Hong Kong are extensively used by InvestHK in its promotion of the benefits of business in Hong Kong and are an indication of how InvestHK can assist prospective and existing investors.

InvestHK will assist investors in making full use of the financial, trade, transportation, communications, information technology, multimedia and manufacturing services that Hong Kong has to offer. InvestHK will be the guide and go-between in order to enable investors to take full advantage of these services. The free market philosophy and business friendly environment that the HKSAR provides is supported by the government by means of a clear regulatory regime and framework with the objective of enabling the private sector to prosper to the benefit of the whole society. InvestHK is committed to helping companies maximise their investment and business opportunities in Hong Kong.

The structure of InvestHK is as follows:

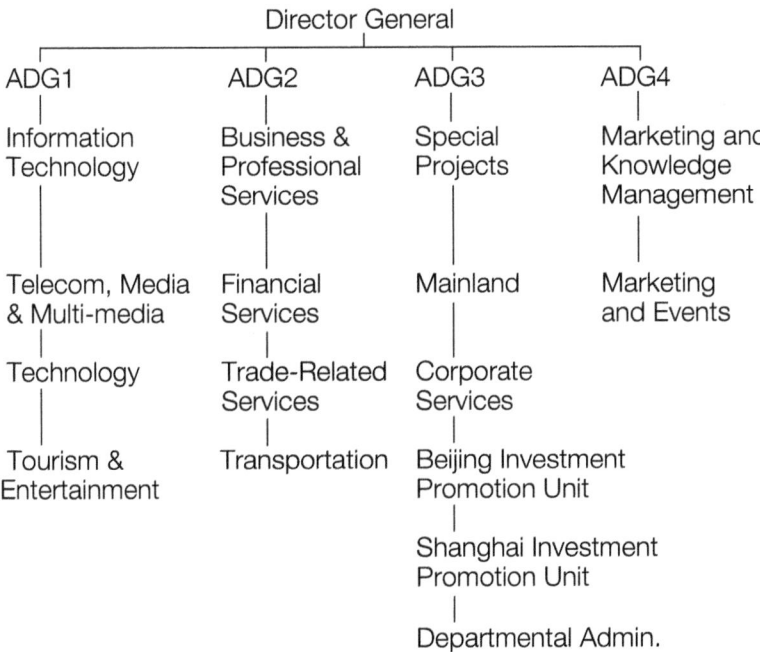

ADG = Assistant Director General

InvestHK is able to provide a vast range of data information and analyses in order to enable companies and potential investors to properly assess business prospects. InvestHK provides an extensive range of services in relation to investment activities including:

- ☐ provision of up to date information regarding Hong Kong's business and investment environment,

- ☐ provision of economic sector profiles; business incorporation requirements; appropriate contacts dependent upon the nature of the investment intended; employment data as appropriate; costing and availability of land, factories, offices and residential housing,

- ☐ provision of government information regarding business support services, taxation levels, import/export regulations and requirements, employment legislation, immigration regulations and government projects where relevant,

- ☐ provision of listings of potential business partners in Hong Kong with whom the investor may consider working; arranging meetings with potential partners; site visits where appropriate; visiting government departments and trade and industrial organisations,

- ☐ helping investors communicate with government departments on matters such as visa applications, trade mark registration, business incorporation, safety requirements, etc.,

- ☐ InvestHK provides a continuous form of assistance to investors that starts before the investment is made, is present during the investment period, and continues after the investment has been made. In this way a continuous and long lasting friendship and relationship is built, and

- ☐ InvestHK is also very cognisant of the feedback from investors regarding the services that it provides and makes every attempt to continue to improve those services.

InvestHK conducts overseas promotions including seminars, sponsorships, information dissemination regarding investment in Hong Kong, visits to prospective companies with an interest in investing in Hong Kong, working with consulates and chambers of commerce, assisting companies of all types in the investment process at all stages from initial decision making to establishing operations and providing aftercare services to ensure that business is running smoothly. InvestHK seeks to raise the profile of Hong Kong by promoting its advantages thereby strengthening its position as a destination for investment. The CEPA agreement between Hong Kong and China means that InvestHK is also promoting Hong Kong to mainland Chinese companies seeking to expand operations overseas as well as overseas companies considering Hong Kong and the Pearl River Delta as business opportunities.

InvestHK also runs a Business Concierge Service whereby the organisation will provide a list of business concierge service providers to those investors interested in exploring business opportunities in the Greater Pearl River Delta. These service providers have all been pre-qualified by the organisation, but InvestHK will not take part in any negotiations between the investor and the service providers. These service providers will, for a negotiated fee, help with the planning, arrangements and implementation of all visit programmes to the Greater Pearl River Delta. Companies requiring business concierge services should contact InvestHK for the names, addresses and contact numbers of concierge service providers and an updated list will be provided.

Part of the service of InvestHK is to help connect investors with potential business partners with the right aspirations in the correct field. This is a very efficient function of InvestHK and leads to a great saving in time and expense of the parties involved. InvestHK will facilitate meetings and visits to all relevant government and commercial organisations that could possibly be related or involved with the investment programme being considered and negotiated. This helps establish a network of contacts of interested parties so as to make the investment programme more smooth and essentially more successful.

When an overseas company (investor) plans to set up a regional headquarters or regional office in Hong Kong, InvestHK is prepared to assist with all the necessary contacts with relevant organisations. This would include government departments and the necessary ancillary services such as trademark registration, work visa applications, business incorporation, fire regulations, legal and financial services as required, etc. The objective of InvestHK is to ensure that all investors in Hong Kong working with InvestHK experience a very smooth and efficient establishment of corporate operations in Hong Kong.

Companies of all sizes seek investment opportunities in lucrative markets so as to further their business aims. A favourable business orientated environment is the ideal location for such investment because of the opportunities it will offer. Companies must consider locations from a strategic viewpoint with regard to corporate objectives. Companies will seek locations that have an advanced business infrastructure; firm economic and social stability; developed technologies; an educated and capable workforce; and increasingly a global orientation within the community. Companies will naturally be cautious before committing themselves to investing in facilities and will also consider deeply the extent of their investment. Hong Kong offers an extensive range of business orientated environmental features that multinationals normally seek including :

- ☐ a world class infrastructure,
- ☐ the busiest sea and air cargo terminals in the world,
- ☐ complete absence of exchange controls, trade barriers and tariffs,
- ☐ free flow of information,
- ☐ level playing field for business,
- ☐ free press and freedom of speech,
- ☐ rule of law,
- ☐ low and simple tax system that is efficient and predictable,
- ☐ advanced telecommunications system that enables companies to be in full contact with other offices anywhere in the world,
- ☐ numerous institutions in various business sectors employing advanced technologies,
- ☐ a dense sea and air route transportation network with connections worldwide,
- ☐ hard working, educated and very cosmopolitan society,
- ☐ etc.

Hong Kong is a city that means business and has the necessary resources and structures to ensure that business objectives are achieved within defined and agreed time frames. InvestHK was established with the objective of attracting inward investment and ensuring that those inward investment objectives are achieved.

Invest Hong Kong

The organisation will assist in all types of inward investment programmes.

The organisation provides an investment promotion service designed to offer solutions to investors by guiding, encouraging and facilitating investment programmes. It has a precise investment promotion strategy whereby specific business sectors are targeted in which Hong Kong has a clear advantage over other Asian cities. Invest Hong Kong also uses a proactive marketing strategy to target specific companies within specific market sectors. The organisation regards aftercare service as particularly important because it helps strengthen the bonds between the investor and Hong Kong and as such helps retain investment as well as facilitate and encourage further investment and possible product development activities. This in turn increases Hong Kong's attractiveness and competitiveness.

According to current analysis Hong Kong has nine key business sectors in which it is envisaged that companies would do particularly well if located in Hong Kong. These sectors are:

- Financial services.
- Trade related services.
- Telecommunications.
- Media and multi-media.
- Transportation.
- Business and professional services.
- Information technology.
- Technology (especially electronics and biotechnology).
- Tourism and entertainment.

In conjunction with regional headquarters development these key business sectors will receive very comprehensive attention from InvestHK. The organisation will assist in the research and decision making processes of inward investors in order to ensure that corporate investment objectives are achieved.

InvestHK, promotes inward investment, and works closely with regional headquarters and regional offices in order to ensure that companies are fully provided with all the support services they require. Even though the organisation is targeting nine specific sectors, regional headquarters and regional offices across all industries will be assisted as required.

In order to facilitate its corporate marketing programme, in 2001 Invest Hong Kong commenced an image building programme to publicise the advantages of Hong Kong's investment environment as well as the organisation's corporate identity. In 2002, the corporate marketing programme included participation in the Transatlantic Yacht Race 2002 as a sponsor of the vessel entitled 'Spirit of Hong Kong'. This race included numerous stops at specific cities where promotional events and functions were held thereby enabling sponsors such as Invest Hong Kong to promote themselves and their services. As such this represented very positive public relations activities for both Hong Kong and Invest Hong Kong. Another very important promotional activity hosted by Invest Hong Kong was the Forbes Global CEO Conference from 24th to 26th September 2002. This event was held at the Hong Kong Convention and Exhibition Centre and was a successful function enabling delegates from world famous companies to interact with each other and experience Hong Kong's world renowned facilities.

Invest Hong Kong has also been strengthening its investment promotion activities in Mainland China by creating two investment promotion units. One of these units deals with companies in the Shanghai area including Jiangsu and Zhejiang provinces, whilst the other promotion unit deals with companies in Beijing and Tianjin. This promotion in Mainland China has led to expansion in the Hong Kong headquarters as a dedicated team has now been created to cover all matters regarding Mainland China.

Key performance measures under the investment promotion programme for Invest Hong Kong are:

- [ ] The market value of the in-flow of foreign direct investment into Hong Kong,

- [ ] Hong Kong's percentage share of foreign direct investment inflows into South, East and South-East Asia,

- [ ] The number of projects pursued,

- [ ] The number of pursuable leads,

- [ ] The number of projects generated as a result of aftercare services, and

☐ The number of projects completed.

Invest Hong Kong has a broad range of plans including:

☐ Participation in public relations events and activities in order to continue the promotion of Invest Hong Kong's corporate identity and image.

☐ Close cooperation with Hong Kong's overseas Economic and Trade Offices as well as the Hong Kong Trade Development Council offices around the world in order to implement various planned business campaigns.

☐ Further enhancement and upgrading of the promotion of investment opportunities in Hong Kong as well as China.

Hong Kong Economic and Trade Offices

Commercial Relations Programme

Hong Kong has a number of Economic and Trade Offices in cities around the world including London, New York, Washington, Geneva, Brussels, San Francisco, Guangdong, Tokyo, Toronto, Sydney and Singapore. The objective of these offices is to develop and enhance Hong Kong's trade and economic interests by cultivating relations with host governments, representing Hong Kong at all types of national and international trade associations and organisations, as well as maintaining active liaison with regional governments and organisations. Hong Kong's Economic and Trade Offices (HKETOs) continually monitor all types of developments in their respective regions with regard to likely affects on trade and report such developments to the head office in Hong Kong.

The offices lobby and conduct negotiations with their respective host governments regarding all types of trade issues as well as provide assistance to Hong Kong officers in trade agreement negotiations. The primary aim of the Hong Kong Economic and Trade Offices is therefore to represent Hong Kong overseas and to promote the development of the city's trade and commercial interests on an international basis.

Key performance measures under the commercial relations programme for the HKETOs are:

☐ Number of meetings on trade related matters attended.

- [ ] Number of visits to host governments and trade organisations.

- [ ] Number of seminars, exhibitions and workshops organised and in which participated.

- [ ] Number of public speeches given.

- [ ] Number of media interviews and briefings given.

- [ ] Number of circulars, newsletters and press releases issued.

Apart from promoting Hong Kong overseas, the HKETOs are active in opposing protectionism in the territory's major markets. They also monitor trade and market developments as well as consumption trends, and provide diplomatic, commercial and intellectual support to the Hong Kong Trade and Industry Department in bilateral as well as multilateral trade negotiations around the world.

Public Relations Programme

The HKETOs are very effective in public relations activities. A range of publicity events and public relations activities to promote Hong Kong are regularly organised in overseas countries and regions. The HKETOs also closely monitor and report on the reactions of host countries to events taking place in Hong Kong. An important function of the public relations programme is for the HKETOs to provide a very comprehensive information and enquiry service to host countries so that companies in the host countries can easily find information regarding Hong Kong in order to initiate and develop contacts.

The HKETOs are very active in facilitating procedures for overseas companies to develop contacts with organisations and companies in Hong Kong. One of the aims of the HKETOs is to promote Hong Kong as a World City and the ideal location for business. Hong Kong is presented to host countries as a very reliable trade partner and the best gateway to China.

Key performance measures under the public relations programme for the HKETOs are:

- [ ] Number of calls on senior government officials/organisations.

- [ ] Number of public relations functions/events organised and in which participated.

☐ Number of newsletters, pamphlets and press releases issued.

☐ Number of visitors assisted.

☐ Number of public speeches given.

☐ Number of media interviews and briefings given.

☐ Number of enquiries handled.

Each HKETO will develop its own public relations plan for the country or region in which it is active. These plans will then be reviewed by the Invest Hong Kong headquarters. The organisation of Hong Kong Economic and Trade Offices is active in all the countries and regions where it has offices with performance being continually monitored against set targets.

Investment Promotion Programme

As a leading international finance and business centre, the aim of the Investment Promotion Programme is not only to attract new foreign direct investment, but also to retain existing foreign direct investment. In this way the Investment Promotion Programme maintains as well as develops Hong Kong's reputation worldwide. The HKETOs promote Hong Kong as an attractive business environment and an ideal location for inward investment funds to be used either in Hong Kong or elsewhere. Hong Kong's very professional financial management capabilities are highlighted.

The HKETOs provide detailed advice and assistance to all companies regarding the formulation as well as implementation of investment plans concerning Hong Kong. A core aim of the HKETOs is to encourage investors to consider both Hong Kong and China as investment targets.

Key performance measures under the investment promotion programme for the HKETOs are:

☐ Number of companies visited to encourage inward investment.

☐ Number of companies targeted through direct mailings.

☐ Number of seminars and presentations organised and in which participated.

- ☐ Number of newsletters, pamphlets and press releases issued.
- ☐ Number of public speeches given.
- ☐ Number of media interviews and briefings given.
- ☐ Number of enquiries handled.

InvestHK now commissions an annual Global Perception Audit with the objective of determining what exactly are Hong Kong's strengths and weaknesses as a location for inward investment. According to reports released in 2006, the second of these audits found that Hong Kong is regarded as having the best environment in the region for investments. It is seen as being a leading city for potential investors and is now more highly rated than it was in 2004.

Some of the main strengths of Hong Kong were stated as being its low restrictions on imports, its status as the main business hub in the Asia Pacific and its easy access to the Chinese market. However, the city's financial facilities and infrastructure were seen as its best strengths. Nevertheless, the report did reveal negative concerns regarding the cost of office space, apartments and staff as well as worries regarding the future availability of high calibre managerial and executive staff.

Invest Hong Kong

20. Hong Kong Trade Development Council

The Hong Kong Trade Development Council (HKTDC) was established in 1966 as a government sponsored organisation with the objective of promoting the products and services of Hong Kong companies and raising the international profile of Hong Kong as a business city. Since then the Hong Kong Trade Development Council has evolved into a multinational organisation with offices in many countries around the world. Its resources and utility have burgeoned as Hong Kong has grown in stature to that of a World City.

The HKTDC now organises and takes part in a great many international exhibitions, events, seminars, promotions, etc. with the objective of promoting the products and services of Hong Kong companies as well as promoting Hong Kong as the ideal investment location for South East Asia, as the best and main gateway to China, as the perfect location for an Asia Pacific regional headquarters or regional office, and also as the World City of the Asia Pacific.

One of the fundamental functions of the HKTDC is to work closely with Hong Kong companies as well as overseas companies in the development of business opportunities not just in Hong Kong, but throughout the region. A vital part of this function is to promote Hong Kong as the world renowned regional business centre that is an ideal location for international multinational companies seeking to develop business relations in China and Asia.

The HKTDC's global network of offices seeks to encourage overseas companies to source products and services from Hong Kong as well as sell and manufacture product in Hong Kong, China and the region, and also develop partnerships with Hong Kong companies as well as make use of Hong Kong's vast range of business services. As such the HKTDC is particularly gifted in helping companies, particularly small and medium sized companies, based in overseas markets develop successful business strategies for the Chinese and Asian markets. The HKTDC has often been regarded from a corporate level as the global marketing arm of Hong Kong due to its active presence in many varied business functions around the world.

The stated mission of the HKTDC is to develop international trade opportunities for Hong Kong companies, particularly the small and medium-sized companies

(SMEs), as well as to positively promote the image and reputation of Hong Kong. In order to achieve this mission there are a number of definite objectives. The HKTDC will seek market development and diversification for Hong Kong companies. It will endeavour to gain worldwide promotion of Hong Kong products and services. The HKTDC will seek to help in the further promotion of Hong Kong's established position as a leading international business centre with an extensive range of business services.

It will promote Hong Kong's position as a World City and the best and main gateway to the Chinese market and hence as the pre-eminent and most developed international business city in China. Another of its objectives will be to enhance the city's position as a fervent believer in the advantages of free trade and a confirmed partner and platform for the development of global business aspirations.

The HKTDC is governed and controlled by a 19 member Council composed of well respected and highly experienced business leaders and senior government officials. The Council plans and supervises the organisations global operational activities, promotion plans and services programme. The HKTDC is geared towards powering the success of businesses in international trade by providing a range of services including marketing opportunities, business matching services, market intelligence, SME development programmes, database information, exhibitions, seminars, corporate events, etc.

The HKTDC's extensive global network of offices enables it to act as the eyes, ears and matchmaker in world markets. The network enables the HKTDC to scour markets for business opportunities, organise a vast range of overseas promotional activities, develop business relations and contacts in many markets and absorb and feedback an extensive amount of market intelligence regarding overseas market developments and prospects. The HKTDC is often the starting point for both overseas and mainland Chinese companies seeking suppliers, buyers and partners from Hong Kong.

The organisation is also active in its support of Hong Kong Business Associations around the world due to their strong relations with Hong Kong. The Federation of Hong Kong Business Associations Worldwide currently comprises a network of 28 Hong Kong business associations based in 22 countries and regions. This organisation can be contacted via its website at http://www.hkfederation.org.hk. The HKTDC has also developed its position as the Hong Kong secretariat for bilateral committees established with the objective of developing closer business links between Hong Kong and the USA, the European Union, Japan and South Korea. These committees enable high-level private sector exchanges to be undertaken regarding opportunities, challenges and issues affecting Hong Kong's business relations with major trading partners from these territories.

A listing of the HKTDC's global network of offices around the world is provided in the appendix with details regarding postal addresses, telephone and facsimile numbers, and e-mail addresses.

Hong Kong's position as the exhibition and convention capital of Asia has been built on the basis of its Convention and Exhibition Centre. In the early 1980s the government designated prime land along the Wan Chai harbour front as a desired location for the Convention and Exhibition Centre. In 1984 the HKTDC council joined together with the construction company New World Company Ltd. with the intention of building the project. The centre opened in November 1988 to much acclaim as Asia's largest steel building and an innovative facility.

The Hong Kong Convention and Exhibition Centre (HKCEC) was more than just an exhibition hall, it also included an office tower, serviced apartments and two hotels thereby enabling overseas exhibitors and buyers to stay within the facility. Also instead of being constructed horizontally outwards like many exhibition centres in Europe and the USA, the HKCEC was constructed vertically due to Hong Kong's natural space limitations.

In March 1994, the Hong Kong government authorised the further expansion of the centre by reclaiming land from the harbour and this expansion was completed in 1997 just prior to the handover of sovereignty. The centre is now approaching saturation point for some of its major exhibitions and space utilisation in general within the centre is increasing by approximately 10 percent each year for its exhibition usage.

The Hong Kong Convention and Exhibition Centre is recognised as being the best convention and exhibition facility in Asia and also one of the best in the world. The centre stages many major international exhibitions of world renown attracting both exhibitors and visitors from all over the world. Some of the exhibitions are so popular that the facility is almost bursting at the seams and as a consequence this has created a demand for more space. In order to deal with this situation, new plans have recently been put forward for the expansion and the Convention and Exhibition Centre. This expansion would create an additional 19,400 square metres of exhibition space which would be roughly equivalent to an additional 1,000 standard size exhibition booths. Under the plan, construction work would start in early 2006 and be completed in early 2009 at a cost of HK$1.2 billion.

With this expansion the HKTDC would no longer be required to have waiting lists for exhibitors due to space limitations. It would also mean that for a number of the major exhibitions held in Hong Kong, the territory would become the number one exhibition site in the world for those particular exhibitions in terms of the number of exhibitors participating. It is projected that undertaking this expansion would have major economic benefits for Hong Kong because it would ensure that trade fairs would not drift away to other locations and financially it would lead to a surge in expenditure within the economy of the order of HK$40 billion between 2009 and 2025. It would also lead to substantial job creation. The total cost of the expansion would be recuperated extremely quickly within the first year or two. With this expansion, Hong Kong's position as the exhibition capital of Asia would be even more acclaimed.

A central theme of the HKTDC's annual plan in 2003-04 was 'partnering for success'. Based on a rolling three year planning horizon, the HKTDC's vision is to increase Hong Kong's world trade potential by being a partner that sources, sells, manufactures for and services all types of markets worldwide. The HKTDC's mission is to enhance Hong Kong's position as a global trade platform; to create business opportunities and facilitate international trade; to be the primary source of market information, contacts, marketing opportunities and practical training; and to cooperate and assist others in increasing the critical mass of international companies using Hong Kong's global trade platform and infrastructure in order to develop business throughout the region.

The HKTDC actively promotes Hong Kong as the best location from which companies can sell products and services to China and the Asia Pacific; source products and services throughout the region; manufacture products in China under Hong Kong control; as well as develop, manage and expand Asia Pacific business operations. The HKTDC's objectives and strategies include developing China as a domestic market for Hong Kong companies; helping to further build Hong Kong's already renowned global trade platform; to promote the abundant competitive advantages of Hong Kong's SMEs particularly from a corporate strategical position; and to further enhance its own position and reputation as a leading trade promotion organisation throughout the world.

According to the proposed 2004-05 annual plan of the HKTDC, the council plans a number of key objectives including:

- Using the CEPA agreement with China in order to assist Hong Kong companies to enter and become more involved in mainland Chinese markets.

- Place a greater emphasis upon the global marketing of Hong Kong and the Pearl River Delta as the ideal business base.

- Develop the potential of Hong Kong companies to expand into emerging markets around the world.

- Continue the development of Hong Kong as a business platform and trade fair capital ideally suited for SMEs to promote their businesses.

☐ Use e-commerce to increase the competitiveness of Hong Kong's SMEs.

☐ Establish the HKTDC as the world's premier trade promotion organisation capable of providing marketing support in a wide variety of formats to an extensive range of companies.

The development of the Chinese market in recent years together with its spectacular growth in GDP coupled with its accession to the WTO and the implementation of the Closer Economic Partnership Arrangement (CEPA) with Hong Kong has made China a prime and vast domestic market that Hong Kong companies, including Hong Kong based multinationals, must make every effort to profitably develop. The HKTDC is therefore making every effort to increase understanding and raise awareness of the business opportunities that are available as a result of CEPA. This was a major priority for the organisation's 2004/05 programme. The HKTDC is also placing great emphasis upon promoting Hong Kong's clear links with the Pearl River Delta, which has received enormous investment capital from Hong Kong.

The HKTDC will also be promoting Hong Kong's links with other major distribution hubs such as the Yangtze River Delta and the Bohai region. The HKTDC will be promoting Hong Kong as a regional trendsetter with a modern, cosmopolitan, fast paced lifestyle offering a wonderful range of products and services. Emphasis will be placed on sector specific partnerships so as to highlight Hong Kong's unique advantages. A range of activities will be undertaken by the HKTDC in China including roadshows, expos, department store promotions, seminars, workshops, service centres, business missions, etc. The HKTDC seeks to raise the profile of Hong Kong companies, products and services on the mainland so as to make such companies, products and services more acceptable and desirable to the Chinese population thereby raising demand for Hong Kong products and services and as such developing business opportunities.

The HKTDC will continue to promote the many business advantages that have evolved as a result of the close and integrated links between Hong Kong and the Pearl River Delta. Hong Kong's well established business services will be promoted in conjunction with the growing dynamic manufacturing capability of the Pearl River Delta region together with its burgeoning consumer markets. The HKTDC has already scheduled an extensive list of marketing activities regarding the Hong Kong Pearl River Delta link, including roadshows, seminars, information exchanges, close and coordinated work with the global network of Hong Kong Business Associations, business missions in and out of Hong Kong, an advisory service, business matching programmes, expos, etc. It is expected that the Hong

Kong Pearl River Delta linkage will see a tremendous growth in business and overseas inward investment in the near future.

As part of its promotional efforts the HKTDC continually monitors global competition and protectionist trends in overseas markets. The organisation is continually exploring new regions and new market opportunities with regard to Hong Kong products and services. Market specific studies are regularly performed so as to develop market intelligence. Market research and promotional materials are continually supplied by the HKTDC to Hong Kong companies. Both on line and off line marketing activities are conducted.

Inward buying missions and outward selling missions are always supported by the HKTDC in a variety of ways. The HKTDC is always continually looking for new and exciting ways to promote Hong Kong and its many attributes and business potential. The HKTDC regularly takes part in exhibitions around the world and is responsible for arranging for large groups of Hong Kong companies to take part in overseas exhibitions and promotional events.

Over the last 25-30 years and ever since China started to open up to the rest of the world, Hong Kong has become the crossroads for China and the rest of the world. This has led to a great expansion in the number of overseas companies with regional headquarters or regional offices in Hong Kong. There are also an increasing number of Chinese companies seeking to establish regional offices in Hong Kong. Hong Kong is therefore the meeting point for overseas companies seeking business opportunities in China and throughout South East Asia, and Chinese companies seeking business opportunities in the rest of the world. It is the HKTDC's objective to further enhance this unique position for Hong Kong by promoting Hong Kong's business platform and highly successful business services.

Hong Kong is now recognised as being Asia's trade fair, exhibition and convention capital with a wealth of world class facilities. The Hong Kong Convention and Exhibition Centre is owned and managed by the HKTDC and therefore it is in the organisation's own interest to promote the quality, versatility and functional efficiency of this facility. The exhibitions staged by the HKTDC represent an ideal opportunity for both overseas companies as well as Chinese companies together with Hong Kong companies to promote their products and services and develop business relations throughout the world.

Hong Kong's exhibitions are truly international in character with exhibitors and visitors coming from around the world. The HKTDC has a continuous programme of exhibitions and conventions planned many months in advance and its promotion of these events is a guaranteed success.

In 2003 the HKTDC website, www.tdctrade.com, was declared as being the best trade promotion website in Asia. The HKTDC is committed to further developing its on line facilities so that buyers and investors around the world can have 24 hour access to HKTDC services. A primary aim of the HKTDC website is to promote and enhance the competitiveness of Hong Kong companies. It also helps in the Hong Kong campaign for greater e-commerce in Hong Kong and the region. The HKTDC is collaborating with various strategic partners and organisations in order to provide greater value added services via its website as well as in its other services.

The Hong Kong Trade Development Council offers a sourcing guide via its website, http://www.tdcenterprise.com, with online sourcing of products & brands from over 100,000 Hong Kong companies. One of the services offered by the HKTDC is a business matching service whereby it will attempt to match the requirements of overseas companies with the products and services of Hong Kong companies. The business matching service is operated via the website, http://www.tdctradepartners.com, and is an Internet based matching service for business partners. The HKTDC's promotions are of course on a worldwide basis.

The HKTDC is now offering Hong Kong companies a free web conferencing facility in order to facilitate easy contact with overseas customers. The facility is based at web video conferencing booths in the Convention and Exhibition Centre and is absolutely free to Hong Kong companies. In order that this facility can be used productively it is provided with extended opening hours so as to synchronise with European and North American time zones. A technical support service is also provided for this facility. The idea of cyber marketing is another facility that the HKTDC is currently considering.

HKTDC overseas offices also conduct catalogue shows by inviting potential buyers and importers to examine marketing materials and catalogues from Hong Kong companies at their respective offices, and then relaying useful information back to Hong Kong as well as creating an online version of each catalogue show on the HKTDC website http://www.hkenterprise.com. HKTDC overseas offices are also active in making initial contact with potential international buyers and importers on behalf of Hong Kong companies. Direct mailing campaigns and telemarketing campaigns are also conducted by the HKTDC in Hong Kong and overseas.

The HKTDC is committed to further developing and enhancing its position as a leading trade promotion organisation with the objective of being the best in the world. The organisation has a comprehensive marketing strategy geared to promoting Hong Kong and its vast range of products and services. The organisation has a vast range of market specific trade journals greatly facilitating the speedy location of required products and services. An extensive database of both suppliers and potential buyers is readily available for interested parties.

Further developments can be expected in the HKTDC's Business InfoCentre as demand for such a resource increases. The HKTDC also provides a call centre service and SME centre service. It works closely with other organisations such as InvestHK, the Hong Kong Productivity Council and Chambers of Commerce in order to ensure a coordinated, strong and consistent message is produced and initiatives are carried out effectively to the required standard.

The organisation also closely monitors its performance so that amendments and corrections can be made to the way work is carried out so as to continually improve performance and raise the profile of Hong Kong. As the corporate marketing arm of Hong Kong, the HKTDC is an indispensable and extremely valuable Hong Kong asset.

In November 2000, the HKTDC was actively involved in the formation of the Federation of Hong Kong Business Associations Worldwide. This federation of business associations was started by traders and buyers overseas having a strong connection with Hong Kong and has now become an important network for communication and information exchange regarding Hong Kong and business prospects. The Federation is a non-profit organisation that aims to promote cooperation, communication and synergy on a global basis amongst the various associations. It is believed that by acting in unison it will enhance Hong Kong's position as a business and investment platform.

Information regarding the Federation can easily be obtained from its website at http://www.hkfederation.org.hk. This website is linked to other relevant websites regarding Hong Kong, trade and business. A fundamental objective of the Federation is partnership building so as to enhance business opportunities. It also provides extensive opportunities for interaction with business leaders and opinion formers in both the public and private sectors in Hong Kong and worldwide. Business contacts are readily available via the associates' directory on the website.

For many companies, China is still seen as a foreign and somewhat mysterious market due to lack of experience, but recent developments have made China a very compelling market and Hong Kong an ideal platform from which to enter this market. The Federation of Hong Kong Business Associations is an easy means to access Hong Kong's platform and its members can provide substantial knowledge regarding their extensive experiences and insight to facilitate such a venture. Through close association with the Federation companies can see the benefits that the Federation has to offer.

HKTDC, Business Advisory Service

The Hong Kong Trade Development Council provides a free comprehensive business advisory service regarding trends and developments in China and in overseas markets. The China business advisory service covers a number of issues including investment procedures, business law, customs declaration, trade marks and patents, taxation, product inspection requirements, credit risk management, brand marketing and development, etc.

Other subjects also covered regarding overseas markets include export credit management, letter of credit operations, trade laws, international marketing strategies, market prospects and trends, etc.

HKTDC Business InfoCentre

The Hong Kong Trade Development Council (HKTDC) Business InfoCentre at the Hong Kong Convention and Exhibition Centre is an extremely comprehensive business information centre of world class standard. The centre has the latest state of the art computer technology for online research and gathering of information. The latest trade information, business directories, books, periodicals, journals, etc. from around the world covering markets all around the world are freely available at the centre.

There is also very detailed information regarding China and its developments, prospects and needs. The HKTDC produces many trade reports each year and these can be purchased in hard copy format or else accessed online. The HKTDC also organises many workshops, seminars and focus groups regarding market developments, trends and business opportunities.

Hong Kong Trade Development Council

21. The Promotion of Hong Kong

Hong Kong's economy is no longer restricted to the political borders of its territory. Instead Hong Kong's economy incorporates much more including its overseas manufacturing facilities throughout southern China, South East Asia, Europe, Africa, the Americas and elsewhere. These business structures are owned, managed and directed from offices in the HKSAR controlling business activity in these overseas dominions.

Hong Kong is a city often regarded as having the characteristics of a nation due economic developments during its colonial history. It has its own currency, its own tax system, legal system and customs authority just like a nation. It is also a member of organisations such as the World Trade Organisation (WTO) and the Asia Pacific Economic Cooperation (APEC) just like a nation. However, its physical size, structure, population total and population density make it a city, and like all major cities its economic structure is very similar with agriculture playing a negligible role, manufacturing now accounting for a very small amount and the preponderance of economic activity being in the services sector.

Hong Kong is attempting to position itself as Asia's premier international city for the 21st century under the title of World City. It has passed the stage of being described as a metropolitan economy and is now being classified as a World City of a similar status as New York, London and Tokyo. According to much urban economic development literature, the concept of a city being classified as a 'World City' requires the incorporation of distinctive characteristics that are not normally found simultaneously in individual cities. Whilst a city may have one or two of these characteristics it is rare to find all of the distinctive characteristics in an individual city.

However, there are a few cities that do possess all of these distinctive characteristics. The characteristics include:

- ☐ the city is primarily externally oriented,

- ☐ the city is more integrated into the activities of international business rather than local business,

- ☐ most of the city's economic activities relate to providing a detailed range of business services, including financial services, in order to facilitate the development of trade and manufacturing,

☐ the city will have clusters of different types of business services within its realm.

Hong Kong currently possesses all of these distinctive characteristics and can therefore be classified as a World City.

World cities have commonly lost manufacturing jobs as manufacturing facilities have been pushed out to nearby hinterlands. In Hong Kong's case this includes Southern China, South East Asia and other locations around the world. World cities generally have a large number of small and medium sized active companies. These SMEs often have a symbiotic relationship with clusterings of business service providers as non-core business activities are outsourced. Nevertheless world cities tend to have a higher number of business start ups and failures due to risk levels. All these aspects are present in Hong Kong, thereby supporting the proposition that Hong Kong is a World City.

Hong Kong has the critical mass of skilled personnel and company clusters to raise it above all other Asian business locations. Its trade related services are seen as the most comprehensive available in Asia. Globalisation of trade and manufacture has added greatly to the growth of regional trade and development of business hubs. Manufacturers, exporters, importers, distributors and retailers often attempt to reduce their total transaction costs by reducing the number of locations and companies they need to contact when developing and arranging their business webs.

This has led to core business activities like planning, finance, insurance, marketing, etc. being clustered in a relatively few business hubs. Hong Kong has become Asia's global business hub because it has the critical mass of companies together with many active and willing entrepreneurs capable of making business deals happen. When this is added to a recognised and respected legal system it makes Hong Kong the business centre for companies from around the world.

Interestingly many world cities do not restrict the flow of labour, but Hong Kong does due to the size and density of its population. All non-Hong Kong residents are required to obtain a work permit in order to work in Hong Kong. This applies to people from mainland China as well as other countries around the world. Therefore when a multinational corporation sets up a regional headquarters or regional office in Hong Kong and employs staff that are not permanent Hong Kong residents, those staff members will require work permits.

An ID card is normally sufficient for the purpose of obtaining a work permit. World cities are often the educational centre and political capital of the country, but in Hong Kong's case as in New York's case this is not the situation. Hong Kong is a part of China and the political capital is Beijing, which is also the educational centre. Hong Kong companies just like overseas multinationals that have set up manufacturing facilities in China must acquaint themselves with the ramifications of the legal system in China. This would obviously apply regarding any country in which manufacturing facilities are set up by an external multinational company. It is nevertheless very important to have a proper understanding of the country's legal system and its implications for commercial activities.

During its relatively short and dynamic history Hong Kong has gained an immeasurable wealth of business knowledge and experience that has raised its profile above that of surrounding cities and regions. Hong Kong's trade and trade supporting services demand the close and careful attention of multinationals seeking to develop and establish themselves in South East Asia.

Hong Kong has developed into a world city with global aspirations. Some would argue that London, New York and Tokyo are global cities because of their worldwide connections and interactions with places around the world. Hong Kong is attempting to develop along the same or very similar lines with worldwide connections and interactions. Multinationals are to a great extent concerned regarding the global connections and aspirations of the cities in which they locate their offices because this reflects on their company's image and position.

A multinational with an office located in a somewhat run down and backward locality will have a much lower if not maligned image when compared to a multinational with an office located in a highly developed and modern world class city with superb infrastructure and communications network. Image is an important element in the corporate marketing program of most companies.

Competitive advantage is a keen objective of most multinationals. How to achieve such competitive advantage needs to be very carefully assessed. Multinationals need to fully determine their core competencies as well as their peripheral competencies, and fully assess the level of competition, its ramifications and likely competitive counter strategies. Although price is an important element in a competitive strategy it cannot be the sole core element of the competitive strategy otherwise it runs the risk of being undermined when competitors seek to reduce their costs and prices. Intense price competition destroys margins and is generally very unproductive. Multinationals will therefore seek competitive advantage in many different aspects such as :

- ☐ Corporate growth

- ☐ Market dominance

- ☐ Market entry

- ☐ Brand image building
- ☐ Corporate image building
- ☐ Asset acquisition
- ☐ Countering competitive threats
- ☐ Countering growth in competition
- ☐ Market development
- ☐ Sector entry, development or dominance
- ☐ Product reputation and image
- ☐ Company reputation and image
- ☐ Advertising proficiency
- ☐ Public relations activities
- ☐ Customer relationship management and customer service
- ☐ Coordinating corporate structure and activities
- ☐ Distribution and Agency relations
- ☐ Etc.

Hong Kong's development has created many trade and trade supporting services. This rich tapestry is something that multinationals can very easily draw upon when located in Hong Kong.

Due to its close relationship with China, there are many companies in Hong Kong with a wealth of knowledge and business experience in relation to China that are seeking to act as partners and guides for overseas multinational companies seeking to enter the Chinese market. Contact with these companies can easily be made through the InvestHK government funded organisation.

The rapid growth in offshore trade has not only stimulated demand for trade supporting services in Hong Kong, it has enabled Hong Kong to consolidate its position as the most important trading hub in the region. Although there has been an inevitable increase in the number of companies seeking trade supporting services in mainland China, the vast majority of companies located in Hong Kong will continue to maintain their regional headquarters or offices in Hong Kong because of the strategic coordination and management opportunities the territory offers for widely dispersed business activities.

The Annual Survey of Regional Offices Representing Overseas Companies in Hong Kong conducted by the Census and Statistics Department which investigates the number of regional headquarters, regional offices and local offices in Hong Kong found that as at 1st June 2002, there were 948 regional headquarters, 2171 regional offices and 1748 local offices. The presence of so many multinational corporations in Hong Kong with either regional headquarters or regional offices clearly demonstrates that the city has global characteristics. China's accession to the WTO will inevitably attract many more MNCs to the city and the region.

Hong Kong is a very popular place for locating regional headquarters or regional offices whether they be local Hong Kong companies or overseas multinationals. Being based in Hong Kong offers companies a number of advantages when they operate as the control centre, or brain, of regional operations. Having the regional headquarters, or control centre, in Hong Kong, companies can and do control the complete range of business operations including marketing and sales; market research; order placement; product development; material sourcing and procurement; production control and operational output; quality control; inspection and certification; trade finance; packing; transport, freight forwarding and transhipment; logistics; and customer service. This has led to an enormous demand for trade supporting services in all the aforementioned operational activities and Hong Kong has developed a plethora of companies engaged in conducting these operational services.

On 10th May 2001, Mr. Tung Chee Hwa, the Chief Executive of the Hong Kong Special Administrative Region launched the Brand Hong Kong programme. The objective of the programme was to promote Hong Kong internationally as Asia's World City. As part of the programme, Hong Kong was represented with a new modern visual identity and a stylised dragon was used to represent the dynamism and creative spirit of Hong Kong.

It has been argued by some that due to China's emergence into the global market, its prolific economic growth rate in recent years and the expectation that in years to come it will be the largest economy in the world, Hong Kong is well positioned to evolve into being the business capital of the world. That was the finding of CLSA, an eminent investment banking brokerage company. According to the company's chief economist Dr. Jim Walker, capital from China is now being spent in Hong Kong, which automatically raises the profile of Hong Kong and increases economic activity. This is happening because the well established institutions in Hong Kong cannot be quickly replicated in China and therefore China is obliged to make use of Hong Kong's institutions. These institutions include a well established legal system that fully upholds contract law, a convertible currency, the free and unrestrained movement of capital, free and unrestricted flow of information that is essential for good business, low taxation, an efficiently monitored economy and strong stock market, highly developed telecommunications and transportation infrastructures, and a well capitalised privately owned banking system.

A recent report co-authored by Dr. Walker sees Hong Kong as being a substantial beneficiary of China's modernisation with its financial services sector becoming an important coordinating centre for hard currency capital raising activities on behalf of the mainland. Capital surplus from the mainland is now moving into Hong Kong in order to relieve pressure in the mainland. The report points out that Hong Kong companies as well as overseas multinationals based in Hong Kong will benefit greatly from China's accession to the WTO because of the opening up of investment opportunities in service sectors such as accounting, commercial banking, law, insurance, education, engineering, medicine, etc. Hong Kong is moving into the position of becoming a services sector investment attractor of the same magnitude as London and New York if not bigger. The report considers Hong Kong as an investment boomtown that is perfect for corporate location of regional headquarters or regional offices.

The Industry Department helps to promote and facilitate overseas investment in Hong Kong and works closely with seven overseas Investment Promotion Units in North America, Europe, Japan and Australia providing advice and assistance to potential overseas investors. At the end of 1996 there were 403 foreign owned manufacturing companies and 4477 foreign owned non-manufacturing companies in Hong Kong, as well as 2307 overseas companies with regional headquarters or regional offices in Hong Kong to coordinate activities across the region. "To provide additional assurance to overseas investors, Hong Kong has concluded many bilateral investment promotion and protection agreements with its major investment partners including Australia, Austria, Belgium/Luxembourg, Denmark, France, Germany, Italy, Japan, Korea, the Netherlands, New Zealand, Sweden and Switzerland." (Hong Kong Government Publications, 1998, P.93).

Hong Kong has established a number of representative offices in various countries/markets around the world including Europe, the USA, the UK, Japan, Singapore and Australia in order to promote the economic and trade interests of the territory. The territory is also a founding member of the WTO and several other international organisations. Its separate membership of the WTO is indicative of the level of autonomy that the city has in conducting its external commercial relations, which is guaranteed under the Joint Declaration and the Basic Law.

According to Government sources, it is the statutory role of the Hong Kong Trade Development Council to globally promote the image of Hong Kong as a business partner as well as to promote and expand Hong Kong's trade with China and the rest of the world. The Hong Kong Trade Development Council has an extensive network of offices in countries throughout the world and effectively serves as the international marketing arm of Hong Kong's manufacturers and service providers. Extension of the Convention Centre, which is owned by the HKTDC, consolidated the territory's position as the trade fair capital of Asia.

This facility is extensively used throughout the year to host many exhibitions and conventions on an international basis and very effectively helps to promote Hong Kong as Asia's World City. The HKTDC organises many promotional trade events worldwide each year including inward and outward trade missions thereby providing cost effective channels for local manufacturers and traders to reach international markets.

The Hong Kong Export Credit Insurance Corporation (ECIC) provides a wide range of insurance facilities and services to Hong Kong exporters of both goods and services. During 1996-97 the ECIC was awarded ISO 9002 certification, making it the world's first credit insurer to receive such an award and recognition. The corporation is very actively involved in Hong Kong's export trade and is regarded by many as an indispensable service.

Hong Kong has a wide range of trade and industrial organisations including the Federation of Hong Kong Industries, the Chinese Manufacturers Association of Hong Kong, the Hong Kong General Chamber of Commerce, the Chinese General Chamber of Commerce, the Hong Kong Management Association, the Hong Kong Chinese Enterprises Association, the Hong Kong Exporters Association and various chambers of commerce providing a wide range of services including issuance of certificates of origin, handling trade enquiries, organising trade promotion activities, seminars and training courses, trade missions, informational programmes, quality certification and shipment inspection, etc.

Even though some Fortune 500 companies had wrongly dismissed Hong Kong as finished as a result of the handover of sovereignty in 1997, Hong Kong hosted the Fortune Global Forum in May 2001 clearly demonstrating to all Fortune 500 companies and organisations that Hong Kong is very truly a dynamic and industrial economy that is clearly alive and prospering.

On 4th June 2001, the World Association of Newspapers held a 3 day congress in Hong Kong. The congress confirmed Hong Kong's position as a well developed international media centre and also demonstrated Hong Kong's commitment to press freedom and the freedom of speech.

Hong Kong is a very important tourist location with many world class standard hotels. In 2001 there were 13.7 million visitors to the territory. The territory offers many tourist attractions including Hong Kong Disneyland, Ocean Park, Stanley, Repulse Bay, Tung Chung cable car, scenic parks, hiking trails, nature conservation areas, street markets such as Temple Street and Tung Choi Street, Lan Kwai Fong a popular area with the expatriate community, temples such as Wong Tai Sin and Chung Ching Koon, etc. The Hong Kong life style is also a very popular attraction because of its energy, liveliness and cosmopolitan character.

Hong Kong is also very popular because of its abundant shopping facilities and cheap prices as well as the opportunity to haggle in certain quarters. The Hong Kong Tourism Board and Commission have been very thorough in their promotion of Hong Kong as a tourist destination with the result that tourist arrivals have increased considerably since the drop in 1998 which was due to the Asian Financial Crisis.

Business Satisfaction and Recent Reports

According to a recent report issued by the British Chamber of Commerce in Hong Kong regarding a survey conducted of its members in 2003, there is a high degree of confidence in the business environment in Hong Kong on both a short term and medium term basis. There is also good optimism regarding long term prospects. It is considered that the decrease in the cost of doing business in Hong Kong due to the recent deflation experienced by the territory has led to an increase in Hong Kong's regional competitiveness.

Compared to a survey conducted 12 months before in 2002, there was a 1% increase from 86% to 87% concerning overall satisfaction regarding the business environment in Hong Kong. Levels of optimism in relation to business outlook for the future experienced a dramatic increase from 51% to 80%. The medium term outlook was also regarded more positively than before with 90% of respondents considering medium term prospects as good. Long term prospects for the next 5 years were regarded as optimistic by 85% of respondents.

In view of the fact that Hong Kong experienced very adverse economic conditions during the period of 1998 to 2003 due to a number of external factors, it is now considered by many that the territory is experiencing a good recovery. Most see this recovery as a clear indication to the international business community that Hong Kong is still the ideal location for conducting business both in China and the Asia Pacific region. However, it is also considered by many that the Hong Kong government needs to deliver on policies recently introduced as well as balance the budget and that the Hong Kong work force needs to continue to improve its skills so as to remain attractive to international companies in order to attract investment.

The year 2003 is generally regarded as having been a difficult time for Hong Kong, but 90% of the chamber's members considered the outlook for the next 2 years as very positive, which was a substantial increase on the 75% recorded in the previous year. China is now an integral part of the Hong Kong economy and 71% of the chamber's members expect to invest in China within the next three years. Up to 65% of the chamber believe that the Closer Economic Partnership Arrangement (CEPA) recently entered into by Hong Kong and China will have a positive effect on business in the territory.

With regard to satisfaction ratings, the British Chamber of Commerce Annual Business Confidence Survey in 2003 revealed that various aspects of conducting business in Hong Kong were regarded as being of particular note. Public security and safety scored a satisfaction rating of 99%, communications network scored 98%, geographic location scored 98%, infrastructure scored 97% and the taxation system scored 97%. The survey results are virtually identical with survey results from previous years and clearly demonstrate the very positive business attributes that Hong Kong has to offer the international community.

Another aspect of the economy that also received a noticeable finding was the level of satisfaction regarding the pegging of the Hong Kong dollar to the United States of America dollar which experienced a satisfaction increase of 12% from 79% in 2002 to 91% in 2003. This was no doubt due to the stability that it provided to the economy. Freedom of the press also saw an increase in satisfaction rating from 79% to 89% and satisfaction with intellectual property rights protection experienced a notable increase of 16% from 74% in 2002 to 90% in 2003.

However, there did seem to be a certain level of dissatisfaction with government leadership as well as the level of air quality in the territory. Despite this, it would be a little harsh to be too critical of the government, because since the handover of sovereignty in 1997, the Hong Kong government has experienced a number of difficult external factors that have had a definite effect upon the territory. The government has nevertheless maintained control and safely managed the economy, and now provided that the external global environment shows signs of peace and prosperity Hong Kong will experience growth.

Regarding financial matters it must also be noted that decreasing commercial office rents and decreasing property rents have led to increased levels of satisfaction due to their beneficial effect on economic business circumstances. The report issued by the British Chamber of Commerce in Hong Kong in 2003 clearly sees good optimism in Hong Kong's future and rates the territory as a very attractive place in which multinationals can locate offices and conduct business locally as well as regionally.

The 2004 World Investment Report by the United Nations Conference on Trade and Development states that Hong Kong is the second largest recipient of foreign direct investment in Asia after China and also is the 11th largest recipient in the world. The report also states that Hong Kong is the best performing host economy for foreign direct investment in Asia and number three in the world. Hong Kong's foreign direct investment inflow in recent years has been as follows:

Year	1996	1997	1998	1999	2000	2001	2002	2003
US$ Billion	10.5	11.4	14.8	24.6	61.9	23.8	9.7	13.5

The exceptionally high figure for 2000 was due to exceptional mergers and acquisitions.

The report predicts that foreign direct investment (FDI) will increase in Asia in the short term as faster economic growth is experienced together with improving corporate profitability. Asian growth rates have been amongst the best in the world recently and Hong Kong is in a particularly advantageous investment position due to its location and economic infrastructure. It should also be noted that whilst the majority of FDI is coming from western countries, there is nevertheless a growth in FDI from China thereby making Hong Kong a very cash rich society.

Hong Kong is of course still conducting investment initiatives and promotions overseas via InvestHK and the Economic and Trade Offices. A new investment facilitation policy recently announced by the Ministry of Commerce is geared towards encouraging mainland Chinese companies and organisations to invest in Hong Kong.

The Economic Freedom of the World Annual Report 2003 by The Fraser Institute ranked Hong Kong as the freest economy in the world followed by Singapore, the USA, New Zealand and the UK.

According to a report released by CB Richard Ellis entitled Global Market Rents in January 2004, Hong Kong was ranked 31st in the Global 50 Index regarding occupancy cost per annum. This in effect means that the cost of office space in Hong Kong is cheaper than many other cities around the world including London, Sydney, Tokyo, Seoul, Mumbai, etc. This makes Hong Kong a very appealing locational prospect for many of the world's multinationals.

The World Heritage Foundation in 2004 again voted Hong Kong the freest economy in the world for the 10th consecutive year. As one of the largest trading entities in the world with a duty free port, Hong Kong is the model of free trade according to the report.

Hong Kong: The World City and International Business Centre

22. Regional Headquarters and Setting up a Company

According to the 2004 Annual Survey of Regional Offices Representing Overseas Companies in Hong Kong conducted by the Census and Statistics Department, on 1st June 2004 there were 1098 overseas companies with regional headquarters in Hong Kong, representing a 13.66% increase on the figure of 966 for 2003. On the same date there were 2511 overseas companies with regional offices in Hong Kong, representing a 12.05% increase on the figure of 2241 for 2003. The survey also showed that on 1st June 2004 there were 2334 overseas companies with local offices in Hong Kong, representing a 5.75% increase on the figure of 2207 for 2003.

Analysis conducted by the survey showed that the main countries or territories of incorporation of the parent company of the regional headquarters, regional offices and local offices were the United States, Japan, China and the United Kingdom. The main lines of business for these headquarters and offices were wholesale, retail and import/export; business services; transport and transport related services; finance and banking.

The survey noted that there were a number of favourable factors regarding the establishment of a regional headquarters, regional office or local office in Hong Kong including the free flow of information, low and simple tax system, absence of exchange controls, corruption free government, well established communication and transport infrastructures, geographical location, free port status, availability of a wide range of business and professional support services, business opportunities in China, availability of financial services, etc.

Nevertheless the cost and availability of business and residential accommodation were regarded as being something of a negative factor. However, in general Hong Kong is viewed as having an improved business environment compared with the previous survey in 2003.

Many of the regional headquarters and regional offices in Hong Kong are not just responsible for business in Hong Kong, but also cover China and South East Asia.

Of the regional headquarters 233 were from the United States of America, 159 were from Japan, 96 were from China, 80 were from the United Kingdom and 52 were from Germany. Of the regional offices 471 were from Japan, 437 were from the United States of America, 170 were from China, 163 were from the United

Kingdom and 121 were from Taiwan. Of the local offices 296 were from Japan, 290 were from China, 272 were from the United States of America, 138 were from the United Kingdom and 86 were from Singapore.

The major lines of business conducted by these regional headquarters in 2002 were 486 in wholesale, retail and import/export trades; 227 in business services; 87 in finance and banking; 63 in transport and related services; 53 in manufacturing; 29 in construction, architectural and civil engineering; 20 in insurance; 17 in telecommunications services; 7 in real estate; and 6 in restaurants and hotels. The major lines of business conducted by the regional offices in 2002 were 1133 in wholesale, retail and import/export trades; 535 in business services; 177 in finance and banking; 123 in transport and related services; 75 in manufacturing; 68 in construction, architectural and civil engineering; 61 in insurance; 36 in telecommunications services; 14 in real estate and 12 in restaurants and hotels. The major line of business conducted by local offices in 2002 were 576 in wholesale, retail and import/export trades; 438 in business services; 335 in finance and banking; 112 in transport and related services; 92 in construction, architectural and civil engineering; 83 in insurance; 54 in manufacturing; 49 in real estate; 24 in restaurants and hotels; and 12 in telecommunications services. It should be noted that some of the offices are in more than one major line of business.

It should be noted that a regional headquarters is an office that has control over regional operations covering Hong Kong and one or more other places, and that management of the business is done without frequent referrals to the parent company outside Hong Kong. A regional office is an office that coordinates regional operations covering Hong Kong and one or more other places and that management of the business is done with frequent referrals to the parent company outside Hong Kong or to the regional headquarters. A local office is an office that takes charge of business conducted solely in Hong Kong. A parent company outside Hong Kong is a company with final management control over all the operations and activities of one or more offices in the region.

The most popular and commonly used trade supporting services in Hong Kong are freight forwarding and consolidation, which also incorporates warehousing activities. Other popular trade supporting services include trade finance facilities and documentation; market research; research and development; advertising; business negotiation; product design; insurance cover; testing and certification of shipments; and arbitration. These trade supporting services are used for shipments from China as well as other third country origin sources.

Recent surveys have indicated that many companies both local and overseas multinationals place overwhelming importance on Hong Kong as an ideal location for strategic coordination and management of widely dispersed business operations. Many companies have recently revealed their intention of maintaining their regional headquarters or regional offices in Hong Kong, with a sizeable percentage planning to further expand their offices in Hong Kong because of its ideal location for corporate objectives.

It is the objective of many Hong Kong traders and overseas multinationals to oversee the whole process of value creation from start to finish, from sourcing to final delivery to the buyer. In this way companies can monitor progress and make immediate improvements where appropriate. Action can be taken immediately whenever required. A major advantage of having the company regional headquarters in Hong Kong is the opportunity to closely monitor and control flexible and very efficient production when it is being carried out in China or South East Asia. An increasing number of Hong Kong companies use the city as a control centre base.

Very often the entire manufacturing process is controlled from the headquarters in Hong Kong. This includes order placement, material sourcing, product development, sales, marketing, market research, operations management, trade finance, quality control, inspection and certification, shipping and freight forwarding, logistics, etc. This has led to an enormous demand for trade supporting services, which has in turn greatly stimulated the overall economy. Hong Kong's trading cluster is now moving more towards being a global integrator in international trade with a growing control over many of the parts of the entire supply chain.

The opening up of mainland China's economy in the late 1970s helped transform Hong Kong into an international business centre and China's accession to the WTO will lead to a further structural change and development of the Hong Kong economy. Increased liberalisation in China will facilitate further economic expansion of companies in Hong Kong, both local and overseas multinationals, and greater penetration of the mainland market even though there will be greater competition from mainland companies. China's WTO entry will raise the level and intensity of trade both to and from China. The Chinese market will be a lucrative market for those companies that are prepared to venture into the market.

Hong Kong service providers are currently expanding into mainland China in increasing numbers in the same manner that manufacturers have done over the past 25 years. With China's entry into the WTO this expansion will be made much easier and quicker as obstacles are removed regarding foreign participation in service sector activities. Research indicates that many Hong Kong service providers plan to increase the level of their activities with regard to business negotiation, market research, insurance, trade finance and documentation, product development and design.

Hong Kong's role as a prime location for regional headquarters has a long history, but it was not until the 1980s that this role began to assume some significance with the rate at which regional headquarters and regional offices were being established tending to speed up. Nevertheless recent survey data has indicated that regional headquarters and regional offices consider that there are certain aspects which need government attention. These aspects include government support for business development, economic conditions, the education system, unemployment and pollution problems. The cost and availability of residential accommodation, business accommodation and staff are also issues to be considered carefully.

Nowadays multinational corporations are tending to look at areas and territories on a regional basis as part of a drive towards globalization and a global strategy. As such multinational corporations are seeking to locate their regional headquarters or regional offices in places ideally suited to conveniently, efficiently and completely cover a particular region. Hong Kong is centrally positioned in South East Asia with quick, convenient and easy access to the whole of South East Asia and all other business centres in the region. This central location is a distinct advantage for companies located in Hong Kong.

Globalization drivers and the demand for cheap cost effective manufacturing facilities have resulted in South East Asian countries as a whole achieving a significant advantage in the manufacturing sector. This has greatly increased the springboard potential of Hong Kong as well as its control centre function. Today Hong Kong is only moderately attractive as a potential sales market or even as a production base, but it is very attractive as a strategic location because of its role as a gateway to China and also as a management control centre for broader operations. Multinational corporations cannot afford to miss the greatest market opportunity the world currently has in the form of China which is set to grow at a very rapid pace to become the largest economy in the world within the next 20 years. The strategic importance of China cannot be ignored.

Hong Kong and Singapore are clearly the chosen places for multinationals in South East Asia with Hong Kong normally being the preferred option. This is because both of these cities have the independent spirit to operate functionally as a base for regional headquarters or regional offices and both of these cities are well acquainted with the global processes of multinational corporations and more importantly the global culture of these corporations. It is recognised that in South East Asia it is Hong Kong and Singapore that have the most effective and efficient channels of distribution both globally and regionally. Overseas companies seeking to develop sophisticated distribution systems in the region should consider these cities first before any other locations.

Over the last 25 years Hong Kong has transformed itself from being a production site to being a base for managing and controlling manufacturing and production operations in China and elsewhere in South East Asia. With regard to regional marketing operations, Hong Kong's communications and transportation infrastructures are the best in Asia and make Hong Kong a very exciting city in which to live and work. They are also very cost effective infrastructures that are not a burden to the population. As regional distribution centres both Hong Kong and Singapore are highly rated regarding distribution infrastructure and distance requirements, but with Hong Kong probably being the better, subject to the objectives of the particular multinational corporation. With regard to customer service operations, again both Hong Kong and Singapore are the best choices in South East Asia. Both have good communications infrastructures as well as multilingual capabilities, which are obviously key determinants in this particular aspect of business.

With regard to the location of regional headquarters, the major concerns of multinationals are the communications and transportation infrastructures, the proximity of the markets to be entered or developed by the regional headquarters, the projected cost of such a regional headquarters on corporate budgets, the marketing activities to be conducted and their relevance and importance to corporate plans both short and long term, as well as the quality of life and availability of appropriate staff both expatriate and local for conducting regional headquarters operations. On these points Hong Kong is clearly the best option in South East Asia: its communications and transportation infrastructures are the best in Asia; its strategic location means that it has quick and easy access to all other cities in Asia; it is the best location for entry into the Chinese market and has a number of organisations that can assist with this entry; it is an ideal location for marketing activities and has companies that can assist in all types of marketing activities; it is also the best place in South East Asia for exhibitions and conventions with probably the best convention and exhibition centre in Asia; it offers an exciting life for those living and working in Hong Kong, both short term and long term; and it has an abundance of highly educated and qualified labour capable of performing without difficulty the vast number of business jobs and functions.

For those multinational companies not seeking to establish a regional headquarters or regional office, Invest Hong Kong can help to establish partnership relations between the multinational company and an appropriate Hong Kong company so as to develop opportunities in the Chinese market as well as regional markets. This is a distinct advantage for overseas multinationals and is very cost effective. Multinational corporations must realise that the Asia Pacific region is certainly extremely important from a global perspective and multinationals must include the region in their global strategies otherwise they will lose out to their competitors not just on a cost basis, but also on a brandname development and total sales basis. MNCs must be fully cognisant with competitor corporate strategies and the short as well as long term effects that these strategies will have on their own business fortunes. Corporate growth dictates that China and South East Asia must be incorporated into the global strategies of multinationals that wish to survive in the long term. At present, China and South East Asia represent the most economically active areas in the world with tremendous growth prospects and therefore multinationals cannot afford to ignore these areas.

Many MNCs promoting and selling in China now use Hong Kong as a regional base in order to control sales and distribution activities over the border. In 1999 the Industry Department reported that of the 2,490 overseas MNCs with regional headquarters or offices in Hong Kong more than 50 per cent were active in the distributive trade sector, and of those companies more than 90 per cent covered the Chinese market. Over a thousand MNCs with regional headquarters or offices in Hong Kong in 1999 were active in sales and distribution in China. Provided that Hong Kong is able to maintain the quality and world class standard of its professionals and the quality of its managerial staff as well as make every effort to control the cost of conducting business in the territory, its attraction as a regional base will continue to flourish.

It has been reported in a recent comparative study performed by the Hong Kong Government that living costs for expatriate personnel are lower in Hong Kong than in other cities such as London, New York and Tokyo. This is just one of the factors that helps Hong Kong in being a more attractive place for establishing an overseas headquarters or office.

Security is often an aspect that is overlooked when considering the location of a regional office overseas. However, it must be pointed out that Hong Kong is one of the safest cities in Asia, if not the world. The Hong Kong police are an extremely efficient and even-handed force that for many years has ensured the safety of all people living in the territory. It is perfectly safe to go out on the streets at any time of day without fear of being mugged or assaulted. Unfortunately this is not possible in many Western societies. Of course Hong Kong, like all cities, has its criminal elements, but petty crime is not the problem that it is in many western countries. Hong Kong is a very safe city, which should be an important consideration for multinational companies planning to set up an office in the city and have staff stationed in Hong Kong.

In 2002, Hong Kong received world class recognition for its facilities, which further emphasized its position and reputation for being an excellent international business centre. The territory received three renowned prestigious accolades:

- ☐ The Hong Kong Convention and Exhibition Centre was again voted for the ninth consecutive year as being the world's Best Overseas Conference Centre,

☐   Hong Kong International Airport at Chek Lap Kok was voted Cargo Airport of the Year, and

☐   The University of Science and Technology School of Business and Management in Hong Kong was rated as being the best business school in Asia.

Hong Kong's trading companies provide a very high quality service to their overseas customers and are currently experiencing a growth in demand from mainland China. Hong Kong has an extensive range of efficient business support services and is expected to maintain its position as a competitive business partner for many companies, organisations and regions. It is expected that many foreign importers will continue to maintain their regional headquarters in Hong Kong because of its support structures.

Hong Kong is a very strategic location having quick and easy access to many other Asian business centres. Coupled with this fact is the city's world class infrastructure and extensive business services, which together have propelled Hong Kong into the ranks of world cities. London serves as Europe's business capital whilst New York serves as the United States of America's business capital and both are recognised as world cities. Hong Kong is in the same niche as these two cities and serves as South East Asia's business capital and world city. In June 2003 there were 3,207 overseas companies with regional operations in Hong Kong. These comprised 966 regional headquarters and 2,241 regional offices which at that time represented a record high for the territory since the annual survey of Regional Offices Representing Overseas Companies in Hong Kong began.

Hong Kong has thrived due to its belief in the free trade of goods and services. The territory does not offer companies financial incentives to locate in the city as is common in many western countries. Instead Hong Kong offers what is probably one of the freest and best business environments in the world with an abundance of business support services that are geared towards helping companies that locate in the city to prosper in their chosen field. This independent business spirit is the life force of Hong Kong and has been so ever since the 1840s when Hong Kong was founded. The city has been a free port for more than 150 years, which has enabled companies to freely move product in and out of the territory as required. Much of Hong Kong is privately owned and run, but regulated by a government with a hands off approach so that business can freely flourish and the community can reap the rewards.

Many multinational companies regard Hong Kong as a very suitable location for a regional headquarters or regional office due to a number of reasons. A recent report on the Annual Survey of Regional Offices Representing Overseas companies in Hong Kong found that the most favourable factor for setting up a regional headquarters or regional office in Hong Kong was the low and simple tax system. Companies have found that it is a decided advantage to know in advance how much ones tax bill is going to be. Also the fact that the corporate as well as personal tax rate is so low means that overall operational costs of multinationals is reduced to a very manageable level. Hong Kong has for many years prided itself on the efficiency and cost effectiveness of its tax system and the fact that its tax rates are noticeably lower than competing locations. This is without doubt one of the prime reasons why Hong Kong has more multinationals stationed in its territory than all other cities in Asia.

Other favourable factors for locating a regional headquarters or regional office in Hong Kong cited by many companies in the survey included the political stability and security of the territory; free flow of information; rule of law and independent judiciary; corruption free government; absence of exchange controls; communication, transport and other infrastructure as well as the territory's free port status.

When establishing a regional headquarters or regional office in Hong Kong, many multinational corporations have listed the following factors as being very important attractions in determining there choice of Hong Kong as their preferred location:

- ☐ Low, simple and predictable tax system;

- ☐ Free and unrestrained flow of information;

- ☐ A stable political system and personal security;

- ☐ A clean and corruption free government;

- ☐ An independent impartial judiciary supported by the rule of law;

- ☐ World class banking and financial facilities;

- ☐ Highly developed communications and transportation infrastructures.

Whereas other cities have restrictive and some would argue protectionist regimes, Hong Kong is a very free and open society where the rule of law is supreme and the safety of the individual is paramount.

In order to be regarded as a world city, the structures and institutions within the city have to be geared towards the international or global market. The city has to be receptive to all the actions and influences from the global market place, but at the same time able to assert its own position within the global market. Much of the business, as is the case with Hong Kong, has to be conducted at an international level with many interactions with other countries around the world. Active participation in global forums and associations is also another aspect of being a world city.

For many years Hong Kong has been very actively involved in the international market having trade relations with many countries around the world. The city's growth as a leading business centre in Asia has attracted a great interest from companies and countries from around the world. According to recent reports its position now and forecast growth prospects within the next 20 years mean that Hong Kong will be propelled to an even higher level as the main business centre of Asia and the world. China is placing a greater reliance on Hong Kong as its primary financial centre and an increasing number of companies and countries are placing a greater reliance on Hong Kong as a means to enter China. This two way flow of trade interests automatically raises demand for Hong Kong's services sector and gives rise to a much greater flow of finance through the city. This in turn enriches the city thereby increasing its appeal. The very cosmopolitan character of Hong Kong also helps to raise its image as a world city, because there are people from all over the world now living and working in Hong Kong. This gives rise to a very diverse cultural image that is highly respected and even cherished in the city.

Hong Kong is now seen as the regional headquarters for regional and global operations by an increasing number of companies. Its business environment is amongst the best in the world with companies free to actively pursue their corporate objectives with very little if any government interference. It is this freedom of action for companies to pursue legally acceptable corporate objectives that has made Hong Kong an extremely attractive city for many companies. Its simple and low tax system has also greatly contributed to its corporate attractiveness because companies can very quickly and easily assess their income and expenditure requirements in order to justify their corporate actions. Added to this, the efficiency and reach of the financial services sector has meant that Hong Kong automatically becomes a magnet for investment capital. As such Hong Kong is a very attractive location for foreign direct investment (FDI) and is the second most popular site for FDI in Asia. It is also recognised internationally as providing a very good return on such investment capital.

According to a Hong Kong Trade Development Council report in 2000, China's WTO accession is certain to attract many more MNCs to the region and Hong

Kong's ability to serve MNCs with substantial interests in China will be unrivalled. Nevertheless some of the larger MNCs may decide to enter the Chinese market directly, but will in all probability maintain a regional headquarters or regional office in Hong Kong. MNCs will find that Hong Kong remains an advantageous location for conducting business in China and South East Asia. Hong Kong is set to remain the most favourite location for a regional headquarters or regional office. China's WTO accession is not going to change this position, if anything it will strengthen it. It is wrong to assume that China's WTO accession means that MNCs no longer need Hong Kong as a gateway to China and that these MNCs will relocate into China.

The economic environment in China is not the same or even comparable with that of Hong Kong. China does not have the business infrastructures that Hong Kong has developed over many years. It is true that perhaps a few MNCs may relocate from Hong Kong into China, possibly to Shanghai. However, the majority of MNCs will maintain a presence in Hong Kong, but no doubt with a growth in activity in China. China's WTO accession is set to attract many MNCs to the region and facilitate other MNCs in their further expansion into China. The smaller MNCs with their leaner corporate structures and greater propensity to outsource services will find Hong Kong is the ideal location for a regional headquarters or office, because of its extensive range of business services of a world class professional calibre.

According to an Industry Department survey in 2000, it was found that most MNCs with regional headquarters in Hong Kong are responsible for operations covering a wider area than just Hong Kong and China. Many are also covering South East Asia and the Asia Pacific region.

New Regional Headquarters and Regional Offices

When planning to establish a regional headquarters or regional office overseas in a city like Hong Kong there are many points and aspects for the company to consider in order to facilitate a smooth and productive investment process. These points of consideration will include:

- ☐ Cost

- ☐ Personnel (expatriate & local)

- ☐ Language (communications)

- ☐ Marketing objectives
- ☐ Corporate objectives
- ☐ Marketing budgets
- ☐ Term of the office - how long is it planned to run the office
- ☐ Tax implications
- ☐ Potential profits expected
- ☐ Level and nature of competition
- ☐ Corporate brandname development potential
- ☐ Product brandname development potential
- ☐ Forecast market development
- ☐ Forecast market demand for company product or service and expected future development
- ☐ Product / service pricing strategies
- ☐ Etc.

Over the last three years it has been reported that many companies have now moved to Hong Kong. The companies listed below are just a small number of the total number of companies that have either established regional headquarters or regional offices in Hong Kong within the last three years.

	Company	Country	Sector
1.	Fila	USA	Retail
2.	Tanberg ASA	Norway	Marketer of Video Conferencing Systems
3.	IEE (Institution of Electrical Engineers)	UK	Professional Body

Company	Country	Sector
4. Financial Times	UK	Media
5. Royal Ten Cate	Holland	Supplier of Industrial Products
6. Fortinet	USA	IT
7. Hong Kong Yamazaki Diecast	Japan	Diecast Manufacturer
8. EMC	USA	Information Storage and Management
9. Fujisawa Pharmaceutical	Japan	Pharmaceuticals
10. CompTIA (Computing Technology Industry Association)	USA	Global IT Industry Association
11. University of Ulster	UK	Education
12. ITX E-Globaledge	Japan	Technology Solution Provider
13. ACI (Airports Council International)	Switzerland	Professional Body
14. Perbio Science AB	Sweden	Biotechnology
15. Schema	Israel	IT
16. Metro AG	Germany	Retail
17. PBEC (Pacific Basin Economic Council)	Asia Pacific	Largest independent business association in Asia Pacific
18. Hamburg Sud	Germany	Container Shipping Group

19. Olympus	Japan	Maker of Home Appliances
20. Alladin Knowledge Systems	Israel	Software Security
21. Mailprove	New Zealand	Anti-Spam and Security Services
22. Nanomuscle	USA	Technology
23. Renesas Technology Corporation	Japan	Semiconductors
24. UFI (Global Association of the Exhibition Industry)	France	Union of Exhibition Industry
25. Nutech Company Ltd	Mainland China	Supplier of Container Inspection Systems
26. Byford	Malaysia	Retail
27. KBC Asset Management Ltd.	Belgium	Financial Services
28. Peribit Networks	USA	Telecommunications
29. IndeCorp Corporation	USA	Hotel Marketing
30. Dragon River	USA	Manufacturer of herbal-health supplements
31. Acterna	USA	Telecommunications
32. Air Plus International	Germany	Tourism
33. James Thomas Engineering	UK	Engineering
34. Topcom	Belgium	Telecommunications

35. Citrix Systems	USA	Access Infrastructure Provider
36. United Commercial	USA	Banking
37. Benesse Corporation	Japan	Provider of Education Products and Services
38. Musiwave	France	Mobile Music Entertainment Service Provider
39. Altea	Italy	Fashion (Ties)
40. Boubon Watch	France	Watchmaker
41. DePfa Bank	Ireland	Banking
42. Frontier Silicon	UK	Semiconductor Manufacturer
43. illy	Italy	Food and Beverage
44. Kingdee	China	IT
45. Tokyo Style Hong Kong Co. Ltd.	Japan	Fashion
46. Hansgrohe	Germany	Homeware
47. Look (HK) Ltd.	Japan	Fashion
48. Mingkeda	China	Retailer of Electrical Appliances
49. OppenheimerFunds Inc.	USA	Asset Management
50. Ermenegildo Zegna	Italy	Fashion
51. Bayer MaterialScience	Germany	Biochemical

52. ECCO	Denmark	Shoes and Apparel
53. Braccialini	Italy	Fashion
54. Pianegonda	Italy	Jewellery
55. STX Pan Ocean	Korea	Transportation
56. Yokohama	Japan	Automobile Parts
57. Richard Mille	Switzerland	Watches
58. Network Appliance, Inc.	USA	IT
59. Methanex	Canada	Chemicals
60. Megabite	Singapore	Restaurant
61. Gatineau	France	Beauty
62. Belkin Corporation	USA	Technology
63. Oriola	Spain	Law
64. Sisley	France	Cosmetics
65. The Executive Centre	UK	Professional serviced offices
66. SM Entertainment	Korea	Entertainment
67. MiniCo Self-Storage	USA	Logistics
68. Ingenious Coaching	Australia	Professional business services

During 2003 142 foreign companies either established themselves in Hong Kong or expanded operations in Hong Kong making it the most successful year for inward investment promotion in Hong Kong. All the companies were assisted by InvestHK in fulfilling their investment objectives which collectively resulted in at least HK$2.49 billion in direct investment and substantial job creation. Hong Kong is without doubt the preferred location for many multinationals regarding international business in the Asia Pacific region. According to the Census and Statistics Department, foreign direct investment (FDI) inflow in 2003 was HK$105.6 billion, which represented a 39% increase on 2002. These figures show that Hong Kong is definitely a preferred destination for FDI and the fundamentals of Hong Kong are very attractive for foreign investors. InvestHK is therefore busily promoting the advantages of Hong Kong and the Pearl River Delta in order to attract foreign multinationals.

Business Registration

Companies are allowed a period of one month to obtain their business registration certificate after commencing business operations. In 2004, a one year business certificate of registration fee was HK$2,600 whilst a three year business certificate of registration fee was HK$7,000 and the over the counter processing time for the certificate was normally 30 minutes.

A postal application for business registration normally requires two working days. A locally incorporated limited company or a company incorporated overseas must be registered with the correct submission of relevant documents. The Business Registration Office is situated in the Inland Revenue Building in Wan Chai at:

Business Registration Office
Inland Revenue Department
4/F, Revenue Tower
5 Gloucester Road
Wan Chai
Hong Kong
T: (852) 187 8088
F: (852) 2824 1482
E: taxbro@ird.gov.hk
W: http://www.info.gov.hk/ird/eng/tax/bre.htm

Prior to incorporating a new company and obtaining a business registration certificate, a search must be conducted at the Companies Registry to ensure that the proposed name for the company is not already registered and being used by another company. The Registrar of Companies maintains an index of company names for all companies in Hong Kong. The search is conducted free of charge at the Public Search Section of the Companies Registry which is located at:

Companies Registry
13/F, Queensway Government Offices
66 Queensway
Hong Kong

Information to be presented to the Registrar of Companies after conducting a search at the Companies Registry includes the following documents:

- ☐ Memorandum of Association

- ☐ Articles of Association

- ☐ Declaration of Compliance

- ☐ Proforma indicating company name, presenter's name, address, telephone number and facsimile number

The printed Memorandum of Association must contain the following information:

- ☐ The company name in English or Chinese or both,

- ☐ The word limited must be used for an English name or 4 Chinese characters indicating limited for a Chinese name (the format of Chinese characters is available from the Inland Revenue Department),

- ☐ The Hong Kong registered office address,

- ☐ A statement that the liability of members is limited,

- ☐ An indication of the amount of authorised share capital at the time of incorporation,

- ☐ An indication of the number of shares possessed by subscribers,

- ☐ The signatures of all the subscribers with attestation by a witness.

The printed Articles of Association must be in consecutively numbered paragraphs. The following must be observed:

- [ ] For a private company, the Articles must contain a statement indicating that it is private,

- [ ] The First Schedule of the Companies Ordinance indicates regulations that companies may adopt. These may be adopted completely or in part. Table A Part I of the Ordinance is for companies that are not private, whilst Table A Part II is for companies that are private,

- [ ] Each subscriber given in the Memorandum of Association must sign the Articles of Association and the signature must be attested by a witness.

The specified form NC1A 'Statement of Compliance on Incorporation of a Company' must also be signed by the relevant people named in the Articles of Association who individually may be a subscriber, a director or secretary. This form is signed after the Memorandum of Association and Articles of Association have both been signed. It takes approximately 6 working days to incorporate a local limited company.

Incorporation fees in 2004 were HK$1,720 upon application plus HK$1.00 for every HK$1,000 or part thereof of nominal share capital up to a maximum of HK$30,000. For companies without share capital the charge was from HK$170 to HK$1,025 depending on the number of members. For information regarding fees, the New Companies Section of the Companies Registry should contacted at:

New Companies Section of the Companies Registry
14/F, Queensway Government Offices
66 Queensway
Hong Kong
T: (852) 2867 2587
F: (852) 2526 9843

Private limited companies and registered branches of overseas companies are the two most common forms of business entity for overseas investors. It is a legal requirement that overseas companies must within one month of commencing business apply for registration with the Inland Revenue Department.

The Registrar of Companies requires that the following documents must be submitted at the time of registration:

- [ ] The Memorandum of Association and Articles of Association defining the company's constitution. These documents must be certified.

☐ For registration of an overseas company in Hong Kong form F1 must be submitted clearly indicating details of the directors, the secretary and authorised representative in Hong Kong; the Hong Kong address of the business; the business address in the place of incorporation and the registered office address in the place of incorporation.

☐ A copy of the Certificate of Incorporation of the company which must be certified.

☐ A copy of the latest accounts of the company which must be certified unless exemption to this submission has been granted by the Registrar of Companies.

Form F1 must be completed in either English or Chinese. Form F1 may be purchased at the Companies Registry or downloaded from the Companies Registry Internet website (http://www.info.gov.hk/cr/). Original documents or certified documents should be submitted with the application. The latest accounts documents should be in English or Chinese, or a certified translation.

A notary public should be used to certify the competence of the translation. It normally requires 22 working days to register an overseas company in Hong Kong. The application/registration fee in 2004 was HK$1,720 plus HK$20 registration fee for each additional document to be registered in support of the application. Further information regarding the registration of an overseas company in Hong Kong can be obtained from:

Overseas Companies Section of the Companies Registry
29/F, Queensway Government Offices
66 Queensway
Hong Kong
T: (852) 2867 4655
F: (852) 2523 5629

The Business Licence Information Service (BLIS) is provided by the Trade and Industry Department and is a one stop service providing a complete array of information on licensing requirements for all types of businesses in Hong Kong, such as restaurants, factories, trading companies, retail shops, etc. The purpose of this service is to assist investors in their planning and investment, save time and reduce the risk of discrepancies and non-compliance with regulations stipulated by the government. The full service may be obtained from:

Trade and Industry Department
M/F, Trade and Industry Department Tower
700 Nathan Road
Kowloon
Hong Kong
T: (852) 2398 5133
F: (852) 2737 2377
W: http://www.info.gov.hk/licence

When establishing a company, matters regarding the rules and regulations concerning the Memorandum of Association, Articles of Association and registration of companies, both local and overseas, companies should contact the Trade and Industry Department in order to obtain details of the latest and most current requirements so as to ensure that the company satisfactorily complies with all legal obligations. Rules and regulations change over time and therefore the Trade and Industry Department should be the primary source of contact when establishing a company.

Banking, Currency and Credit

When applying for banking, currency and credit facilities, the directors of a locally registered company in Hong Kong, must submit in person to the bank the following documents:

- ☐ Identification in the form of passports or identity cards;

- ☐ A certified copy of the board of directors resolutions for regulating the account;

- ☐ A certificate of Business Registration;

- ☐ For an unlimited company, notification of compliance with Hong Kong Business Registration Form 1(a), (b), (c) and (d);

- ☐ For a limited company - Certificate of Incorporation, Memorandum of Association, Articles of Association and details of all the directors registered with the Companies Registry; and

- ☐ The company chop

These requirements will vary depending upon which bank is used.

When a company registered as a foreign company applies for banking, currency and credit facilities in Hong Kong, it must provide the same information as provided by a locally registered company plus:

☐ The Overseas Company Certificate of Registration; and

☐ A list of all the directors and secretary together with any Companies Registry amendments.

Banks will freely provide full details of their requirements regarding company accounts and banking facilities, and companies should carefully check these requirements. Bank credit and facilities are freely available to foreign investors in the same way as they are to local investors and on the same terms. However, terms will vary from bank to bank based on the perceived credit risk.

Funding Schemes

Under the government's maximum support philosophy there are a number of funding support schemes available to the business sector including :

i) *The Innovation and Technology Fund*

This fund is administered by the Innovation and Technology Commission and is responsible for financing projects geared towards upgrading and developing innovative technology to be used in the manufacturing and services industries.

The government has established an Innovation and Technology Fund of US$640 million in order to support projects that have the objective of enhancing innovation and technology in industry as well as those projects regarded as essential for the future development and upgrading of industry. Up to 75% of the cost for training staff in new technologies is supported by the fund. The aim of the fund is to increase productivity, added value content and competitiveness in manufacturing and service industries. It seeks to encourage technology ventures and R & D activities so as to raise the technological profile of the city. A grant may also be provided for patent applications. A HK$250 million fund has been established creating a DesignSmart initiative with the objective of assisting design ventures and providing training in design and branding. A Design and Innovation Centre has also been established and companies are now allowed a tax deduction relating to the costs of research and development expenses regarding design related activities.

ii) The Applied Research Fund

This is controlled and administered by the Applied Research Council, which is owned by the Government. The objective of the fund is to encourage technology ventures and applied R & D that have commercial potential. This will raise the technological capability and competitiveness of industry leading to higher value added output. The fund is private sector managed with proposals being assessed on the basis of technical and commercial viability. Investment proposals are also determined by the private sector.

iii) The New Technology Training Scheme

This is administered by the Vocational Training Council. It provides assistance to companies seeking to have staff trained in new technologies that would be beneficial to the business sector and to Hong Kong in general. Training may be overseas, local or by means of work attachment.

iv) The Patent Application Grant

The Hong Kong Productivity Council is the implementation agent for this scheme. The Patent Application Grant has been devised with the objective of assisting companies in applying for patents to cover their inventions. In 2004 patent applicants could obtain a grant of up to US$12,820 or 90 per cent of the cost of the patent application depending upon which was the least. The grant is awarded to cover the patent application costs including attorney fees, technical appraisal, consultancy fees, filing, etc.

Regional Headquarters and Setting up a Company

23. Recent Examples of Companies Setting Up in Hong Kong

Leading fashion hair designer comes to Hong Kong

Toni & Guy, the UK-based fashion hair design chain have now opened a salon in Hong Kong as a first step in expanding into the Greater China region. According to the director, Susan Roberts, the international lifestyle in Hong Kong together with its very discerning clientele meant that the city was the ideal point at which to commence its expansion programme. As an international brand, Toni & Guy found that there was considerable demand for their product in such an international city like Hong Kong.

Hong Kong as a launchpad for regional expansion

London based sandwich chain store Pret A Manger is using Hong Kong as a launchpad for expansion into the Asia-Pacific region. Its first store was opened in 2002 with plans for a further 4 stores to be opened in due course. According to Andrew Rolfe, the company chairman and chief executive, Hong Kong, like London and New York, where the company also has branches, has the same high values including good customer service, speed of delivery and a passion for high quality food.

Growth in certification authorities in Hong Kong

According to the Financial Times dated 12th October 2001, BTI Consultants which is part of Kelly Services Inc., a Fortune 500 company with 2,200 offices worldwide, established it's North Asia regional office in Hong Kong.

According to the Financial Times dated 20th January 2003, KEMA BV established it's Greater China Headquarters in Fanling, New Territories, Hong Kong. It was stated that the organisation had a commitment to Hong Kong as a central base for its Greater China operations. The reasons given for this position were Hong

Kong's strategic location, world class infrastructure, skilled workforce, transparent government and regulatory framework. KEMA BV is a technical service provider and consultancy.

IT Industry Association establishes Regional HQ

The largest global IT industry association, CompTIA (The Computing Technology Industry Association), in March 2004, established its regional headquarters in Hong Kong. CompTIA is the world's main supplier of vendor neutral information and communication technology skills certification. CompTIA regards Hong Kong as the launch pad to establish contacts throughout the region. It's decision to choose Hong Kong was due to its strategic location and the fact that the IT industry in the region is booming. Also the region is home to 3 billion people so the growth potential is tremendous.

Hong Kong as a Regional IT hub

According to Ornit Avidar, the commercial attache for the Israeli Consulate, the growth in the number of Israeli high-tech companies based in Hong Kong demonstrates that the Hong Kong Special Administrative Region functions as a regional information technology hub as well as a good base location for expansion in the Asia-Pacific. Hong Kong is seen as the pivotal hub due to its excellent infrastructure and communications capability. Some 25 Israeli high-tech companies already have their regional headquarters located in Hong Kong. Hong Kong is seen as a stable operating base with quick and convenient access to all regional locations due to the territory's extensive air network infrastructure.

VDE Global Services GmbH in Hong Kong

In April 2004 VDE Global Services GmbH established its Greater China centre in Hong Kong under the name VDE Global Services HK Ltd. This regional headquarters is planned as an important base for regional expansion. The Hong Kong office will be responsible for the business operations of regional representative offices in Shenzhen, Guangzhou, Shanghai, Beijing, Suzhou and Taiwan. Product certification is extremely important in order to meet market requirements and in the past many Hong Kong manufacturers have struggled to obtain certification because of the communication gap due to the distance away from the market. Now that VDE have established a regional base in Hong Kong it will greatly facilitate the smooth and efficient process of obtaining product certification approvals. VDE is a major technical and scientific association in Europe covering many product sectors. The company regards Hong Kong as a strategic location from an operational point of view particularly with regard to the dramatic developments in the mainland China market.

Top Japanese company uses Hong Kong as a springboard for entry into China and the region

According to a recent report in February 2004, the Japanese company ITX E-Globaledge Corporation is using Hong Kong as a springboard in order to develop business in China and the surrounding region. The company has selected Hong Kong as a regional base in order to take advantage of the huge market potential of China and the region. The Hong Kong company that has been established by the Japanese head office is ITX E-Globaledge Hong Kong & China Limited and this will oversee all business operations in China as well as the activities of the representative office in Shanghai.

ITX E-Globaledge is one of Japan's major IT business creation companies, and is a leading electronics and networking solution provider that is a key player in a number of fields including networking and computing, PC peripherals, mobile and wireless communications, power supplies, etc. The company regards China as the future of the electronics industry. The Hong Kong office is envisaged as an important key step in business development for the company that will enable it to expand in China using advanced technology and business models from the rest of the developed world whilst also enabling it to bring out product from China to the rest of the world. Hong Kong therefore functions as a two way means of entry and exit for development of the China market.

According to the company president of ITX E-Globaledge Corporation, Hong Kong offers unique advantages that other Asian markets cannot match. These include a pool of local available talent with expertise in the IT industry and fluent language capability in English, Chinese and Japanese. The Hong Kong business environment is also seen as being particularly advantageous for the company. The geographic location of Hong Kong is also seen as being particularly strategic with it being able to serve as a window to the international market and able to handle all trading business to overseas markets.

The establishment of a regional office in Hong Kong, by such a major Japanese company, has further strengthened Hong Kong's position as the main international business hub in Asia. This will inevitably encourage other foreign companies to likewise consider setting up a regional headquarters or regional office in order to access the Chinese market as well as that of other surrounding regional Asian markets.

Leading Chinese technology company uses Hong Kong as a strategic base for global expansion

Nutech Company Limited, during March 2004, established its first regional office, outside Mainland China, in Hong Kong. The company is one of the world's leading suppliers of container inspection systems and is a renowned leader in the research and development of X-ray inspection technology. Nutech acknowledges that Hong Kong is an ideal location for technology companies seeking to expand and develop relations overseas due to its well established international networks and relations. Nutech's Hong Kong office will be responsible for business coordination and development with overseas companies and liaison with agencies around the world.

Nutech was established in 1997 and has concentrated on the development, manufacture and marketing of civil security applications for nuclear technology and high tech products. The company has the largest professional X-ray inspection system manufacture in the world and its proprietary X-ray inspection system has been exported to many markets around the world. Nutech chose to locate its first regional office outside China in Hong Kong because of Hong Kong's recognised and well established advantages in various sectors including trade, finance, transportation and technology. Hong Kong is able to offer many mainland Chinese companies unique advantages in their desire to expand globally, because of its well established business environment, geographical location, talented labour with international experience, well developed communications infrastructure, its legal system and fair play environment, its well established financial infrastructure, etc.

Regional HQ for ED.UK.8 Kids Ltd.

In April 2004, ED.UK.8 Worldwide Ltd. established its regional headquarters in Hong Kong under the name ED.UK.8 Kids Ltd. The company has been established to market the organisations educational toys, tools, media and appliances for young children in Hong Kong and the region as well as to use Hong Kong as a vehicle for entry into the Chinese market.

Hong Kong was chosen because of its business friendly reputation as well as its central location in Asia, level playing field for business, simple and low tax regime and its corruption free government. Hong Kong is also seen as a good market to obtain customer feedback regarding product features and innovations that can be used in future product developments.

Good growth in the regional insurance sector

In November 2001, Swiss Re, the top life re-insurance company in the world, established its Asian Division headquarters in Hong Kong. The company has been active in Hong Kong for 45 years, but in November 2001 decided to expand its regional operations by creating a headquarters in Hong Kong. The insurance sector in Hong Kong is seen as offering strong benefits for the company with it expected that there will be strong long term growth in Hong Kong and the region. Hong Kong was seen as the natural choice for a regional headquarters because of its close proximity to China and its well developed financial and insurance sectors. Hong Kong was also seen as offering a talented pool of employees, a good legal environment with the rule of law and a good level of maturity in the financial services sector that makes it an ideal business location.

Part of the reason for Swiss Re's move was because of the globalisation process and the trend towards a stronger concentration of resources in Asia due to the growth and potential of the market. China is seen as a rich and potential market to be developed in the next few years. The Swiss Re office is a very multinational environment with approximately 60% of the staff being Hong Kong Chinese and the remaining 40% being a variety of nationalities including Indians, French, Germans, Italians, Swiss, Malaysians and Swedish. Two other large insurance groups have also recently set up regional headquarters in Hong Kong - these are the Standard Life Investments Group from the UK and the Axa Group from France.

In October 2001, the largest insurance company in the world, the Axa Group from France, established their Asia Pacific headquarters in Hong Kong. Axa's strategic decision of choosing Hong Kong for an Asia Pacific headquarters was due to its functional expertise, regional potential, growth prospects and ability to serve the region. The region is seen as offering tremendous business opportunities with Hong Kong as the gateway to China and other Asian markets due to it being an international hub for financial services. It is also recognised that compared to all the other cities in Asia, Hong Kong offers the most competitive position with regard to mainland China which is seen as becoming the largest potential market in the world.

Hong Kong is also seen as being an unrivalled location from which multinational organisations can develop and manage business growth in China and the Asia

Pacific region. As a leading insurance centre in Asia, Hong Kong has attracted many leading insurers and China's accession to the WTO and progressive liberalisation offers further business opportunities that will inevitably lead to an intensification of competition in the sector and elsewhere.

During September 2001, Standard Life Investments decided to establish their Asia Pacific regional headquarters in Hong Kong after conducting a comparative locational analysis between Hong Kong and Singapore. Hong Kong was selected because its financial markets have a high degree of liquidity and operate effectively under a transparent regulatory system. Hong Kong is a very open insurance centre and an important regional base for portfolio management activities.

As more high profile insurance companies locate in Hong Kong it raises the reputation of the city. Management at Standard Life also note that as a result of China's accession to the WTO, Hong Kong's position as the gateway to China and the region will inevitably gain importance because of its world class infrastructure and very comprehensive banking and financial systems. Another reason why Standard Life chose Hong Kong as its base was because so many other multinationals are also seeking to locate in Hong Kong in expectation of business opportunities to emerge in the vast Chinese market which is in the process of opening up to the world.

The Importance of Fund Management

In June 2002 a leading European bank Westdeutsche Landesbank Girozentrale (WestLB), established a Business Development and Client Servicing office in Hong Kong for its fund management unit WestAM. The company chose Hong Kong because it is recognised as being a sophisticated regional market for financial services with a very attractive and rich potential clientele. Hong Kong was also seen as having an extremely talented pool of employees very capable of helping business grow.

The company revealed that even though whilst conducting its corporate location analysis and other cities in the region appeared to offer a lower cost, it was firmly decided that long term business potential was by far much greater if the company chose Hong Kong as its regional base. Hong Kong was also seen as being a springboard for regional expansion and therefore it was decided that the Hong Kong office would be responsible for the entire Asian region, with the exception of Japan.

When the office opened in June 2002, the speed of the business environment, its efficiency, openness, work attitude and dynamic lifestyle were fully noted by the

German management. It was stated that things could be achieved very quickly in Hong Kong that would probably take twice as long in Europe. Another aspect of Hong Kong that was welcomed by the company was the safety of the Hong Kong environment, which was regarded as particularly suitable for young families.

WestAM is a fund management company with over 500 institutional clients worldwide including pension funds, banks, insurance companies, corporations, endowments, government agencies, etc. It is considered that WestAM will be yet another reason for Hong Kong to maintain its position as the leading financial services centre in Asia.

Hong Kong is well recognised as offering fund managers numerous advantages in the form of free flow of capital and information, a clear and transparent regulatory system, an independent legal system based on English common law, an absence of government bureaucracy, sophisticated telecommunications infrastructure, low and simple corporate tax regime, and a highly qualified array of fund management professionals. These aspects of Hong Kong were no doubt well considered by WestAM prior to establishing its regional base in Hong Kong.

Growth in Mexican interest in Hong Kong

Many Mexican companies have tried to develop direct relations with mainland Chinese companies, but have so often found themselves having to come to Hong Kong for expertise and talent that is available in Hong Kong, but not in China. As a result Hong Kong is becoming a base for Mexican companies and an increasing number of partnerships are being formed.

Innovative software solutions provider chooses Hong Kong

In April 2004, the US based innovative software solutions provider Blackpearl, Inc. established its Asia Pacific headquarters in Hong Kong. The company provides software solutions to companies in the financial services industry with the objective of eliminating costly and inefficient processes, improving service quality and identifying revenue opportunities and risks. The company considered that as a global financial centre Hong Kong's financial services industry is well developed and as such is a prime target for the company. Hong Kong has over 380 banking institutions, 2,100 securities dealers, 200 insurers and 1,600 unit trusts and mutual funds and as such presents a good opportunity for the company.

All of these institutions are seeking to develop a competitive edge in a very competitive market and therefore will be able to use the services of Blackpearl,

Inc. It was also noted that Hong Kong has an unrivalled position as a springboard to China and the whole of Asia and therefore presents good development opportunities for the company.

Chinese Software Company seeking global growth expands Hong Kong operations

In March 2004, China's number one software applications provider, Kingdee International Software Group Co. Ltd. decided to expand its Asia Pacific headquarters in Hong Kong in a determined attempt to expand globally into overseas markets. Ever since 2001 the company has been providing local Hong Kong and multinational companies with enterprise software and professional services. The company regards Hong Kong as the window to the world and considers Hong Kong as offering a strategic opportunity to sell globally because of its well developed institutions and infrastructures.

Kingdee is a provider of enterprise software in China's commercial market and is currently in the process of building strong partnership networks outside China so as to develop software sales in resource planning, knowledge management, customer relationship management and business performance management. The company serves many industrial sectors including electronics, banking and finance, telecommunications, pharmaceuticals, property development, automotive and travel. Hong Kong is seen as a major strategic stepping stone to global development.

Kingdee was the first Chinese software company to list on the Growth Enterprise Market index in Hong Kong. It was stated that Kingdee can provide localised enterprise software to Hong Kong and multinational companies seeking entry into China as well as supply best price enterprise software to other markets in the Asia Pacific. Kingdee's expansion of its facilities in Hong Kong is seen as a strong endorsement of the city as an international business hub for Chinese companies.

Leading IT company opens regional headquarters in Hong Kong

In February 2004, EMC Corporation opened its new regional headquarters in Hong Kong covering the Asia Pacific and Japan. The company is a world renowned leader in information storage and management. In selecting Hong Kong as its regional base it was decided that Hong Kong's strategic location at the centre of the region together with its well developed telecommunications infrastructure and excellent world class international airport made the city the ideal location in order to remain competitive. China was also seen as a huge potential market with its fast GDP growth and therefore location on its door step in Hong Kong was an ideal vantage point for entry into the mainland market. Hong Kong was also seen as having a skilled workforce with international exposure and a good IT talent. It was also considered that the strategic move by a major player like EMC Corporation was a strong endorsement of Hong Kong's position as a regional business hub and would help Hong Kong move further up the technology ladder.

Communication Boom

In December 2001 Communication Asia Network (CAN) selected Hong Kong as its worldwide headquarters. CAN is a US/European broadcasting company that has located in Hong Kong with the intention of broadcasting a vast range of cultural, informational and educational material to the Asian market. The decision to choose Hong Kong was greatly assisted by InvestHK who understood the needs of the company, introduced it to the community at the Science and Technology Park and also created opportunities by opening business meetings with key industrial players relevant to CAN's industry.

As a result CAN has now formed a partnership with the Hong Kong University of Science and Technology in order to establish a state-of-the-art digital multimedia institute for the 21st century. The company regards Hong Kong as a definite launchpad for regional operations and considers prospects to be exciting.

Philips streamlined expansion

In April 2002 Philips Electronics China Group streamlined its South East Asian operations and integrated its Hong Kong and Singapore operations into one Asia Pacific headquarters in Hong Kong. According to the company, Hong Kong is an excellent location due to the regional emphasis of the hi-tech industry being more on North East Asia and China. Hong Kong's sophisticated communications and transport infrastructures together with its world class airport helps the company keep in close contact with its target markets. Also Hong Kong's position as the Asian conference and exhibition centre is another plus point.

Hong Kong is an important purchasing hub for the Philips operation due to Southern China being an important source of product. Philips is a very multicultural and international company employing people of many different nationalities in the same location. Staff in Hong Kong whether local or expatriate enjoy a good quality of life in Hong Kong as well as access to good schools and health care. The company has had a long history in Hong Kong having first opened an office in 1948 and since then has seen considerable development and expansion. The HKSAR is Philips world headquarters for portable audio and sound accessories products. It is envisaged that there will be further regional expansion in the coming years with Hong Kong being the central control centre.

Major USA Pharmaceutical company locates new Asian Headquarters in Hong Kong

Eli Lilly, a major United States of America pharmaceutical company, has had a sales office in Hong Kong since 1976. However, in December 2001 the company established its Asian headquarters in Hong Kong. It was stated that the structural move was because Hong Kong is an ideal central location from which the company can oversee and coordinate its considerable regional sales and clinical activities throughout Asia. The Asian headquarters will be responsible for corporate and government affairs, human resources, legal aspects, finance requirements, medical functions and marketing in the region.

According to the company, the Chinese pharmaceutical market is the fastest growing in the world, and Hong Kong will provide the necessary springboard function to actively enter the Chinese market. The company feels confident because it is envisaged that with China's accession to the WTO there will be definite improvements in intellectual property rights, tariffs and regulatory systems. Hong Kong will have a very important position in the company's expansion into the Chinese market.

Canadian company creates Asia Pacific Headquarters in Hong Kong

In June 2002, Northern Digital Inc. established its Asia Pacific headquarters in Hong Kong. The company develops, manufactures and sells a range of advanced measurement systems for a wide range of applications from image guided surgery to industrial quality inspection and reverse engineering. Its new office is located in the commercial district of Wan Chai and is regarded as being a permanent base in the region. According to the company Hong Kong was an obvious choice for a regional base because of its excellent infrastructure and extremely well developed IT, telecommunications, transport and shipping sectors.

It was also appreciated that Hong Kong has an abundance of professional services in the legal, financial and marketing communications sectors with highly trained personnel. Northern Digital Inc. regards Asia as being a very important growth market and Hong Kong as an efficient and international business environment from which the company can market its products on a regional basis with particular emphasis upon China. It was stated at the opening ceremony of the new office that the company seeks to work in close partnership with its customers so as to adapt its technology to meet customer specific needs.

InvestHK also highlighted the fact that Hong Kong is very important as a sales and marketing location for many multinational companies that seek to develop and expand their business operations in Asia and that as an ideal location with excellent infrastructures the vast majority of companies find that it is quite easy to maintain close and developed contact with regional target markets.

Leading wireless broadband company chooses Hong Kong

In May 2004, Navini Networks, a leading American wireless broadband technology company set up its regional headquarters in Hong Kong in order to develop networks throughout the Asia Pacific region. According to the company Hong Kong was chosen for three specific reasons:

1. It has the best logistics system in the region enabling companies to reach customers easily across the region from Australia to India and everywhere in between.

2. It is the natural gateway to China, an important target market.

3. It is a telecommunications hub and enables Navini Networks to remain in close contact with developments in the trade.

Navini Networks uses wireless broadband technology of a wide area format that is patented in order to deliver to its customers multi-megabit speeds with up to a range of eight miles from its base station. The company has been recognised in the industry as playing a major role in innovation, technological development and corporate strategy for the sector.

It was noted that as an important well developed financial, trading and transport centre, Hong Kong has a great need of the types telecommunication services that are clearly a part of Navini's product sector. Also Hong Kong's comprehensive broadband coverage and user base represent an ideal launch pad for all types of new technologies and associated applications across Asia. Hong Kong was also considered as being the ideal base from which to approach the Chinese market.

Recent examples of companies setting up in Hong Kong

Europe's No.1 telecom company moves into Hong Kong

In November 2002, Deutsche Telekom Group, the leading European telecommunications company, established its Greater China office in Hong Kong confirming Hong Kong as being of tremendous strategic importance for multinational telecommunications companies aiming at serving the strong growth market in China.

The new company T-Systems China Ltd., is a subsidiary of the Deutsche Telekom Group and is involved in creating solutions by means of the merging of information technology and telecommunications for its corporate customer base in Greater China. This company's corporate investment endorses Hong Kong's position as the regional telecommunications centre. It was noted that Hong Kong's excellent geographical position coupled with its telecommunications infrastructure made Hong Kong a global communications centre with a perfect international network. Hong Kong has been ranked as number one by the International Telecommunication Union regarding its Mobile/Internet Index meaning that the territory is the best productive location for developing business in this sector.

T-Systems China Ltd. can now make full use of Hong Kong's experienced pool of telecommunications specialists and China business partners/operators, as well as take full advantage of Hong Kong's simple and low taxation system, its stable monetary infrastructure and transparent corruption free legal system. The company is confident that its global communications infrastructure and international set up will enable it to follow its customers to any market in the world. Deutsche Telekom is yet another company of a world class character that has decided to establish a strong base in Hong Kong in order to expand its Asian operations with particular emphasis upon China.

Major telecoms group locates its Asia Pacific Headquarters in Hong Kong

The BT group moved its Asia Pacific headquarters from Australia to Hong Kong in July 2002. This was a strategic corporate move so that the company could be more centrally located in order to deal with the Asia Pacific market and give particular attention to the strongly developing China market. The company is the business services and solutions section of the BT group and a recognised high profile information and communications technology service provider. BT has been operational in Hong Kong for over 15 years and regards its localised approach to Hong Kong and China as gaining strength.

The company's corporate mentality is to think global at a corporate level, but to act local at an operational level and this has facilitated successful development of business within the region. The Asia Pacific region is seen as being critical to corporate development.

Hong Kong is recognised as being the premier location for multinational headquarters due to its geographical location, world class infrastructures in many sectors, international cosmopolitan environment, multilingual workforce of a high capability and its professional support services in finance, transport and legal aspects. As such Hong Kong is a superb location for foreign multinationals with ambitions on the China market. Hong Kong is generally the preferred business base for the Asia Pacific region and BT is yet another company taking advantage of this fact.

It was noted that the Asia Pacific region is currently seen as the best potential growth market for the next decade. The increasing number of companies deciding to establish their regional headquarters in Hong Kong is set to increase business spending in the economy and lead to the creation of more high value added jobs in the city thereby boosting the Hong Kong economy. An increasing number of multinational companies like the BT Group are using Hong Kong as their base for an Asia Pacific regional headquarters or regional office in order to cover operations in the Asia Pacific region and China.

Hong Kong is seen as being a corporate decision making control centre for regional operations by many multinationals in the growing Asia Pacific market. The expanding presence of companies like BT will add to the strength of Hong Kong as a world class telecommunications centre. InvestHK have of course been of assistance to BT Plc in the corporate relocation of their Asia Pacific headquarters.

New Asian Headquarters established in Hong Kong for USA satellite tracking company

In July 2002, Aprize Satellite Limited established its Asian headquarters in Hong Kong. The new company is a Sino-US joint venture under the name Aprize Asia Ltd. and has been established with the objective of using the China business experience and relations of the Hong Kong partners in order to explore and develop the Chinese market quickly and efficiently with minimal risk.

Aprize Satellite Limited produces systems designed for the monitoring as well as tracking of assets whether fixed or mobile by means of low-Earth orbit satellites. The systems are extremely reliable and very low cost and hence very market competitive. Aprize uses a very innovative, proprietary system for efficient data transmission over the Internet at a reduced fee and equipment cost. The Aprize system represents a good development in asset tracking and data monitoring and is regarded as being particularly suitable for use in the shipping container, truck trailer and oil tanker markets.

China's accession to the WTO is seen as the opening of a huge potential market with very good business opportunities and Hong Kong is regarded as being the ideal operations centre for development of the China market as well as a good base for servicing the region as a whole. Hong Kong was regarded as the natural choice for Aprize in Asia, because of its well developed business environment, its flexibility of operations and its support services. Hong Kong has a well developed and cost effective telecommunications and IT infrastructure supported by an efficient international business environment that is ideal for the satellite communication business. It was stated by InvestHK Ltd. that Aprize having chosen Hong Kong as its regional headquarters is yet another example of a leading international company realising Hong Kong's advantages as a central business location for efficiently and effectively coordinating business operations throughout the Asia Pacific region and China as well as taking advantage of Hong Kong's capital raising facilities.

Famous Japanese restaurant opens first restaurant in Hong Kong

In April 2004, the Japanese restaurant Mi-ne Sushi opened its first restaurant in Hong Kong, regarding the city as a very good potential market. The company regards Hong Kong as the true culinary capital of Asia because there are so many restaurants providing such a variety of cuisine. As a very cosmopolitan city it is only natural that there should be such a wide variety of cuisine in Hong Kong to cater for the diverse range of nationalities. It was noted that Hong Kong's multi-cultural consumer base was always seeking more choice together with a wider variety of choice particularly in quality cuisine and that when a good quality restaurant is established, news of its presence quickly passes along the grapevine leading to a surge in clientele.

The company plan to open more restaurants in Hong Kong due to the demand for quality Japanese food in an attractive environment. It was stated that the Hong Kong consumer is very open to international cuisine because it is such an international city. The company regards Hong Kong as its main business base outside Japan and further expansion within the region or possibly globally is envisaged.

Ace Hardware opens Hong Kong buying office

In April 2004, Ace Hardware Corporation of the USA opened its international buying office, AGD Asia Ltd., in Hong Kong. Ace is the largest hardware retailer-owned cooperative in the USA. The new office is seen as an important step in corporate strategy and will facilitate sourcing and procurement of products for the co-operative's members. The organisation regards Hong Kong as an important window to China and the region. The telecommunications and transportation infrastructures in Hong Kong are seen as being very modern, up to date and sophisticated.

Therefore Hong Kong is seen as being an excellent platform for AGD Asia Ltd. to use as a base for sourcing, purchasing and effectively delivering a wide range of products from the region to its dealer countries. The organisation sees tremendous business opportunities in Asia and believes that its presence in Hong Kong will help it meet those opportunities. Hong Kong is regarded as the international sourcing hub in Asia due to its excellent business environment. Hong Kong's central geographic location, world renowned infrastructures, multilingual and proficient workforce and the availability of professional support services mean that Hong Kong is the prime location in which multinational companies seek to base their regional offices and this fact was well recognised by Ace Hardware Corporation when it established its buying office.

Top ladies fashion store opens in Hong Kong

In March 2004, the leading Belgian ladies fashion brand SCAPA started business in Hong Kong. The store will be operated by Look (HK) Ltd., which is a subsidiary of a Japanese leading ladies fashion company. SCAPA can be found in the ifc Mall and will offer ladies fashion items, handbags and accessories. Hong Kong was chosen because of the city's sophisticated retail, distribution and management structures. Three further SCAPA stores are planned, all to open within the next two years.

It was noted that Hong Kong is Asia's leading fashion centre as well as style capital and therefore is the best place for established retailers to build brand awareness. It was also stated that Hong Kong consumers are very fashion conscious and therefore receptive to new fashion products and brands entering the market. The company sees Hong Kong as a means of developing a position in China, which is regarded as offering enormous potential, and therefore by opening a store in Hong Kong in order to showcase their products it will in time build brand awareness and lead to expansion into the Chinese market.

Airports Council International moves its Pacific Regional Office to Hong Kong

In June 2004, the Airports Council International office in Vancouver was relocated to Hong Kong as the new Pacific Regional Office. The Airports Council International is a non-profit organisation whose role is to develop cooperation between member airports and world aviation authorities including airlines, governments and aircraft manufacturing companies. The organisation has 535 members covering 1,500 airports in 165 countries.

Hong Kong was chosen as the new Pacific Regional office because of its unique location, the growth rate of China's air travel market, and the high number of air routes centred on Hong Kong. It is expected that the office will serve as a base for technology transfer, learning and the sharing of experience of airport members which will help business growth in general. It was noted that the regional office being located in Hong Kong would strengthen the city's position as the aviation hub on both a regional and global basis. Being based in Hong Kong is testimony to the fact that Hong Kong is such a strategic location with much connectivity to important markets where prospects are developing well.

The strengthening of Hong Kong's role as international shipping centre

In May 2004, Operasia Forwarding Ltd. from Spain set up its regional office in Hong Kong. The company is a subsidiary of the leading Spanish international freight forwarder Operinter, S.A. It is planned that the company's Hong Kong office will be responsible for both seafreight and airfreight shipments to customers located in regional markets. It was stated that the Hong Kong office will be used for planned expansion into the Chinese market because Hong Kong provides an ideal position for companies like Operasia, which specialise in transportation and logistics, to enter the Chinese market and take advantage of business growth opportunities.

Operasia were attracted to Hong Kong because of its well established business, legal and banking environment as well as its strategic location and the expertise of its workforce. Hong Kong is the world's busiest container port and its international air cargo handling facility is the largest in the world. Business activity in this industry is enormous and very competitive. Also in January 2004 Hong Kong and China implemented the CEPA arrangement, which is scheduled to lead to greater business flows between Hong Kong and the Pearl River Delta region. The Hong Kong government in expectation of growing demand for business facilities between Hong Kong and China is committed to developing the infrastructure and resources. Hong Kong is without doubt, due to its highly developed business environment and resources, the natural springboard for foreign multinational companies like Operasia Forwarding Ltd. seeking to enter into or expand operations in China and throughout the region.

Bayer MaterialScience chooses Hong Kong

In January 2006, after having studied many cities in the region, Bayer MaterialScience (BMS) which is one of the 300 companies in the Bayer group decided to select Hong Kong as the base for its new Asian business operations. The Hong Kong office will be responsible for the management functions of its business and service units as well as its regional service centre. The objective of this move is to establish central control of operations. This links in very closely with Hong Kong's development as a control centre for many companies with regional operations.

Bayer MaterialScience revealed that its reasons for choosing Hong Kong as its base included the services orientation of the city, its central geographic position in the region and its well developed transport connections throughout the region, its level of information technology and communications infrastructure, together with the international outlook of its citizens. Hong Kong's integrated economic links with China and the advantages under the CEPA arrangements with China were also important considerations.

ECCO and Footwear Development

ECCO, the Danish footwear manufacturer is experiencing good growth in Hong Kong. The company set up its regional Asia Pacific headquarters in Hong Kong in 2002 to control retail, distribution, sales, sourcing and management functions. The Hong Kong office is responsible for all activities and functions conducted throughout the Asia Pacific region. Since 2002 the company has expanded substantially. In March 2003 ECCO opened its first shop and in 2006 has now opened its fifth shop in Telford Plaza, Kowloon. There are further plans for development of a flagship shop together with concept shops. The company regards Hong Kong as an ideal strategic market that offers good potential for long term business development in the region and is therefore committed to further investment. ECCO regard brand name development as the key to regional success.

> Recent examples of companies setting up in Hong Kong

Other Corporate Developments in Hong Kong:

The IT company Network Appliance Inc. from the USA has recently opened its regional headquarters in Hong Kong in order to support distribution activities and partners across the region.

The jewellery company Pianegonda from Italy has opened its first store in Hong Kong. The company chose Hong Kong for its store because of the city's infrastructure and logistics. The city is also seen as a fashion and accessories trend leader, Asia's main business hub and an ideal doorstep to China.

SGS the Swiss inspection, testing and certification organisation was set up in Hong Kong in 1959 and has very recently strengthened its Hong Kong base in line with developments in the Pearl River Delta. All management and support services are now from Hong Kong, which functions as the company's regional headquarters.

The Korean shipping company STX Pan Ocean has 270 vessels calling at ports all over the world. The company has recently set up a subsidiary office in Hong Kong due to the tremendous growth in the import and export trade between the Pearl River Delta and the rest of the world. Its Hong Kong office will mainly be involved in sales activities and the provision of services for container traffic.

Hong Kong's number one provider of serviced offices is the UK organisation The Executive Centre, which has now launched two more centres in Central district and Hong Kong Eastern district. These centres are part of a HK$156 million investment programme for Asia and Europe. The organisation forecasts strong long term growth in demand for serviced office space in Hong Kong from both foreign companies and local Hong Kong companies seeking offices that are cost effective. In 2006, The Executive Centre was providing services to over 1,000 companies in Hong Kong and was regarded as being the leading provider of serviced offices in the Asia Pacific with 19 centres in 10 cities.

The Canadian chemical company Methanex has very recently moved its Asia Pacific base from Auckland, New Zealand to Hong Kong. Methanex is the world's leading manufacturer of methanol and has moved to Hong Kong because Asia is now experiencing the fastest growth of demand for methanol in the world. The company sees the move as a means of being closer to its customers in order to ensure the quality of service.

The USA logistics company MiniCo Self-Storage has now opened its second unit in Hong Kong. The 65,000 sq. ft. storage facility is located in Chai Wan in Eastern Hong Kong. The company is geared towards providing safe, secure, private and clean storage facilities for both commercial and residential customers in a convenient and cost effective manner.

The Italian fashion company Braccialini has now simultaneously opened its regional head office in Hong Kong together with two retail stores. The company designs and manufactures shoes, leather goods, handbags and accessories. It sees Hong Kong's central geographic location and international trading expertise as the best means of developing its various brands on a regional basis. Sales, marketing, finance, logistics and retail functions will be controlled from the Hong Kong office.

The Singapore restaurant company Megabite first established a bakery chain in Hong Kong called Breadtalk in June 2005. Now in 2006, the company has established a food court called 'Food Republic' with the objective of developing a new concept in Asian food. Hong Kong is regarded as being something of a food paradise and this development is seen as being a good move in the company's long term corporate development in Asia.

Recent examples of companies setting up in Hong Kong

24. Useful Addresses and Contacts

Invest Hong Kong and Hong Kong Economic and Trade Offices

InvestHK Head Office:
Suites 1501-6, Level 15
One Pacific Place, 88 Queensway
Hong Kong
T: (852)-3107-1000
F: (852)-3107-9007
E: enq@InvestHK.gov.hk
W: http://www.InvestHK.gov.hk

Economic and Trade Offices of the Government of the Hong Kong Special Administrative Region

Brussels Office
Rue d'Arion, 118 Arlon
B-1040 Brussels
Belgium
T: 32-2-775-0088 (general)
F: 32-2-770-0980
E: general@hongkong-eu.org
W: http://www.hongkong-eu.org

London Office
6 Grafton Street
London, W1S 4EQ
UK
T: 44-20-7499-9821
F: 44-20-7495-5033
E: general@hketolondon.gov.hk
W: http://www.hketolondon.gov.hk

New York Office
115 East 54th Street, 5th Floor
New York, NY 10022
U.S.A.
T: 212-752-3320
F: 212-752-3395
E: hketony@hketony.gov.hk
W: http://www.hongkong.org/new_york.html

San Francisco Office
130 Montgomery Street
San Francisco, CA 94104
U.S.A.
T: 415-835-9300
F: 415-421-0646
E: hketosanfrancisco@hketosanfrancisco.gov.hk
W: http://www.hongkong.org/san_francisco.html

Washington, DC Office
1520, 18th Street, N. W.
Washington
DC 20036
U.S.A.
T: 202-331-8947
F: 202-331-8958
E: hketo@hketowashington.gov.hk
W: http://www.hongkong.org/washington_dc.html

Sydney Office
Level 1, Hong Kong House
80 Druitt Street
Sydney, NSW 2000
Australia
T: 612-9283-3222
F: 612-9283-3818
E: enquiry@hketosydney.gov.hk
W: http://www.hketosydney.org.au

Useful Addresses and Contacts

Singapore Office
9 Temasek Boulevard
#34-01, Suntec Tower Two
Singapore 038989
T: 65-6338-1771
F: 65-6339-2112
W: http://www.hketo.org.sg

Guangdong Office
Flat 7101, Citic Plaza
233 Tian He North Road
Guangzhou
Guangdong, 510 613
China
T: 8620-3891-1220
F: 8620-3891-1221
E: general@gdeto.gov.hk
W: http://www.gdeto.gov.hk

Tokyo Office
Hong Kong Economic and Trade Office Building
30-1 Sanban-cho, Chiyoda-ku
Tokyo 102-0075
Japan
T: 81-03-3556-8961
F: 81-03-3556-8960
E: Invest@hketototyo.gov.hk
   tokyo_enquiry@hketotyo.gov.hk
W: http://www.hketotyo.or.jp

Overseas Consultants

Canada
Shirley Wong, Principal Consultant,
Investment Promotion, Canada
14 College Street, Toronto
Ontario, M5G 1K2
Canada
T: 416-596-7500
F: 416-596-7501
E: swong@investhk.ca

Germany
Geert Hovens,
Investment Promotion Executive, Germany
Hardstrasse 8,
78256 Steisslingen
Germany
T: 31-478-50-81-65
F: 31-478-50-81-66
E: ghovens@lancebv.com

Italy
Stefano De Paoli,
Investment Promotion Executive, Italy
Piazza Bertarelli, 1
20122 Milano
Italy
T: 39-02-8953-4108
F: 39-02-8460-841
E: stefano@depaoliassociati.com

Korea
Jennifer Lee, Consultant
#201, 2F, Trade Tower,
159-1, Samsung-Dong
Kangnam-Ku, Seoul
Korea
T: 82-2-6000-6320
F: 82-2-551-7060
E: Jennifer@InvestHK.co.kr

France
Lorna Lennon,
Investment Promotion Executive, France
9 Cité Dipetit Thouars
75003 Paris
France
T: 33-1-42-77-12-84
F: 33-1-43-56-12-05
E: llennon@bailiwickonline.com

India
Shammi Hattangdi,
Senior Consultant, India
A.F. Ferguson & Co.
Maker Tower "E", 4th Floor
Cuffe Parade
Mumbai 400 005
India
T: 91-22-2218-6412
F: 91-22-2218-6567
E: shammi@investhk-in.com

Japan
Tommy Hirano, Senior Consultant
Western Japan Consulting Office
c/o Hong Kong Trade Development Council
10/F Osaka Kokusai Building,
2-3-13 Azuchimachi, Chuo-ku
Osaka 541-0052
Japan
T: 81-6-4705-7019
F: 81-72-727-5537
E: westjpn@investhk.jp

Middle East
Dr Sunil Gupta, Senior Consultant
Muscat Office:
Way No 2107, Villa No. 223, PO Box 308
P.C. 114, Jibroo
Sultanate of Oman
T: 968-791-876 / 968-798-881
F: 968-704-394

Dubai Office:
A1 Sahel Building, Flat #6, 2nd Floor
Deira, PO Box 35264, Dubai
The United Arab Emirates
T: 971-4-273-7034
F: 971-4-273-7035
E: sgupta@ideas-consulting.com

Useful Addresses and Contacts

Nordics
Mats Gerlam, Consultant
Västra Hamngatan 14
411 17 Goteborg
Sweden
T: 46-31-7117100
F: 46-31-7117107
E: mats.gerlam@investhk.se

Singapore
SITOH Yih Pin
Investment Promotion Director, Singapore
5 Shenton Way
#23-03 UIC Building
Singapore 068808
T: 65-6534-5700
F: 65-6538-8745
E: sitoh@investhk.com.sg

Consulates

Consulate General of the Argentine Republic
2018 Jardine House
1 Connaught Road
Central
Hong Kong
T: (852) 2523 3208
F: (852) 2877 0906
E: consarhk@netvigator.com

The Austrian Consulate General
Ms. Dr. Brigitta Blaha-Silva,
Consul General
Room 2201 Chinachem Tower
34-37 Connaught Road
Central
Hong Kong
T: (852) 2522 8086
F: (852) 2521 8773
E: hongkong-gk@bmaa.gv.at

Honorary Consulate of the Kingdom of Bahrain in HKSAR
15/F, Chevalier House
45 Chatham Road
Tsim Sha Tsui
Kowloon
Hong Kong
T: (852) 2733 9868
F: (852) 2368 2399
E: info@bahrainconsulate.org.hk

Barbados Consulate
9/F, Cheung Kong Centre
9 Queen's Road
Central
Hong Kong
T: (852) 2128 8888

Benin Consulate
Room 2007, 20/F, Westin Centre
26 Hung To Road
Kwun Tong
Kowloon
Hong Kong
T: (852) 2191 3843

Australian Consulate General
23-24/F, Harbour Centre
25 Harbour Road
Wan Chai
Hong Kong
T: (852) 2827 8881
F: (852) 2585 4457
E: acghkadm@netvigator.com
W: http://www.australia.org.hk

Bahamas Consulate General
Room 704, 7/F, Sino Plaza
255-257 Gloucester Road
Causeway Bay
Hong Kong
T: (852) 2147 0202
E: bahacghk@netvigator.com
W: http://www.bahamas.org.hk

Bangladesh Consulate
Room 3501, China Resources Building
26 Harbour Road
Wan Chai
Hong Kong
T: (852) 2827 4278
E: bangladt@netvigator.com

Belgium Consulate
9/F, St. John's Building
33 Garden Road
Central
Hong Kong
T: (852) 2524 3111
E: hongkong@diplobel.org

Brazil Consulate General
Rooms 2014-21, Sun Hung Kai Centre
30 Harbour Road
Wan Chai
Hong Kong
T: (852) 2525 7004
E: cgbrahkg@netvigator.com

Useful Addresses and Contacts

British Consulate General
1 Supreme Court Road
Admiralty
Hong Kong
T: (852) 2901 3000
F: (852) 2901 3066
E: information@britishconsulate.org.hk
    consular@britishconsulate.org.hk
W: http://www.britishconsulate.org.hk

Cameroon Consulate
Suite 503, 5/F, Cosmos Building
8-11 Lan Kwai Fong
Central
Hong Kong
T: (852) 2525 2005
E: cameroonchk@netvigator.com

Chile Consulate General
Suite 1408, Great Eagle Centre
23 Harbour Road
Wan Chai
Hong Kong
T: (852) 2827 1826
E: cgchile@netvigator.com

Congo Consulate
24/F, China Merchants Tower
Shun Tak Centre
168-200 Connaught Road
Central
Hong Kong
T: (852) 2793 1313
E: shufaito@mfth.com.hk

Cyprus Consulate
Room 902, Tower 1, Silvercord
30 Canton Road
Tsim Sha Tsui
Kowloon
Hong Kong
T: (852) 2375 5153
E: cyprus@pci.com.hk

Cambodia Consulate General
Unit 616, 6/F, Star House
3 Salisbury Road
Tsim Sha Tsui
Kowloon
Hong Kong
T: (852) 2546 0718
E: cacghk@netvigator.com

Canadian Consulate General
11-14/F, One Exchange Square
8 Connaught Place
Central
Hong Kong
T: (852) 2810 4321
W: http://www.hongkong.gc.ca

Columbian Consulate
Unit 3102, 31/F, Office Tower
Convention Plaza
1 Harbour Road
Wan Chai
Hong Kong
T: (852) 2541 2217
E: chongkong@minrelext.gov.co

Cuban Consulate
Room 1112, Jardine House
1 Connaught Place
Central
Hong Kong
T: (852) 2525 6320

Czech Republic Consulate
Room 1204-5, Great Eagle Centre
23 Harbour Road
Wan Chai
Hong Kong
T: (852) 2802 2212
E: hongkong@embassy.mzv.cz
W: http://www.mfa.cz/hongkong

Danish Consulate General
Room 2402B, Great Eagle Centre
23 Harbour Road
Wan Chai
Hong Kong
T: (852) 2827 8101
E: hkggkl@um.dk

Democratic Republic of Congo Consulate
24/F, Yardley Commercial Building
3 Connaught Road West
Central
Hong Kong
T: (852) 2850 5692

Equatorial Guinea Consulate
37/F, Vicwood Plaza
199 Des Voeux Road
Central
Hong Kong
T: (852) 2543 1943

Ethiopian Consulate
Unit 24, 3/F, Block B, Focal Industrial Centre
21 Man Lok Street
Hung Hom
Kowloon
Hong Kong
T: (852) 2363 0200
E: ethiopia@on-nets.com

Fiji Consulate
Room 1401-1402, Parkes Commercial Centre
2-8 Parkes Street
Yau Ma Tei
Kowloon
Hong Kong
T: (852) 2375 1618
E: info@fiji-worldchallenge.com.hk

Consulate General France
25/F & 26/F, Admiralty Centre Tower II
18 Harcourt Road
Admiralty
Hong Kong
T: (852) 3196 6100
F: (852) 3196 6101
E: hongkong@dree.org
W: http://www.france.com.hk/
    http://www.consulfrance-hongkong.org

Democratic People's Republic of Korea
Room 4007, 40/F, China Resources Building
26 Harbour Road
Wan Chai
Hong Kong
T: (852) 2803 4447

Egyptian Consulate General
Suite No. 1, 22/F, Sino Plaza
255-257 Gloucester Road
Causeway Bay
Hong Kong
T: (852) 2827 0668
E: egyptcg@netvigator.com

Estonian Consulate
4/F, Eltee Building
3 Ning Foo Street
Chai Wan
Hong Kong
T: (852) 2898 7337

Office of European Commission in Hong Kong and Macau SARs
19/F, St. John's Building
33 Garden Road
Central
Hong Kong
T: (852) 2537 6083
E: mailto@delhkg.cec.eu.int
W: http://www.delhkg.cec.eu.int/

Finland Consulate
Room 2405-8, Dah Sing Financial Centre
108 Gloucester Road
Wan Chai
Hong Kong
T: (852) 2525 5385
E: sanomat.hng@formin.fi
W: http://www.finland.org.hk

Gabon Consulate
c/o Sino-Oceans Limited
22/F, Jade Centre
98-102 Wellington Street
Central
Hong Kong
T: (852) 2851 0973
E: cassam_goolijarry@sino-oceans.com

Useful Addresses and Contacts

German Consulate General
21/F, United Centre
95 Queensway
Admiralty
Hong Kong
T: (852) 2105 8712
E: germancg@netvigator.com
W: http://www.germanconsulate-hongkong.org

Greece Consulate General
Suite 2503-2504, Two Pacific Place
Admiralty
Hong Kong
T: (852) 2774 1682
E: greekcg@biznetvigator.com

Hungary Consulate
Suite 3202, Citibank Tower
3 Garden Road
Central
Hong Kong
T: (852) 2878 7555
E: hunconsulate@huconhgk.com.hk

Indian Consulate General   and
Chancery, Information Wing and
Consul General's Office
Unit D, 16/F, United Centre
95 Queensway
Admiralty
Hong Kong
T: (852) 2528 4028
F: (852) 2865 4617
E: cg@indianconsulate.org.hk
W: http://www.indianconsulate.org.hk

Indonesian Consulate General
6-8 Keswick Street
Causeway Bay
Hong Kong
T: (852) 2890 4421
E: kjrihkg@netvigator.com

Ghana Consulate
Room 610, Wing On House
71 Des Voeux Road
Central
Hong Kong
T: (852) 2530 3448
E: ghanahk@ghana.org.com
W: http://www.ghana.org.hk

Guinea Consulate
Room 2101, CRE Building
303 Hennessy Road
Wan Chai
Hong Kong
T: (852) 3110 3232
E: guineahk@netvigator.com

Iceland Consulate
12/F, Warwick House
East Taikoo Place
979 King's Road
Quarry Bay
Hong Kong
T: (852) 2876 8888

Indian Consulate General
Consular, Economic and Commercial Wings
26A United Centre
95 Queensway
Admiralty
Hong Kong
T: (852) 2866 4027
F: (852) 2529 0421
E: commerce1@indianconsulate.org.hk
W: http://www.indianconsulate.org.hk

Iranian Consulate General
Rooms 4010-12, 40/F, Office Tower
Convention Plaza
1 Harbour Road
Wan Chai
Hong Kong
T: (852) 2845 8002
E: irancghk@netvigator.com

Ireland Consulate
6/F, Chung Nam Building
1 Lockhart Road
Wan Chai
Hong Kong
T: (852) 2527 4897
E: iceconhk@netvigator.com

Consulate General of Italy
Suite 3203-06, 32/F
Asia Pacific Finance Tower
3 Garden Road
Central
Hong Kong
T: (852) 2522 0033
F: (852) 2845 9678
E: consolato.hongkong@esteri.it
    italconshk@italianconsulate.org.hk
W: http://www.italianconsulate.org.hk/

Consulate General of Japan
46-47/F, One Exchange Square
8 Connaught Place
Central
Hong Kong
T: (852) 2522 1184
F: (852) 2845 5360
W: http://www.hk.emb-japan.go.jp/

Korean Consulate
5-6/F, Far East Finance Centre
16 Harcourt Road
Admiralty
Hong Kong
T: (852) 2529 4141
E: korcon@netvigator.com

Laos Consulate
Room 1402, Arion Commercial Centre
2-12 Queen's Road West
Sheung Wan
Hong Kong
T: (852) 2544 1186

Consulate General of Israel
Rm 701, Admiralty Centre Tower II
18 Harcourt Road
Admiralty
Hong Kong
T: (852) 2821 7500
F: (852) 2865 0220
E: info@hongkong.mfa.gov.il
W: http://www.mfa.gov.il
     http://www.israeltrade.gov.il/hongkong

Jamaican Consulate
10/F, Manulife Tower
169 Electric Road
North Point
Hong Kong
T: (852) 2510 1233
E: rhlhh@ryoden.com.hk

Kazakhstan Consulate
Unit 3106, 31/F, Shun Tak Centre
200 Connaught Road
Central
Hong Kong
T: (852) 2548 3841

Kuwait Consulate
Suite 5, 28/F, Sino Plaza
255-257 Gloucester Road
Causeway Bay
Hong Kong
T: (852) 2832 7866
E: kuconshk@netvigator.com

Lithuanian Consulate
2/F, 79 Wyndham Street
Central
Hong Kong
T: (852) 2522 2852
E: exports@styleasia.com.hk

Useful Addresses and Contacts

Luxembourg Consulate
c/o Chekiang First Bank Centre
G/F, 1 Duddell Street
Central
Hong Kong
T: (852) 2877 1018
E: conluxhk@netvigator.com

Malaysian Consulate
24/F, Malaysia Building
50 Gloucester Road
Wan Chai
Hong Kong
T: (852) 2821 0800
E: mwhkong@netvigator.com

Mali Consulate
Unit 5011, 5/F, United Centre
95 Queensway
Admiralty
Hong Kong
T: (852) 2109 8111
E: mdoffice@hongthai.com

Mauritius Consulate
Suite 1006A, Bank of America Tower
12 Harcourt Road
Central
Hong Kong
T: (852) 2744 4063
E: osman@hk.gin.net
   maurcon@hk.gin.net

Monaco Consulate
Room 3203A, Central Plaza
18 Harbour Road
Wan Chai
Hong Kong
T: (852) 2893 0669

Moroccan Consulate
Marine Deck, Ocean Terminal
Canton Road
Tsim Sha Tsui
Kowloon
Hong Kong
T: (852) 2736 7286

Madagascar Consulate
Penthouse, East Ocean Centre
98 Granville Road
Tsim Sha Tsui East
Kowloon
Hong Kong
T: (852) 2316 0888
E: mdgr@afasia.com

Maldives Consulate
Room 201-205, Kowloon Centre
29-43 Ashley Road
Tsim Sha Tsui
Kowloon
Hong Kong
T: (852) 2376 2114

Malta Consulate
Room 504, Chinachem Golden Plaza
77 Mody Road
Tsim Sha Tsui East
Kowloon
Hong Kong
T: (852) 2739 1515
E: synflex@hkstar.com

Mexico Consulate
Room 1304, Great Eagle Centre
23 Harbour Road
Wan Chai
Hong Kong
T: (852) 2511 3305
E: mexicohk@netvigator.com

Mongolian Consulate
3/F, Crystal Industrial Building
71 How Ming Street
Kwun Tong
Kowloon
Hong Kong
T: (852) 2264 6173
E: mongolia_consulate@hotmail.com

Mozambique Consulate
Suite 25, New Henry House
10 Ice House Street
Central
Hong Kong
T: (852) 2521 1444
E: info@alitom.com.hk

Myanmar Consulate General
Room 2421-2425, Sun Hung Kai Centre
30 Harbour Road
Wan Chai
Hong Kong
T: (852) 2827 7929
E: myancghk@pacific.net.hk
W: http://myanmar.e-consulate.org

Nepalese Consulate General
Unit 715, North Tower, Concordia Plaza
1 Science Museum Road
Tsim Sha Tsui East
Kowloon
Hong Kong
T: (852) 2369 7813
E: rncghk@netvigator.com

New Zealand Consulate General
Room 6501, Central Plaza
18 Harbour Road
Wan Chai
Hong Kong
T: (852) 2525 5044
E: nzcghk@netvigator.com
W: http://www.nzembassy.com/hongkong

Nigeria Consulate
Rooms 3309-10, 33/F, China Resources Building
26 Harbour Road
Wan Chai
Hong Kong
T: (852) 2827 8813
E: ngrconhk@netvigator.com
W: http://www.nigeria-consulate.org.hk

Pakistan Consulate
Room 3706, 37/F, China Resources Building
26 Harbour Road
Wan Chai
Hong Kong
T: (852) 2827 1966
E: parephk@netvigator.com

Peru Consulate
Suite 3308, 33/F, China Resources Building
26 Harbour Road
Wan Chai
Hong Kong
T: (852) 2868 2622
E: peruhkmc@netvigator.com

Namibia Consulate
Room 509, Manning House
38-48 Queen's Road
Central
Hong Kong
T: (852) 2586 1339
E: drhenrychan@hotmail.com
W: http://namibia.e-consulate.org

Netherlands Consulate General
Suite 5702, 5/F, Cheung Kong Centre
2 Queen's Road
Central
Hong Kong
T: (852) 2522 5127
E: information@netherlands-cg.org.hk
W: http://www.netherlands-cg.org.hk

Niger Consulate
Unit B, 1/F, Kowloon Centre
29-39 Ashley Road
Tsim Sha Tsui
Kowloon
Hong Kong
T: (852) 2376 2112

Oman Consulate
19/F, Gee Chang Hong Centre
65 Wong Chuk Hang Road
Wong Chuk Hang
Hong Kong
T: (852) 2873 0888
E: fidcr@netvigator.com

Papua New Guinea Consulate
Unit 602B, 6/F, 1 Hysan Avenue
Causeway Bay
Hong Kong
T: (852) 2499 3611

Philippines Consulate General
14/F, United Centre
95 Queensway
Admiralty
Hong Kong
T: (852) 2823 8500
E: pcg@philcongen-hk.com

Useful Addresses and Contacts

Polish Consulate
Suite 2009, Two Pacific Place
88 Queensway
Admiralty
Hong Kong
T: (852) 2840 0779
E: kgrphk@netvigator.com

Rwandan Consulate
Suite 1102, 11/F, 148 Electric Road
North Point
Hong Kong
T: (852) 2545 9898
E: rwandahk@netvigator.com
W: http://www.embarwanda-china.com

Seychelles Consulate
12B Bowen Road
Hong Kong
T: (852) 2354 3669
E: seychelles@ffreefire.com

Slovak Republic Consulate
11/F, Milo's Industrial Building
2-10 Tai Yuen Street
Kwai Chung
New Territories
Hong Kong
T: (852) 2484 4568

South African Consulate General
27/F, Sunning Plaza
10 Hysan Avenue
Causeway Bay
Hong Kong
T: (852) 2577 3279
E: sacghgk@netvigator.com

Sri Lankan Consulate
22/F, Dominion Centre
43 Queen's Road East
Wan Chai
Hong Kong
T: (852) 2876 0828
E: drthcc@pacificgroup.com.hk

Russian Consulate
Room 2106-2123, 21/F, Sun Hung Kai Centre
30 Harbour Road
Wan Chai
Hong Kong
T: (852) 2877 7188
E: russia@hknet.com
W: http://www.russia.com.hk

Saudi Arabian Consulate
Suite 6401, Central Plaza
18 Harbour Road
Wan Chai
Hong Kong
T: (852) 2520 3200
E: cncon@mofa.gov.sa

Singaporean Consulate
Room 901, 9/F, Admiralty Centre Tower I
18 Harcourt Road
Admiralty
Hong Kong
T: (852) 2527 2212
E: sporecon@sg.corp.com.hk
W: http://www.mfa.gov.sg/hongkong

Slovenian Consulate
9/F, Fu Hing Building
10 Jubilee Street
Central
Hong Kong
T: (852) 2545 2107
E: phlandpt@netvigator.com

Spanish Consulate General
8/F, Printing House
18 Ice House Street
Central
Hong Kong
T: (852) 2525 3041
E: espcghk@asiaonline.net

Swedish Consulate General
8/F, The Hong Kong Club Building
3A Chater Road
Central
Hong Kong
T: (852) 2521 1212
E: generalkonsulat.hongkong@foreign.ministry.se

Swiss Consulate General
Suite 6206-7, Central Plaza
18 Harbour Road
Wan Chai
Hong Kong
T: (852) 2522 7147
E: swisscg@hon.rep.admin.ch
W: http://www.eda.admin.ch/hongkong

Thailand Consulate General
8/F, Fairmont House
8 Cotton Tree Drive
Central
Hong Kong
T: (852) 2521 6481-5
E: thaicghk@thai-consulate.org.hk
W: http://www.thai-consulate.org.hk

Trinidad and Tobago Consulate
Room 1108, Stanhouse, 734-738 King's Road
Quarry Bay
Hong Kong
T: (852) 2834 4988
   (852) 2833 9091
F: (852) 2838 7796

Turkish Consulate General
Room 301, Sino Plaza
255-257 Gloucester Road
Causeway Bay
Hong Kong
T: (852) 2572 1331
E: turkcons@netvigator.com

United Arab Emirates Consulate General
Unit 2205-6, Mass Mutual Tower
38 Gloucester Road
Wan Chai
Hong Kong
T: (852) 2866 1823

Uruguay Consulate
30/F, Entertainment Building
30 Queen's Road
Central
Hong Kong
T: (852) 2168 0832
E: Afreris@pacific.net.hk

Tanzanian Consulate
Room 404-405, 4/F, Metropole Building
57 Peking Road
Tsim Sha Tsui
Kowloon
Hong Kong
T: (852) 2311 8828
E: jkingdom@ctimail.com
W: http://www.tanzania.go.tz

Togo Consulate
Units A & E, 7/F, Wah Shun Industrial Centre
4 Cho Yuen Street
Yau Tong Bay
Kowloon
Hong Kong
T: (852) 2340 0285/7

Tunisian Consulate
1/F, Annex Building
The Wharney
57-73 Lockhart Road
Wan Chai
Hong Kong
T: (852) 2523 2323
F: (852) 2523 2366

Ugandan Consulate
1811 Star House
3 Salisbury Road
Kowloon
Hong Kong
T: (852) 2572 868
E: ugandahk@netvigator.com

United States of America Consulate General
26 Garden Road
Central
Hong Kong
T: (852) 2523 9011
F: (852) 2845 1598
W: http://www.usconsulate.org.hk
   http://www.hongkong.usconsulate.gov

Venezuelan Consulate
Room 5405, Central Plaza
18 Harbour Road
Wan Chai
Hong Kong
T: (852) 2730 8099
E: consulve@netvigator.com

Vietnamese Consulate
15/F, Great Smart Tower
230 Wan Chai Road
Wan Chai
Hong Kong
T: (852) 2591 4510
E: vnconsul@netvigator.com

Chambers of Commerce, Business Associations and Business Councils

The Hong Kong General Chamber of Commerce
22/F, United Centre
95 Queensway
Hong Kong
T: (852) 2529 9229
F: (852) 2527 9843
E: chamber@chamber.org.hk
W: http://www.chamber.org.hk/

Australian Chamber of Commerce in Hong Kong
4/F, Lucky Building
39 Wellington Street
Central
Hong Kong
T: (852) 2522 5054
F: (852) 2877 0860
E: austcham@austcham.com.hk
W: http://www.austcham.com.hk

Canadian Chamber of Commerce in Hong Kong
Suite 1301, 13/F, Kinwick Centre
32 Hollywood Road
Central
Hong Kong
T: (852) 2110 8700
F: (852) 2110 8701
E: canada@cancham.org
W: http://www.cancham.org

Chinese Chamber of Commerce, Kowloon
2/F, 8 Nga Tsin Long Road
Kowloon City
Kowloon
Hong Kong
T: (852) 2382 2309

The American Chamber of Commerce in Hong Kong
Rm 1904, Bank of America Tower
12 Harcourt Road
Central
Hong Kong
T: (852) 2526 0165
F: (852) 2810 1289
E: amcham@amcham.org.hk
W: http://www.amcham.org.hk

The British Chamber of Commerce in Hong Kong
1201 Emperor Group Centre
288 Hennessy Road
Wan Chai
Hong Kong
T: (852) 2824 2211
F: (852) 2824 1333
E: info@britcham.com
W: http://www.britcham.com

China Council for the Promotion of International Trade / China Chamber of International Commerce (HK) Representative Office
Rm 1902, Great Eagle Centre
23 Harbour Road
Wan Chai
Hong Kong
T: (852) 2827 7038
F: (852) 2827 4701
E: ccpithk@hkstar.com
W: http://www.ccpit.org

Chinese General Chamber of Commerce
4/F, 24-25 Connaught Road
Central
Hong Kong
T: (852) 2525 6385
F: (852) 2845 2610
E: cgcc@cgcc.org.hk
W: http://www.cgcc.org.hk

Useful Addresses and Contacts

The Dutch Business Association
Suite 5702, 57/F, Cheung Kong Centre
2 Queen's Road
Central
Hong Kong
T: (852) 2815 2801
F: (852) 2815 2173
E: info@dba.com.hk
W: http://www.dba.com.hk

The French Chamber of Commerce and Industry in Hong Kong
Unit 702-03, 7/F, Ruttonjee House
Ruttonjee Centre
11 Duddell Street
Central
Hong Kong
T: (852) 2523 6818
F: (852) 2524 1428
E: info@fccihk.com
W: http://www.fccihk.com

The Hoi Ping Chamber of Commerce of Hong Kong
Flat A-A1, 13/F, Central House
270-276 Queen's Road
Central
Hong Kong
T: (852) 2543 9378
F: (852) 2815 1321
E: hoipinghk@hknet.com

Indian Chamber of Commerce Hong Kong
Main Office:
2/F, Hoseinee House
69 Wyndham Street
Central
Hong Kong
T: (852) 2523 3877, 2845 4612
F: (852) 2845 0300, 2845 9916
E: indcham@icchk.org.hk
W: http://www.icchk.org.hk
Kowloon Office:
Rm 1006, Albion Plaza
2-6 Granville Road
Tsim Sha Tsui
Hong Kong
T: (852) 2301 3681
F: (852) 2723 9884

Finnish Business Council
Suite 1001, Tower 1
Lippo Centre
89 Queensway
Hong Kong
E: fbc@fbc.com.hk
W: http://www.fbc.com.hk

German Chamber of Commerce, Hong Kong
Rm 3601, Tower One
Lippo Centre
89 Queensway
Admiralty
Hong Kong
T: (852) 2526 5481
F: (852) 2810 6093
E: info@hongkong.ahk.de
W: http://www.china.ahk.de
http://www.ahk.org.hk

Hong Kong Chiu Chow Chamber of Commerce Ltd.
9/F, Chiu Chow Association Building
81-85 Des Voeux Road West
Sheung Wan
Hong Kong
T: (852) 2559 2188
F: (852) 2559 8426
E: mail@chiuchow.org.hk
W: http://www.chiuchow.org.hk

Hung Hom Office:
Rm 1308, Tower B
Hung Hom Commercial Centre
37-39 Ma Tau Wai Road
Hung Hom
Kowloon
Hong Kong
T: (852) 2356 0122
F: (852) 2356 0978

International Chamber of Commerce Hong Kong, China Business Council
12/F, Kwong Fat Hong Building
1 Rumsey Street
Sheung Wan
Hong Kong
T: (852) 2973 0006
F: (852) 2869 0360
E: generl@icchkcbc.org
W: http://www.iccwbo.org/home/national_committees/asia_pacific/hong_kong.asp
   http://www.icchkcbc.org

Italian Chamber of Commerce in Hong Kong
Unit 902-3, Wilson House
19-27 Wyndham Street
Central
Hong Kong
T: (852) 2521 8837
F: (852) 2537 4764
E: icc@icc.org.hk
W: http://www.icc.org.hk

The Hong Kong Japanese Chamber of Commerce & Industry
38/F, Hennessy Centre
500 Hennessy Road
Causeway Bay
Hong Kong
T: (852) 2577 6129
F: (852) 2577 0525
W: http://www.hkjcci.com.hk

Kowloon Chamber of Commerce
3/F, K.C.C. Building
2 Liberty Avenue
Homantin
Kowloon
Hong Kong
T: (852) 2760 0393
F: (852) 2761 0166
E: kcc02@hkkcc.biz.com.hk
W: http://www.hkkcc.org.hk

Mexican Business Association of Hong Kong Ltd.
Suite 3203A Central Plaza
18 Harbour Road
Wan Chai
Hong Kong
T: (852) 2877 3434
F: (852) 2877 6607
E: tradecommhk@mexitrade.com.hk

New Zealand - Hong Kong Business Association
Rm 6A, Kingpower Commercial Building
409-413 Jaffe Road
Wan Chai
Hong Kong
T: (852) 2536 4469
F: (852) 2810 9068
W: http://www.nzhkba.org.hk

Norwegian Chamber of Commerce
Rm 2405-8, Dah Sing Financial Centre
108 Gloucester Road
Wan Chai
Hong Kong
T: (852) 2289 0607
F: (852) 2810 1232
E: info@ncchk.org.hk
W: http://www.ncchk.org.hk

The Singapore Chamber of Commerce
23/F, China Hong Kong Tower
8-12 Hennessy Road
Wan Chai
Hong Kong
T: (852) 2838 3733
F: (852) 2838 3390
E: director@scchk.com.hk
W: http://www.scchk.com.hk

South African Business Forum
Rm 2706-10, Great Eagle Centre
23 Harbour Road
Wan Chai
Hong Kong
T: (852) 2577 3279
F: (852) 2577 4532
W: http://www.sabusinessforumhk.com

Useful Addresses and Contacts

Spanish Chamber of Commerce
Rm 1103, Jubilee Centre
18 Fenwick Street
Wan Chai
Hong Kong
T: (852) 2763 6236
F: (852) 2763 6279
E: info@spanish-chamber.com.hk
W: http://www.spanish-chamber.com.hk

**Taiwan Business Association
(Hong Kong) Ltd.**
Rm 701-2, 7/F, Hang Seng Wanchai Building
200 Hennessy Road
Wan Chai
Hong Kong
T: (852) 2802 2824
F: (852) 2583 7913
E: hktbase@netvigator.com
W: http://www.hktba.com/

Swedish Chamber of Commerce in Hong Kong
Rm 4401, 44/F, China Resources Building
26 Harbour Road
Wan Chai
Hong Kong
T: (852) 2525 0349
F: (852) 2537 1843
E: info@swedcham.com.hk
W: http://www.swedcham.com.hk

Hong Kong Taiwan Chamber of Commerce
5/F, Chevalier House
45 Chatham Road
Kowloon
Hong Kong
T: (852) 2721 7636
F: (852) 2721 3470

Associations, Federations, Institutes, Commissions, Councils, Committees and Agencies

The Hong Kong Advertisers Association
Rm 1001, 10/F, Tak Woo House
17-19 D'Aguilar Street
Central
Hong Kong
T: (852) 2882 2555
F: (852) 2882 4673
E: hkaa@hotmail.com

Hong Kong Agriculture, Fisheries and Conservation Department
Cheung Sha Wan Government Offices
5/F to 7/F, part 8/F, part 9/F
303 Cheung Sha Wan Road
Kowloon
Hong Kong
T: (852) 2708 8885
F: (852) 2311 3731
E: mailbox@afcd.gov.hk
W: http://www.afcd.gov.hk

Hong Kong Association of Banks
Rm 525 Prince's Building
Central
Hong Kong
T: (852) 2521 1169
F: (852) 2868 5035
E: info@hkab.org.hk
W: http://www.hkab.org.hk

Hong Kong Article Numbering Association
22/F, OTB Building
160 Gloucester Road
Wan Chai
Hong Kong
T: (852) 2861 2819
F: (852) 2861 2423
E: info@hkana.org
W: http://www.hkana.org

Hong Kong Association of Freight Forwarding and Logistics Ltd.
8/F, China Hong Kong Centre
122-126 Canton Road
Tsim Sha Tsui
Kowloon
Hong Kong
T: (852) 2796 3121
F: (852) 2796 3719
E: alice@haffa.com.hk
W: http://www.haffa.com.hk

Hong Kong Association of International Co-operation of Small and Medium Enterprises
Rm 308, Kai Tak Commercial Building
317-319 Des Voeux Road
Central
Hong Kong
T: (852) 2893 5449
F: (852) 2834 5519
E: info@isme.com.hk
W: http://www.isme.com.hk

Useful Addresses and Contacts

Hong Kong Austrian Association Ltd.
GPO Box 8031
Central
Hong Kong
T: (852) 2534 1240
F: (852) 2832 7807
E: info@aa.com.hk
W: http://www.austrian-association.com.hk

British Council
Supreme Court Road
Admiralty
Hong Kong
T: (852) 2913 5100
F: (852) 2913 5102
E: enquiries@britishcouncil.org.hk
W: http://www.britishcouncil.org.hk

Hong Kong Capital Markets Association (HKCMA)
HKCMA Secretariat
c/o International Conference Consultants, Ltd.
Unit 301, 3/F, The Centre Mark
287-299 Queen's Road
Central
Hong Kong
T: (852) 2543 7343
F: (852) 2547 9528
E: hkcma@icc.com.hk
W: http://www.hkcma.org

China-Britain Business Council
Abford House
15 Wilton Road
London
SW1V 1LT
T: 44 (0) 20 7828 5176
F: 44 (0) 20 7630 5780

Hong Kong Bar Association
LG2, High Court
38 Queensway
Admiralty
Hong Kong
T: (852) 2869 0210
F: (852) 2869 0189
E: info@hkba.org
W: http://www.hkba.org

Business and Professionals Federation of Hong Kong
Suite 1501-02 World Trade Centre
280 Gloucester Road
Causeway Bay
Hong Kong
T: (852) 2810 6611
F: (852) 2810 6661
E: info@bpf.org.hk
W: http://www.bpf.org.hk

Chartered Institute of Marketing (Hong Kong)
Rm 2702 Lippo Centre Tower One
89 Queensway
Admiralty
Hong Kong
T: (852) 2868 1110
F: (852) 2868 1438
E: info@cimhk.org.hk
W: http://www.cimhk.org.hk

Hong Kong Chinese Enterprises Association
Rm 2104-6 Harbour Centre
25 Harbour Road
Wan Chai
Hong Kong
T: (852) 2827 2831
F: (852) 2827 2606
E: info@hkcea.com
W: http://www.hkcea.com

Chinese Manufacturers' Association of Hong Kong
5/F, CMA Building
64-66 Connaught Road
Central
Hong Kong
T: (852) 2545 6166
F: (852) 2541 4541
E: info@cma.org.hk
W: http://www.cma.org.hk

Constitutional Development Task Force Secretariat
Constitutional Affairs Bureau
3/F, Main Wing
Central Government Offices
Lower Albert Road
Central
Hong Kong
T: 212 752 3320
F: (852) 2523 3207
E: views@cab-review.gov.hk
W: http://www.cab-review.gov.hk

Hong Kong Designer Association
23/F, Po Wah Commercial Centre
226 Hennessy Road
Wan Chai
Hong Kong
G.P.O. Box 9780
Hong Kong
T: (852) 2527 3968
F: (852) 2527 5468
E: info@hongkongda.com
W: http://www.hongkongda.com

Hong Kong Educational Publishers Association Ltd.
18/F, Warwick House East
Taikoo Place
Quarry Bay
Hong Kong
T: (852) 2516 3252
F: (852) 2565 8491
E: wongpaks@oupchina.com.hk

The Hong Kong Coalition of Service Industries
22/F, United Centre
95 Queensway
Hong Kong
T: (852) 2529 9229
F: (852) 2527 9843
E: csi@hkcsi.org.hk
W: http://www.hkcsi.org.hk

Design Council of Hong Kong
4/F, Hankow Centre
5-15 Hankow Road
Tsim Sha Tsui
Kowloon
Hong Kong
T: (852) 2732 3188
F: (852) 2721 3494
E: dpc@fhki.org.hk
W: http://www.fhki.org.hk

Hong Kong Economic & Trade Association Ltd.
11/F Kee Shing Centre
74-76 Kimberley Road
Tsim Sha Tsui
Kowloon
Hong Kong
T: (852) 2723 6223
F: (852) 2722 6705
E: hketa@hkjt.com.hk
W: http://www.hketa.org.hk

Electoral Affairs Commission
Registration and Electoral Office
10/F, Harbour Centre
25 Harbour Road
Wan Chai
Hong Kong
T: (852) 2827 4644
F: (852) 2891 1001
E: reoenq@reo.gov.hk
W: http://www.info.gov.hk/eac

Useful Addresses and Contacts

Hong Kong Electronic Industries Association
Rm 1201, 12/F, Harbour Crystal Centre
100 Granville Road
Tsim Sha Tsui East
Kowloon
Hong Kong
T: (852) 2778 8328
F: (852) 2788 2200
E: hkeia@hkeia.org
W: http://www.hkeia.org

Hong Kong Exporters Association
Rm 825, Star House
3 Salisbury Road
Tsim Sha Tsui
Kowloon
Hong Kong
T: (852) 2730 9851
F: (852) 2730 1869
E: exporter@exporters.org.hk
W: http://www.exporters.org.hk

Federation of Hong Kong Hotel Owners Ltd.
Rm B201, B2, Grand Stanford Inter-Continental
70 Mody Road
Tsim Sha Tsui East
Kowloon
Hong Kong
T: (852) 2369 1887
F: (852) 2367 7805

The Hong Kong Financial Markets Association
Unit 501-3 Far East Consortium Building
121 Des Voeux Road
Central
Hong Kong
T: (852) 2543 7668
F: (852) 2547 9552
E: hkfma@icc.com.hk
W: http://www.hkfma.org.hk

Hong Kong - European Union Business Cooperation Committee
38/F, Office Tower, Convention Plaza
1 Harbour Road
Wan Chai
Hong Kong
T: (852) 2584 4333
F: (852) 2583 9275
E: hktdc@tdc.org.hk
W: http://www.tdctrade.com

Federation of Hong Kong Business Associations Worldwide Ltd.
38/F, Office Tower, Convention Plaza
1 Harbour Road
Wan Chai
Hong Kong
T: (852) 2584 4333
F: (852) 2824 0249
E: hkfederation@tdc.org.hk
W: http://www.hkfederation.org.hk

Federation of Hong Kong Industries
4/F Hankow Centre
5-15 Hankow Street
Tsim Sha Tsui
Kowloon
Hong Kong
T: (852) 2732 3188
F: (852) 2721 3494
E: fhki@fhki.org.hk
W: http://www.fhki.org.hk

Hong Kong Hotels Association
Rm 508-511, Silvercord Tower Two
30 Canton Road
Tsim Sha Tsui
Kowloon
Hong Kong
T: (852) 2375 3838
F: (852) 2375 7676
E: info@hkha.org
W: http://www.hkha.org

Hotel Reservation Centres
Buffer Halls A & B
Passenger Terminal Building
Hong Kong International Airport
Lantau
Hong Kong
T: Buffer Hall A (852) 2383 8380
   Buffer Hall B (852) 2769 8822
F: (852) 2362 2383
E: hrc@hkha.org

Hong Kong / Japan Business Co-operation Committee, and Hong Kong / United States Business Council
38/F, Office Tower, Convention Plaza
1 Harbour Road
Wan Chai
Hong Kong
T: (852) 2584 4333
F: (852) 2583 9275

Hong Kong Logistics Association
4/F, Network of Networks
Hong Kong Productivity Council Building
78 Tat Chee Avenue
Kowloon Tong
Kowloon
Hong Kong
T: (852) 2777 9656
F: (852) 2194 5082
W: http://www.hkla.org.hk

Management Consultancies Association of Hong Kong
Rm 1403 14/F, 9 Queen's Road
Central
Hong Kong
T: (852) 2856 3487
F: (852) 2565 6628
E: mcahk@mca.org.hk
W: http://www.mca.org.hk

Hong Kong Plastics Industry Council
Rm 407-411, Hankow Centre
5-15 Hankow Road
Tsim Sha Tsui
Kowloon
Hong Kong
T: (852) 2732 3188
F: (852) 2721 1494
E: tsd@fhki.org.hk

Hong Kong Investment Funds Association
Rm 1505, Tak Shing House
20 Des Voeux Road
Central
Hong Kong
T: (852) 2537 9912
F: (852) 2877 8827
E: hkifa@hkifa.org.hk
W: http://www.hkifa.org.hk

The Law Society of Hong Kong
3/F, Wing On House
71 Des Voeux Road
Central
Hong Kong
T: (852) 2846 0500
F: (852) 2845 0387
E: sg@hklawsoc.org.hk
W: http://www.hklawsoc.org.hk

The Hong Kong Management Association
14/F, Fairmont House
8 Cotton Tree Drive
Central
Hong Kong
T: (852) 2526 6516
F: (852) 2868 4387
E: hkma@hkma.org.hk
W: http://www.hkma.org.hk

Hong Kong Observatory
134A Nathan Road
Tsim Sha Tsui
Kowloon
Hong Kong
T: (852) 2926 8200
F: (852) 2311 9448
E: mailbox@hko.gov.hk
W: http://www.hko.gov.hk

Political and Economic Risk Consultancy, Ltd.
Rooms 1603-1604, Hollywood Centre
233 Hollywood Road
Hong Kong
G.P.O. Box 1342
Hong Kong
T: (852) 2541 4088
F: (852) 2815 5032
E: info@asiarisk.com
W: http://asiarisk.com/

Useful Addresses and Contacts

Hong Kong Productivity Council
Hong Kong Productivity Council Building
78 Tat Chee Avenue
Kowloon Tong
Kowloon
Hong Kong
T: (852) 2788 5678
F: (852) 2788 5900
W: http://www.hkpc.org
Customer Services Hotline : (852) 2788 6128

Hong Kong Publishing Federation Ltd.
Rm 904, SUP Tower
75-83 King's Road
North Point
Hong Kong
T: (852) 2578 6000
F: (852) 2578 6838

Hong Kong Retail Management Association
Unit B, 22/F, United Centre
95 Queensway
Admiralty
Hong Kong
T: (852) 2866 8311
F: (852) 2866 8380
E: hkrma@netvigator.com

Hong Kong Securities Institute
Rm 2403-08, 24/F, Wing On Centre
111 Connaught Road
Central
Hong Kong
T: (852) 3120 6100
F: (852) 2899 2611
E: info@hksi.org
W: http://www.hksi.org

Hong Kong Publishers & Distributors Association
Flat C, 4/F, National Building
240-246 Nathan Road
Kowloon
Hong Kong
T: (852) 2367 4412
F: (852) 2367 4412

Quick Response Centre for the Textiles and Clothing Industries
Clothing Technology Demonstration Centre Co., Ltd.
9/F, CITA Building
63 Tai Yip Street
Kowloon Bay
Kowloon
Hong Kong
T: (852) 2751 6925   Kimberley Chan
F: (852) 2795 6023
E: kimchan@ctdc.org
W: http://www.qrc.org/

Roadshow Media Ltd.
1 Po Lun Street
Lai Chi Kok
Kowloon
Hong Kong
T: (852) 2746 5266
F: (852) 2744 7055
W: http://www.roadshow.com.hk

Hong Kong Shippers' Council
Rm 2407 Hopewell Centre
183 Queen's Road East
Wan Chai
Hong Kong
T: (852) 2834 0010
F: (852) 2891 9787
E: shippers@hkshippers.org.hk
W: http://www.hkshippers.org.hk

The Taxation Institute of Hong Kong
21/F, Kam Sang Building
255-257 Des Voeux Road
Central
Hong Kong
T: (852) 2810 0438
F: (852) 2523 1263
E: tihkadm@tihk.org.hk
W: http://www.tihk.org.hk

Hong Kong Tourism Board
9-11/F, Citicorp Centre
18 Whitfield Road
North Point
Hong Kong
T: (852) 2807 6543
F: (852) 2806 0303
E: info@hktourismboard.com
W: http://www.discoverhongkong.com

Hong Kong Toys Council
Rm 407-411, Hankow Centre
5-15 Hankow Road
Tsim Sha Tsui
Kowloon
Hong Kong
T: (852) 2732 3188
F: (852) 2721 3494
E: hktc@fhki.org.hk
W: http://www.toyshk.org

Hong Kong Venture Capital Association
Rm. 4010, Jardine House
1 Connaught Place
Central
Hong Kong
T: (852) 2845 6100
F: (852) 2526 2713
E: enquiry@hkvca.com.hk
W: http://www.hkvca.com.hk

Textile Council of Hong Kong Ltd.
3/F, 63 Tai Yip Street
Kowloon Bay
Kowloon
Hong Kong
T: (852) 2305 2893
F: (852) 2305 2493
E: textclhk@netvigator.com
W: http://www.textilecouncil.com

Hong Kong Tourism Commission
2/F, East Wing
Central Government Offices
Lower Albert Road, Central
Hong Kong
T: (852) 2810 3507
F: (852) 2523 1973
E: tcenq@edlb.gov.hk
W: http://www.tourism.gov.hk

The Toys Manufacturers' Association of Hong Kong Ltd.
Rm 1302, Metroplaza, Tower 2
223 Hing Fong Road
Kwai Chung
New Territories
Hong Kong
T: (852) 2422 1209
F: (852) 2422 1639
E: tmhk@harbourring.com.hk

Vocational Training Council
VTC Tower
27 Wood Road
Wan Chai
Hong Kong
T: (852) 2836 1000
F: (852) 2838 0667
E: csd@vtc.edu.hk
W: http://www.vtc.edu.hk

Useful Addresses and Contacts

Hong Kong Trade Development Council (HKTDC) Offices

Hong Kong Trade Development Council
Head Office
38/F, Office Tower, Convention Plaza
1 Harbour Road
Wan Chai
Hong Kong
T: (852) 2584 4333
F: (852) 2824 0249
E: hktdc@tdc.org.hk
W: http://www.tdctrade.com
   http://www.tdctrade.com.hk
   http://www.tdc.org.hk

Hong Kong Trade Development
Council Publications Department
31/F, Wu Chung House
213 Queen's Road East
Wan Chai
Hong Kong
T: (852) 2892 4888
F: (852) 2575 0303
E: enquiry@tdcenterprise.com
   publications@tdc.org.hk
W: http://www.hkenterprise.com

TDC Business Info Centre
Hong Kong Convention and Exhibition Centre
1 Expo Drive
Wan Chai
Hong Kong
T: (852) 2248 4000
F: (852) 2248 4111
W: http://www.infocentre.tdctrade.com

TDC Customer Service Centre
Hong Kong Convention and Exhibition Centre
1 Expo Drive
Wan Chai
Hong Kong
T: (852) 1830 668
F: (852) 2248 4888

China Trade & Investment Resource Centre
Hong Kong Convention & Exhibition Centre
G/F, 1 Expo Drive
Wan Chai
Hong Kong
T: (852) 2248 4000
W: http://infocentre.tdctrade.com

Hong Kong Trader monthly news bulletin
http://www.hktrader.net

Hong Kong Trade Development Council Enterprise
Sourcing Guide, Trade Fairs, Business Matching, Business Contacts
http://www.hkenterprise.com

Hong Kong Trade Development Council Offices around the World

Europe

Amsterdam
Prinsengracht 771, G/F
1017 JZ Amsterdam
The Netherlands
T: (31)-20-627-7101
F: (31)-20-622-8529
E: amsterdam.office@tdc.org.hk

Barcelona
Diagonal Avenue, 512 Bajos
08006 Barcelona
Spain
T: (34)-93-236-0930
   (34)-93-236-0942
F: (34)-93-236-0944
E: barcelona.consultant@tdc.org.hk

Budapest
Rozsa utca 55
H-1064 Budapest
Hungary
T: (36)-1-322-0624
　(36)-1-342-0159
F: (36)-1-341-4798
E: budapest.consultant@tdc.org.hk

London
16 Upper Grosvenor Street
London
W1K 7PL
England
T: (44)-20-7616-9500
F: (44)-20-7616-9510
E: london.office@tdc.org.hk

Moscow
Energeticheskaya St., 6
Moscow
111116 Russia
T: (7)-095-918-1550
　(7)-095-918-1770
F: (7)-095-956-0552
E: moscow.consultant@tdc.org.hk

Frankfurt
Kreuzerhohl 5-7
60439 Frankfurt
Germany
P.O. Box 500551
60394 Frankfurt
Germany
T: (49)-69-95772-0
F: (49)-69-95772-200
E: frankfurt.office@tdc.org.hk

Milan
Via Orefici, 2
20123 Milan
Italy
T: (39)-02-865-405
　(39)-02-865-715
F: (39)-02-860-304
E: milan.office@tdc.org.hk

Asia

Bangkok
42 Tower, 17th Floor
65 Sukhumrit 42 Road
Klong toey
Bangkok 10110
Thailand
T: 66-2713-6258
　66-2713-6259
　66-2713-6260
　66-2713-6261
　66-2713-6262
F: 66-2-651-8088
E: bangkok.consultant@tdc.org.hk

Beijing
Room 918, Tower 2
Bright China Chang An Building
7 Jianguomen Nei Avenue
Dongcheng District
Beijing 100005
People's Republic of China
T: 86-(10)-6510-1700
F: 86-(10)-6510-1760
E: beijing.office@tdc.org.hk

Useful Addresses and Contacts

Chengdu
Room 603, 6/F, Sheraton Chengdu
Lido Hotel No.15, Section 1
Ren Min Zhong Road
Chengdu 610015
Sichuan
People's Republic of China
T: 86-(28)-8676-8999
 (Ext.3568 - 3570)
F: 86-(28)-8676-8262
E: chengdu.office@tdc.org.hk

Fuzhou
Unit 11, 21/F, Worldwide Plaza
158 Wusi Road
Fuzhou 350003
People's Republic of China
T: 86-(591)-8780-8191
 86-(591)-8780-8192
 86-(591)-8780-8193
F: 86-(591)-8780-8194
E: fuzhou.office@tdc.org.hk

Ho Chi Minh City
Suite 1201,
Saigon Tower Office Building
29 Le Duan Street, Dist. 1
Ho Chi Minh City
Vietnam
T: 84-(8)-823-5883
 84-(8)-823-6196
F: 84-(8)-823-5884
E: hochiminh.city.office@tdc.org.hk

Kunming
Room 602, 6th Floor, Hongta Mansion
155 Beijing Road
Kunming 650011
Yunnan
People's Republic of China
T: 86-(871)-357-9599
 86-(871)-357-9598
 86-(871)-357-9597
F: 86-(871)-357-9596
E: kunming.office@tdc.org.hk

Dalian
Room 1505
Dalian Gold Name Commercial Tower
68 Renmin Road
Dalian 116001
People's Republic of China
T: 86-(411)-8271-4991
F: 86-(411)-8271-4234
E: dalian.office@tdc.org.hk

Guangzhou
23/F, Guangdong International Building
Annex A, 339 Huanshi Dong Lu
Guangzhou 510098
People's Republic of China
T: 86-(20)-8331-2889
F: 86-(20)-8331-1081
E: guangzhou.office@tdc.org.hk

Kuala Lumpur
Suite 35-1, Level 35, Menara Dion
27 Jalan Sultan Ismail
50250 Kuala Lumpur
Malaysia
T: 60-(3)-2381-1061
F: 60-(3)-2381-1062
E: kuala.lumpur.office@tdc.org.hk

Osaka
Osaka Ekimae Dai-San Building
10/F Osaka Kokusai Bldg.
2-3-13 Azuchimachi, Chuo-ku
Osaka 541-0052
Japan
T: 06-4705-7030 (Reception)
F: 06-4705-7015
E: osaka.office@tdc.org.hk

Qingdao
25A-B,
Qingdao International Finance Centre
No.59 Xiang Gang Zhong Lu
Qingdao, 266071
People's Republic of China
T: 86-(532)-5793658
F: 86-(532)-5793659
E: qingdao.office@tdc.org.hk

Shanghai
23/F, East Ocean Centre
588 Yanan Road East
Shanghai 200001
People's Republic of China
T: 86-(21)-6352-8488
F: 86-(21)-6352-3454
E: shanghai.office@tdc.org.hk

Singapore
50 Raffles Place
#35-01 Singapore Land Tower
Singapore 048623
T: 65-6538-7376
F: 65-6538-7167
E: singapore.office@tdc.org.hk

Tokyo
Trusty Kojimachi Building
6/F, 3-4 Kojimachi, Chiyoda-ku
Tokyo 102-0083
Japan
T: 81-(3)-5210-5850
F: 81-(3)-5210-5860
E: tokyo.office@tdc.org.hk

Seoul
2/F, KWTC Building
159-1 Samsung-dong
Kangnam-ku
Seoul
Korea
T: 82-(2)-551-7062-70
F: 82-(2)-551-7059/60
E: seoul.consultant@tdc.org.hk

Shenzhen
Unit 06, 15/F
Shenzhen Development Centre Building
2010 Renminnan Road
Shenzhen 518001
People's Republic of China
T: 86-(755)-8228-0112
   86-(755)-8228-0113
   86-(755)-8228-0144
   86-(755)-8228-0282
F: 86-(755)-8228-0114
E: shenzhen.office@tdc.org.hk

Taipei
Unit B, 7/F, #2 Exchange Square
97 Sung Jen Road
Taipei 110
Taiwan
T: 886-(2)-8788-4545
F: 886-(2)-8788-4209
E: taipei.consultant@tdc.org.hk

Wuhan
Unit 06, 7/F
Wuhan International Trade Commerce Centre
566 Jian She Avenue
Hankou,
Wuhan 430022
People's Republic of China
T: 86-(27)-8575-7121/2
   86-(27)-8577-4572 (Ext.5081)
F: 86-(27)-8575-7120
E: wuhan.office@tdc.org.hk

| Useful Addresses and Contacts |

Xian
Room 611
Shaanxi Zhong Da International Mansion
No. 30 Nanda Jie,
Xian
Shaanxi 710002
People's Republic of China
T: 86-(29)-8720-3081
　 86-(29)-8720-3082
　 86-(29)-8720-3083
F: 86-(29)-8720-3589
E: xian.office@tdc.org.hk

Australia

Sydney
Level 3, Hong Kong House
80 Druitt Street
Sydney
N.S.W. 2000
Australia
T: 61-2-9261-8911
F: 61-2-9261-8966
E: sydney.office@tdc.org.hk

Middle East and Africa

Dubai
Suite 602, 6/F, Twin Towers
Beniyas Road, Deira
Dubai
United Arab Emirates
T: (971)-4-2233-499
F: (971)-4-2232-331
E: dubai.office@tdc.org.hk

Johannesburg
137 Daisy Street, cnr Grayston Drive
Sandown, Private Bag X28
Benmore 2010
South Africa
T: (27)-11-322-4898
F: (27)-11-322-4899
E: johannesburg.consultant@tdc.org.hk

North America

New York
219 East 46th Street
New York
NY 10017
U.S.A.
T: (1)-212-838-8688
F: (1)-212-838-8941
E: new.york.office@tdc.org.hk

Chicago
Suite 2028, 333 North Michigan Avenue
Chicago
IL60601
U.S.A.
T: (1)-312-726-4515
F: (1)-312-726-2441
E: chicago.office@tdc.org.hk

Los Angeles
Los Angeles World Trade Centre
Suite #282, 350 South Figueroa Street
Los Angeles
CA 90071-1386
U.S.A.
T: (1)-213-622-3194
F: (1)-213-613-1490
E: los.angeles.office@tdc.org.hk

Miami
Suite No.509, Courvoisier Center II
601 Brickell Key Drive
Miami
FL 33131
U.S.A.
T: (1)-305-577-0414
F: (1)-305-372-9142
E: miami.office@tdc.org.hk

Toronto
G/F, Hong Kong Trade Centre
9 Temperance Street
Toronto
Ontario, M5H 1Y6
Canada
T: (1)-416-366-3594
F: (1)-416-366-1569
E: toronto.office@tdc.org.hk

Central and South America

Mexico City
Manuel E. Izaguirre #13
3er piso, Ciudad Satelite
Estado de Mexico 53100
Mexico
T: 1527-55-5572-4113
   (52)-55-5572-4131
F: (52)-55-5393-5940
E: mexico.city.consultant@tdc.org.hk

Panama City
Condominio Plaza Interntacional
Primer Alto, Oficina No. 27
Edifico del Banco Nacional de Panama
Via Espana y Calle 55
Panama City
Republica de Panama
Postal Address:
Apartado Postal 6-4510, El Dorado
Panama City
Republica de Panama
T: (507)-269-5894
   (507)-269-5611
   (507)-269-6183
E: panama.city.consultant@tdc.org.hk

Santiago
Fidel Oteiza 1916 Of. 701
Providencia
Santiago
Chile
T: (56)-2-225-5015
   (56)-2-244-3864
F: (56)-2-225-1044
E: santiago.consultant@tdc.org.hk

Sao Paulo
Rua Cel. Xavier de Toledo
316 - Cj. 10A - lo.andar
CEP 01048-000
Sao Paulo-SP
Brazil
T: (55)-11-3159-0765
   (55)-11-3258-1269
F: (55)-11-3159-0778
   (55)-11-3258-5858
E: sao.paulo.consultant@tdc.org.hk

Useful Addresses and Contacts

Important Offices and Organisations

Office of the Chief Executive of the Hong Kong Special Administrative Region
5/F, Central Government Offices
Main Wing
Lower Albert Road
Central
Hong Kong
T: (852) 2878 3300
F: (852) 2509 0577
E: ceo@ceo.gov.hk
W: http://www.info.gov.hk/ce/eng/office.htm

Company Registration

Business Licence Information Service (BLIS)
Trade and Industry Department
M/F, Trade and Industry Department Tower
700 Nathan Road
Kowloon
Hong Kong
T: (852) 2398 5133
F: (852) 2737 2377
W: http://www.info.gov.hk/licence

Companies Registry and New Companies Section
14/F, Queensway Government Offices
66 Queensway
Hong Kong
T: (852) 2867 2600 (General Office)
F: (852) 2869 6817
W: http://www.info.gov.hk/cr
Enquiry Hotline: (852) 2234 9933
Incorporation New Companies Section
T: (852) 2867 2587

Oversea Companies Section of the Companies Registry
29/F, Queensway Government Offices
66 Queensway
Hong Kong
T: (852) 2867 4655
F: (852) 2523 5629
E: crenq@cr.gov.hk

Business Registration Office
Inland Revenue Department
4/F, Revenue Tower
5 Gloucester Road
Wan Chai
Hong Kong
T: (852) 187 8088
F: (852) 2824 1482
E: taxbro@ird.gov.hk
W: http://www.info.gov.hk/ird/eng/tax/bre.htm

Help in Setting Up Business in Hong Kong
Hong Kong Regional Office
OCRA (Hong Kong) Limited
Rm 3908, 39/F, Two Exchange Square
8 Connaught Place
Central
Hong Kong
T: (852) 2522 0172
F: (852) 2522 4720
E: hongkong@ocra.com.hk
W: http://www.investukasia.org

Trade Regulation and Information Support Offices

Census & Statistics Department
16/F - 22F & 25/F, Wanchai Tower
12 Harbour Road
Wan Chai
Hong Kong
T: (852) 2582 4733
F: (852) 2827 1708
E: fax-stat@censtatd.gov.hk
W: http://www.info.gov.hk/censtatd

Census & Statistics Department - Publications Unit
19/F, Wanchai Tower
12 Harbour Road
Wan Chai
Hong Kong
T: (852) 2582 3025
F: (852) 2827 1708
E: publications@censtatd.gov.hk
W: http://www.info.gov.hk/censtatd

Customs and Excise Department
Executive Officer (General) 2
General Section / Office of
Department Administration
8/F, Harbour Building
38 Pier Road
Central
Hong Kong
T: (852) 2852 3326
24-hour telephone hotline: (852) 2815 7711
F: (852) 2541 7820
24-hour facsimile hotline: (852) 2542 3334
E: customsenquiry@customs.gov.hk
W: http://www.info.gov.hk/customs

Hong Kong Export Credit Insurance Corporation
2/F, Tower 1, South Seas Centre
75 Mody Road
Tsim Sha Tsui East
Kowloon
Hong Kong
T: (852) 2732 9988
F: (852) 2722 6277
W: http://www.hkecic.com

Hong Kong International Airport
Airport Authority Building
1 Cheong Yip Road
Hong Kong International Airport
Lantau
Hong Kong
T: (852) 2188 7111
Enquiry hotline: (852) 2181 0000
F: (852) 2824 0717
W: http://www.hongkongairport.com

Hong Kong Monetary Authority
55/F, Two International Finance Centre
8 Finance Street
Central
Hong Kong
T: (852) 2878 8196
   (852) 2878 8203
F: (852) 2878 8197
Telex: 74776 XFUND HX
E: hkma@hkma.gov.hk
W: http://www.info.gov.hk/hkma
Public Enquiries:
T: (852) 2878 8222
F: (852) 2878 2010

HKMA Information Centre:
T: (852) 2878 1111
F: (852) 2147 9408
E: infocentre@hkma.gov.hk
W: http://www.info.gov.hk/hkma/eng/
   info_centre/index.htm

Useful Addresses and Contacts

Small and Medium Enterprises Information Centre
M/F, Trade & Industry Department Tower
700 Nathan Road
Kowloon
Hong Kong
T: (852) 2398 5133 (Support centre for SMEs)
F: (852) 2737 2377
E: smeenq@tid.gov.hk
W: http://www.sme.gcn.gov.hk
SME Committee Secretariat
T: (852) 2398 5144

Trade & Industry Department
Departmental Customer Services Manager
Rm 908, Trade & Industry Department Tower
700 Nathan Road
Kowloon
Hong Kong
T: (852) 2392 2922
F: (852) 2787 7422
E: enquiry@tid.gov.hk
W: http://www.info.gov.hk/tid
 http://www.tid.gov.hk

Transport Department
41/F, Immigration Tower
7 Gloucester Road
Wan Chai
Hong Kong
T: (852) 2804 2600
F: (852) 2824 0433
E: tdenq@td.gov.hk
W: http://www.info.gov.hk/td

Business Groups in Hong Kong
http://www.info.gov.hk/link/business.htm

Census & Statistics Department Statistical Bookstore
http://www.statisticalbookstore.gov.hk

The Mainland and Hong Kong Closer Economic Partnership Arrangement (CEPA) Initial Phase of Tariff Preference - Mainland 2004 tariff Codes, product description and origin criteria
http://www.tid.gov.hk/english/aboutus/tradecircular/all_in_one/2003/files/Mainland2001_2004_e.pdf

Commerce & Industry Branch
http://www.info.gov.hk/cib/ehtml/main.html

Commerce & Industry Bureau
http://www.info.gov.hk/cib

Communications and Technology Branch of Commerce, Industry and Technology Bureau
http://www.info.gov.hk/citb/ctb
http://www.citb.gov.hk/ctb

Electronic Service Delivery Scheme
http://www.esd.gov.hk
http://www.info.gov.hk/digital21

Government Information Centre (GIC)
http://www.info.gov.hk
http://search.info.gov.hk/
http://www.info.gov.hk/eindex.htm

Government Information Centre
T: (852) 2810 3824
F: (852) 2147 5770
E: budget@fstb.gov.hk
W: http://www.budget.gov.hk for information regarding current and previous budgets.

Government Information Centre homepage
http://www.search.info.gov.hk (portal website)

Government & Related Organisations
http://www.info.gov.hk/orgindex.htm

Information Service Department, Publicity and Promotions Division
Room 405, Murray Building
Garden Road
Central
Hong Kong
T: (852) 2842 8828 (Various departments given in website)
F: (852) 2905 1572
E: internet@isd.gov.hk
W: http://www.info.gov.hk/isd/
http://www.isd.gov.hk/

http://www.hongkong.org

http://www.hongkong.org/hktrans07.html

News from Hong Kong's Information Services Department
Rm 805, Murray Building
Central
Hong Kong
http://www.news.gov.hk

Trade & Industry Department - CEPA Details
http://www.tid.gov.hk/english/cepa/index.html
http://www.tid.gov.hk/english/cepa/trade_goods.html

Taxation

Inland Revenue Department
Revenue Tower
5 Gloucester Road
Wan Chai
Hong Kong
T: (852) 187 8088
F: (852) 2519 9316
E: taxinfo@ird.gov.hk
W: http://www.info.gov.hk/ird
http://www.ird.gov.hk/index.htm

Dispute Resolution

The District Court
Wan Chai Law Courts
Wan Chai Tower
12 Harbour Road
Wan Chai
Hong Kong
T: (852) 2845 5696
F: (852) 2824 1641
W: http://www.judiciary.gov.hk

The High Court
High Court Building
38 Queensway
Hong Kong
T: (852) 2530 4411
F: (852) 2869 0640
E: enquiry@judiciary.gov.hk
W: http://www.judiciary.gov.hk/en/others/contactus.htm

Useful Addresses and Contacts

Hong Kong International Arbitration Centre
38/F, Two Exchange Square
8 Connaught Place
Central
Hong Kong
T: (852) 2525 2381
F: (852) 2524 2171
E: adr@hkiac.org
W: http://www.hkiac.org
  http://www.hkiac.org/main.html

The Small Claims Tribunal
Wan Chai Law Courts
4/F, Wan Chai Tower
12 Harbour Road
Wan Chai
Hong Kong
T: (852) 2582 4084
F: (852) 2587 9139
W: http://www.info.gov.hk/jud/guide2cs
  /index.htm

Labour

Public Liaison Officer
Labour Department
16/F, Harbour Building
38 Pier Road
Central
Hong Kong
T: (852) 2717 1771 or 2852 4125
F: (852) 2850 5310
W: http://www.info.gov.hk/labour
  http://www.labour.gov.hk

Immigration Department

HKSAR Immigration
http://www.info.gov.hk/immd/
http://www.immd.gov.hk/index.html

Information and Liaison Section
Immigration Department
2/F, Immigration Tower
7 Gloucester Road
Wan Chai
Hong Kong
T: (852) 2824 6111
F: (852) 2877 7711
E: enquiry@immd.gov.hk
W: http://www.info.gov.hk/immd/index.htm
  http://www.immd.gov.hk

Information on the Right of Abode: Hong Kong Immigration Department
Immigration Tower
7 Gloucester Road
Wan Chai
Hong Kong
T: (852) 2824 4055
F: (852) 2598 8388
E: roa@immd.gen.gov.hk
W: http://www.info.gov.hk/immd/

The Office of the Government of the HKSAR in Beijing
21/F, Tower 1
Henderson Centre
18 Jianguomen Nei Avenue
Dongcheng District
Beijing 100005
T: (8610) 6518 6318 extension 033
F: (8610) 6518 6321

Intellectual Property Protection

Intellectual Property Department
24/F, Wu Chung House
213 Queen's Road East
Wan Chai
Hong Kong
T: (852) 2961 6901
F: (852) 2838 6276
E: enquiry@ipd.gov.hk
W: http://www.info.gov.hk/ipd

Exhibition Facilities

AsiaWorld-Expo
Hong Kong International Airport
Lantau
Hong Kong
T: (852) 2838 8808
F: (852) 2561 2822
E: info@asiaworld-expo.com
W: http://www.asiaworld-expo.com

Hong Kong Exhibition Centre
3-4/F, Low Block
China Resources Building
26 Harbour Road
Wan Chai
Hong Kong
T: (852) 2827 9908
F: (852) 2827 5776
E: hkec@crchkec.com.hk
W: http://www.crchkec.com.hk

Hong Kong International Trade and Exhibition Centre (HITEC)
1 Trademart Drive
Kowloon Bay
Kowloon
Hong Kong
T: (852) 2620 2838
F: (852) 2620 2307
E: enquiry@hitec.com.hk
W: http://www.hitec.com.hk

Hong Kong Convention and Exhibition Centre (HKCEC)
1 Expo Drive
Wan Chai
Hong Kong
T: (852) 2582 8888
F: (852) 2802 7284
E: info@hkcec.com
W: http://www.hkcec.com

Hong Kong Exhibition & Convention Industry Association (HKECIA)
16/F, Wayson Commercial House
70 Lockhart Road
Wan Chai
Hong Kong
T: (852) 2878 1368
F: (852) 2869 6103
E: enquiry@exhibitions.org.hk
W: http://www.exhibitions.org.hk

Quality and Certification Laboratories

Hong Kong Association of Certification Laboratories Ltd.
1/F, CMA Building
64-66 Connaught Road
Central
Hong Kong
T: (852) 2542 8620
F: (852) 2541 8154
E: acl@cma.org.hk
W: http://www.hkacl.org/

Hong Kong Quality Assurance Agency
19/F, K. Wah Centre
191 Java Road
North Point
Hong Kong
T: (852) 2202 9111
F: (852) 2202 9222
E: hkqaa@hkqaa.org
W: http://www.hkqaa.org

Hong Kong Q-Mark Council
Federation of Hong Kong Industries
4/F, Hankow Centre
5-15 Hankow Road
Tsim Sha Tsui
Kowloon
Hong Kong
T: (852) 2732 3188
F: (852) 2721 3494
E: fhki@fhki.org.hk
W: http://www.fhki.org.hk

CMA Testing & Certification Laboratories Ltd.
Rm 1302, Yan Hing Centre
9-13 Wong Chuk Yeung Street
Fotan
Shatin
New Territories
Hong Kong
T: (852) 2698 8198
F: (852) 2695 4177
E: info@cmatcl.com
W: http://www.cmatcl.com

Hong Kong Quality Management Association
SHW 3-4, Sheung Wan Station
Mass Transit Railway
Hong Kong
T: (852) 2581 2210
F: (852) 2581 2212
E: info@hkqma.org.hk
W: http://www.hkqma.org.hk

Science and Technology

Hong Kong Association for the Advancement of Science and Technology
2A Tak Lee Commercial Building
113-117 Wan Chai Road
Wan Chai
Hong Kong
T: (852) 2891 3388
F: (852) 2838 1823
E: info@hkaast.org.hk
W: http://www.hkaast.org.hk

Biotechnology Research Institute
The Hong Kong University of Science and Technology
Clear Water Bay
Kowloon
Hong Kong
T: (852) 2358 6000
W: http://www.ust.hk/en/aa/index.html

China Information & Technology Industry Association
Rm 538-543, 1 Science Park West Avenue
Hong Kong Science Park
Pak Shek Kok
New Territories
Hong Kong
T: (852) 2370 8818
F: (852) 2370 8829

Hong Kong Industrial Technology Centre Corporation
1/F. Hong Kong Industrial Technology Centre
72 Tat Chee Avenue
Kowloon Tong
Kowloon
Hong Kong
T: (852) 2788 4433
F: (852) 2788 4261

Innovation and Technology Commission Quality Services Division
35/F & 36/F, Immigration Tower
7 Gloucester Road
Wan Chai
Hong Kong
T: (852) 2829 4800
F: (852) 2824 1302

Hong Kong & Mainland Software Industry Cooperation Association
P.O. Box 28155
Gloucester Road Post Office
Wan Chai
Hong Kong
T: (852) 2838 2773
F: (852) 2866 7275
E: enquiries@hmsica.com
W: http://www.hmsica.com

Hong Kong Cyberport Development Holdings Ltd.
Units 1103-1104, Level II
Cyberport 2
100 Cyberport Road
Hong Kong
T: (852) 3166 3800
F: (852) 3166 3118
E: enquiry@cyberport.com.hk
W: http://www.cyberport.com.hk

Innovation and Technology Commission
20/F, Wu Chung House
213 Queen's Road East
Wan Chai
Hong Kong
T: (852) 2737 2208
F: (852) 2730 4633
E: enquiry@itc.gov.hk
W: http://www.info.gov.hk/itc

Hong Kong Institute of Biotechnology Ltd.
2 Biotechnology Avenue
12 Miles, Tai Po Road
Shatin
New Territories
Hong Kong
T: (852) 2603 5111
F: (852) 2603 5012
E: enquiry@hkib.org.hk
W: http://www.hkib.org.hk/

Hong Kong Plastics Technology Centre Ltd.
Unit 509, Hong Kong Polytechnic University
Hung Hom
Kowloon
Hong Kong
T: (852) 2766 5577
F: (852) 2766 0131
E: ptc@polyu.edu.hk
W: http://www.plastics-ctr.org.hk

Useful Addresses and Contacts

Provisional Hong Kong Science Park Co. Ltd.
Suite 3402-06, 34/F, Tower 1
The Gateway
25 Canton Road
Tsim Sha Tsui
Kowloon
Hong Kong
T: (852) 2629 1818
F: (852) 2629 1833
E: enquiry@hksciencepark.com
W: http://www.hksciencepark.com

Science Park Office
Unit 301-2, Innovation Centre
6 Science Park West Avenue
Hong Kong Science Park
Pak Shek Kok
New Territories
Hong Kong

Tech Centre Office
1/F, Tech Centre
72 Tat Chee Avenue
Kowloon Tong
Kowloon
Hong Kong
T: (852) 2788 4433
F: (852) 2788 4261

Hong Kong Wireless Development Centre
Unit 403, IT Street, Cyberport 3
100 Cyberport Road
Hong Kong
T: (852) 2989 9163
F: (852) 2989 9166
E: contact@hkwdc.org
W: http://www.hkwdc.org

The Hong Kong Science and Technology Parks Corporation
Suite 1905-13, 19/F, Tower 6
The Gateway
9 Canton Road
Tsim Sha Tsui
Kowloon
Hong Kong
T: (852) 2629 1818
F: (852) 2629 1833
W: http://www.hkstp.org

Corporate Communications
Contact Person: Ms. Vega Wong
T: (852) 2629 6692
E: vega.wong@hkstp.org

Other Services

Telecommunications and Postal Services

General Post Office
Hongkong Post, Hongkong Post Headquarters
2 Connaught Place
Central
Hong Kong
T: (852) 2921 2222
F: (852) 2868 0094
E: hkpo@hkpo.gov.hk
W: http://www.hongkongpost.com

Hongkongpost
Kowloon East Post Office Box 68777
Kowloon
Hong Kong
T: (852) 2921 6633
F: (852) 2775 9130
E: enquiry@hongkongpost.gov.hk
W: http://www.hongkongpost.gov.hk

Public Utilities

China Light and Power Hong Kong Limited
CLP Holdings
147 Argyle Street
Mong Kok
Kowloon
Hong Kong
T: (852) 2678 8111
F: (852) 2760 4448
E: clp_info@clp.com.hk
W: http://www.clpgroup.com

Electrical and Mechanical Services Dept
98 Caroline Hill Road
Causeway Bay
Hong Kong
T: (852) 2333 3762
E: info@emsd.gov.hk
W: http://www.emsd.gov.hk

Housing, Planning and Lands Bureau
9/F, Murray Building
Garden Road
Central
Hong Kong
T: Not Available
F: (852) 2186 7832
W: http://www.hplb.gov.hk

Drainage Services Department
43/F, Revenue Tower
5 Gloucester Road
Wan Chai
Hong Kong
T: (852) 2877 0660
F: (852) 2827 8605
E: enquiry@dsd.gov.hk
W: http://www.info.gov.hk/dsd
   http://www.dsd.gov.hk

Hongkong Electric Holdings Limited
44 Kennedy Road
Admiralty
Hong Kong
T: (852) 2843 3111
F: (852) 2810 0506
E: mail@hec.com.hk
W: http://www.hec.com.hk

Water Supplies Department Head Office
48/F, Immigration Tower
7 Gloucester Road
Wan Chai
Hong Kong
T: (852) 2829 4500
F: (852) 2824 0578
E: wsdinfo@wsd.gov.hk
W: http://www.info.gov.hk/wsd

Education for Expatriate Children

Education and Manpower Bureau
15/F, Wu Chung House
213 Queen's Road East
Wan Chai
Hong Kong
T: (852) 2892 5777
F: (852) 2893 0858
W: http://www.info.gov.hk/ed
   http://www.ed.gov.hk
   http://www.emb.gov.hk

English Schools Foundation
43B Stubbs Road
Hong Kong
T: (852) 2574 2351
F: (852) 2838 0957
E: fmoffice@esf.edu.hk
W: http://www.esf.edu.hk

Useful Addresses and Contacts

Schools

http://www.classmateasia.com

Chinese International School
http://www.cis.edu.hk

French International School of Hong Kong
http://www.lfis.edu.hk

German Swiss International School
http://www.gsis.edu.hk

Hong Kong International School
http://www.hkis.edu.hk

Standing Committee on Language Education and Research (SCOLAR Support Unit)
http://www.language-education.com

Other Useful Websites

Useful associations

Website with listing of Associations in Hong Kong taken from TDC Information Service
http://www.tdctrade.com/hksar/order.htm

America Hong Kong Electronics Association
http://www.ahkea.org

Hong Kong Background Information
http://www.info.gov.hk/hkbi/eng/index.htm

Information regarding the Basic Law
http://www.info.gov.hk/basic_law

Business
http://www.business.gov.hk - Chinese
http://www.business.gov.hk/english/f0202.htm - English

2003 - 04 Budget
http://www.budget.gov.hk/2003/eng/index.htm
http://www.budget.gov.hk2004/eng/speech.htm

China Daily
http://www.chinadaily.com.cn/english/home/index.html
http://www.chinadaily.com.cn/english/hkedition/hkhongkong.html

Electoral Affairs Commission
http://www.info.gov.hk/eac

Financial Times - Asia-Pacific
http://www.ft.com/asiapacific

General Information Regarding Hong Kong
http://www.info.gov.hk/ef3.htm

Centre for health protection
http://www.chp.gov.hk

Department of Health website
http://www.info.gov.hk/dh

The Heritage Foundation
214 Massachusetts Avenue, NE
Washington DC 20002-4999
USA
http://www.heritage.org/research/features/index/

HKSAR general website
http://www.gov.hk

Useful Addresses and Contacts

ID Cards - Hong Kong Facts and Statistics
http://www.immd.gov.hk/ehtml/home.htm

Smartid - The new identity card
http://www.smartid.gov.hk

Hong Kong Institute of Public Accountants
http://www.hkicpa.org.hk

SME Export Marketing Fund / SME Training Fund / SME Funding Schemes
http://www.smefund.tid.gov.hk

South China Morning Post
http://www.scmp.com

World Factbook - Hong Kong Information
http://www.odci.gov/cia/publications/factbook/geos/hk.html

Bibliography

Abbas, A. (1997), *Hong Kong Culture and the Politics of Disappearance*, Minneapolis: University of Minnesota Press.

Allen, J. (1997), *Seeing Red China's Uncompromising Takeover of Hong Kong*, Singapore: Butterworth-Heinemann Asia.

American Chamber of Commerce (2000), *2000 Business Outlook Survey*, Hong Kong: American Chamber of Commerce in Hong Kong.

Ashworth, G.J. and Voogd, H. (1990), *Selling the City: Marketing Approaches in Public Sector Urban Planning*, London: Belhaven Press.

Baker, M.J. (1985), *Marketing An Introductory Text*, London: Macmillan Publishers Ltd., 4th edition.

Bell, E. (1998), *Afraid of the dragon - but mauled by the bear*, Business Section, The Observer, 27th September 1998, London: The Observer.

Bereuter, D. (2000), *Seventh Report of the Speaker's Task Force on the Hong Kong Transition*, USA: Internet - http://www.hongkong.org/hktrans07.html

Bertelsen, L. (2000), *Finding the silver lining, China-Britain Trade Review* December 2000, London: China-Britain Business Council.

British Broadcasting Corporation (1998), *China - Into the Red,* The Money Programme, BBC1, 4th October 1998, London: British Broadcasting Corporation.

British Broadcasting Corporation (1998), *The effect of the recession in Hong Kong*, The Money Programme, BBC1, 8th November 1998, London: British Broadcasting Corporation.

British Chamber of Commerce (2000), *2000 Business Confidence Survey*, Hong Kong: British Chamber of Commerce in Hong Kong.

British Chamber of Commerce (2003), *Business Confidence Survey 2003*, Hong Kong: British Chamber of Commerce in Hong Kong.

Camdessus, M. (1997), *Globalisation and Asia: The Challenges for Regional Co-operation and the Implications for Hong Kong* extract from Financial Integration in Asia & the Role of Hong Kong, Hong Kong: Hong Kong Monetary Authority and International Monetary Fund.

Census and Statistics Department (2001), *External Direct Investment Statistics of Hong Kong 2001*, Hong Kong: Government of the Hong Kong Special Administrative Region.

Census and Statistics Department (2002), *Hong Kong as an Information Society*, Hong Kong: Government of the Hong Kong Special Administrative Region.

Census and Statistics Department (2001), *Hong Kong Social and Economic Trends*, Hong Kong: Government of the Hong Kong Special Administrative Region.

Census and Statistics Department (2002), *2000 Survey of Regional Offices Representing Overseas Companies in Hong Kong*, Hong Kong: Government of the Hong Kong Special Administrative Region.

Census and Statistics Department (2002), *Report on 2001 Annual Survey of Regional Offices Representing Overseas Companies in Hong Kong*, Hong Kong: Government of the Hong Kong Special Administrative Region.

Census and Statistics Department (2002), *Report on 2002 Annual Survey of Regional Offices Representing Overseas Companies in Hong Kong*, Hong Kong: Government of the Hong Kong Special Administrative Region.

Cheng, L.K. and Wu, C. (1998), *Competition Policy and the Regulation of Business*, Hong Kong: City University of Hong Kong Press.

CIA (2002), *The World Factbook*, USA: Internet - http://www.odci.gov/cia/publications/factbook/geos/hk.html

Cohen, W.I. and Li, Z. (1997), *Hong Kong under Chinese Rule*, Cambridge: Cambridge University Press.

Commerce, Industry and Technology Bureau (2004), *Mission*, Hong Kong: Internet - http://www.citb.gov.hk

Davis, K. (1996), *Hong Kong after 1997*, London: The Economist Intelligence Unit.

Debell, C. (2001), *SMEs with designs on China*, International Trade Today, March 2001, London: Hemming Information Services.

Department of Justice (1998), *Legal System in Hong Kong*, Hong Kong: Department of Justice, Government of the Hong Kong Special Administrative Region.

Duffy, H. (1995), *Competitive Cities, Succeeding in the Global Economy*, London: E&FN Spon.

Easterby-Smith, M., Thorpe, R. and Lowe, A. (1991), *Management Research: An Introduction*, London: Sage.

Economic Surveys Development Section (3) Census and Statistics Department (2000), *2000 Survey of Regional Offices Representing Overseas Companies in Hong Kong*, Hong Kong: Hong Kong Government Information Services Department.

Editor (1999), *Chinese Law*, 1st March 1999, London: The Financial Times Ltd.

Enright, M.J., Scott, E.E. and Dodwell, D. (1997), *The Hong Kong Advantage*, Hong Kong: Oxford University Press.

Fenby, J. (2000), *Dealing with the Dragon - A year in the new Hong Kong*, London: Little, Brown & Company (UK).

Financial Secretary (2002), *The 2002-03 Budget Speech*, Hong Kong: Government of the Hong Kong Special Administrative Region.

Financial Services Bureau (2000), *2000 Economic Prospects*, Hong Kong: Government of the Hong Kong Special Administrative Region.

Financial Services Bureau (2000), *Third Quarter Economic Report 2000*, Hong Kong: Government of the Hong Kong Special Administrative Region.

Financial Times (2004), *Hong Kong GDP up 7.2% on tourist spending*, Hong Kong: Internet - http://news.ft.com

Gittings, J. (1998), *Hong Kong eyes first place in Asia's race for the skies*, The Guardian, 14th December 1998, London: The Guardian.

Gold, J.R. and Ward, S.V. (1995), *Place Promotion: The use of Publicity and Marketing to Sell Towns and Regions*, Chichester: John Wiley & Sons Ltd.

Government Chief Information Officer (2004), *2004 Digital 21 Strategy*, Hong Kong: Internet - http://www.info.gov.hk/digital21/

Government of the Hong Kong Special Administrative Region (2000), *Third Quarter Economic Report 2000*, Hong Kong: Hong Kong Government Information Services Department.

Government Information Centre (2004), *Applications on Smart ID Card*, Hong Kong: Internet - http://www.smartid.gov.hk

Government Task Force on Services Promotion (1997), *Hong Kong at Your Service, Final Report of the Government Task force on Services Promotion*, Hong Kong: Hong Kong Government Information Services Department.

Henderson, C. (1998), *Asia Falling*, New York: McGraw-Hill Companies Inc.

HKMA & IMF (1997), *Financial Integration in Asia & the Role of Hong Kong*, Hong Kong: Hong Kong Monetary Authority and the International Monetary Fund.

Hollensen, S. (2001), *Global Marketing, A market-responsive approach*, Harlow: Pearson Education Limited, 2nd edition.

Hong Kong Export Credit Insurance Corporation (2004), *About ECIC Corporate Background*, Hong Kong: Internet - http://www.hkecic.com

Hong Kong General Chamber of Commerce (2004), *CEPA and SMEs*, Hong Kong: Internet - http://www.chamber.org.hk

Hong Kong Government Publications (1998), *Hong Kong - A New Era*, Hong Kong: Hong Kong Government Information Services Department.

Hong Kong International Arbitration Centre (2004), *Ways to Resolve a Dispute*, Hong Kong: Internet - http://www.hkiac.org

Hong Kong Monetary Authority (1999), *Annual Report 1999*, Hong Kong: Hong Kong Monetary Authority.

Hong Kong Monetary Authority (2003), *HKMA Annual Report 2003*, Hong Kong: Internet - http://www.info.gov.hk/hkma

Hong Kong Monetary Authority (1997), *Money and Banking in Hong Kong Vol. 2*, Hong Kong: Hong Kong Monetary Authority.

Hong Kong Productivity Council (2004), *Mission and Why is Productivity Important*, Hong Kong: Internet - http://www.hkpc.org

Hong Kong Science and Technology Parks Corporation (2004), *Corporate Profile and Business Review*, Hong Kong: Internet - http://www.hkstp.org

Hong Kong Special Administrative Region Government (2000), *Hong Kong The City that Means Business*, Hong Kong: Hong Kong Government Information Services Department, 2000-2001 edition.

Hong Kong Trade Development Council (2000-2003), *TDC Corporate Web - We Create Opportunity*, Hong Kong: Internet - http://www.tdctrade.com

Hong Kong Trade Development Council Research Department (2000), *China's WTO Accession and Implications for Hong Kong*, Hong Kong: Hong Kong Trade Development Council.

Information Technology and Broadcasting Bureau (2000), *Cyberport News*, Hong Kong: Hong Kong Government Information Services Department.

Invest Hong Kong (2004), *Business and Professional Services*, Hong Kong: Internet - http://www.investhk.gov.hk

InvestHK (2000), *Hong Kong Investment Guidebook*, Hong Kong: The Government of the Hong Kong Special Administrative Region.

InvestHK (2004), *Hong Kong Investment Guidebook*, Hong Kong: The Government of the Hong Kong Special Administrative Region.

InvestHK (2000), *Hong Kong Your Business Focus*, Hong Kong: The Government of the Hong Kong Special Administrative Region.

Invest Hong Kong (April 2004), *Investment Update - Kingdee regional HQ expansion in Hong Kong*, Hong Kong : Government of the Hong Kong Special Administrative Region.

InvestHK (2000), *"Which International Business Centre in Asia?"*, Hong Kong : The Government of the Hong Kong Special Administrative Region.

Ip, S. (2004), *HK enjoys unique advantages*, Information Service Department, Hong Kong: Internet - http://www.news.gov.hk

Jacob, R. (1999), *Asian centres jostle for supremacy in e-commerce battle*, The Financial Times, 23rd March 1999, London: The Financial Times Ltd.

Jacob, R. and Parkes C. (1999), *Disney and HK unveil joint park venture*, The Financial Times, 3rd November 1999, London: The Financial Times Ltd.

Jacob, R. (2001), *FDI is Hong Kong's $64bn question*, The Financial Times, 30th March 2001, London: The Financial Times Ltd.

Jain, S.C. (1996), *International Marketing Management*, Ohio: South-Western College Publishing, 5th edition.

Jao, Y.C. (1997), *Hong Kong as an International Financial Centre, Evolution, Prospects and Policies*, Hong Kong: City University of Hong Kong Press.

Kan, F. (1998), *The Business Guide to Hong Kong*, Singapore: Reed Academic Publishing Asia.

King, A.D. (1990), *Global Cities*, London: Routledge.

Kotler, P. (1980), *Marketing Management, Analysis, Planning and Control*, New Jersey: Prentice-Hall, Inc., 4th edition.

Kotler, P., Asplund, C., Rein, I. and Haider, D. (1999), *Marketing Places Europe: How to attract investments, industries, residents and visitors to cities, communities, regions and nations (in Europe)*, London: Financial Times/Prentice Hall.

Kotler, P., Haider, D.H. and Rein, I. (1993), *Marketing Places, Attracting Investment, Industry and Tourism to Cities, States, and Nations*, New York: The Free Press.

Labate, J. (1998), *Hong Kong link-up concludes a strong year for the Nasd*, 18th December 1998, London: The Financial Times Ltd.

Lamb, D. (1998), *Chop, chop goes the market!* Money Management, August 1998, London: Financial Times Business.

Leahy, J. (2001), *Disney expected to draw 6m HK visitors a year*, The Financial Times, 21st February 2001, London: The Financial Times Ltd.

Leong, H.L. (1998), *A political-economy analysis of the Asian financial crisis*, Journal of the Asia Pacific Economy, Vol. 3, No. 3, 1998, London: Routledge Journals.

Lingle, C. (1997), *The Rise & Decline of the Asian Century*, Hong Kong: Asia 2000 Ltd.

Lucas, L. (1998), *Authorities retreat from stock market*, 1st September 1998, London: The Financial Times Ltd.

Lucas, L. (1999), *China and Hong Kong in bond pact*, 19th January 1999, London: The Financial Times Ltd.

Lucas, L. (1999), *Disillusioned Hong Kong starts to ask for more government*, 6th January 1999, London: The Financial Times Ltd.

Lucas, L. (1999), *Exposure in China at £25bn*, 16th January 1999, London: The Financial Times Ltd.

Lucas, L. (1998), *Go-ahead for HK container terminal*, 9th December 1998, London: The Financial Times.

Lucas, L. and Montagnon, P. (1999), *Stocks and futures exchanges to be merged*, 4th March 1999, London: The Financial Times Ltd.

Mandatory Provident Fund Schemes Authority (2004), *Investment: Common MPF Funds*, Hong Kong: Internet - http://www.mpfahk.org

Martinson, J. (1999), *Investors back Asia, Pacific*, The Financial Times, 13th January 1999, London: The Financial Times Ltd.

McDonald, M. (1999), *Marketing Plans, How to Prepare Them, How to Use Them*, Oxford: Butterworth-Heinemann Ltd.

Meyer, D.R. (2000), *Hong Kong as a Global Metropolis*, Cambridge: Cambridge University Press.

Millar, T. (2004), *Scheme review ensures effectiveness*, Hong Kong: Internet - http://www.news.gov.hk

Ng, S.K. and Lethbridge, D.G. (2000), *The Business Environment in Hong Kong*, New York: Oxford University Press Inc.

Oatley, N. (1998), *Cities, Economic Competition and Urban Policy*, London: Paul Chapman Publishing Ltd.

Panitchpakdi, S. & Clifford, M.L. (2002), *China and the WTO*, Singapore: John Wiley & Sons (Asia) Pte Ltd.

Patten, C. (1998), *East and West*, London: Macmillan Publishers Ltd.

Porter, M.E. (1988), *The Competitive Advantage of Nations*, London: Macmillan Press Ltd.

Ratcliff, T. (2000), *Say hi to Hong Kong's new image*, International Trade Today, November 2000, London: Hemming Information Services.

Research Department (2001), *China's WTO Accession and Implications for Hong Kong*, Hong Kong: Hong Kong Trade Development Council.

Research Department (1998), *Hong Kong's Manufacturing Industries: Current Status and Future Prospects*, Hong Kong: Hong Kong Trade Development Council.

Research Department (2002), *Hong Kong's Trade and Trade Supporting Services: New Developments and Prospects*, Hong Kong: Hong Kong Trade Development Council.

Research Department (2003), *Hong Kong's Trade Outlook for 2003*, Hong Kong: Hong Kong Trade Development Council.

Research Department (1999), *Profiles of Hong Kong's Major Service Industries*, Hong Kong: Hong Kong Trade Development Council.

Ridding, J. (1998), *HK dollar peg faces a test of confidence*, The Financial Times, 17th June 1998, London: The Financial Times Ltd.

Ridding, J. (1998), *Ripples from a bursting bubble*, Financial Times Survey -World Economy and Finance, 2nd October 1998, London: The Financial Times Ltd.

Scott, E.E. (2001), *First Choice Hong Kong - Your Asia Pacific Platform*, Hong Kong: Hong Kong Trade Development Council / Invest Hong Kong.

Seventh National People's Congress of the People's Republic of China (1990), *The Basic Law of The Hong Kong Special Administrative Region of The People's Republic of China*, China: The Consultative Committee for The Basic Law of The Hong Kong Special Administrative Region of The People's Republic of China.

Standing Committee on Language Education and Research (2003), *Action Plan to Raise Language Standards in Hong Kong,* Hong Kong: Government of the Hong Kong Special Administrative Region.

Terpstra, R.H. (1994), *Manual of the Hong Kong Securities Industry*, Hong Kong: The Hong Kong Stock Exchange Limited, 2nd edition.

The European Commission (1999), *First Annual Report by the European Commission on the Special Administrative Region of Hong Kong*, 11th January 1999, Brussels: The European Commission.

The Hong Kong Trader, No. 174 (October 2000), *Hong Kong moves ahead as regional logistics centre*, Hong Kong: Hong Kong Trade Development Council.

The Hong Kong Trader, No. 174 (October 2000), *InvestHK embarks on global promotion*, Hong Kong: Hong Kong Trade Development Council.

The Hong Kong Trader, No. 175 (November 2000), *Chief Executive forecasts huge economic impetus from China's WTO entry*, Hong Kong: Hong Kong Trade Development Council.

The Hong Kong Trader, No. 175 (November 2000), *Cyberport spearheads growth of regional IT hub*, Hong Kong: Hong Kong Trade Development Council.

The Hong Kong Trader, No. 175 (November 2000), *IMF and World Bank open offices*, Hong Kong: Hong Kong Trade Development Council.

The Hong Kong Trader, No. 175 (November 2000), *Irish companies look east*, Hong Kong: Hong Kong Trade Development Council.

The Hong Kong Trader, No. 175 (November 2000), *Massive investment pledged for railway expansion*, Hong Kong: Hong Kong Trade Development Council.

The Hong Kong Trader, No. 175 (November 2000), *Projects on Course to build Hong Kong into a "world-class city"*, Hong Kong: Hong Kong Trade Development Council.

The Hong Kong Trader, No. 175 (November 2000), *Survey confirms Hong Kong as engine of regional growth*, Hong Kong: Hong Kong Trade Development Council.

The Hong Kong Trader, No. 176 (December 2000), *Foreign companies prepare for opening of China market*, Hong Kong: Hong Kong Trade Development Council.

The Hong Kong Trader, No. 176 (December 2000), *Global trading partners invited to share SAR's "first mover" advantage in China*, Hong Kong: Hong Kong Trade Development Council.

The Hong Kong Trader, No. 176 (December 2000), *Hong Kong "ideally situated" as base for regional business, says Chief Executive*, Hong Kong: Hong Kong Trade Development Council.

The Hong Kong Trader, No. 176 (December 2000), *Vigorous trade pushes growth forecast up to 10 per cent*, Hong Kong: Hong Kong Trade Development Council.

The Hong Kong Trader, No. 178 (February 2001), *Airport acts to consolidate hub role*, Hong Kong: Hong Kong Trade Development Council.

The Hong Kong Trader, No. 178 (February 2001), *China signals strong commitment to rule of law after WTO entry*, Hong Kong: Hong Kong Trade Development Council.

The Hong Kong Trader, No. 178 (February 2001), *HKEx in tie-up with overseas exchanges*, Hong Kong: Hong Kong Trade Development Council.

The Hong Kong Trader, No. 178 (February 2001), *New initiatives enhance investment climate in Chinese mainland*, Hong Kong: Hong Kong Trade Development Council.

The Hong Kong Trader, No. 178 (February 2001), *Sharp rise in companies setting up regional operations*, Hong Kong: Hong Kong Trade Development Council.

The Hong Kong Trader, No. 179 (March 2001), *Hong Kong gaining ground as region's e-commerce hub*, Hong Kong: Hong Kong Trade Development Council.

The Hong Kong Trader, No. 179 (March 2001), *Rapid growth in mainland's GDP heralds vast trade opportunities, says Chief Executive*, Hong Kong: Hong Kong Trade Development Council.

The Hong Kong Trader, No. 190 (March 2002), *A cosmopolitan city where the living is easy*, Hong Kong: Hong Kong Trade Development Council

The Hong Kong Trader, No. 190 (March 2002), *Flagship salon heads China expansion*, Hong Kong: Hong Kong Trade Development Council

The Hong Kong Trader, No. 190 (March 2002), *Pearl River Delta set for logistics boom,* Hong Kong: Hong Kong Trade Development Council

The Hong Kong Trader, No. 190 (March 2002), *The executive good life costs less in Hong Kong*, Hong Kong: Hong Kong Trade Development Council

The Hong Kong Trader, No. 190 (March 2002), *World-class honours*, Hong Kong: Hong Kong Trade Development Council

Thompson, Dr. E.R. (2003), *Competitive Advantage Dynamics in the Asia-Pacific Project*, Japan: Internet - http://www.apu.ac.jp/~thompson/Feb24PR.htm

TVB Hong Kong (1997), *Hong Kong - End of An Era*, 30th June 1997, Hong Kong: TVB Hong Kong.

TVB Hong Kong (1997), *Hong Kong - A New Era*, 1st July 1997, Hong Kong: TVB Hong Kong.

Ward, S.V. (1998), *Selling Places The Marketing and Promotion of Towns and Cities 1850-2000*, London: E & FN Spon.

Welsh, F. (1997), *A History of Hong Kong*, London: HarperCollins Publishers, revised edition.

Wesley-Smith, P. (1993), *An Introduction to the Hong Kong Legal System*, Hong Kong: Oxford University Press.

Wilcox, S. (1999/2000), *China In Your Hands*, Export Today, December1999/ January 2000, P.23, Kent: Nexus Media Limited.

Williamson, H., (2000), *Asia recovery 'exceeds expectations'*, The Financial Times, 26th April 2000, P.11, London: The Financial Times Ltd.

Wilson, R.M.S., Gilligan, C. and Pearson, D.J. (1993), *Strategic Marketing Management, Planning, implementation and control*, Oxford: Butterworth-Heinemann Ltd.

Yip, G.S. (1999), *Asian Advantage, Key Strategies for Winning in the Asia-Pacific Region*, New York: Perseus Books Group.

Zhang, A. (2001), *China gears up to a market economy*, International Trade Today, January 2001, P.12, London: Hemming Information Services.

Index

Accountancy – see Financial Management
Addresses & Contacts 332-376
Advertising, Publicity & Market Research 52-54, 72-73, 81, 238-239, 281
Agencies 53, 112-124, 350-356
Air Passenger Transport & Air Cargo 12, 21-24, 37, 73, 200-203, 210, 225, 231, 260
Ansoff Growth Vector Matrix 2
Applied Science & Technology Research Co (ASTRI) 75
Arbitration – see HKIAC
Architects & Architecture 56, 238, 290
Asia Pacific Laboratory Accreditation Cooperation (APLAC) 94
Asiaclear 62
Asian Financial Crisis (1997-1998) 12, 16-20, 33, 46, 103, 107, 130, 218
Asia-Pacific Economic Corporation (APEC) 114, 278
AsiaWorld – Expo 150, 156-158
Associations 53, 54, 60-61, 77, 80, 82, 94, 159-160, 206-207, 269, 284, 346-349
ATM (Automatic Teller Machines) 182
Audit & Accountancy Services – see Financial Management

Bad Debts 12
Balance of Payments 19, 93
Banks & Banking 16, 19, 32, 35, 49, 57, 59-60, 62-64, 93, 106, 125-133, 141, 146, 237-238, 244, 249, 290, 296, 308-309
Bar Codes 70
Bauhinia 12
Bibliography 377-387
Bill of Rights Ordinance 10
Biotechnology 74
Bonds – see Stock Market
Boston Consulting Group Matrix 2, 35
Brand Names 1-3, 5, 44, 86-87, 118, 238, 281, 299, 308
Broadband 70-71, 157, 168, 172, 176, 236
Broadcasting Ordinance (2000) 71
Building & Construction Services 56-57
Business & Professional Services 20, 49-101

Business & Services Promotion Unit 89-90, 112-123
Business Associations 346-349
Business Licence Information Service (BLIS) 307
Business Registration 304-308
Business Reports – see Reports
Business Sectors 49-101
Buyer Power Analysis 3

CAMEL rating 130
Cash & Capital Flows – see Income Flows
Cash Cows 35
Certificate of Origin 16
Chambers of Commerce 108, 123, 275, 285-286, 346-349
Chek Lap Kok Airport 12, 22-23, 77, 79, 150, 156-157, 179, 190, 200-203, 206, 225, 295
Chiang Kai Shek 15
China Factor, The 215-241
China, Integration with 247-255
China, Transport links with 211
Chinese Economy, The 15-16, 18, 20-21, 26, 31-36, 43, 45, 52, 57, 59, 66-67, 70, 79, 82, 117, 169, 198-199, 208, 215-241, 243-245, 247-254, 273, 282-283, 291, 298
Civil Service 10
Climate 6
Closer Economic Partnership Agreement (CEPA) 52, 54-55, 58, 82, 114, 145, 206, 209, 251-253, 259, 271-272, 286
Clothing & Garment Industry (see also – Textiles) 16, 20-21, 43, 54-55, 84-85, 87
Coastline – see Geography
Commerce & Industry Bureau 90, 112-114
Commissions (Trade) 65, 76, 263, 350-356
Committees 71, 91, 127, 130, 350-356
Communications (see also Telecommunications) 20-21, 25-26, 46, 67-72, 88, 102, 112, 231-232, 257, 289, 293, 296, 298
Companies, Setting-up & Operating 1-2, 31, 49, 84, 102, 289-327
Company Registration – see Business Registration
Computer Usage (Software & Hardware) 69-70, 73-75, 91, 102, 131, 157, 168, 172, 175-176, 178-179, 181, 236
Conferences 262
Constitution 8-10

Index

Construction – see Building
Consulates 108, 336-345
Consultants 57-58, 238, 334-335
Contacts 332-376
Conventions – see Exhibitions
Core Competences 4
Corporate & Investment Banking Services 59-60
Councils 10-11, 80, 99, 114-118, 121, 123, 158, 210, 268-277, 284, 332, 350-362
Courts – see Legal System
Crime & Security 188, 294, 296
Customs Regulations & Duty 21, 27, 37-38, 147-148, 203, 278, 289
Cyberport Development 55, 67-68, 165, 169

Deng Xiao Ping 9, 16, 216, 251
Design Services & Associations 54-55, 239
Debt Market, The 17, 62-63, 138
Digital 21 IT Strategy (1998 & 2001) 67, 69, 71, 165, 169, 176, 182
Distribution 4, 94, 234
Dollar, The Hong Kong 12, 60, 62, 81, 93, 125, 127-129, 134, 286
Dollar, The USA 12, 60, 81, 125, 127-129, 133, 286
Driving 188
Dual Nationality 187
Dutiable Commodities Ordinance 99

e-Cash & EPS (Easy Pay System) 182
e-Cert 175-176, 180
e-Commerce & e-Business 67, 69-70, 91, 169, 176, 180, 237, 272, 274
e-Government 176-180
Education & Training 8, 55, 69-70, 89, 92, 104, 134, 177, 193-197, 216, 284, 292
Elections & Electorate, The 9, 13
Electrical Parts & Machinery 20-21
Electronic Service Delivery Scheme (ESD) (2000) 69, 176-180, 182
Electronic Tendering System (ETS) 177, 179
Electronics Industry 16, 19, 43-44, 74-75, 85, 87, 151, 153, 215, 224
Employment & Employees – see Workforce
Engineering & Producer Services 57, 238
English Schools Foundation (ESF) 194-195
European Economic Community (EEC) 83

Exchange Rate, System & Control 12, 93, 125-136, 296
Exhibitions, Conventions, & Trade Fairs 150-162, 273, 293
Export – see Trade

Factor Inflow & Outflow 19
Fairs – see Exhibitions
Farming 6
Fashion – see Clothing
Federations 269, 275, 350-356
Film Services & Film Industry 71, 77
Financial & Business Cluster 42, 49, 88-89, 92
Financial Management & Accountancy 1, 25, 33, 50-52, 91, 226, 240, 243, 247, 261
Financing 18, 35, 44, 50, 60-62, 63-64, 90, 125-136, 226, 231
Flag 12
Food, Beverage, & Cuisine 19, 102, 189, 290
Footwear 21, 235
Foreign Exchange (& Currency) Market 49, 59-60, 62-63, 125-136, 152, 220, 231, 249
Freedom of Expression 10, 72, 284
Freeport Status 37-38, 78, 81, 147, 289, 295
Freight Forwarding 69-70, 206-207, 252, 282, 291
Fund Management 65-66, 231, 237-238, 248
Funding Schemes 49, 60-61, 248, 309-310
Futures – see Stock Market

Garment Industry – see Clothing
General Agreement of Tariffs and Trade (GATT) 83, 219
Geography 5-6, 14, 22, 24-25, 103, 169, 211
Global Market & Globalisation 31, 51, 86, 94, 118, 203, 227, 233, 250, 262, 266, 269, 273, 279-280, 282, 284, 292, 297
Gold Bullion Market 49, 132
Government Electronic Trading Services (GETS) 115, 177, 179
Grand Strategy Matrix 2
Gross Domestic Product (GDP) 16-19, 33, 36, 41-42, 44-45, 49, 56-57, 67, 88, 92, 117, 127, 215, 217, 221, 249-250, 252, 272
Growth Enterprise Market (GEM) 64, 220
Growth, Rates & Markets 13, 18, 50, 53, 56, 60, 64, 71, 73-74, 88, 92, 168, 171, 181, 199, 201, 203, 207, 223-224, 237-240, 252, 281, 287, 294, 297

H.K. Airport Authority (AA) 62
H.K. Convention & Exhibition Centre (HKCEC) 77, 150-151, 153-154, 156-157, 262, 270, 273-274, 276, 294
H.K. Economic and Trade Offices (HKETOs) 263-266
H.K. Education City (HKEdCity) 177, 179
H.K. Export Credit Insurance Corporation (ECIC) 284
H.K. Founding (1842-1843) 34, 37, 216
H.K. Freight Forwarding & Logistics Ltd (HAFFA) 69-70, 206-207, 252, 291
H.K. Institute of Architects (HKIA) 56
H.K. International Arbitration Centre (HKIAC) 26, 119-123, 145
H.K. Islands – see Geography
H.K. Laboratory Accreditation Scheme (HOKLAS) 94
H.K. Mandatory Provident Fund (MPF) 63, 65-66, 130-131, 137-142, 237
H.K. Maritime Centre 37
H.K. Mediation Council (HKMC) 121, 123
H.K. Monetary Authority (HKMA) 62-63, 106-107, 125-136
H.K. Mortgage Corporation (HKMC) 62
H.K. Productivity Council (HKPC) 116-118
H.K. Promotion of 112, 123, 265-266, 278-288
H.K. Science & Technology Park (HKSTP) 55, 163-167, 169
H.K. Society of Accountants (HKSA) 50-51
H.K. Special Administrative Region (HKSAR) 8-9, 84, 151, 157, 186-188, 278, 282
H.K. Strategic Advantages 31-48
H.K. TDC Business Advisory Service 276
H.K. Trade Development Council (HKTDC) 77, 114-115, 268-277, 284, 332, 357-362
Hang Seng Index 64, 134
Hotels 46, 77, 153, 156, 218, 270, 290
Human Rights 11
Hustle Strategy 109-110

Identity Cards 174-177, 179-180, 279, 308
Import – see Trade
Income (Capital & Revenue) Flows 5, 19, 33, 51, 53, 59-60, 62-64, 79, 106-107, 125-136, 144-145, 168, 220, 227, 231
Industrial Clustering & Economic Sectors 41-47
Information Technology (IT) 55, 67-71, 74-75, 86, 157, 163-173, 176, 180-182, 210, 231, 236, 243, 257, 261
Initial Public Offering (IPO) Services 52

Institutes & Institutions 50-51, 56, 62, 67, 74-75, 137-142, 276, 350-356
Insurance 18, 36, 49, 66-67, 90, 115, 237, 248, 250, 284, 290
Intellectual Property Protection Department 39-40, 112, 116
International Air Transport Association (IATA) 206-207
International Covenant for Civil & Political Rights (ICCPR) 10
International Covenant on Economic Social & Cultural Rights (ICESCR) 10
International Monetary Fund (IMF) 103, 130
Internet Service Providers (ISPs) & Internet Usage 21, 69-70, 168-169, 172, 176, 178, 180, 236
Invest Hong Kong (InvestHK) 112, 251, 256-267, 275, 281, 287, 303-304, 332,
Investment & Investment Flows 5, 8, 16-17, 19, 25, 32, 35, 51, 59-60, 62, 65, 87, 96, 112, 115, 125-136, 144-145, 168, 216-218, 220, 222, 227, 233, 238, 241, 243-246, 247, 256-267, 286, 297

Jewellery 20, 151, 153, 215, 224
Joint Declaration (1984) 8-10
Joint Electronic Teller Company (JETCO) 132

Kuomintang, The 15

Land Registry 41
Light Manufacturing Cluster 42
Legal Services 144-145
Logistics 26, 78, 91, 198-214, 222, 243, 247, 252, 254, 291
Language(s) 8, 25, 193-194
Law, Basic, & The Legal System 8-10, 13, 26-27, 31, 33, 37, 39, 49-50, 58, 78, 92, 113, 119-123, 143-149, 215, 228-229, 231-232, 251, 257, 260, 278, 280, 284, 296
Legislative Council (LegCo) 10-11

Management Consultancy Services 57-58
Manufacturing 4, 14-19, 44-45, 74-75, 79, 83-88, 94, 109, 222, 227, 257, 290-292
Market Conditions & Demand 1-2, 26, 31, 51, 72-73, 81, 85, 91, 125-136, 145, 168, 218, 299
Market Share & Research Analysis & Strategy, 1-2, 5, 53, 90, 117, 280, 291
McKinsey Market Analysis 2
Medical & Health Provision 7, 12, 184
Military 23-24, 34
Ministry of Commerce (MOFCOM) 248, 287
Ministry of Foreign Trade & Economic Cooperation (MOFTEC) 228

Multilateral Recognition Arrangement (MRA) 94
Multimedia – see Television
Multinationals (MNCs) 4, 19, 31-33, 35, 37, 49, 51-52, 82, 84, 87, 92, 108, 118, 144, 156, 169-170, 189, 194, 203, 217, 221-222, 227, 229-239, 243, 247, 253-254, 280, 282, 291-298, 304

National People's Congress (NPC), Chinese 8, 10, 120, 143
New Entrants Analysis 3
New Territories 15, 21-22, 41, 76, 158, 209, 211-213
News & News Media 72-73, 104, 179
Non-Government Organisations (NGOs) 112-124

Octopus Cards 182-183
Offices & Organisations 363-373
One-country-two-systems 8-9, 122, 251
One-stop Access Portal (OSP) 178-179
Opium Wars 15, 37, 215
Original Design Manufacture (ODM) 74, 76, 86
Original Equipment Manufacture (OEM) 16, 43-44, 54, 74-76, 85-87, 215

Palmerston, Lord 38
Patents, Trade Marks & Copyrights 39-40, 116, 241, 310
Patten, Chris 11-12
Pearl River Delta (PRD) 35-37, 55, 113, 156, 158, 199-200, 207, 209-210, 217, 231-232, 253, 259, 271-273, 304
People's Liberation Army (PLA) 23
PEST Analysis 2
Plastics Industry 16, 87
Political Parties 11
Population 6-8, 17-18, 45, 81, 92-93, 102-103, 137-138, 152, 171, 174-175, 181, 188, 193-194, 215-216, 257, 278
Porters 5-force model analysis 1-2, 4, 85-86
Postal Services 185, 203
Press & Press Freedom 72, 104, 260, 284
Prices & Pricing 2, 18, 44, 81, 91, 106-107, 109, 216, 299
Printing & Publishing 19, 54, 71-73
Production Portfolio & Productivity Mix 1, 19, 44, 74, 85, 110-118, 217, 221
Profit Margins & Profitability 3-5, 16, 35, 44, 93, 97, 131, 216, 234, 299
Property Market 18, 24, 32, 34, 40-42, 56-57, 81, 93, 98-99, 174, 218, 287, 289-290

Public Relations 112-114, 264-265, 281
Public Transport 12, 21-25, 53, 106, 179, 188, 211-213, 219
Public Utilities (Gas, Electricity, Water) 183
Putonghua (Mandarin) 7-8, 193-194, 251

Quality (QA - Assurance, QC - Control, QM - Management) 41, 250, 282, 284, 291
Quota Restrictions 43, 87

Railways 21-22, 106, 179, 188, 211-212
Real Estate – see Property Market
Real Time Gross Settlement (RTGS) 132
Reclamation Projects 24, 56
Regional Headquarters 1-2, 31, 36, 78, 227, 229-230, 232-233, 238, 254, 256, 262, 273, 282, 289-327
Rents – see Property
Reports & Surveys 77-78, 89, 153, 156, 169, 180, 203, 226, 230, 232, 247, 254, 276, 282, 285-287, 289-290, 292, 296-297
Research & Development (R & D) 84, 90, 309-310
Retail & Retailing 4, 46, 80-82, 85-86
Risk Management 64, 130, 229

SARS 12
SEANZA Forum 130
Securities – see Stock Exchange
Securities & Futures Commission (SFC) 65
Service Industries & Sectors 18, 42, 44, 49-101, 112-123
Shipping & Ports 14, 16, 21-27, 36-38, 45, 50, 79, 100, 179, 198-200, 206-209, 212, 225, 231, 253-254, 260, 291
Shopping 80-81, 189, 216, 239
Small & Medium-Sized Enterprises (SMEs) 114-115, 210, 252-253, 268-269, 275, 279
Social Aspects 174-192
Social Life 189-190
Social Security 16, 184
Societies – see Institutes
Sourcing 4-5, 42, 75, 79, 93-94, 217, 229-230, 243, 291
Sovereignty, Transfer of (July 1 1997) 8-9, 12, 16, 32-33, 84, 143, 217, 284, 286
Sports Equipment 20
Standard & Poor 12, 62

Star(s) 35-36
Stock Exchange & Stock Market 12, 32, 34-35, 42, 49, 62-66, 86, 102, 107, 134-135, 146, 218, 220, 231-232, 237, 248
Substitutes Analysis 3
Supplier Power Analysis 3
Supply Chain 3, 206, 229, 291
Surveying 56
Surveys – see Reports
SWOT Analysis 1-2, 4

Tax & The Taxation System 4-5, 31-32, 35, 37, 58, 61, 63, 78, 81, 93, 95-100, 103, 106, 134, 251, 260, 278, 289, 296-297, 299, 310
Technology 73-76, 88, 112-113, 310
Telecommunications 20, 34, 68, 72-73, 79, 92, 112-113, 153, 157, 165, 168-173, 181-182, 224, 236, 238, 260-261, 290
Telephones 21, 34, 168-172, 177, 179, 181, 188
Television Broadcasting & Multimedia 21, 53, 55, 67-68, 70-71, 75, 77, 104, 112, 151, 157, 169, 236, 257, 261
Textiles (see also Clothing) 16, 20-21, 43, 85, 215
Tiger Economies 17, 107
Tobacco 19, 147
Total Factor Productivity (TFP) 107
Tourism Cluster, & Entertainment 16, 25, 45-46, 76-78, 81-82, 91, 153, 156, 160, 186, 216, 218, 240, 243, 252, 261, 285
Toys 16, 20, 85, 87-88, 151, 215, 224, 235
Trade Fairs – see Exhibitions
Trade Related Intellectual Property Rights (TRIPS) Agreement 40, 241
Trade, Import & Export 14-18, 20-21, 24-25, 33, 35-37, 41-44, 57, 78, 83-88, 90, 93-94, 97, 114-115, 181-182, 206, 209, 215, 218, 220, 222-223, 225, 227-228, 241, 247, 290
Trademarks – see Patents
Trading & procurement 78-80
Traffic Conditions 188-189
Transport & Logistics Cluster 42, 228
Transportation 23, 81, 88, 90, 152, 156, 179, 188-189, 198-214, 219, 226, 243, 247, 252, 257, 260-261, 293, 296
Tsang, Donald 13
Tung Chee Hwa 12-13
Typhoons 187

UNCITRAL Model Law 120
Unemployment – see Workforce
Unique combinations 106-111
United Nations (UN) 9, 11, 15, 36, 215, 217, 287

Venture Capital Market, The 35, 42, 49, 60-61, 69, 231, 248
Visa Requirements 186-187

Watches & clocks 16, 84, 88, 150, 153, 215, 224
Websites 69, 80, 121, 135, 158-160, 164, 179, 201, 269, 273-275, 308, 332, 332-376
Why Hong Kong? 102-105
World Bank 43, 62, 235
Workforce & Wages 16-19, 24, 50, 78, 84-85, 91-93, 96, 103, 137, 152, 174, 181, 185-187, 215-223, 243, 247, 279, 293, 304
World Heritage Foundation 287
World Trade Organisation (WTO) & Chinese Accession 43, 50, 52, 54, 58, 67, 73, 75, 78-79, 82, 90, 117, 126, 145-146, 156, 169, 199, 203, 206, 219-220, 224-241, 252, 272, 278, 282-283, 291, 297-298

Yangtze River Delta 231, 272

www.ingramcontent.com/pod-product-compliance
Ingram Content Group UK Ltd.
Pitfield, Milton Keynes, MK11 3LW, UK
UKHW022230230426
12048UKWH00016BA/1164